Reformed Resurgence

Reformed Resurgence

*The New Calvinist Movement and the Battle
over American Evangelicalism*

BRAD VERMURLEN

OXFORD
UNIVERSITY PRESS

OXFORD

UNIVERSITY PRESS

Oxford University Press is a department of the University of Oxford. It furthers
the University's objective of excellence in research, scholarship, and education
by publishing worldwide. Oxford is a registered trade mark of Oxford University
Press in the UK and certain other countries.

Published in the United States of America by Oxford University Press
198 Madison Avenue, New York, NY 10016, United States of America.

© Oxford University Press 2020

Library of Congress Cataloging-in-Publication Data
Names: Vermurlen, Brad, author.
Title: Reformed resurgence : the new Calvinist movement and the battle over American
evangelicalism / Brad Vermurlen.
Description: New York, NY, United States of America : Oxford University Press, 2020. |
"This book is a revised and expanded version of my doctoral dissertation completed
in the Department of Sociology at University of Notre Dame in 2016. " |
Includes bibliographical references and index.
Identifiers: LCCN 2020007115 (print) | LCCN 2020007116 (ebook) |
ISBN 9780190073510 (hardback) | ISBN 9780190073534 (epub) |
ISBN 9780190073541 (online)
Subjects: LCSH : Christian sociology—Reformed Church. | Calvinism—United States—
Sociological aspects. | Evangelicalism—United States—Sociological aspects. |
Big churches—United States—Sociological aspects. |
Religion and sociology—United States.
Classification: LCC BX9423.S63 V47 2020 (print) | LCC BX9423.S63 (ebook) |
DDC 284/.273—dc23
LC record available at https://lccn.loc.gov/2020007115
LC ebook record available at https://lccn.loc.gov/2020007116

1 3 5 7 9 8 6 4 2

Printed by Integrated Books International, United States of America

For Alex

Contents

Contents

Figures and Tables

Acknowledgments

I first heard of Reformed theology in 2007 while reviewing the literature for my undergraduate honors thesis about the Emerging Church movement. So, on one time horizon, I have been digging into this area for quite some time— well over a decade. But this also means, on a different horizon, until late I was unaware of an entire religious tradition with deep roots in United States history and into which, I quickly learned, some Americans are still reared today. My relatively late "discovery" of Reformed theology also means the story told in these pages is, in a way, my own story of learning the ropes of American Protestantism.

This book is a revised and expanded version of my doctoral dissertation completed in the department of sociology at University of Notre Dame in 2016. I first want to thank my dissertation committee at Notre Dame: David Sikkink, Christian Smith, Omar Lizardo, and Kraig Beyerlein. Chris and his books, especially, have served as an outstanding model of scholarship for me since I arrived at Notre Dame as an optimistic twenty-two-year-old. The Center for the Study of Religion and Society was a vital institutional home to me for eight years, even when I was out of town (or out of the office). Omar, as anyone who knows him can attest, is continually a generous and illuminating guide to all things culture and theory.

Funding for this project came primarily in the form of two grants from Notre Dame's Institute for Scholarship in the Liberal Arts. Additionally, grants from the Graduate School at Notre Dame and from Docent Research Group specifically helped to offset the costs of travelling to and from Seattle, New York City, and Minneapolis. A university presidential fellowship at Notre Dame provided additional funds and freed me from departmental responsibilities during the 2012–2013 academic year, which allowed me to commit myself fully to traveling, reading, and writing. The early seeds of this book were presented at the annual meetings of the American Sociological Association as well as the Society for the Scientific Study of Religion on a handful of occasions from 2010 to 2013.

Thanks to Joe Carter for granting permission to use figure 2.1, of John Piper. Photo credit for that image goes to The Gospel Coalition. Figure 2.2 of

Mark Driscoll is used by permission of Alex Murashko, who himself took the photo. Thanks to Matt Schmucker at Together for the Gospel for permission to use figure 2.3. Lastly, figure 4.1 is from page 20 of *A Theory of Fields* and is reproduced with permission of the Licensor through PLSclear.

During the participant observation leg of my research, Samantha MacLaren, Adam MacLaren, Katie Condit, Noel Heikkinen, Jacob Wagner, Ellen Childs, and Megan Mitrovich each went out of their way to help me find short-term housing in unfamiliar cities. In the end, Brian Gong, Josh Wood, Zach Carlson, Ryan Stansky, Drew Allenspach, and Eugene Allred opened up their homes to me. I knew none of them before showing up at their front doors, and I am grateful for their hospitality. Thanks are also due to the dozens of Evangelical leaders across the country who graciously took the time to do interviews for this project. Mark Dever, Andy Naselli, and Tony Jones went above and beyond by helping me to secure additional interviews. Behind the scenes, Phil Wade, Joseph Haugan, and Tracy Wickham each contributed by transcribing a portion of my recorded interviews. Thanks to them as well.

I received encouragement in my work from Dan Price, Suzanne Price, Mike Tinaglia, Lauren Tinaglia, Rey Goicochea, Annika Goicochea, Shannon Nielsen, Austin Choi-Fitzpatrick, Andrew Lynn, and Jeff Guhin. They all made the research and writing process even more enjoyable than it already is. Also, Jeff Guhin and Wes Markofski were kind enough to show me what a successful book prospectus looks like. My father, Rick Vermurlen, has always been there to provide respite, perspective, advice, encouragement, and free housing when I needed it. Thanks, Dad. My mother, Barb Olds, has always expressed interest in my work and let me know how proud she is that her son was writing a book. Many thanks are also owed to Glenn Lucke, who continually and yet graciously demands nothing short of excellence in everything I do. Justin Detmers first got me interested in studying religion sociologically during those Emerging Church years. Over the years, Justin has worked with me, encouraged me, and challenged me in ways only a best man can.

From early on, during my undergrad days at University of Michigan–Ann Arbor, Eric Johnson demonstrated much of the intellectual rigor and faithfulness that motivated my first steps as a scholar. Terence McGinn, who served as my undergrad mentor and introduced me to both sociology of religion and sociological theory, provided a solid foundation and constant care. After I got married and relocated back to Ann Arbor, the department of sociology at University of Michigan welcomed me back as a visiting graduate student for my final two years of graduate work, allowing me to write, use the library, and participate in the intellectual life of the department. Thanks to Sarah Burgard for facilitating that arrangement.

Thanks as well to Theo Calderara at Oxford University Press and two anonymous reviewers. Each of them provided written feedback that pushed me to reorganize some sections and add new material, which ultimately resulted in a better book.

Finally, and most important, I owe the deepest gratitude to my wife and children. Our two new little ones, Evelyn and Steven, have added much joy and cuteness to our home as I put the finishing touches on the manuscript. And throughout the entire process, my wife, Alex Vermurlen, has been an unending source of love, adventure, and support. She has sacrificed time and energy so that this project could finally cross the finish-line and has done so with a glad heart. For these reasons and untold more, this book is dedicated to her.

1

Background, Clarifications, and Overview

Christianity, these days, and in our part of the world, is on the move. Years of racial demographic changes continue to make Christianity in the United States less white. The candidacy and election of Donald Trump have awakened a surge of populist politics and Christian nationalism from the American heartland. Legal fights over abortion, religious liberty, and gender identity, buttressed largely by Christian beliefs, are in the news. "The nones"—American adults who are atheist, agnostic, or nothing in particular—now match Evangelical Protestants as a share of the population, and disaffected "Exvangelicals" are increasingly organizing themselves on-line. Young Christians are becoming more progressive on many hot-button social and cultural issues, while some young conservative Christian men are listening to Jordan Peterson and other figures of the Intellectual Dark Web to piece together a transgressive view of the world through social media and online journalism. And #ChurchToo is bringing attention to problems of sexual abuse and toxic masculinity within American congregational life.[1]

Through all of this, one of the biggest happenings in American Evangelicalism is a groundswell of commitment to the thought of the sixteenth-century French theologian and reformer, John Calvin—especially among the rising generation of Evangelicals. Since 2006, this "New Calvinist" or "neo-Reformed" movement has taken Evangelicalism by storm, representing a conservative push for Protestant orthodoxy amid broader turmoil and change. Calvinism has long been of interest to social scientists as a strict early-modern theological system that eventually led to the rise of modern capitalism,[2] radical politics,[3] and state power.[4] This book

---

[1] The opening line about Christianity being "on the move" is taken from Alvin Plantinga, "Advice to Christian Philosophers," *Faith and Philosophy* 1, no. 3 (1984): 253–271. Quoted from p. 253.
[2] Max Weber, "The Protestant Ethic and the Spirit of Capitalism," in *The Protestant Ethic and the Spirit of Capitalism with Other Writings on the Rise of the West*, 4th ed., ed. Stephen Kalberg (New York: Oxford University Press, 2009 [1904-05]), 59–159.
[3] Michael Walzer, *The Revolution of the Saints: A Study in the Origins of Radical Politics* (Boston, MA: Harvard University Press, 1982 [1965]).
[4] Philip S. Gorski, *The Disciplinary Revolution: Calvinism and the Rise of the State in Early Modern Europe* (Chicago: The University of Chicago Press, 2003).

Reformed Resurgence. Brad Vermurlen, Oxford University Press (2020). © Oxford University Press.
DOI: 10.1093/oso/9780190073510.001.0001

turns the lens on Calvinism more directly, providing a comprehensive sociological account of the increasing prominence of Calvinism in American
Evangelicalism today, especially among Millennials. But to do so, it looks not
mainly at laypeople but at the leaders. This book explains how pastors, seminary professors, and other Calvinistic leaders use and engage with elements
of today's public culture to advance their distinctive early-modern religious
worldview.

A key move this analysis makes is that the New Calvinist movement cannot
be understood or explained in isolation but needs to be viewed in relation to
the wider landscape of Evangelicalism in the United States. The genealogy
of the organizations and leaders constituting the movement, and even the
rising numbers of younger Americans becoming conservative Calvinists, are
ironically the least important aspects of this movement's story. More important for explaining the Reformed resurgence sociologically are the various
ways its leaders engage culture and strategically position themselves vis-à-vis
the rest of the Evangelical field, vying in a game-like contest for orthodoxy
against other expressions of the Evangelical tradition.

Against my own original expectations, there is no magic bullet for
explaining the New Calvinism as a religious phenomenon. There is not only
one or just a few ways the New Calvinist movement has worked toward and
accomplished its own strength, but several. Through strategic, often deliberative engagement with church tradition, innovation, postmodernism, the
Internet, city life, politics, gender and sexuality, individual autonomy, contextualization, impression management, symbolic boundaries, and more,
the sociological strength of the New Calvinism is less a matter of market dynamics of supply and demand or happening to take the best posture toward
culture—and instead is a *direct result of religious leaders' strategic and conflictual actions*. The New Calvinism enjoys a vitality that has been fought for and
won in the context of the broader field of Evangelicalism. Through the analysis in these pages, the Reformed resurgence is shown to be real and strong
and nevertheless relationally constructed.

By accounting for the New Calvinism this way, this project advances a new
paradigm for understanding how conservative religion can be strong and
thriving in the world today, our pluralistic hypermodern Western world.[5]

---

[5] Putting prefixes on "modern" has led to problems about definitions, categories, implications, and
scope. Throughout this book I use "hypermodern" and "hypermodernity" to refer to our current
Western setting (from 9/11 onward) with all of the cultural mores, conflicts, and assumptions that
come along with it. I avoid using "postmodern" and "late-modern" because of what those terms imply
about modernity itself, namely, that it is over or almost over. I similarly avoid "advanced modern"

It is a paradigm using and expanding on *strategic action field theory*, a recent framework proposed for analyzing movements and organizations but rarely applied to religion.[6] However, as we will see, with strength also comes weakness. Because a field-theoretic model of strength is premised upon an underlying current of disunity and conflict, it has baked into it a concomitant element of significant overall religious weakness. In the same storyline by which conservative Calvinistic belief has experienced a resurgence in its field, American Evangelicalism has *turned in on itself*—such that the strength and prominence of this neo-Reformed movement also reveals the increasing weakness, fragmentation, and incoherence of the Evangelical field as a whole, at least in the United States. For an institutional domain of life with no agreed-upon overarching leadership, with very little consensual meanings of important texts, and no real mechanisms of accountability, how is coherence in that arena finally maintained? The short answer is, after much conflict and struggle, it isn't.

Identifying a New Calvinist Movement

A New Calvinist movement? Is there such a thing? A time-tested piece of advice in sociology is "before one proceeds to explain or to interpret a phenomenon, it is advisable to establish that the phenomenon actually exists, that it is enough of a regularity to require and to allow explanation."[7] It would look quite silly to write a book purporting to explain a resurgence of Calvinism in American Evangelicalism when, in reality, there is no such thing. And even

because that term implies improvement. Rather, I understand what is normally called "postmodernity" and "postmodernism" to be an *extension* and *intensification* of the animating assumptions of modernity (having to do with individual autonomy, unconstrained self-direction, consumer capitalism, technology, incredulity toward authorities and tradition, and so on) rather than a radical break from it. "Hypermodern" therefore serves to mean something like "modernity as it has developed and worked itself out over the course of 500 years and now leaves us in our present-day cultural and epistemic situation."

[6] Neil Fligstein and Doug McAdam, *A Theory of Fields* (New York: Oxford University Press, 2012); Kent D. Miller, "Competitive Strategies of Religious Organizations," *Strategic Management Journal* 23, no. 5 (2002): 435–456; Manuel Hensmans, "Social Movement Organizations: A Metaphor for Strategic Actors in Institutional Fields," *Organization Studies* 24, no. 3 (2003): 355–381; John Levi Martin, "What Is Field Theory?" *American Journal of Sociology* 109, no. 1 (2003): 1–49. See chapter 4 of the present work.

[7] Robert K. Merton, "Three Fragments from a Sociologist's Notebooks: Establishing the Phenomenon, Specified Ignorance, and Strategic Research Materials," *Annual Review of Sociology* 13 (1987): 1–28. Quoted from p. 2.

if there is, there is a risk in studying something too idiosyncratic. As John Levi Martin has warned: "Take for granted that you can find one of anything. [...] Unless there was a strong theory that denies that such a thing should *ever* be found, it's just not important. Don't cross the street to look at them, let alone write a dissertation on them."[8] It is necessary therefore to take some space to "establish the phenomenon."

This issue is trickier for the New Calvinism than for many other empirical social phenomena that sociologists are interested in explaining, such as the demonstrated correlation between two variables as measured on a survey (say, education and church attendance). This is because—as we will see in chapters 4 through 6—the questionable ontological status of the New Calvinism is itself a crucial part of the story.[9] The temptation is to think the New Calvinist movement or Reformed resurgence is real only if there are significantly more Calvinists in the American religious landscape today than there were two decades ago. This book resists that temptation by arguing the New Calvinist movement is less about this kind of numerical growth than it is about relational, game-like contestation and the struggle for symbolic capital and power in one's field. At the same time, I am not merely explaining a widespread though ultimately mistaken perception of a religious movement (one that does not actually exist), because the perception of such a movement, including the media attention it receives, is itself an indispensable part of the movement. What is important at the beginning of this analysis therefore is not whether there is an actual numerical resurgence of Calvinism in American Evangelicalism (see chapter 3) but just that a lot of people are talking about one.

Attention to the New Calvinist movement started only in 2006 when *Christianity Today* published a cover story by Collin Hansen in which he argued that "Calvinism is making a comeback" in American Evangelicalism.[10] Two years later, Hansen published a book-length treatment of the New

---

[8] John Levi Martin, *Thinking Through Theory* (New York: W. W. Norton and Company, 2015), 251.

[9] The theory developed in this work is similar to the social construction of social problems, such as the famous myth of poisoned Halloween candy, although I do not want to call the New Calvinism a social problem. See Joel Best and Gerald T. Horiuchi, "The Razor Blade in the Apple: The Social Construction of Urban Legends," *Social Problems* 32, no. 5 (1985): 488–499; Steve Woolgar and Dorothy Pawluch, "Ontological Gerrymandering: The Anatomy of Social Problems Explanations," *Social Problems* 32, no. 3 (1985): 214–227. The theory differs from this literature, however, in that it puts more emphasis on agency, conflict, and symbolic power in the struggle to become "a thing."

[10] Collin Hansen, "Young, Restless, Reformed: Calvinism Is Making a Comeback—And Shaking Up the Church," *Christianity Today*, September 22, 2006, http://www.christianitytoday.com/ct/2006/september/42.32.html, accessed December 28, 2015.

Calvinism with an Evangelical press named Crossway Books (see chapter 2 for the significant role of Crossway itself in the movement).[11] From there, the New Calvinism started to get coverage in the mainstream secular press. In the opening days of 2009, University of North Carolina historian Molly Worthen—while she was still in graduate school at Yale—wrote about the New Calvinism by focusing on one of its leading megachurches, Mars Hill Church (MHC) in Seattle. She wrote:

> [Calvinistic American Evangelicals'] message seems radically unfashionable, even un-American: you are not captain of your soul or master of your fate but a depraved worm whose hard work and good deeds will get you nowhere, because God marked you for heaven or condemned you to hell before the beginning of time. Yet a significant number of young people in Seattle—and nationwide—say this is exactly what they want to hear. Calvinism has somehow become cool.[12]

Two months later, David Van Biema writing for *TIME Magazine* included the New Calvinism on a list of "10 Ideas Changing the World Right Now."[13] Quoting Ted Olsen, managing editor at *Christianity Today*, Van Biema wrote: "'Everyone knows where the energy and the passion are in the Evangelical world'—with the pioneering new-Calvinist John Piper of Minneapolis, Seattle's pugnacious Mark Driscoll and Albert Mohler, head of the Southern Seminary of the huge Southern Baptist Convention." Warren Nozaki followed up with a good summary of the New Calvinism in a 2010 issue of the *Christian Research Journal*, published by the Christian Research Institute.[14] In *The Economist*, Julia Duin was one of the first among several journalists to investigate the rise of—and controversy surrounding—Calvinism in the Southern Baptist Convention, in particular.[15] For *The Christian Science Monitor*, journalist Josh Burek declared that "Calvinism

---

[11] Collin Hansen, *Young, Restless, Reformed: A Journalist's Journey with the New Calvinists* (Wheaton, IL: Crossway, 2008).

[12] Molly Worthen, "Who Would Jesus Smack Down?" *The New York Times*, January 6, 2009, http://www.nytimes.com/2009/01/11/magazine/11punk-t.html, accessed December 28, 2015.

[13] David Van Biema, "The New Calvinism," *Time*, March 12, 2009, http://content.time.com/time/specials/packages/article/0,28804,1884779_1884782_1884760,00.html, accessed December 28, 2015.

[14] Warren Nozaki, "Reformed Theology Resurgence," *Christian Research Journal*, November 3, 2010, http://www.equip.org/article/reformed-theology-resurgence/, accessed December 28, 2015.

[15] Julia Duin, "The New Calvins: Tensions Inside of One of America's Most Successful Churches," *The Economist*, October 7, 2010, http://www.economist.com/node/17204934, accessed December 29, 2015.

Is Back" among American Evangelicals, especially highly educated twenty-somethings.[16] Also in 2010, Kate Shellnutt profiled the New Calvinist movement in an article for *The Houston Chronicle*, focusing on its rising presence in Houston, Dallas, and Austin.[17] "The newest thing in Protestantism," she opened, "is really the oldest thing in Protestantism: Reformed theology." Harkening back to Worthen's essay five years earlier in *The New York Times*, near the end of 2013 Boston University religion professor Stephen Prothero wrote about Mark Driscoll and MHC for *The Wall Street Journal*, focusing on (and lightly criticizing) Driscoll's "macho vision of Christ."[18]

By 2014, the existence and popularity of a New Calvinist movement was firmly established in the American Evangelical psyche, and continuing coverage of it in the secular media was already viewed (by the Evangelical leaders involved) as somewhat late to the game. In *The New York Times*, "Belief" columnist Mark Oppenheimer wrote:

> Evangelicalism is in the midst of a Calvinist revival. Increasing numbers
> of preachers and professors teach the views of the 16th-century French re-
> former. Mark Driscoll, John Piper and Tim Keller—megachurch preachers
> and important evangelical authors—are all Calvinist. Attendance at Calvin-
> influenced worship conferences and churches is up, particularly among
> worshipers in their 20s and 30s.[19]

[16] Josh Burek, "Christian Faith: Calvinism Is Back," *The Christian Science Monitor*, March 27, 2010, http://www.csmonitor.com/USA/Society/2010/0327/Christian-faith-Calvinism-is-back, accessed December 29, 2015.

[17] Kate Shellnutt, "Young Christians Turn to Centuries-Old Teachings of Church Fathers: Next Generation of Theologians Craves Historical Tradition," *The Houston Chronicle*, October 28, 2010, http://www.chron.com/life/houston-belief/article/Young-Christians-turn-to-centuries-old-teachings-1599346.php, accessed December 29, 2015.

[18] Stephen Prothero, "A Cage-Fighting Christ for Our Time: Updating American Tradition by Calling for a More Macho Redeemer," *The Wall Street Journal*, December 12, 2013, http://www.wsj.com/articles/SB10001424052702304073204579167963887805686, accessed December 29, 2015.

[19] Mark Oppenheimer, "Evangelicals Find Themselves in the Midst of a Calvinist Revival," *The New York Times*, January 3, 2014, http://www.nytimes.com/2014/01/04/us/a-calvinist-revival-for-evangelicals.html, accessed December 29, 2015. Oppenheimer interviewed me over the phone for this article and quoted me at the end of it. However, our interactions later in the process over email made it clear he was having trouble understanding a distinction I was making between (quantitative) adherence to Calvinism among American Evangelicals broadly and (somewhat more qualitative) *attention or emphasis given to this "New Calvinism" as a movement*, including media attention like his very own article. His original wording made it sound like I thought the former would soon be in decline, when I really meant that the latter would. His eventual word choice of "the hoopla might level off" is a result of me stressing this.

Denny Burk, professor of biblical studies at Boyce College (the undergraduate school of the Southern Baptist Theological Seminary), perceptively picked up on this and responded to it on his personal blog (http://www.dennyburk.com/check-out-the-new-york-times-fascinating-feature-on-the-resurgence-of-calvinism-among-evangelicals-nytimes-markopp1/, accessed December 30, 2015). Burk wrote:

Following up on Oppenheimer's piece, Martin Marty, professor emeritus at the University of Chicago Divinity School, reflected on the religious conflict and tensions about Calvinism on the website for the Martin Marty Center for the Advanced Study of Religion. His post was quickly picked up and republished by *The Huffington Post*.[20] In addition to the conflict dimension, Marty noted, "[T]he movement has helped place what we might call Calvinist 'theological-theology' on the agenda at seminaries, church growth institutes, and opinion fashioners in the media." When the Jonathan Edwards Center at Yale University[21] made the collected works of Edwards free online in early 2015, Evangelical journalist Jonathan Merritt reported on it for *Religion News Service*, which was then republished with *The Washington Post* and *The Huffington Post*.[22] Merritt explained well the "renewed interest" in the mid-eighteenth-century American Calvinist thinker—"especially among conservative evangelicals and 'New Calvinists.'"

Only recently have academic works made mention of the New Calvinism; however, by now it has clearly entered the scholarly literature. When the movement is mentioned, it is usually in works published by Oxford University Press. Presbyterian historian D. G. Hart, for instance, framed his chapter on the post–World War II legacy of Jonathan Edwards in relation to "the Young,

---

The end- of the article asks whether the reformed resurgence is a fad—a movement that is here and then gone like the emergent church. I think that comparison misses the point. There are many important differences between the two movements that render them apples and oranges. The emergent church represented theological innovation. The reformed resurgence is a rallying around something old. The emergent church comprised a theologically liberal impulse. The reformed resurgence comprises a conservative one— one rooted in the rallying cry of the reformation Sola Scriptura. The emergent movement was here and then for all practical purposes has left us. I predict that will not be the case with reformed resurgence. It has proved to be an enduring tradition over the centuries. To be sure, its popularity may indeed wane in North American evangelicalism. In fact, that is almost surely to happen eventually. But it is not likely to go extinct like other theological flashes in the pan. The tradition will go forward even if its current popularity doesn't. That's the difference.

[20] Martin Marty, "Calvinism and Conflict," *The Huffington Post*, January 28, 2014, http://www.huffingtonpost.com/martin-marty/calvinism-and-conflict_b_4677124.html, accessed December 30, 2015.

[21] http://edwards.yale.edu/

[22] Jonathan Merritt, "Jonathan Edwards' Collected Works Now Available for Download," *The Washington Post*, February 3, 2015, https://www.washingtonpost.com/national/religion/jonathan-edwards-collected-works-now-available-for-download/2015/02/03/5d70cf08-abc8-11e4-8876-460b1144cbc1_story.html, accessed December 30, 2015; Jonathan Merritt, "Fiery Colonial Preacher Jonathan Edwards' Collected Works Now Available Online," *The Huffington Post*, February 4, 2015, http://www.huffingtonpost.com/2015/02/04/jonathan-edwards-works-online_n_6605714.html, accessed December 29, 2015.

Restless, and Reformed."[23] Historian Jon Balserak discusses "New Calvinism" and "New Calvinists," along with John Piper, Tim Keller, and R. C. Sproul, in his 2016 introduction to Calvinism.[24] Fredrik Fällman has published on the "rather unexpected development" of New Calvinism among young intellectuals in China.[25] And a descriptive portrait of the New Calvinism is forthcoming as a chapter from Flynn Cratty, a PhD candidate in European history at Yale.[26] In sociology, Wes Markofski's groundbreaking book on "the New Monasticism"—which, like this book, analyzes Evangelicalism in the United States as its own field of contestation—mentions the New Calvinism in passing twice, but it does not factor into the book's larger analysis.[27] Likewise, in their analysis of the Emerging Church movement, Gerardo Marti and Gladys Ganiel mention "neo-Reformed evangelicals" and the "neo-Calvinists" multiple times[28] (but see the next chapter on "neo-Calvinism" vs. "New Calvinism"), referring to this New Calvinist phenomenon.[29]

Data and Methods

Data for this project come from a mixed-method approach, employing three kinds of qualitative research. The first is participant observation at three New Calvinist megachurches in different regions of the United States (namely, the East Coast, Pacific Northwest, and Midwest).[30] The second is interviews with

[23] D. G. Hart, "Before the Young, Restless, and Reformed: Edwards's Appeal to Post-World War II Evangelicals," in *After Jonathan Edwards: The Courses of the New England Theology*, ed. Oliver D. Crisp and Douglas A. Sweeney (New York: Oxford University Press, 2012), 237–253.

[24] Jon Balserak, *Calvinism: A Very Short Introduction* (New York: Oxford University Press, 2016), xiv, 1, 8, 23, 85, 125.

[25] Fredrik Fällman, "Calvin, Culture, and Christ? Developments of Faith among Chinese Intellectuals," in *Christianity in Contemporary China: Socio-cultural Perspectives*, ed. Francis Khek Gee Lim (New York: Routledge, 2013), 153–168. While the present analysis focuses on the New Calvinism in the United States, I hope to write on New Calvinism outside of the United States in future work.

[26] Flynn Cratty, "The New Calvinism," in *The Oxford Handbook of John Calvin*, ed. Carl Trueman and Bruce Gordon (New York: Oxford University Press), in press.

[27] Wes Markofski, *New Monasticism and the Transformation of American Evangelicalism* (New York: Oxford University Press, 2015), 79, 146.

[28] Gerardo Marti and Gladys Ganiel, *The Deconstructed Church: Understanding Emerging Christianity* (New York: Oxford University Press, 2014), 57, 93, 103–104, 107, 138, 140, 167.

[29] Christian Smith also mentioned the "neo-Reformed" segment of American Evangelicalism in his afterword to *The Bible Made Impossible: Why Biblicism Is Not a Truly Evangelical Reading of Scripture* (Grand Rapids, MI: Brazos Press, [2011] 2012), 180.

[30] On the effect of regional culture on religious life, see, for example, James K. Wellman, Jr. and Katie E. Corcoran, "Religion and Regional Culture: Embedding Religious Commitment within Place," *Sociology of Religion* 74, no. 4 (2013): 496–520; Philip Barlow and Mark Silk, eds., *Religion*

seventy-five Evangelical leaders across the country, including not only New Calvinist figures but also leaders who are peripheral to or even fervently critical of the movement. And the third component of data is content analysis of a host of printed and online materials from within the American Evangelical subculture, including their books, blog-posts, recorded sermons, promotional materials, conference lectures, online videos, pamphlets, orders of worship, and so on.

Participant Observation

The participant observation leg of my project began in October 2012 when I flew from Detroit to Seattle to gather data on MHC, where Mark Driscoll was the senior pastor. For ten weeks, I did everything a heavily involved attendee of MHC would do, and much more. I attended weekend services, often two or three in one day, at the different campuses of MHC across the greater Seattle region. I attended postservice gatherings at pubs and restaurants with the pastoral staff and their congregants. I rode a bicycle to and from community group (Bible study) in the Seattle rain. I attended a weekly junior and senior high ministry at the church's Shoreline campus. Late in the evening, I went out for cocktails and sushi with the worship bands. I sat in on preacher training (for the pastors starting new campuses of MHC), an apologetics seminar, and men's night. I went to a Thanksgiving dinner in the University District for international students and other people who had nowhere else to go. I went to the homes and dinner parties of deacons and musicians. I showed up early, stayed late, and asked questions. Near the end of my stay in Seattle, MHC staff gave me a guided tour behind the scenes of the production side of the church and, the next day, let me shadow them for an afternoon. After two and a half months, I returned home a week before Christmas.

The next month, in late January 2013, I moved into an apartment in the Financial District of Lower Manhattan, in New York City, for participant observation at Redeemer Presbyterian Church (RPC), where Tim Keller was the lead pastor. For two months, I did the things a twenty-something Manhattanite deeply involved at this Evangelical megachurch would do— and, again, probably more. I attended the Sunday services at the church's

and Public Life in the Midwest: America's Common Denominator? (Walnut Creek, CA: AltaMira Press, 2004).

three locations across Manhattan, often two or three in one day. I participated in two of the church's vocational groups, for writers and PhD students. I dove deeply into "Quarters," RPC's twenty-something ministry that organized happy hours and social events throughout the city. I frequented the church's Midtown offices, met with the pastoral staff, and saw congregants waiting for counseling services. I visited a Bible study group in a cramped NoHo apartment. I watched the performers in Central Park, but I avoided Times Square and made sure not to make eye contact on the subway. I attended supplementary lectures on the Upper West Side on topics like work and art and contextualizing the Gospel. I attended praise and worship nights during the week and went to a lunch where newcomers could learn about Redeemer. I listened as entrepreneurs in the church pitched their business plans to potential investors, hoping to win sponsorship from the church. And I wandered Manhattan for hours in the bitter cold with volunteers from Redeemer, looking for homeless people to introduce to the church's social services.

That summer, for June and July 2013, I moved into a house on the edge of downtown Minneapolis to gather data on Bethlehem Baptist Church (BBC), where John Piper was the longtime preacher. Here again, I attended multiple worship services each weekend, including the live services on Saturday evenings at their downtown location and services with prerecorded sermons on Sundays. In addition to services, I got involved in other areas of the church's life. I went to evangelism training dinners. I attended the church's weekly "getting acquainted with Bethlehem" discussion group for newcomers. I sat through classes on Calvinism, and I explored BBC's large bookstore. I participated in the church's pro-life taskforce and watched a panel discussion on how Christians should respond to the legalization of same-sex marriage. I went to a prayer meeting for persecuted Christians around the globe. I walked trails along the Mississippi River. I attended Bethlehem's quarterly strategy meeting and the finale performance of their children's music camp. I went to their community group leader appreciation dinner. Midweek, I joined them downtown in public parks for street evangelism and for well-attended baptism services, where we ate, sang, and dunked people in large tubs of water.

In addition to these three megachurches, I attended other events relevant to the New Calvinist movement as such opportunities arose. Some of those were events hosted by leaders and organizations in other, competing pockets or "tribes" of American Evangelicalism. For instance, near the end of my time in Minneapolis, I attended a six-hour "missional roundtable," which featured leaders from the neo-Anabaptist pocket of American Evangelicalism, including David Fitch, Geoff Holsclaw, and Mark Van Steenwyk. (Neo-Anabaptist Evangelicalism is described in chapter 3.) Likewise, during my final two weeks in Minneapolis, while still participating at BBC, I also attended worship gatherings and social events at Solomon's Porch, a progressive "Emergent" congregation led by Doug Pagitt.[31] (This pocket of American Evangelicalism is also described in chapter 3.) Other supplemental events I attended were thoroughly New Calvinist. For example, in early December 2013, I participated in a two-day Evangelical conference in downtown Lansing, Michigan, titled Sola 13,[32] which celebrated and defended the five solae of the Protestant Reformation.[33] That conference was put on by two large Calvinistic churches in the Lansing area—namely, University Reformed Church (PCA) and Riverview Church (nondenominational)—and featured presentations from New Calvinist figureheads such as Matt Chandler, John Piper, Albert Mohler, Kevin DeYoung, and others. Throughout this entire season, I wrote thorough field-notes documenting and reflecting on all that I was doing and seeing. More details and a complete listing of events for this participant observation aspect of data collection are available in Appendix A.

Personal Interviews

Throughout this time, and continuing for several months later, I also conducted interviews with Evangelical leaders across the United States to hear—in their own words—their perspectives on their religious identities, theology, cultural issues, the New Calvinism, and the current state of the American Evangelical field. In total, the number of interviews conducted was seventy-five, with a slight oversample of the pastoral staff and other leaders (musicians, deacons, etc.) from within the three Calvinistic megachurches where I conducted participant observation. Outside of those three megachurches, I interviewed additional leaders from across the full spectrum of American Evangelicalism, including more New Calvinists in other

---

[31] http://www.solomonsporch.com/
[32] http://sola13.com/
[33] These are five Latin phrases, coalesced in later centuries, that indicate core convictions of the Reformation during the sixteenth century, in protest against Roman Catholic teachings: *Sola Scriptura* (Scripture alone), *Sola Gratia* (Grace alone), *Sola Fide* (Faith alone), *Solus Christus* (Christ alone), and *Soli Deo Gloria* (Glory to God alone).

organizations as well as other, non-Calvinistic pockets and expressions of American Evangelicalism.

From among the New Calvinists, to name just a few, I interviewed Kevin DeYoung, Justin Taylor, Tim Keller, Tim Challies, Mark Dever, Owen Strachan, Collin Hansen, and (a not-so-new-Calvinist) J. I. Packer. Among progressives, I interviewed Tony Jones, Doug Pagitt, Brian McLaren, Christian Piatt, Rachel Held Evans, Jay Bakker, Frank Schaeffer, and Phyllis Tickle, among others. In the neo-Anabaptist corner, I interviewed David Fitch, Geoff Holsclaw, Greg Boyd, Mark Van Steenwyk, Tim Suttle, and Shane Claiborne, among others. Among mainstream American Evangelicals, I interviewed leaders such as Andy Crouch, Austin Fischer, Matt Bennett, and Roger Olson.[34] This wide-reaching pool of interview data added a wealth of rich, personal accounts, insights, and observations directly from the Evangelical leaders themselves to supplement the other data sources.[35] More details, including a list of the interviewees, their affiliations, and the full interview guide, are included in Appendix A.

Printed and Online Content

Much of what happens of sociological interest among the leadership ranks of American Evangelicals today happens in print and, especially, on the Internet. Therefore, any examination of contemporary American Evangelicalism—particularly one, as this is, that tries to capture discourse and infighting among its leaders—would be incomplete without broad-sweeping content analysis. First, print: Over the course of my participant observation, I amassed a pile of printed materials from MHC, RPC, and BBC just under 1.5 feet high which included orders of worship, annual reports, promotional materials, newsletters, and informational pamphlets. These sources supplemented my fieldwork and interviews to help gain a thorough picture of these three megachurches. I also obtained and read several books authored by some of the Evangelical leaders in this study, both Calvinists and non-Calvinists, which (although not a random sample) likewise gave me a broader and deeper vision of the field.

---

[34] Olson's was the only interview conducted in written form.
[35] See Allison J. Pugh, "What Good Are Interviews for Thinking about Culture? Demystifying Interpretive Analysis," *American Journal of Cultural Sociology* 1, no. 1 (2013): 42–68.

The more involved element of content analysis was from the Internet. Over the course of about four years (from autumn 2011 to autumn 2015), I immersed myself in the digital world of the New Calvinism and reactions to it.[36] I started on Facebook, where I systematically "friended" or "liked" the pages of a few hundred Evangelical leaders and organizations, both New Calvinists and otherwise. I also paid close attention to Evangelical elites and organizations on Twitter, eventually creating my own account in March 2015 and "following" several of them. On both Facebook and Twitter, I made a habit of reading their updates, clicking on whatever links they posted, and following their digital trails to find out what they were thinking and talking about. I visited their personal and organizational websites; I read their blogs; I watched their recorded sermons; and I kept up on news about American Evangelicalism by reading outlets such as *The Christian Post, Christianity Today, First Things, CNN, The Atlantic,* and *The New York Times.* I listened to their music, watched their videos on YouTube and Vimeo, and subscribed to their podcasts on iTunes (mostly various kinds of nonsermon lectures, interviews, and discussions), which I regularly listened to while driving and washing the dishes. Through all of this, I became extraordinarily well-versed not only in the ideological and cultural content of the various expressions of American Evangelicalism at the level of leadership, but I also saw precisely who was interacting with or critiquing whom, when, and how.[37]

Analytic Strategy

Much of this sort of qualitative research appeals to "grounded theory," which is an approach that tries to let theoretical insights and explanations emerge inductively from the data using certain analytic strategies, like memo writing and theoretical sampling.[38] My process of data analysis and

---

[36] Seth Giddings and Martin Lister, eds., *The New Media and Technocultures Reader* (New York: Routledge, 2011); T. V. Reed, *Digitized Lives: Culture, Power, and Social Change in the Internet Era* (New York: Routledge, 2014). See also the discussion of the role of the Internet in the New Calvinism in chapter 5.

[37] Scott A. Golder and Michael W. Macy, "Digital Footprints: Opportunities and Challenges for Online Social Research," *Annual Review of Sociology* 40 (2014): 129–152.

[38] Antony Bryant and Kathy Charmaz, eds., *The Sage Handbook of Grounded Theory* (Thousand Oaks, CA: Sage, 2007); Kathy Charmaz, *Constructing Grounded Theory*, 2nd ed. (Thousand Oaks, CA: Sage, [2006] 2014); Juliet Corbin and Anselm Strauss, *Basics of Qualitative Research: Techniques and Procedures for Developing Grounded Theory*, 4th ed. (Thousand Oaks, CA: Sage, 2015).

theoretical discovery[39] did resemble a standard grounded theory approach in many ways. However, my mindset from the beginning differed from some applications of grounded theory in two ways, both of which reflect something of an empiricist bias in the standard grounded theory model. First, grounded theory is typically organized around *induction* as the mode of inference, but instead my analytic strategy relied on *retroduction* and *abduction*. This means I thought hard about what must be the case and what factors must be at play for the phenomenon under study to be the way it is (retroduction) and allowed the empirical data and evidence to "carry me away" to new working hypotheses and possible theories (abduction).[40] Second, I rejected the assumption that any person who looked at the same data and applied the same analytic methods would necessarily arrive at precisely the same conclusions and explanations as I did—as if the "right answer" was buried in the sociological data and all one needed to do was excavate it.[41] A better way to look at it is that I interpreted the dataset as fair-mindedly as possible in light of existing theoretical frameworks and my own social position and intellectual training in order to construct (what I think is) a compelling explanation and argument.[42]

What This Book Is Not

More than a few casual interactions among friends and colleagues while writing this manuscript have made it evident to me that it is as necessary at the outset to make clear not only what this project *is* but also what it *is not*. What follows are five possible misperceptions that I have encountered during the research and writing process.

First, this book is not a theological defense or critique of Calvinism or, for that matter, any other theological approach, worldview, or belief system.

---

[39] Richard Swedberg, *The Art of Social Theory* (Princeton, NJ: Princeton University Press, 2014); Richard Swedberg, ed., *Theorizing in Social Science: The Context of Discovery* (Stanford, CA: Stanford University Press, 2014).

[40] Stefan Timmermans and Iddo Tavory, "Theory Construction in Qualitative Research: From Grounded Theory to Abductive Analysis," *Sociological Theory* 30, no. 3 (2012): 167–186; Iddo Tavory and Stefan Timmermans, *Abductive Analysis: Theorizing Qualitative Research* (Chicago: The University of Chicago Press, 2014).

[41] Ironically, "the inductive method" is a popular method of biblical interpretation, which, as we will see, might explain some of the doctrinal disagreements and infighting among American Evangelicals.

[42] See Paul K. Edwards, Joe O'Mahoney, and Steve Vincent, eds., *Studying Organizations Using Critical Realism: A Practical Guide* (New York: Oxford University Press, 2014).

Even while at certain points it is necessary to describe a position or a dispute in the field of Evangelical theology—or even to articulate a leader's critique of some theological idea—this book itself takes no stances on questions regarding theology. When it comes to social science, this book describes, explains, critiques, and makes arguments; but when it comes to theology, it only describes. Readers will not find in these pages arguments or claims about which religious beliefs are "best" or "true." When appropriate, I do attempt to clarify common misconceptions about doctrines in order to present them as accurately as possible—that is, to present them in the way Evangelical scholars who actually hold those doctrines would express them. Still, the goal throughout is to be impartial (as far as that is possible) and fair-minded toward the various theological systems and beliefs one encounters.

Secondly, this book is not a work of comparative sociology. On multiple occasions, when my interlocutors heard I was gathering data on three influential Calvinistic megachurches in different regions of the country, some assumed my intention was to compare them with one another. Others, when they heard I discuss and analyze the field of American Evangelicalism in terms of its four major "tribes," likewise thought that the primary objective was to compare them. Neither is the case. As with practically any sociological study, some basic comparisons are made (especially in chapter 3), but the comparative method is not the primary approach of this project. Instead, the narrative and argument in this work are far more reliant upon the relational, game-like social contestations and interactions between religious leaders within and over the American Evangelical field.[43]

Similarly, this book is not an exercise in historical sociology. It appears that for some, the words "New" and "Calvinism"—or, by association, Weber[44]—immediately suggest that the analysis deals with long historical processes, reaching deep into the past (e.g., dealing with an older, classic Calvinism). That, too, is not the case. Even though Calvinism and some of its historic theological alternatives are centuries old, most of the processes and actors relevant to the New Calvinist movement emerged no earlier than the 1960s, and many parts of the story, like the Internet and the "Emerging Church,"

---

[43] In this way, the analysis in this book is an example of what Matt Desmond calls "relational ethnography," which "involves studying fields rather than places, boundaries rather than bounded groups, processes rather than processed people, and cultural conflict rather than group culture." See Matthew Desmond, "Relational Ethnography," *Theory and Society* 43, no. 5 (2014): 547–579. Quoted from p. 574.

[44] Stephen Kalberg, *Max Weber's Comparative-Historical Sociology* (Chicago: The University of Chicago Press, 1994).

only began in the 1990s. This is very much a study of *present-day* American Evangelicalism.

At the same time, given the somewhat long timeframe during which this project took form, a challenge during the writing process was keeping up with the ongoing flux in American Evangelicalism, both big and small—especially changes which occurred after I had written the pertinent sections. Since I started this book, megachurches have closed or splintered, pastors have resigned, editors and professors have changed positions, and more. Rather than ignore those changes, on the one hand, or frantically try to keep up with them, on the other, I chose to strike what I hope is a reasonable balance. I updated the manuscript when doing so struck me as necessary and feasible, but in a few subtle ways (such as the numbers in Appendix C) I left the "weight" of the narrative back in 2012 to 2016. So, if a quoted leader feels no longer central or if the newest big thing is left out, that is why.

Fourthly, this book is not an attempt to "prove a hypothesis." By far the most common question I received in the years working on this project was what hypothesis I was trying to prove. The question is innocuous enough, but (aside from the correction that hypotheses in the hard sciences are *tested*, and either supported or not supported, not *proven*) the question assumes a hypothetico-deductive model of the social sciences that I do not adopt in this work nor accept more generally.[45] Thus, this project is not, strictly speaking, an effort to prove or test some hypothesis, as one might do in a chemistry lab or with a psychology experiment. A better way to view the project is as an endeavor to use the best available evidence and sociological theory together in order to describe, analyze, and explain an interesting socio-religious phenomenon—the New Calvinism. I *do* make an argument, but in the process it is best to avoid the language of "hypothesis testing" and "proof."[46]

Finally, this book is not causally exhaustive—that is, this book does not address every cause that might possibly contribute to the rise and resurgence of Calvinism in American Evangelicalism today. As a work of sociology, this project focuses only on *social* causal mechanisms—and therefore causal mechanisms and processes that might be considered "nonsocial" are not accounted for. For instance, during the interviews for this project, some Evangelical leaders stated that they became convinced of the truth of

---

[45] Philip S. Gorski, "The Poverty of Deductivism: A Constructive Realist Model of Sociological Explanation," *Sociological Methodology* 34, no. 1 (2004): 1–33.

[46] Berth Danermark et al., *Explaining Society: Critical Realism in the Social Sciences* (New York: Routledge, 2002).

Calvinism after a period of personal study. They read the Bible for themselves, considered what the text meant, and in the end found Calvinism to be the most compelling theological system. That certainly would make sense as a causal process that has contributed to the rise of Calvinism on the "micro" level, but that sort of isolated personal study and reflection is not the kind of causal mechanism or explanation that is at issue in this investigation.[47]

In a different way, several persons with whom I have spoken (namely, those who view the New Calvinism as a positive and encouraging development) have expressed concern about writing a sociological book about the resurgence of a theology. From their perspective, the resurgence of Calvinism—along with renewed passion among American Evangelicals for theological rigor, the glory and sovereignty of God, the health of local churches, and expositional "Gospel-centered" preaching—is ultimately a miraculous, supernatural work of God sparking revival in the hearts, minds, and lives of people across America. And such a divine act, the concern goes, is not subject to being explained (or explained away) in human terms through social processes. Regardless of whether or not a divine Being is at work behind or through this movement, this book "brackets off" the supernatural as a causal factor and instead proceeds on the premise that there is much to be gained from understanding the social, cultural, and institutional processes involved.

What Follows

The logic and argument of this book build sequentially across the chapters. In this regard, reading any chapter before the ones that come before it will result in at best a partial and "foggy" understanding of the purposes they serve in addressing the New Calvinist movement and in advancing the broader argument. More immediately, this also means that the current section serves a dual purpose—it provides both an overview of the rest of the book as well as a narrative summary of the big-picture argument it makes.

From here, chapter 2 provides an introductory description of the New Calvinism. It begins with short descriptions of the three New Calvinist megachurches at which I conducted participant observation, followed by a number of other key organizations, institutions, conferences, networks,

---

[47] See Ronald Jepperson and John W. Meyer, "Multiple Levels of Analysis and the Limitations of Methodological Individualisms," *Sociological Theory* 29, no. 1 (2011): 54–73.

and religious leaders constituting the Reformed resurgence. These include the Acts 29 Network, Southern Baptist Theological Seminary, The Gospel Coalition, Together for the Gospel, the Passion Conferences, Crossway and the ESV Bible, and the Council on Biblical Manhood and Womanhood, among others. It then describes the beliefs and convictions which taken together delineate the New Calvinism within the broader landscape of Evangelicalism in the United States, including a Calvinistic view of salvation, traditional complementarian views of men and women, and social conservatism. The chapter also addresses taking a "missional" posture toward culture as well as the continuation versus cessation of the miraculous gifts of the Holy Spirit, suggesting these two markers—commonly used in the movement itself—are somewhat less helpful lenses through which to delineate the New Calvinism. The chapter wraps up with four more descriptive and analytical concerns—namely, the holding together of the "religious affections" with "the life of the mind," whether or not the New Calvinism is "truly Reformed," what the difference is between New Calvinism and Kuyperian neo-Calvinism, as well as the significance of a resurgent element to the movement. Altogether, this chapter offers a succinct descriptive introduction to the major organizations, networks, conferences, leaders, doctrines, convictions, and features of the movement.

Having described the New Calvinism substantively and analytically, chapter 3 identifies and details the other tribes or pockets of American Evangelicalism against which the Reformed resurgence is said to be resurging. These are mainstream American Evangelicalism, neo-Anabaptist Evangelicalism, and progressive or Emergent Evangelicalism. Next, this chapter clarifies a possible confusion about how these three alternatives and the New Calvinism relate to the Emerging Church, and then it briefly acknowledges some intermixing and blurring between these four tribes. The latter half of chapter 3 employs the limited data available to address these tribes' comparative sizes and sociological strengths. The conclusion is that although the New Calvinism has indeed grown numerically since the late 1990s, the other expressions and tribes of American Evangelicalism either (a) are large enough to match and overshadow the organizational growth and leadership following of the New Calvinist movement (as is the case with mainstream Evangelicalism) or (b) are significantly smaller in scale but have themselves largely emerged only since the late 1990s and therefore have "resurged" in their field percentage-wise just as much (which is the case for the neo-Anabaptist and progressive Emergent pockets). This conclusion

suggests the New Calvinism enjoys strength and prominence disproportionate to its numerical following and sets the stage for an explanatory model
of institutional religious strength that relies more on the strategic and conflictual efforts of leaders to gain symbolic power in and over their field than
on simple additive growth.

Chapter 4 develops such a model. It starts by revisiting the question of religious strength vis-à-vis the secularization thesis, and then it briefly lays out
the five leading theoretical frameworks currently on offer in the sociology
of religion for making sense of religious vitality (namely, sheltered enclave
theory, status discontent theory, strict church theory, the religious economies framework, and subcultural identity theory). Next, this chapter critically reviews each theory, drawing out the "nugget of truth" in each but finally
showing how each is ill-suited, or at least incomplete, for explaining the New
Calvinist movement sociologically. However, what each framework gets
right, I argue, can be incorporated into a new, field-theoretic model of religious strength. From there, this chapter gives an introduction to field theory
in sociology and suggests one recently developed stream of field theory—
Fligstein and McAdam's "strategic action fields"[48]—is well-suited to explain
the New Calvinism. The crucial insight from strategic action field theory that
helps to explain the New Calvinism is that *through social processes of game-
like contestation, leaders of movements and organizations strategically battle
and vie with their competitors for a more advantageous position in and over
their field, which is defined by possession of symbolic capital and power.* Some
space is taken to work out the "nuts and bolts" of the framework as it relates
to *strategy* (i.e., relational positioning instead of social skill or tactics), *opportunity* (i.e., discursive rather than political), and the undergirding theory of
human *action* (namely, one that is culturalist, not economistic). With all the
parts in place, the chapter concludes with a systematization of the theory/
model, in which seventeen general social mechanisms are specified as causes
that together produced the Reformed resurgence.

The remainder of the book is an explication of this causal model.
Chapters 5 and 6 demonstrate this field-theoretic approach to religious
strength empirically in two parts using the data described earlier in this introductory chapter. In both parts, the social mechanisms identified at the
end of chapter 4 serve as guideposts, which are italicized in the text.

---

[48] Fligstein and McAdam, *A Theory of Fields*.

In chapter 5, Part I focuses on the most powerful social mechanisms and processes that precipitated the rise of the New Calvinist movement. First, I describe three aspects of the American cultural "backdrop" (namely, the gender and sexual revolutions since the 1960s, religious pluralism and fluidity, and "the triumph of the therapeutic"[49]) and three discursive opportunities (namely, the invention and widespread use of the Internet, the terrorist attacks of 9/11, and postmodernism and the Emerging Church), which together facilitated the onset of contention in the American Evangelical field. Following this, I map the correspondence between Evangelical leaders' positions in the field and their corresponding dispositions, which I heuristically term their "first foot forward in their Christian walk" (i.e., *ontology* for the New Calvinists, *epistemology* for the progressives, *ethics* for the neo-Anabaptists, and *pragmatism* among mainstream Evangelicals). I then explain the importance of the multivocality of the Bible as well as the observation that, based on the time I spent in the field, at least one-quarter of congregants involved in neo-Reformed churches seem not to know enough about Calvinism even to have an opinion about it. The chapter ends by empirically establishing the "rules of the game," which are the elements of the Bebbington Quadrilateral[50] (i.e., crucicentrism, biblicism, activism, and conversionism), to which I add the more all-encompassing field-rule of "the Gospel," very broadly defined. These rules are understood to be endogenous to the social system such that the battle over American Evangelicalism is a battle *with* and *over* these rules.

In chapter 6, Part II demonstrates the game-like contest and battle in the American Evangelical field, which functioned to create and fortify the Reformed resurgence. It begins by showing multiple ways New Calvinist leaders strategically positioned themselves in relation to their field competitors to secure a "competitive advantage" (especially among university-educated young people) over other expressions of Evangelical Christianity. These include providing clear "black and white" answers; promoting traditional notions of masculinity and femininity; offering historical rootedness within a tradition of the Church; deemphasizing autonomous will and self-direction; evincing theological seriousness; focusing on elite urban culture; and being apolitical and nonpartisan. As part

---

[49] Philip Rieff, *The Triumph of the Therapeutic: Uses of Faith after Freud* (Chicago: The University of Chicago Press, [1966] 1987).

[50] David W. Bebbington, *Evangelicalism in Modern Britain: A History from the 1730s to the 1980s* (London: Unwin Hyman, 1989), 2–17.

of this positioning, many New Calvinist leaders have also positioned themselves as the gatekeepers of the field's established orthodoxy, trying to enforce who is "in" and who is "out" based on the "rules of the game."[51] As
two examples, I give in-depth accounts of the recent and very public controversies regarding former megachurch pastor Rob Bell (his view on Hell)
and World Vision-USA (their short-lived policy change on gay marriage),
focusing on the strong Calvinist resistance. In these cases and elsewhere,
this chapter also shows religious leaders—in the position as challengers in
the field—pushing back against and criticizing New Calvinist leaders, their
actions, and dispositions. The factors of charismatic authority and regional
contextualization are also highlighted. In total, this chapter demonstrates the
field-theoretic model of religious strength by showing how the Reformed resurgence, the New Calvinist movement, is largely a *relationally constructed
and symbolic strength*—an institutional vitality that has been fought for and
won by Christian leaders' strategic and conflictual actions.

Lastly, chapter 7 takes stock of what the preceding explanation means for
American Evangelicalism today. It starts with comments and evaluations
from Evangelical leaders themselves regarding the state and health, or lack
thereof, of Evangelicalism in the United States. Avoiding the sociologist's
problematic temptation to predict the future, this chapter instead makes explicit what by this point will be clear about Evangelicalism *presently*: that the
strength and resurgence of the New Calvinist movement have unintentionally come at the cost of the increasing weakness, fragmentation, and incoherence of the Evangelical field in the United States as a whole.[52] Not that this
is the New Calvinists' "fault"; the neo-Reformed movement is best understood as a reaction to, not the cause of, Evangelicalism's troubles. In closing,
this chapter offers two brief reflections for the sociology of religion. The first
is simply that to understand and explain religion well sociologists must do
better to understand the theological issues and particularities that matter to
religious people. The second addresses the question of religion in the hypermodern world in light of a field-theoretic model of religious strength (and
weakness). Approaches that evaluate religion and secularization based solely
on factors like religious markets (supply and demand) or survey questions
about church attendance and belief in God overlook a crucial element of

[51] Sorcha A. Brophy, "Orthodoxy as Project: Temporality and Action in an American Protestant
Denomination," *Sociology of Religion* 77, no. 2 (2016): 123–143.
[52] Kenneth J. Collins, *Power, Politics and the Fragmentation of Evangelicalism: From the Scopes Trial
to the Obama Administration* (Downers Grove, IL: InterVarsity Press, 2012).

contemporary religion: its leaders' capacity to fight for their own strength—and to win. In this way, however, American Evangelicalism functions akin to a game of *Calvinball*, from the Calvin and Hobbes comic strip, in which the game itself is a struggle over the rules and players battle to win a contest while it devolves into disorder. The overall vision of Evangelicalism in the United States, in the end, consists of pockets of subcultural and local strength within a broader framework of secularization as "cultural entropy,"[53] as religious meaning and coherence fall apart.[54]

[53] Terence E. McDonnell, *Best Laid Plans: Cultural Entropy and the Unraveling of AIDS Media Campaigns* (Chicago: The University of Chicago Press, 2016).
[54] See Brad S. Gregory, *The Unintended Reformation: How a Religious Revolution Secularized Society* (Cambridge, MA: Belknap Press of Harvard University Press, 2012); Hans Joas, *Faith as an Option: Possible Futures for Christianity* (Stanford, CA: Stanford University Press, 2014).

2

Institutions, Leaders, and Features of the New Calvinist Movement

The first step toward understanding and explaining the New Calvinist movement in American Evangelicalism today—as with any social phenomenon—is to describe it well. This chapter very briefly describes the organizations, institutions, conferences, networks, and religious leaders constituting the movement. It then describes the beliefs and convictions which taken together delineate the movement within the broader landscape of Evangelicalism in the United States. The chapter wraps up with a few more descriptive and analytical concerns.

Organizations, Institutions, and Leaders

Bethlehem Baptist Church

One influential megachurch leading the way in the New Calvinist movement is Bethlehem Baptist Church (BBC) in Minneapolis.[1] Founded in 1871 as the First Swedish Baptist Church of Minneapolis, BBC is widely known for the work and ministry of its longtime (though now former) pastor for preaching and vision, John Piper. Now in his mid-seventies, Piper's intense voice contrasts with his modest stature, grandfatherly wire spectacles, and thinned silvery white hair. Piper is known for developing the concept of "Christian hedonism," which links human happiness and joy with God's glory by teaching that "God is most glorified in us when we are most satisfied in him."[2] Christian hedonism is also reflected in BBC's stated mission, which colors everything at the church: "Bethlehem exists to spread a passion for the supremacy of God in all things for the joy of all peoples through Jesus Christ."

---

[1] https://bethlehem.church/
[2] John Piper, *Desiring God: Meditations of a Christian Hedonist*, revised edition (Colorado Springs, CO: Multnomah Books, [1986] 2011). See also https://www.desiringgod.org/topics/christian-hedonism.

Reformed Resurgence. Brad Vermurlen, Oxford University Press (2020). © Oxford University Press.
DOI: 10.1093/oso/9780190073510.001.0001

Figure 2.1 John Piper teaching at The Gospel Coalition's 2017 national conference.

On a typical weekend in 2012, Bethlehem welcomed about 4,500 people to its three locations across the greater Minneapolis area, although since Piper's departure from the pastorate in early 2013, average attendance has dipped to about 3,300. Still, Piper's influence among Evangelicals reverberates well beyond Bethlehem. He has authored or edited more than fifty books, and Desiring God,[3] which started as a "tape ministry" in 1994, is one of the most popular online hubs for conservative Protestant theological resources, including articles, videos, sermons, podcasts, study guides, free books, and more. Additionally, BBC is the home of Bethlehem College and Seminary, which enrolls about two hundred students in undergraduate and graduate degree programs.[4] After nearly thirty-three years as pastor, Piper transitioned out of his preaching role at Bethlehem in early 2013 and now serves as chancellor of the college and seminary and continues teaching at conferences and through the ongoing online ministry of Desiring God (see Figure 2.1).

[3] https://www.desiringgod.org/
[4] https://bcsmn.edu/

Redeemer Presbyterian Church

Another Calvinist megachurch with far-reaching influence—both in the New Calvinist movement and in Evangelicalism broadly—is Redeemer Presbyterian Church (RPC).[5] Founded on the Upper East Side of Manhattan in 1989, RPC is widely known for the writing and teaching of its longtime senior pastor, Tim Keller.[6] With a calm and professorial temperament, Keller is seen as a Christian intellectual. He has authored multiple best-selling books and has been profiled positively in *The Wall Street Journal*, *The New York Times*, and *The Atlantic*. Keller is popular among Evangelicals for his measured preaching style as he aims to explain the truth and goodness of Christianity to cosmopolitan young professionals in New York.[7]

In addition to weekend services and community groups, major ministries of Redeemer include its Center for Faith and Work (integrating Christianity with career),[8] Hope for New York (mercy and justice efforts),[9] and Redeemer City to City (church planting and movement multiplication),[10] among others. By the time I visited in early 2013, Redeemer had grown to 5,000 people worshipping at three locations across Manhattan— on the Upper East Side in an auditorium of Hunter College, downtown in the Salvation Army building on 14th Street, and on the Upper West Side in a newly constructed five-story building on West 83rd Street. Since then, in early 2017, Redeemer added a fourth congregation in the Lincoln Square neighborhood of Manhattan. Around the same time, RPC announced its congregations would become individual "particularized" churches, and the centralized homepage now describes Redeemer not as a single multisite church but as "a family of churches and ministries for the good of the city."

---

[5] https://www.redeemer.com/

[6] http://www.timothykeller.com/

[7] See William McMillan, "Contextualization, Big Apple Style: Making Conservative Christianity More Palatable in Modern Day Manhattan," *Symposia* 5 (2013): 1–16; William McMillan, *Cosmopolitan Calvinists: Global Religion in a Secular Age* (PhD diss., Department of Sociology, Yale University, 2018).

[8] http://faithandwork.com/

[9] https://www.hfny.org/

[10] https://www.redeemercitytocity.com/

Figure 2.2 Mark Driscoll teaching at the 2013 Resurgence conference.

Mars Hill Church

The first church to spring to many observers' minds when they think of the New Calvinism is Mars Hill Church (MHC), led by Mark Driscoll (see Figure 2.2). MHC was a large nondenominational multisite church based in Seattle. Launched in 1996 from a Bible study that met in Driscoll's home, MHC quickly became one of the nation's fastest growing and most controversial churches. At its peak, in late 2013 and early 2014, MHC welcomed more than 14,000 weekly attendees across fifteen campuses in five states (Washington, California, Oregon, Arizona, and New Mexico). The megachurch was widely recognized for Driscoll's brash preaching style, a clear emphasis on masculinity, and frank talk about sex. Now in his late forties, Driscoll has been called "American evangelicalism's bête noire"[11] and "the football coach of American evangelicalism." Notably, there was an unmistakable "hipster vibe" infusing the megachurch's aesthetic, music, décor, and style. Dim lighting. Warm colors. Thundering music. Good coffee. Thick beards.[12] In this way, MHC as a whole embodied the mixture of urbanism, aesthetics, and masculinity that

---

[11] Worthen, "Who Would Jesus Smack Down?"

[12] On the social significance of beards, see Christopher Oldstone-Moore, *Of Beards and Men: The Revealing History of Facial Hair* (Chicago: The University of Chicago Press, 2016).

Willa Brown described nicely as "the lumbersexual."[13] MHC dissolved at the end of 2014 after a series of very public controversies.[14]

The Acts 29 Network

The Acts 29 Network describes itself as "a diverse, global family of church-planting churches."[15] Cofounded in 1998 by Mark Driscoll and David Nicholas, the network now consists of about 740 local Evangelical churches—mostly in the United States, but also in Europe, Australia, New Zealand, Canada, Central America, South America (mostly Brazil), southern Asia, and Africa.[16] Driscoll served as the president and major figurehead of Acts 29 from shortly after its founding until spring of 2012. At that time, Matt Chandler of The Village Church in Texas was appointed as Acts 29's new president, and its headquarters were relocated from Seattle to Dallas.[17] Acts 29 is interdenominational, including churches belonging to over a dozen denominations—largely Baptist and Presbyterian—as well as several "non-denominational" churches. (Although Acts 29's leadership has emphasized it is not a denomination, observers have pointed out its similarity to a denomination.) Through "boot camps" (regional conferences) and rigorous assessment and training of aspiring church planters, the Acts 29 Network is a crucial part of the "nuts and bolts" of the New Calvinist movement. It is a pivotal way the New Calvinism moves beyond simply being an American, celebrity-driven, megachurch phenomenon and instead forms a global network of smaller churches pastored by lesser-known men.

[13] Willa Brown, "Lumbersexuality and Its Discontents," *The Atlantic*, December 10, 2014, https://www.theatlantic.com/national/archive/2014/12/lumbersexuality-and-its-discontents/383563/, accessed April 19, 2019.

[14] Among lots of media coverage, see Michael Paulson, "Divisive Pastor Quits Post at Seattle Church," *The New York Times*, October 15, 2014, https://www.nytimes.com/2014/10/16/us/mark-driscoll-evangelical-megachurch-mars-hill.html, accessed April 19, 2019; Morgan Lee, "Goodbye, Mars Hill: Mark Driscoll's Multisite Empire Will Sell Properties and Dissolve," *Christianity Today*, October 31, 2014, https://www.christianitytoday.com/news/2014/october/goodbye-mars-hill-multisite-church-dissolve-mark-driscoll.html, accessed April 19, 2019.

[15] https://www.acts29.com/

[16] A global map of all Acts 29 churches is available at https://www.acts29.com/find-churches/.

[17] Ed Stetzer, "Matt Chandler Named New President of Acts 29," *Christianity Today*, March 28, 2012, https://www.christianitytoday.com/edstetzer/2012/march/matt-chandler-named-new-president-of-acts-29.html, accessed April 22, 2019. The headquarters have since moved again to Sheffield, England.

The Southern Baptist Theological Seminary

No seminary is "officially" New Calvinist, but if one figures most prominently in the movement, it is the Southern Baptist Theological Seminary (SBTS),[18] which has been called "ground zero" of the New Calvinism.[19] Located in Louisville, Kentucky, SBTS is the first, largest, and flagship seminary of the Southern Baptist Convention (SBC), which itself is the largest Protestant denomination in the United States. The seminary's president, R. Albert Mohler Jr.,[20] has served in that role since 1993 and helped solidify a concerted internal campaign launched in the late 1970s to steer SBTS and the SBC in a conservative direction.[21] Mohler arrived at SBTS intent on enforcing the seminary's 1858 founding confessional statement, titled the Abstract of Principles.[22] After a few highly contentious years during the mid-1990s, most of the faculty at SBTS had either resigned or been forced out and swiftly replaced with conservatives. Today, Mohler remains a leading voice among Calvinistic Evangelicals and is highly influential among a new generation of seminarians, young pastors, and other ministry leaders. Additionally, Mohler's new faculty—including Denny Burk, Tom Schreiner, and Bruce Ware—are influential in their own right among young theologically inclined Evangelicals.

The Gospel Coalition

Another key organization for the New Calvinist movement is The Gospel Coalition (TGC).[23] First organized in 2005 and officially cofounded in 2007

[18] http://www.sbts.edu/

[19] Hansen, *Young, Restless, Reformed*, 69–93.

[20] https://albertmohler.com/

[21] See, for example, Nancy Tatom Ammerman, *Baptist Battles: Social Change and Religious Conflict in the Southern Baptist Convention* (New Brunswick, NJ: Rutgers University Press, [1990] 1995); Nancy Tatom Ammerman, ed., *Southern Baptists Observed: Multiple Perspectives on a Changing Denomination* (Knoxville: The University of Tennessee Press, 1993); Grady C. Cothen, *What Happened to the Southern Baptist Convention? A Memoir of the Controversy* (Macon, GA: Smyth and Helwys, 1993); James C. Hefley, *The Conservative Resurgence in the Southern Baptist Convention* (Garland, TX: Hannibal Books, [1991] 2005); David T. Morgan, *The New Crusades, the New Holy Land: Conflict in the Southern Baptist Convention, 1969–1991* (Tuscaloosa: University of Alabama Press, 1996); Ellen M. Rosenberg, *The Southern Baptists: A Subculture in Transition* (Knoxville: The University of Tennessee Press, 1989); Jerry Sutton, *The Baptist Reformation: The Conservative Resurgence in the Southern Baptist Convention* (Nashville, TN: B&H, 2000); Gregory A. Wills, *Southern Baptist Theological Seminary, 1859–2009* (New York: Oxford University Press, 2009).

[22] http://www.sbts.edu/about/abstract/

[23] https://www.thegospelcoalition.org/

by Tim Keller and D. A. Carson, TGC is at once a community of like-minded "broadly Reformed" Evangelical pastors and leaders as well as a consistent online presence for Calvinistic resources, blogs, articles, sermons, videos, and book reviews. TGC includes more than fifty council members—most of whom are senior pastors of churches but who also include, for example, the presidents of Wheaton College (Phil Ryken) and SBTS (Al Mohler).[24] These pastors represent churches belonging to various denominational families, including Evangelical Free, Baptist, Reformed, Presbyterian, Anglican, and others, or none at all. Beyond its council, TGC puts on a number of conferences attended by pastors and interested laypersons, including a large biannual national conference (the first of which was held in May 2007), regional conferences throughout the United States and Canada, and conferences targeted exclusively to—and in large part taught by—women.[25]

Moreover, TGC runs a significant International Outreach effort, which they call "theological famine relief." This initiative, in partnership with a variety of Christian publishers, crowd-funds the translation of particular books on theology and ministry—many written by John Piper but also books by Tim Keller, Mark Dever, D. A. Carson, and others—as well as the ESV Study Bible, which are then distributed to pastors in Africa, Asia, and South America.[26]

In addition to these more "on the ground" elements, The Gospel Coalition is likewise prominent in the digital realm. From day to day, TGC is just as much a website and online resource hub as it is a flesh-and-blood network of councilmen, conferences, and international work. The website hosts blogs from a dozen leading voices in the Reformed Evangelical world,[27] as well as a seemingly endless stream of articles, videos, book reviews, various podcasts (available on iTunes), and free online courses. Other digital resources include a newly adapted catechism,[28] a church directory,[29] and a jobs board.[30] TGC is also home of a peer-reviewed academic journal of theology, published three times a year, named *Themelios*.[31] In total, through both its "real-life" community and its strong online presence, The Gospel Coalition is

---

[24] https://www.thegospelcoalition.org/about/council/
[25] https://www.thegospelcoalition.org/events/
[26] https://www.thegospelcoalition.org/io/
[27] https://www.thegospelcoalition.org/blogs/
[28] http://newcitycatechism.com/
[29] https://www.thegospelcoalition.org/churches/
[30] https://jobs.thegospelcoalition.org/
[31] http://themelios.thegospelcoalition.org/

Figure 2.3 Promotional material for the 2012 Together for the Gospel conference.

a central organizing force—in many ways the organizational mastermind—of the New Calvinism.

Together for the Gospel

Among the organizations constituting the New Calvinist movement, Together for the Gospel (T4G)[32] is an important but relatively simple one (see Figure 2.3). T4G is a three-day national conference held every two years in Louisville, Kentucky, at which leading Calvinistic pastors and theologians speak to an audience composed mostly of other pastors. The first T4G conference was held in 2006 in the Grand Ballroom of the Galt House Hotel and drew about 2,800 attendees. Four leaders—Mark Dever, Al Mohler, C. J. Mahaney, and Ligon Duncan—teamed up to organize the first T4G conference, but its speakers in 2006 and subsequent years have included other men such as John Piper, Matt Chandler, R. C. Sproul, Thabiti Anyabwile, John MacArthur, Kevin DeYoung, David Platt, Greg Gilbert, and Carl Trueman, among others.

The conferences are structured around a combination of main sessions, panel discussions, and breakout sessions. Sample topics include "Why the Reformation Isn't Over," "Future Theological Threats," "The Power of the Articulated Gospel," "The Pastor as Public Theologian in an Increasingly Hostile Culture," and sessions on the inerrancy of the Bible, gay marriage,

[32] https://t4g.org/

complementarianism, contextualization, celebrity pastors, suffering, denominationalism, and more. The T4G conferences have grown over the years, in 2018 drawing approximately 12,600 attendees. Through its conferences and repository of sessions on its website, T4G has added much of substance and a sense of unity to the New Calvinist movement.

The Passion Conferences

Another notable series of conferences are the Passion conferences.[33] Whereas T4G targets pastors and other ministry leaders, Passion is aimed at emerging adults aged eighteen to twenty-five years, and especially university students. Louie Giglio, lead pastor of Passion City Church—a nondenominational megachurch in Atlanta, Georgia—launched the Passion conferences in 1997. (Giglio made national headlines in January 2013 for being pressured to back out of delivering the benediction at Barack Obama's second presidential inauguration because he holds to the traditional Christian view of human sexuality.[34]) The Passion conferences bring together well-known conservative Evangelical leaders and speakers from across the United States. In addition to sermons, times of prayer, and high-energy contemporary worship music performances, the Passion conferences also raise awareness of and work toward ending sex trafficking and other forms of modern-day slavery.[35]

Unlike the other organizations and events described in this chapter, the Passion conferences reach further into mainstream American Evangelicalism, featuring speakers such as Andy Stanley, the late Bill Bright (founder of Campus Crusade for Christ), Carl Lentz (of Hillsong NYC), and Christine Caine, and contemporary worship leaders like Chris Tomlin and the David Crowder Band. Still, while the Passion conferences are not narrowly a Calvinist event, they nevertheless have been one of the most influential vehicles through which a rising generation of (primarily college-educated) twenty-somethings has been exposed to Calvinistic teachers and preachers. Noteworthy among these are Francis Chan and Matt Chandler. But even more significantly, the Passion conferences have further extended

---

[33] https://passionconferences.com/

[34] Sheryl Gay Stolberg, "Minister Backs Out of Speech at Inaugural," *The New York Times*, January 10, 2013, https://www.nytimes.com/2013/01/11/us/politics/minister-withdraws-from-inaugural-program-after-controversy-over-comments-on-gay-rights.html, accessed March 7, 2019.

[35] https://enditmovement.com/

the preaching platform of John Piper, who has preached at nearly every stateside Passion conference since 1997. Through these youth meetings, which fill stadiums year after year, tens of thousands of religiously interested emerging adults in the United States have been introduced to Piper's teaching.

Crossway and the English Standard Version Bible

The organization producing many of the books for the New Calvinism should not be overlooked as an essential aspect of the movement itself. While other Evangelical publishers like Zondervan, Eerdmans, and InterVarsity also publish several books by New Calvinist writers, Crossway stands out as the movement's go-to publisher.[36] What would later become Crossway started in 1938 as Good News Publishers, a family-owned business that designed and printed evangelistic Gospel tracts. Today, Good News distributes more than sixteen million tracts each year. Additionally, the book-publishing division of Good News Publishers launched in 1979 as Crossway Books and since then has produced more than 1,500 titles. Now located in Wheaton, Illinois, the original founders' son, Lane Dennis, serves as the president of Crossway. Another notable leader connected with Crossway is Justin Taylor, who serves as executive vice president for book publishing. His blog, *Between Two Worlds*, is hosted on The Gospel Coalition's website and is one of the most widely read blogs for the New Calvinist movement.[37]

In addition to numerous books, Crossway has contributed to the New Calvinism by producing the English Standard Version (ESV) of the Bible, first published in 2001.[38] The ESV was intended as a more "word-for-word" or "essentially literal" translation of the original Hebrew and Greek texts, as opposed to looser "idea-for-idea" translations. For the endeavor of creating a new translation of the Bible, based on the existing RSV, Crossway commissioned more than fifty Evangelical scholars as "Translation Review Scholars," who each worked with the text in their area of expertise.[39] A twelve-member "Translation Oversight Committee," led by J. I. Packer as the general editor,

---

[36] https://www.crossway.org/
[37] https://www.thegospelcoalition.org/blogs/justin-taylor/
[38] https://www.esv.org/
[39] https://www.esv.org/translation/review-scholars/

organized the review and revision process.[40] Later, an additional team of ninety-five Christian scholars worked to add notes, articles, illustrations, and maps, which resulted in 2008 in the 1.4 million-word *ESV Study Bible*.[41] The ESV Bible is now the translation of choice for so many of the "Young, Restless, and Reformed" that a few of the movement's key leaders have jokingly called it the "Elect Standard Version."

The Council on Biblical Manhood and Womanhood

On questions of gender and sexuality, the most important organization for the New Calvinist movement is the Council on Biblical Manhood and Womanhood (CBMW),[42] located in Louisville, Kentucky. CBMW was founded in 1987 by a group of Evangelical pastors and scholars—led by John Piper and Wayne Grudem—who were concerned about the widening influence of feminist thought within American Evangelicalism.[43] After an initial meeting earlier that year in Dallas, the group met for the second time at the Sheraton Ferncroft Resort in Danvers, Massachusetts, just prior to the 1987 meeting of the Evangelical Theological Society. There they incorporated the council and adopted a statement—called the Danvers Statement—articulating ten rationales for why CBMW was needed and ten affirmations about gender in the home and the Church.[44] They named their traditional view "complementarianism."

The president of Crossway, Lane Dennis, was involved in this meeting and that weekend commissioned Piper and Grudem to assemble an edited volume definitively laying out the complementarian position. In 1991, Crossway published *Recovering Biblical Manhood and Womanhood*, which won the "Book of the Year" award from *Christianity Today* in 1992 and to this day is nicknamed "the blue book" among younger complementarians.[45] Although

---

[40] https://www.esv.org/translation/oversight-committee/. At the age of eighty-nine, Packer called the ESV Bible "the most important bit of service to the Church that I've been involved in in the whole of my working life," https://www.youtube.com/watch?v=uMo14MIOkyQ, accessed April 2, 2019.

[41] http://esvstudybible.org/

[42] https://cbmw.org/

[43] https://cbmw.org/about/history/; see Sally K. Gallagher, "The Marginalization of Evangelical Feminism," *Sociology of Religion* 65, no. 3 (2004): 215–237; Gallagher (p. 228) makes a normative suggestion when she says the gender views of Piper and Grudem are "reminiscent of [racial] segregationists in the 1950s."

[44] https://cbmw.org/about/danvers-statement

[45] John Piper and Wayne Grudem, eds., *Recovering Biblical Manhood and Womanhood: A Response to Evangelical Feminism* (Wheaton, IL: Crossway, [1991] 2006).

the CBMW was founded almost twenty years before "New Calvinism" or "neo-Reformed" entered the Evangelical lexicon, this council—along with its journal, podcast, website, conferences, and the more recent Nashville Statement[46]—has been indispensable to the Reformed resurgence.

Other Key Leaders

The descriptions to this point get us far down the road in describing the actual persons and organizations involved in the New Calvinist movement. But for the sake of space, this chapter rounds out the picture simply by providing brief bullet-point descriptions of a few more of the relevant actors. Among others still, those actors include the following.

- D. A. Carson is emeritus professor of New Testament at Trinity Evangelical Divinity School (TEDS). Carson cofounded The Gospel Coalition with Tim Keller and serves as the organization's president. He is the author of several academic-level books and articles.
- Tim Challies is a pastor at Grace Fellowship Church, a small church in Toronto, Ontario. He is more widely known for his popular personal website, challies.com. He is additionally a cofounder of Cruciform Press and has written five books.
- Francis Chan is currently a pastor with We Are Church, a house church network in northern California. Chan is better known as the former teaching pastor of Cornerstone Community Church in Simi Valley, California, as well as for his popular pastoral books and speaking at national conferences, including Passion.
- Matt Chandler is teaching pastor at The Village Church—a Southern Baptist megachurch headquartered in Flower Mound, Texas—and president of the Acts 29 Network. The Village Church welcomes 11,000 congregants across five campuses. He has also authored multiple books.
- Mark Dever is senior pastor of Capitol Hill Baptist Church in Washington, DC. He is the president of 9Marks (a ministry to foster church health), an emeritus council member with The Gospel Coalition, and the author of several books and articles. As of fall 2019, Dever is also a professor at Southern Baptist Theological Seminary.

---

[46] https://cbmw.org/nashville-statement

- Kevin DeYoung is senior pastor of Christ Covenant Church (PCA) in Matthews, North Carolina, and assistant professor of systematic theology at Reformed Theological Seminary in Charlotte. He is the author of several theological books and is board chairman of The Gospel Coalition, which hosts his blog. Previously he served as senior pastor at University Reformed Church in East Lansing, Michigan, near Michigan State University.

- Collin Hansen is editorial director for The Gospel Coalition. Formerly associate editor for *Christianity Today*, his September 2006 article titled "Young, Restless, Reformed: Calvinism Is Making a Comeback—And Shaking Up the Church" was the first publication to describe the New Calvinist movement. This work was then expanded into a book-length description, published in 2008 from Crossway.[47]

- James MacDonald is founder and, until recently, senior pastor at Harvest Bible Chapel, a nondenominational megachurch of 13,000 people meeting in seven locations in and around Chicago. He oversaw what was formerly Harvest Bible Fellowship, a network of more than one hundred churches affiliated with Harvest, and has authored several books. MacDonald was fired in February 2019 "for engaging in conduct that the Elders believe is contrary and harmful to the best interests of the church."[48]

- C. J. Mahaney is senior pastor at Sovereign Grace Church of Louisville, in Kentucky. He is the former pastor of Covenant Life Church in Gaithersburg, Maryland, and the former president of Sovereign Grace Ministries (now Sovereign Grace Churches). He also served on the Council on Biblical Manhood and Womanhood.[49]

- Darrin Patrick was the founder and former senior pastor of The Journey, a multisite, nondenominational megachurch in St. Louis, Missouri.

---

[47] Collin Hansen, "Young, Restless, Reformed: Calvinism Is Making a Comeback—And Shaking Up the Church," *Christianity Today*, September 22, 2006, http://www.christianitytoday.com/ct/2006/september/42.32.html, accessed September 20, 2015; Collin Hansen, *Young, Restless, Reformed: A Journalist's Journey with the New Calvinists* (Wheaton, IL: Crossway, 2008).

[48] Quoted from https://www.harvestbiblechapel.org/2019/02/13/february-2019-elder-update-2/, accessed March 4, 2019. See also Kate Shellnutt, "James MacDonald Fired from Harvest," *Christianity Today*, February 13, 2019, https://www.christianitytoday.com/news/2019/february/james-macdonald-fired-harvest-bible-chapel.html, accessed March 4, 2019.

[49] Mahaney's ministry career has been embroiled in controversy surrounding the alleged mishandling and cover-up of child sexual abuse, allegations which he denies. See Kate Shellnutt, "Sovereign Grace Disputes Rachel Denhollander's Remarks," *Christianity Today*, February 6, 2018, https://www.christianitytoday.com/news/2018/february/sovereign-grace-rachael-denhollander-sgm-abuse-ct-interview.html, accessed March 4, 2019.

Patrick served as vice president of the Acts 29 Network and was a council member of The Gospel Coalition—until The Journey removed Patrick from "all internal and external leadership positions" in April 2016 for "a historical pattern of sin."[50] He was then a teaching pastor at Seacoast Church until his unexpected death in May 2020.

- Sam Storms is lead pastor for preaching and vision at Bridgeway Church in Oklahoma City, Oklahoma. He is on the board of directors for Desiring God, a council member of The Gospel Coalition, and the author of several books and articles.

- Tullian Tchividjian is best known as the former senior pastor of Coral Ridge Presbyterian Church (PCA), a megachurch in Ft. Lauderdale, Florida. He was a lecturer of pastoral theology at the church's Knox Theological Seminary and a contributing editor to Christianity Today's *Leadership Journal*. Tchividjian is the author of eight books and formerly blogged for The Gospel Coalition. He resigned from Coral Ridge in 2015 after revelations that he and his wife both had extramarital affairs.[51] He is the grandson of famed evangelist Billy Graham.

The Black Component

A significant component of the New Calvinist movement consists of various African American pastors, professors, and other church leaders. Among these are Thabiti Anyabwile, who is a pastor at Anacostia River Church in southeast Washington, DC, and who blogs for The Gospel Coalition (and formerly served as assistant pastor for church planting at Capitol Hill Baptist

---

[50] Leonardo Blair, "Pastor Darrin Patrick Fired from The Journey Megachurch; Resigns from Acts 29 for 'Historical Patterns of Sin,'" *The Christian Post*, April 15, 2016, http://www.christianpost.com/news/pastor-darrin-patrick-fired-from-the-journey-megachurch-resigns-from-acts-29-for-historical-patterns-of-sin-161816/, accessed August 1, 2016; Kate Shellnutt, "Darrin Patrick Removed from Acts 29 Megachurch for 'Historical Pattern of Sin,'" *Christianity Today*, April 13, 2016, http://www.christianitytoday.com/gleanings/2016/april/darrin-patrick-removed-acts-29-megachurch-journey.html, accessed August 1, 2016.

[51] Sarah Pulliam Bailey, "Billy Graham's Grandson Steps Down from Florida Megachurch after Admitting an Affair," *The Washington Post*, June 21, 2015, https://www.washingtonpost.com/news/acts-of-faith/wp/2015/06/21/billy-grahams-grandson-steps-down-from-florida-megachurch-after-admitting-an-affair/; Bob Smietana and Morgan Lee, "Tullian Tchividjian Resigns after Admitting 'Inappropriate Relationship,'" *Christianity Today*, July 30, 2015, https://www.christianitytoday.com/news/2015/june/tullian-tchividjian-resigns-after-admitting-inappropiate-re.html; Morgan Lee, "Tullian Tchividjian Confesses Second Affair Concealed by Two Coral Ridge Elders," *Christianity Today*, March 21, 2016, https://www.christianitytoday.com/news/2016/march/tullian-tchividjian-confesses-second-affair-coral-ridge.html, accessed March 7, 2019.

Church in Washington, DC, with Mark Dever); Voddie Baucham, Jr., who was the preaching pastor at Grace Family Baptist Church in Spring, Texas, and a council member of The Gospel Coalition before moving to Lusaka, Zambia, to be Dean of the Seminary at African Christian University; and Trillia Newbell, a popular speaker, author, and the director of community outreach for the Ethics and Religious Liberty Commission with the Southern Baptist Convention.

Other notable black voices include Anthony (Tony) Carter, who is the senior pastor of East Point Church, on the southwest side of Atlanta; Crawford Loritts, Jr., who serves as the senior pastor of Fellowship Bible Church in Roswell, Georgia, and a council member of The Gospel Coalition; Charlie Dates, senior pastor at Progressive Baptist Church in Chicago; Louis Love, Jr., the senior pastor with New Life Fellowship Church in Vernon Hills, Illinois; and Eric Redmond, a Southern Baptist, and now assistant professor of Bible at Moody Bible Institute and a former council member of The Gospel Coalition; among others.

There is also a noteworthy portion of the movement that produces theologically rich Christian hip-hop, spoken word poetry, and accompanying music videos. The most widely known among these Calvinistic hip-hop artists is Grammy-winner Lecrae, but this phenomenon also includes rappers such as Trip Lee, KB, and Tedashii with Lecrae's record label, Reach Records; Flame and Mike Real with Clear Sight Music; Shai Linne, Json, and Stephen the Levite with Lamp Mode Recordings; Propaganda, Sho Baraka, and Jackie Hill-Perry with Humble Beast Records; Eshon Burgundy with NFTRY; and approximately a dozen others.[52] One Christian hip-hop artist—William Branch, also known as The Ambassador—explained the spirit behind Calvinist hip-hop:

What has been titled "Reformed rap," or that same emphasis that you see in Reformed circles and Reformed theology—when it hit rap, it was a great antidote as well as an antithesis to the rap that we commonly know as just secular rap. And, rap is a boasting platform. That's the nature of the art. [. . .] When we came with an emphasis on the exalted Christ and the glory

---

[52] For more details, see my paper, "Structural Overlap and the Management of Cultural Marginality: The Case of Calvinist Hip-Hop," *American Journal of Cultural Sociology* 4, no. 1 (2016): 68–106.

of God, it was our way of saying, "We both boast, but our boasts are different." And our boast was in Jesus Christ. Our boast was in God's glory.[53]

Two other important organizations need acknowledging. The first is the Reformed African American Network (RAAN), which was cofounded in fall 2011 by Jemar Tisby and Phillip Holmes, and in late October 2017 changed its name to The Witness: A Black Christian Collective.[54] The second is The Front Porch,[55] where Thabiti Anyabwile, Tony Carter, and Louis Love facilitate conversations about Reformed theology and African American churches. Together, these artists, leaders, and organizations help to establish the New Calvinism as a movement with traction and appeal beyond only white Americans.[56]

Despite the presence of several prominent black leaders in the New Calvinism, the race story in recent years—particularly since research for this book began in 2012—has been dominated by what has been called the "quiet exodus" or "black exodus" from (majority white) Evangelicalism.[57] Many black leaders previously within the orbit of the Reformed resurgence have distanced themselves from Evangelicalism (without abandoning their doctrinal or moral convictions) due to what they perceive as various race-based grievances, injustices, and frustrations, among them underrepresentation in leadership, tokenism, unsympathetic responses to police shootings of black men, the election of Donald Trump, lack of concrete advancement in racial reconciliation, and recurrent microaggressions and other insensitivities.[58]

[53] Staff Post, "How Has 'Reformed Rap' Contributed to the Reformed Resurgence?" *The Gospel Coalition*, January 12, 2018, https://www.thegospelcoalition.org/video/reformed-rap-contributed-reformed-resurgence/, accessed January 12, 2018.

[54] Jemar Tisby, "The Journey from RAAN to 'The Witness: A Black Christian Collective,'" *The Witness*, October 31, 2017, https://thewitnessbcc.com/raan-witness-black-christian-collective, accessed January 15, 2018.

[55] https://thefrontporch.org/

[56] For insider, confessional analyses of this component of Reformed Evangelicalism, see for example, Thabiti M. Anyabwile, *The Decline of African American Theology: From Biblical Faith to Cultural Captivity* (Downers Grove, IL: InterVarsity Press, 2007); Thabiti M. Anyabwile, *The Faithful Preacher: Recapturing the Vision of Three Pioneering African-American Pastors* (Wheaton, IL: Crossway, 2007); Anthony B. Bradley, *Liberating Black Theology: The Bible and the Black Experience in America* (Wheaton, IL: Crossway, 2010); Anthony J. Carter, *On Being Black and Reformed: A New Perspective on the African-American Christian Experience* (Phillipsburg, NJ: P&R, 2003); Anthony J. Carter, ed., *Experiencing the Truth: Bringing the Reformation to the African-American Church* (Wheaton, IL: Crossway, 2008); Anthony J. Carter, ed., *Glory Road: The Journeys of 10 African-Americans into Reformed Christianity* (Wheaton, IL: Crossway, 2009).

[57] Campbell Robertson, "A Quiet Exodus: Why Black Worshipers Are Leaving White Evangelical Churches," *The New York Times*, March 9, 2018, https://www.nytimes.com/2018/03/09/us/blacks-evangelical-churches.html, accessed February 27, 2019.

[58] Anthony B. Bradley, ed., *Aliens in the Promised Land: Why Minority Leadership Is Overlooked in White Christian Churches and Institutions* (Phillipsburg, NJ: P&R, 2013); Jemar Tisby, *The*

Nationally recognized black leaders who have, in one way or another, given up on or stopped trying to engage (white) Evangelicalism in just the last few years include Lecrae, Jemar Tisby, Anthony Bradley, Léonce Crump, Jr., and Eric Mason, among others.[59]

(Anthony Bradley is a professor of religious studies and chair of the program in Religious and Theological Studies at The King's College, a Christian college in New York City; Léonce Crump, Jr., is founder and lead pastor of Renovation Church in Atlanta; and Eric Mason is the founder and senior pastor of Epiphany Fellowship in Philadelphia. Both Crump and Mason were formerly board members of the Acts 29 Network.)

Distinctive Beliefs and Convictions

Calvinist Soteriology

The most significant feature of the New Calvinism, unsurprisingly, is a traditional Calvinist view of how salvation happens.[60] Calvinism today is commonly represented using the acronym TULIP. It has become customary to recognize that TULIP is an imperfect summary of—or mnemonic device

---

Color of Compromise: The Truth about the American Church's Complicity in Racism (Grand Rapids, MI: Zondervan, 2019); Eric Mason, *Woke Church: An Urgent Call for Christians in America to Confront Racism and Injustice* (Chicago, IL: Moody Publishers, 2018).

[59] The names listed here are based on a combination of journalistic news coverage and comments I observed on Twitter. On Tisby, see his own op-ed, "How Ferguson Widened an Enormous Rift between Black Christians and White Evangelicals," *The Washington Post*, August 9, 2019, https://beta.washingtonpost.com/religion/2019/08/09/how-ferguson-widened-an-enormous-rift-between-black-christians-white-evangelicals/, accessed August 28, 2019; On Lecrae, see John Piper, "My Hopeful Response to Lecrae Pulling Away from 'White Evangelicalism,'" *Christianity Today*, October 9, 2017, http://www.christianitytoday.com/ct/2017/october-web-only/john-piper-lecrae-white-evangelicalism-gives-me-hope.html, accessed January 12, 2018; CT Editors, "The Significance of Lecrae Leaving White Evangelicalism," *Christianity Today*, October 12, 2017, https://www.christianitytoday.com/ct/2017/october-web-only/significance-of-lecrae-leaving-white-evangelicalism.html, accessed January 12, 2018. Additionally, Anthony Bradley tweeted: "[B]lack evangelicals really, really tried after WWI and it failed. Why are black evangelicals still trying what hasn't been done in over 100 years? Why?" Accessed February 27, 2019 from https://twitter.com/drantbradley/status/1096236522909650944. Responding to a related thread by Anthony Bradley, Eric Mason tweeted: "I have given up on evangelicalism period. The construct is a facade! Your comments on the multiethnic church have validity. [Our church] lost all but a few whites the 'freer' I became as a black man. We are now a black church w/ African diaspora." Accessed February 27, 2019, from https://twitter.com/pastoremase/status/1096916909486997505.

[60] Piper, *Five Points: Towards a Deeper Experience of God's Grace* (Ross-shire, UK: Christian Focus Publications, 2013); Michael Horton, *For Calvinism* (Grand Rapids, MI: Zondervan, 2011); Balserak, *Calvinism*.

for—the Canons of Dort (1619), and that the Canons of Dort are themselves a summary of only certain aspects of John Calvin's theology. And summaries of summaries are typically not the best way to grasp what someone thought and wrote. As Kenneth Stewart has shown, even though there is substantial continuity in the way the five disputed doctrines have been expressed over the centuries since Dort, the TULIP acronym did not crystallize into its present-day layout until 1913.[61] Still, because the goal of this book is to explain the New Calvinist movement, and because both the leaders and critics of that movement recurrently frame Calvinism using TULIP, I will stick with the received mnemonic.

- T stands for *total depravity*, which means every aspect of every person— including one's mind, body, and will—has been distorted and marred from its originally good design by humanity's fall into sin. This doctrine is a consequence and extension of the Christian doctrines of the fall and original sin, and it is about the scope (extensiveness) of the world's brokenness, not its depth (intensiveness). Importantly, total depravity makes people morally unable by their own initiative to place their faith in Jesus for salvation.[62]
- U stands for *unconditional election*, which means God, before the foundation of the world, chose particular persons to be rescued from their fallen, sinful condition and reconciled to Him. And this election was not conditional upon anything about the persons saved—not even foreseen faith or repentance. This doctrine, which can be most closely aligned with "predestination," is often treated as Calvinism's central dogma.[63]

[61] Kenneth J. Stewart, "TULIP Is the Yardstick of the Truly Reformed," in *Ten Myths About Calvinism: Recovering the Breadth of the Reformed Tradition* (Downers Grove, IL: InterVarsity Press, 2011), 75–96.

[62] Marguerite Shuster, *The Fall and Sin: What We Have Become as Sinners* (Grand Rapids, MI: William B. Eerdmans, 2004), esp. 159–170; Piper, *Five Points*, 17–24. From the Calvinist view, a generic, partial, nonsalvific knowledge of God is possible due to the "sense of divinity" (*sensus divinitatis*) that remains in all persons even after the fall—but in the fallen condition, and apart from God's saving grace, this innate capacity is distorted and misdirected in the form of unbelief, superstition, idolatry, and false religions. Paul Helm, "John Calvin, the *Sensus Divinitatis*, and the Noetic Effects of Sin," *International Journal for Philosophy of Religion* 43, no. 2 (1998): 87–107.

[63] Horton dissuades against such an emphasis, however, arguing that the doctrine of predestination or election, while clearly important, was neither unique to Calvin nor noticeably elevated in his writings. Horton, *For Calvinism*, 28–31. Forster too advises against this, pointing to the sufficiency of Augustine's thought on predestination, and suggesting instead that John Calvin's pioneering contribution was the emphasis he placed on the work of the Holy Spirit in regeneration. Forster, *The Joy of Calvinism*, 40–44. See also Peter J. Thuesen, *Predestination: The American Career of a Contentious Doctrine* (New York: Oxford University Press, 2009).

- L stands for *limited atonement*, but it is better called "particular redemption" or "definite atonement." This doctrine regards the causal efficacy of the cross, claiming that Jesus's death served the specific targeted purpose of making some persons actually saved, securing their salvation, not merely making all persons savable. The salvific work of Jesus on the cross, on this teaching, is "definite in its intention and scope."[64]
- I stands for *irresistible grace*, also called "effectual calling." This doctrine says God, by His grace and through the work of the Holy Spirit, extends a special inward call only to the elect, by which they are inescapably drawn toward Christ for salvation. This call, not human will or cooperation, is the decisive cause of spiritual regeneration (being "born again").[65] God's elect are awakened, "made willing by His grace."[66]
- P stands for *perseverance of the saints*, which means once someone is truly regenerate or "born again," that person will not and cannot revert to an unregenerate state or, in other words, lose his or her salvation. Stated positively, God's saving grace perseveres throughout a Christian's life and sustains his or her saving faith to final completion. In short, "Once saved, always saved."[67]

These five points of Calvinism together are sometimes called "the doctrines of grace." They are also sometimes framed in theological discourse—especially in relation to the alternatives—using the categories "monergism" ("one working") versus "synergism" ("working together").[68] Monergism, the Calvinist position, refers to the view that salvation is a unilateral act of God's grace that reorients personal wills toward Himself and therefore infallibly produces in the elect regeneration, faith, repentance, and perseverance. In contrast, synergism refers to other theological perspectives in which

---

[64] Horton, *For Calvinism*, 80. See also David Gibson and Jonathan Gibson, eds., *From Heaven He Came and Sought Her: Definite Atonement in Historical, Biblical, Theological, and Pastoral Perspective* (Wheaton, IL: Crossway, 2013); Piper, *Five Points*, 37–52.

[65] Piper, *Five Points*, 25–36; Grudem, *Systematic Theology*, 692–708. See also Matthew Barrett, *Salvation by Grace: The Case for Effectual Calling and Regeneration* (Phillipsburg, NJ: P&R, 2013).

[66] Westminster Confession, X.I., http://www.reformed.org/documents/wcf_with_proofs/.

[67] Thomas R. Schreiner and Ardel B. Caneday, *The Race Set before Us: A Biblical Theology of Perseverance and Assurance* (Downers Grove, IL: InterVarsity Press, 2001); Thomas R. Schreiner, *Run to Win the Prize: Perseverance in the New Testament* (Wheaton, IL: Crossway, 2010); Piper, *Five Points*, 63–76.

[68] Horton, *For Calvinism*, 16.

salvation is the result of cooperation, in various ways, between the grace of God and human free will.

Although Calvinism has a robust history within American Evangelicalism—from the Puritans up to many of the leading mid-twentieth century neo-Evangelicals—today it remains a minority position. Other views on salvation, and the spectrum of will and grace, include Arminianism/Wesleyanism, Lutheranism, Molinism, N. T. Wright's "new perspective on Paul," semi-Pelagianism, open theism, emphasizing practice over belief, and generic indifference or agnosticism toward soteriology and God's providence over human affairs. Readers unfamiliar with these views should consult Appendix B on "Nine (or So) Alternatives to Calvinism."

Gender Complementarianism

Aside from Calvinist soteriology, the leading (and arguably most controversial) distinctive belief of the New Calvinist movement is a traditional, conservative view of men and women, of masculinity and femininity.[69] They hold that men and women are equal, different, and complementary. Since the late 1980s, as conservative Evangelical leaders began responding to the increasing presence and pressures of second-wave feminism, this traditional stance on sex/gender has been called "complementarianism." On this view, men and women are equal in dignity and worth as persons made "in the image of God." At the same time, men and women are different and naturally complement one another in their God-given proclivities and roles, particularly in the home and the Church. (There is much less emphasis on gender roles and relations in the public sphere, such as workplaces and in the government.)

In the home, complementarianism holds a husband is called to lovingly lead and protect his wife and children, while a wife is to submit herself intelligently and graciously to the leadership of her husband. (This teaching does not hold that *all* women should submit to *all* men.) This structure for family life is justified in part by Ephesians 5: 22–33, where the Apostle Paul draws a parallel between husbands sacrificially, lovingly leading their wives

---

[69] By "distinctive belief" I do not mean only Calvinists, let alone only New Calvinists, embrace complementarianism. Many non-Calvinist conservative Evangelical leaders hold the same view. Instead, I mean New Calvinists uniformly embrace complementarianism, which in combination with other distinctive beliefs, delimits the movement.

and that Jesus loved and gave Himself up for His Bride, the Church—along with wives respectfully submitting to their husbands the way the Church itself submits to and follows Jesus.[70] In the Church, complementarianism likewise means men are in positions of authority. Women may not serve in the offices of pastor or elder; those roles are reserved only for qualified men. As noted on previous pages, the leading organization articulating and defending complementarianism among American Evangelicals today is the Council on Biblical Manhood and Womanhood.[71]

A Note on "Missional Churches"

Among leaders of the New Calvinism, taking a "missional" posture toward culture is sometimes said to be a distinctive of their movement. Pastors, seminary professors, and missiologists have used the word "missional" since the early 1980s.[72] It was then developed more systematically in the 1990s,[73] until it finally burst into popular Evangelical discourse throughout the first decade of the new millennium.[74] Despite a large literature on the "missional" church in Evangelicalism, the word remains notoriously difficult to define. Different authors and pastors use the word differently. Ed Stetzer, a researcher and missiologist at Wheaton College, described the word as a Rorschach test, in which people see whatever they already find problematic or right with the Church.[75] The word "missional" has been commonly used—even gaining "buzzword" status—in multiple pockets and expressions of Evangelicalism, from Calvinist to Arminian, whether complementarian or egalitarian.

Although the word "missional" is amorphous and difficult to define, it is usually used in relation to the words "missions" and "missionary." If

---

[70] For a recent, slightly longer discussion of complementarianism, see Samuel L. Perry, *Addicted to Lust: Pornography in the Lives of Conservative Protestants* (New York: Oxford University Press, 2019), 90–93.

[71] https://cbmw.org/

[72] Francis M. DuBose, *God Who Sends: A Fresh Quest for Biblical Mission* (Nashville, TN: Broadman Press, 1983).

[73] Charles Van Engen, *God's Missionary People: Rethinking the Purpose of the Local Church* (Grand Rapids, MI: Baker Books, 1991); Darrell L. Guder, ed., *Missional Church: A Vision for the Sending of the Church in North America* (Grand Rapids, MI: William B. Eerdmans, 1998).

[74] It did not take much time to find more than thirty-five books from Evangelical publishers with the word "missional" it their titles, a list which I will not reproduce here.

[75] Ed Stetzer, "What Does 'Missional' Mean?" *Christianity Today*, June 9, 2014, https://www.christianitytoday.com/edstetzer/2014/june/what-does-missional-mean.html, accessed March 5, 2019.

the terms "missions" and "missionary" typically bring to mind the image of evangelists going to faraway places to share the Gospel, the newer term "missional" is meant to invoke evangelistic fervor, strategic engagement, and possibly also service—all in one's own local community or context. Stated differently, in addition to local churches *sending* missionaries, the missional concept is intended to emphasize that local churches (and the people in them) are themselves *sent* to be on mission where they live and work every day. For some churches, the concept of missional helped to shift their philosophy of ministry from "come and see" (also called *attractional*) to "go and be" (*incarnational*).

The missional approach can be viewed in sharper relief when it is contrasted with three ideal-typical alternatives: First, the culturally withdrawn fundamentalist church that sends foreign missionaries but whose engagement with the local community rarely moves beyond somewhat abrasive "street evangelism"; second, the mainline liberal Protestant congregation that over time has lost zeal for evangelistic outreach and whose engagement with the local community is service and work for social justice; and third, the booming suburban Evangelical megachurch, where attendees are "consumers" more than local missionaries.

In this light, it makes sense that leaders of the Reformed resurgence would underscore their movement's "missional" posture toward their communities and cities, especially if they wanted to distance themselves from the culturally withdrawn Calvinists that constitute American fundamentalism. The problem this raises for this study, however, is that out of seventy-five personal interviews with Evangelical leaders from all sorts of traditions and tribes, not a single one rejected the missional label as I have defined it. Whether they were Calvinistic or anything else, whether complementarian or not, conservative or self-professed progressive, every person interviewed for this book affirmed this point. Even the Calvinist pastors that other New Calvinist pastors said were not very missional (because they were more fundamentalist) said they were, or hoped they were, missional.

Driscoll listed Mark Dever and Kevin DeYoung as two Calvinist leaders who are not missional.[76] I spoke with Dever and DeYoung about this. Dever told me: "I don't like the word 'missional,' but when you break it down in specifics of what guys mean by it, I'm not only fine with it; I hope that's what

[76] Mark Driscoll, *A Call to Resurgence: Will Christianity Have a Funeral or a Future?* (Carol Stream, IL: Tyndale House, 2013), 308–309.

I try to do in my own life and in our church's life." Similarly, DeYoung said, "If 'missional' simply means God has given the Church a mission, then I'm fine with 'missional.'" He referenced a different leading New Calvinist pastor who had said that "missional" is "a junk-drawer term." DeYoung said he understands the mission of the Church—qua the Church—to be proclaiming the Gospel and making disciples and not primarily "redeeming the city" or "transforming the culture" or working for various admittedly good social causes. Still, he said, "Given the right people and the right circumstances, I don't mind the term 'missional.'" Elsewhere, DeYoung and Greg Gilbert explained their position as "not anti-missional." The word "missional," they say, "is often shorthand for 'get out of your holy huddle and go engage your community with the gospel.' We are all for that. Every Christian should be."[77]

And that is precisely what the rest of the interviews for this book revealed. The "missional" label is widely accepted—whether wholesale or in cautious and qualified ways—among all sorts of Evangelical leaders from a variety of traditions and theological perspectives. The term "missional" *does* describe the New Calvinism. And the term helps to set the New Calvinist movement apart analytically from both American fundamentalism and mainline liberal Protestantism.[78] But fundamentalist and mainline organizations enter into this study only in passing, when necessary. When the focus of examination is *within* and *across* Evangelicalism, saying a church or ministry is "missional" does not add much clarity or insight. Australian missiologists might say these leaders (or this book) fail to grasp the full meaning of "missional." But empirically, when the task is to delineate the New Calvinism from other expressions and pockets of American Evangelicalism, "missional" adds very little analytical leverage.

Social Conservatism

If being "missional" is a proposed marker of the New Calvinism that in fact doesn't really set the movement apart, then the opposite can be said for being socially conservative. That is, being socially conservative is a factor that is not

[77] Kevin DeYoung and Greg Gilbert, *What Is the Mission of the Church? Making Sense of Social Justice, Shalom, and the Great Commission* (Wheaton, IL: Crossway, 2011), 20–25.

[78] Robert D. Woodberry and Christian S. Smith, "Fundamentalism et al: Conservative Protestants in America," *Annual Review of Sociology* 24 (1998): 25–56; George M. Marsden, *Understanding Fundamentalism and Evangelicalism* (Grand Rapids, MI: William B. Eerdmans, 1991).

typically used in Evangelicals' public discourse to delineate the New Calvinism from other expressions of Evangelicalism but in fact *does* help analytically to distinguish it from other groups. Of course, as "conservative Protestants," the leadership of mainstream (and especially white) American Evangelicalism tends already to be more socially conservative on average than the American populace, especially on abortion and homosexuality.[79] But even with this overlap between New Calvinists and the rest of Evangelicalism, it is New Calvinist leaders who are most likely to "hold the pole" on social and cultural matters. This has already been noted with strict gender complementarity in the home and Church, where male initiative and female submissiveness are prescribed.

Beyond gender, leaders of the New Calvinism are conservative on several other social issues. On abortion, they are uniformly pro-life; most if not all would like to see *Roe v. Wade* overturned. On sexual ethics, they uniformly believe any sexual activity other than one man and one woman in marriage is sinful. There may be New Calvinist leaders who are *not against* redefining civil marriage to include gay and lesbian couples, but if there is, they have not stated as much publicly (and if they did, they undoubtedly would be cast out of the movement's leadership ranks). One might hear New Calvinists employ arguments from Catholic political and legal theorists to make the case that traditional man-woman marriage is objectively best for promoting societal flourishing and the common good.[80] New Calvinists have been active in the recent uptick in discourse on religious liberty (in light of former President Obama's contraception mandate and legal victories for gay marriage), and they supported Hobby Lobby in its controversial Supreme Court case.[81] They believe religious freedom applies not only to "pews, homes, and hearts," as one progressive columnist for *The New York Times* recently put it,[82] but also to the public square.[83] The

[79] Corwin E. Smidt, *American Evangelicals Today* (Lanham, MD: Rowman and Littlefield, 2013), 191–192, 202–205.

[80] Sherif Girgis, Robert P. George, and Ryan T. Anderson, "What Is Marriage?" *Harvard Journal of Law and Public Policy* 34, no. 1 (2011): 245–287; Sherif Girgis, Ryan T. Anderson, and Robert P. George, *What Is Marriage? Man and Woman: A Defense* (New York: Encounter Books, 2012); Patrick Lee and Robert P. George, *Conjugal Union: What Marriage Is and Why It Matters* (New York: Cambridge University Press, 2014).

[81] Steven D. Smith, *Getting over Equality: A Critical Diagnosis of Religious Freedom in America* (New York: New York University Press, 2001); Steven D. Smith, *The Rise and Decline of American Religious Freedom* (Cambridge, MA: Harvard University Press, 2014).

[82] Frank Bruni, "Your God and My Dignity: Religious Liberty, Bigotry, and Gays," *The New York Times*, January 10, 2015, https://www.nytimes.com/2015/01/11/opinion/sunday/frank-bruni-religious-liberty-bigotry-and-gays.html, accessed March 13, 2019.

[83] Albert Mohler has made this point in, among other texts, "Religious Liberty vs. Erotic Liberty—Religious Liberty Is Losing," *AlbertMohler.com*, January 12, 2015, https://albertmohler.com/2015/01/12/religious-liberty-vs-erotic-liberty-religious-liberty-is-losing/, accessed March 13, 2019.

Southern Baptist Convention's Ethics and Religious Liberty Commission is a key player on this front.[84]

New Calvinist leaders are conservative in other areas as well, but less vocally than on issues of gender, abortion, sexuality, marriage, and religious liberty. In fall 2013, for instance, Mark Driscoll started an online skirmish when he argued, "God is not a pacifist."[85] In response, several Anabaptist-leaning Evangelicals (on whom more in the next chapter), known for their commitment to pacifism and nonviolence, wrote critical replies.[86] On the question of war, "just war theory" is the normative position. On the death penalty, Driscoll, John Piper, Wayne Grudem, and Albert Mohler have each made public statements supporting capital punishment. There isn't room to provide a full catalogue of New Calvinists' positions on social and economic issues, but one such project is Wayne Grudem's *Politics—According to the Bible*.[87] Given the influence of Grudem's *Systematic Theology* on the movement,[88] it is not surprising also to find broad agreement with Grudem's conservative arguments across a full range of concerns.

Nevertheless, it is possible to find people further to the right. In the past few years, several Calvinist leaders have reinvigorated their energies toward social responsibility and social justice, including racial reconciliation and loving the poor, as reflected (for example) in their conference on the fiftieth anniversary of Martin Luther King Jr.'s assassination.[89] Among some exceptionally conservative Baptists and Presbyterians—where the Evangelical field shades into fundamentalism—this renewed social effort has led to allegations

[84] https://erlc.com/

[85] http://theresurgence.com/2013/10/22/is-god-a-pacifist

[86] See, for example, Greg Boyd's three-part series, the first of which is "Responding to Driscoll's 'Is God a Pacifist?' Part I," *ReKnew*, October 24, 2013, http://reknew.org/2013/10/responding-to-driscolls-is-god-a-pacifist-part-i/; See also Scot McKnight, "Fights about Pacifism," *Jesus Creed*, October 25, 2013, http://www.patheos.com/blogs/jesuscreed/2013/10/25/fights-about-pacifism/ ; Jonathan Merritt, "Mark Driscoll Makes Pacifists Fighting Mad" (with responses from Shane Claiborne, Scot McKnight, and Jonathan Wilson-Hartgrove), *Religion News Service*, October 24, 2013, http://jonathanmerritt.religionnews.com/2013/10/24/mark-driscolls-pansy-post-outrages-christian-pacifists/; Mike Skinner, "Jesus Is Cruciform, Not Octagonal (A Response to Mark Driscoll)," *Cruciform Theology*, October 22, 2013, https://cruciformtheologyblog.com/2013/10/22/jesus-is-cruciform-not-octagonal-a-response-to-mark-driscoll/; Preston Sprinkle, "Driscoll's DeJesus Uncrossed," *Theology for Real Life*, October 23, 2013, http://facultyblog.eternitybiblecollege.com/2013/10/driscolls-dejesus-uncrossed/; Brian Zahnd, "You're Not a Pacifist, Are You?" *BrianZahnd.com*, October 22, 2013, http://brianzahnd.com/2013/10/youre-pacifist/.

[87] Wayne Grudem, *Politics—According to the Bible: A Comprehensive Resource for Understanding Modern Political Issues in Light of Scripture* (Grand Rapids, MI: Zondervan, 2010).

[88] Wayne Grudem, *Systematic Theology: An Introduction to Biblical Doctrine* (Grand Rapids, MI: Zondervan, 1994).

[89] Available at http://mlk50conference.com/ and https://www.thegospelcoalition.org/conference/mlk50/.

the New Calvinist movement (especially Tim Keller, Thabiti Anyabwile, and The Gospel Coalition more generally) has succumbed to racial identity politics, intersectionality, and "cultural Marxism"—in short, that they've *gone woke*.[90] In October 2018, Keller responded on Twitter: "Do I really need to defend that I'm not a Marxist? The internet is a strange place."[91] But that is a matter for another book. For present purposes, attending not to conservative Protestant polemicists on the Internet but instead looking toward the bigger Evangelical landscape in the United States, the New Calvinism can be set apart analytically and empirically as conservative, by and large, on most social issues.

Continuationism versus Cessationism

Another potential movement-defining benchmark has to do with the ways the Holy Spirit—the third member of the Trinity—operates (or not) in human life today. This theological question is much discussed among leaders of the New Calvinism, at least when they are talking about or attempting to analyze their own movement. On one level, there are several ways the Holy Spirit is believed to be active today that are entirely uncontroversial among New Calvinists. Practically all would say the Holy Spirit is the agent in regeneration (getting "born again"), convicts Christian believers of their sins, helps them to interpret the Bible, empowers them to live lives pleasing to God, and seals them for salvation. But on top of these, there is some debate about the revelatory *gifts* of the Holy Spirit, such as speaking in tongues, healings, visions, and prophecy. The question is whether those supernatural gifts ceased after the writers of the New Testament died (cessationism) or whether they continue to be operative in the lives of Christians even up to the present (continuationism).[92] The cessationist perspective is dominant among fundamentalist dispensational Calvinists and much of the "older" Reformed world. The continuationist stance animates much of Charismatic and Pentecostal expressions of Christianity. The primary reason this issue

---

[90] The influence of Jordan Peterson seems to be lurking behind the scenes here.

[91] https://twitter.com/timkellernyc/status/1047920810990739457

[92] See Wayne Grudem, ed., *Are Miraculous Gifts for Today? Four Views* (Grand Rapids, MI: Zondervan, 1996); Samuel E. Waldron, *To Be Continued? Are the Miraculous Gifts for Today?* (Merrick, NY: Calvary Press, 2007); Thomas R. Schreiner, *Spiritual Gifts: What They Are and Why They Matter* (Nashville, TN: B&H, 2018).

is talked about so much among New Calvinist leaders is that one of the movement's figureheads, Mark Driscoll, identified continuationism as one of the movement's identifying traits.[93]

However, when I actually spoke with New Calvinist leaders, a strange thing happened. Almost every leader said they hold a somewhat unusual position on this issue somewhere between continuationism and cessationism. What that means is an "atypical" position is, in fact, the typical position. For example, when I asked Mark Dever where he landed on this issue, he said the entire conversation arose as an "extra-biblical construct" among Protestants as a response to continuing revelation in the Catholic Church (when the Pope speaks authoritatively *ex cathedra*). Instead, Dever said he wants to defend the authority and sufficiency of the Bible alone, but he also has no reason to say God will not work in a particular way at a particular time. He concluded: "In my mind, it's just a non-issue. I am disinterested in the conversation." Kevin DeYoung's answer was similar to Dever's. He rejected the idea of continuing revelation ("the canon is closed"), but he also explained he believes God still gives special gifts and works through miracles and healings. "I can agree with and disagree with each of the terms," he said. Furthermore, Collin Hansen told me, "I'm not a cessationist, so I guess that makes me a continuationist," but he also added that he does not actively seek to incorporate gifts of healing, prophecy, or tongues into his Christian life. One professor at John Piper's seminary said the miraculous gifts of the Spirit, like speaking in tongues and prophecy, are "possible but very rare." Piper himself has said the gifts of tongues, healing, and prophecy are certainly possible but that they are most appropriate in smaller groups, not in the corporate church setting.[94] At a recent conference, Tim Keller said: "I'm about 80 percent a cessationist, myself. I'm actually pretty skeptical about an awful lot of the claims of miracles and healing."[95] And when I interviewed Keller he stated, "[Our church] really [is] on the border. I would be a moderate continuationist, I think." Another well-known Calvinist pastor said: "Guys who are continuationist often think I'm a cessationist, and guys who are cessationist often think I'm a continuationist." Justin Taylor told me he leans toward a variety of "cessationism that understands that God still does very unusual things." Danny Akin told me that he is "cautious but open" to the

---

[93] Driscoll, *A Call to Resurgence*, 105–108, 112–113.
[94] https://www.youtube.com/watch?v=nfyuc0D9H_E, accessed March 20, 2019.
[95] https://www.youtube.com/watch?v=xIRSzsUSRZA, accessed March 20, 2019.

miraculous gifts of the Holy Spirit. In short, these are the sorts of answers I got over and over on this topic.

It is evident from the interviews, then, that the New Calvinism is neither staunchly cessationist nor fully continuationist (i.e., charismatic). One exception is Tim Challies, who simply told me he is cessationist. But most leaders appear to hold a position somewhere in between the two ideal-typical views, blending the two together with various nuances and caveats. An apt label for the vast majority of this movement's leadership would be "cautious continuationists."[96] So, if the desire is to differentiate the New Calvinists from fundamentalist Baptists and old-school Presbyterians (both of which are Calvinists), then highlighting the continuationism part of cautious continuationism is helpful. Likewise, understanding the cautious aspect of cautious continuationism would be beneficial for differentiating the New Calvinism from Charismatic and Pentecostal expressions of American Evangelicalism. There is certainly a notable continuationist impulse in the New Calvinism, especially among pastors like Mark Driscoll, John Piper, C. J. Mahaney, and Sam Storms, along with Wayne Grudem.[97] But given the ways New Calvinist leaders themselves actually talk about this topic—with consistent qualifications, caveats, hesitancies, and sometimes dismissal—it is hard to avoid the conclusion that it is not a very clear or well-defined analytical choice for conceptualizing the movement.

Four Other Comments

Mind and Heart, Together

Reformed Christians are a notoriously academic and bookish crowd. Perhaps in an attempt to counteract that overarching predisposition, leaders of the New Calvinist movement aim to strike the right balance between the roles of mind and heart in Christian living. Far from being anti-intellectual, New Calvinists are active in "the life of the mind," as evidenced for example in the many books

---

[96] See Robert L. Saucy, "An Open But Cautious View," in Grudem, *Are Miraculous Gifts for Today?*
[97] See Mark Driscoll, *Spirit-Filled Jesus: Live by His Power* (Lake Mary, FL: Charisma House, 2018), especially the Appendix; Sam Storms, *Practicing the Power: Welcoming the Gifts of the Holy Spirit in Your Life* (Grand Rapids, MI: Zondervan, 2017).

their movement has produced. But New Calvinist leaders also are attuned to the role of emotions and affections in Christian life, and self-consciously try to foster those without devolving into the flimsy sentimentality prevalent in much of mainstream American Evangelicalism.[98]

The theme of *joy* in John Piper's preaching and writing is the clearest example of this effort. Tim Keller, as well, has written and spoken against sentimentality in worship and preaching, but also the need to "preach to the heart"[99] and to promote *awe* and *wonder* of God through music.[100] For New Calvinist leaders, eighteenth-century colonial Calvinist preacher and theologian Jonathan Edwards (1703–1758) serves as a model in balancing mind and heart, especially his 1746 book *Religious Affections*.[101] Piper and Keller have both publicly highlighted the impact that Edwards's life, writing, and preaching have had not only on their doctrinal views but also on their understanding of the heart, the affections, in Christian faithfulness.[102] Kevin DeYoung likewise advised his followers on Twitter: "Head and heart, doctrine and affection, doxology and orthodoxy, never pull those things apart. Beware of churches that do."

None of this is to suggest today's non-Calvinist Evangelical leaders are not engaged in the life of the mind, writing their own academic books (several are). Nor is it to say that older generations of American Calvinists were unaware of the importance of rightly ordered affections in life (they were not). In this sense, the holding together of the mind and the heart is not *distinctive* of the New Calvinism, but it is undoubtedly a notable *feature* of the movement.

[98] Todd M. Brenneman, *Homespun Gospel: The Triumph of Sentimentality in Contemporary American Evangelicalism* (New York: Oxford University Press, 2014).

[99] This was the topic of Keller's hour-long workshop at The Gospel Coalition's 2015 National Conference in Orlando, Florida.

[100] Timothy J. Keller, "Reformed Worship in the Global City," in *Worship by the Book*, ed. D. A. Carson (Grand Rapids, MI: Zondervan, 2002), 193–239.

[101] Dane C. Ortlund, *Edwards on the Christian Life: Alive to the Beauty of God* (Wheaton, IL: Crossway, 2014); Harry S. Stout, *The New England Soul: Preaching and Religious Culture in Colonial New England*, 25th anniversary edition (New York: Oxford University Press, [1986] 2012).

[102] As Piper put it during the seventh annual Gaffin Lecture in March 2014 at Westminster Theological Seminary: "The New Calvinism puts a priority on pietism or piety in the Puritan vein, with an emphasis on the essential role of the affections in Christian living, while esteeming the life of the mind and being very productive in it, and embracing the value of serious scholarship. Jonathan Edwards would be invoked as a model of this combination of the affections and the life of the mind more often than John Calvin, whether that's fair to Calvin or not." Accessed February 25, 2019, from https://www.youtube.com/watch?v=vB5q6qIwJLk. See also John Piper and David Mathis, eds., *Thinking. Loving. Doing: A Call to Glorify God with Heart and Mind* (Wheaton, IL: Crossway, 2011).

On Being Reformed-ish

When the New Calvinism is framed using either of its two alternative names—that is, the neo-Reformed or the Young, Restless, Reformed[103]—it is common for adherents in the Presbyterian and Reformed traditions to suggest this New Calvinist movement ought not be called Reformed. To be actually Reformed, the thinking goes, a church has to be connected to the confessional heritage and denominational lineage stretching back to Calvin and the other early reformers. From this perspective, being truly Reformed includes not merely adhering to the Calvinistic doctrines of salvation (like the New Calvinism does), but also a commitment to the sixteenth- and seventeenth-century confessional statements, the practice of infant baptism, covenant theology (as opposed to dispensationalism), and a conciliar model of church governance within a historically Reformed denomination.[104]

Stated differently, some pastors and theologians say it is impossible for a Baptist church or a nondenominational church to be Reformed. And if the criteria just mentioned make a Reformed church, they would be correct. This is why one occasionally hears New Calvinist leaders call themselves "Reformed-ish." Another layer of confusion gets added by the fact that the New Calvinism, although heavily Baptist, is a mixture of churches that lack the aforementioned criteria (Baptist and nondenominational churches) and other churches that meet them (certain popular Presbyterian churches). For a book whose aim is to understand and explain the New Calvinist movement sociologically, the question of whether or not this movement is "Truly Reformed" is neither here nor there. Theologians and church historians may take up the question and might cringe when I use the words "Reformed" and "Calvinist" interchangeably, but it is an issue that I can only note upfront and ask that the reader interpret "Reformed" with generosity.

---

[103] Hansen, *Young, Restless, Reformed.*
[104] Michael Allen and Scott R. Swain, *Reformed Catholicity: The Promise of Retrieval for Theology and Biblical Interpretation* (Grand Rapids, MI: Baker Academic, 2015); Bryan Chapell, *Why Do We Baptize Infants?* (Phillipsburg, NJ: P&R, 2006); R. Scott Clark, *Recovering the Reformed Confession: Our Theology, Piety, and Practice* (Phillipsburg, NJ: P&R, 2008); Richard A. Muller, *After Calvin: Studies in the Development of a Theological Tradition* (New York: Oxford University Press, 2003); Stephen E. Smallman, *What Is a Reformed Church?* (Phillipsburg, NJ: P&R, 2003); R. C. Sproul, *What Is Reformed Theology? Understanding the Basics* (Grand Rapids, MI: Baker Books,

New Calvinism versus Neo-Calvinism

A distinction should be made between New Calvinism and neo-Calvinism. Decades before the present-day New Calvinist movement emerged within American Evangelicalism, the term "neo-Calvinism" referred to a school of thought in the Dutch Reformed tradition, developed most forcefully by former Dutch Prime Minister and theologian Abraham Kuyper (1837–1920). Dutch thinkers Herman Bavinck (1854–1921), Herman Dooyeweerd (1894–1977), and Dirk Vollenhoven (1892–1978) also had a formative influence on the neo-Calvinist movement. In addition to having a Calvinistic doctrine of salvation, neo-Calvinism emphasized the sovereignty of God over all of creation, the need for Christians to create and engage with culture in all spheres of human life (the "cultural mandate"), the differentiated authority and responsibilities of different sectors of human life ("sphere sovereignty"), a distinctly "Christian worldview," a rationalistic *reductio ad absurdum* strategy for defending the truth of the Christian faith (called "presuppositional apologetics"), as well as a cosmic all-encompassing understanding of redemptive history (not merely individuals' sin, salvation, and piety).[105]

Neo-Calvinism is still around today as a part of the Dutch Reformed tradition. Its figurehead thinkers include leading Protestant intellectuals (many of whom are philosophers) and higher education administrators, such as Alvin Plantinga, Cornelius Plantinga, Nicholas Wolterstorff, George Marsden, Richard Mouw, Albert Wolters, James W. Skillen, Calvin Seerveld, Michael Goheen, Craig Bartholomew, James K. A. Smith, Ray Pennings, and the late H. Evan Runner. Institutions associated with the neo-Calvinist tradition include Calvin College (now University) and Calvin Theological Seminary, Kuyper College in Michigan, Dordt College in Iowa, Trinity Christian College in Illinois, Cardus (a think-tank in Canada), the CCO (Coalition for Christian Outreach) and its annual Jubilee Conference, Redeemer University College and the Institute for Christian Studies, both in Ontario, and the Center for Public Justice in Washington, DC, among others.[106]

1997); Carl R. Trueman, *The Creedal Imperative* (Wheaton, IL: Crossway, 2012); Malcolm H. Watts, *What Is a Reformed Church?* (Grand Rapids, MI: Reformation Heritage Books, 2011).

[105] See Craig G. Bartholomew, *Contours of the Kuyperian Tradition: A Systematic Introduction* (Downers Grove, IL: InterVarsity Press, 2017); Richard J. Mouw, *Abraham Kuyper: A Short and Personal Introduction* (Grand Rapids, MI: William B. Eerdmans, 2011).

[106] Tim Keller, *Center Church*, 192n22, helped with this list. A generation before most of the men listed here, Cornelius Van Til and Gordon Clark were important neo-Calvinist philosophers.

Aside from working out of different religious institutions, the differences between Kuyperian neo-Calvinism and the New Calvinism are largely a matter of emphasis rather than of kind. The easiest way to grasp the differences is that the former movement emphasizes the sovereignty of God over all of *creation* (and what that entails for Christians working vocationally and making culture in "secular" fields) while the latter movement tends to emphasize the sovereignty of God specifically over *salvation*. These two orientations are not mutually exclusive ideological positions, and leaders of both movements, if asked explicitly, would very likely affirm what the other one emphasizes. (New Calvinist leaders agree that God is sovereign over all of creation.) But this difference in emphasis shapes the way leaders in the New Calvinism tend to think about cultural engagement, the biblical narrative, and the purpose of the local church. Without tackling the nuances involved, suffice it to say that in the New Calvinism (and especially in its Baptist components) all three tend to be more individualistic and less institutional or corporate.[107] Another big difference is that Kuyperian neo-Calvinists tend to be egalitarian rather than complementarian about gender roles.

If all this sounds like Greek, the reader can move on without much loss. But for those curious about this matter, the point is simply that Kuyperian neo-Calvinism and the New Calvinist movement examined in this book are similar and related but not the same thing.

The Importance of Resurgence

It is not exactly right analytically to say the New Calvinist movement is just the combination of the particular cultural and theological features outlined in this chapter, or even the aggregate of the persons and organizations that hold to and promote them. It is more precise instead to think of the New Calvinism as *the increasing presence and prominence* of those convictions and leaders, all held together, in American Evangelicalism since the turn of the new millennium, and particularly among persons in their twenties and thirties. In short, without the "resurgent" dimension, there is no New Calvinism, rightly understood.

The term "resurgence" gained traction within the New Calvinism—and among the interested observers of it—around 2008 or 2009 as a way to

---

[107] This is less the case in the Presbyterian component of the New Calvinist movement.

describe and frame the movement. This framing arose largely because one of the movement's leading megachurches, MHC in Seattle, operated a very popular although now defunct resources and leadership development website named The Resurgence.[108] It appears that the name for that website seeped into the wider consciousness of the New Calvinism and became a way to understand what was going on. So, for example, when Ligon Duncan, the chancellor and CEO of Reformed Theological Seminary, asked Kevin DeYoung what the "New Calvinism" is, DeYoung answered: "The New Calvinism is a resurgence of Reformed theology, mainly in soteriology [. . .] Mainly it's a new sense, especially among young people, that God's sovereignty is biblical and massively important, that God loved us before we loved Him."[109]

To speak of the New Calvinism as a phenomenon necessarily involves a claim to a distinct sociological change over time, and specifically a marked increase of some kind since roughly the year 2000. So any focus on the "new" in this movement's name should not be seen as indicating some major *revision* or *alteration* of Calvinism but a *resurgence* of it. The basic heartbeat of the New Calvinist movement as a religious phenomenon is the idea that Calvinism—along with the other traits described earlier—has surged back onto the American Evangelical scene with renewed popularity and strength.

Conclusion

British pastor and author Iain Murray—himself a Calvinist—has suggested it is a "regrettable misnomer" to call the collection of pastors, theologians, congregations, networks, conferences, and convictions described in this chapter "the New Calvinist movement."[110] He contends this serious Calvinistic zeal is neither *new* nor a *movement*, but is rather old, organic, and decentralized. Other readers may find other problems (for example, some pastors included in this chapter undoubtedly would be hesitant to place much personal stock in the label "New Calvinism"). Whatever merits such concerns might hold, they are not at issue at this juncture. Even just offering the descriptions on previous pages and labeling these actors collectively

---

[108] Through the end of 2014, the website was http://theresurgence.com; today an inactive archive exists at http://theresurgencereport.com.

[109] https://www.youtube.com/watch?v=jscdlO1BUj0, accessed March 4, 2019.

[110] Iain Murray, "Thoughts on the 'Together for the Gospel' Conference 2014," June 6, 2014, https://banneroftruth.org/us/resources/articles/2014/thoughts-together-gospel-conference-2014/, accessed April 29, 2019.

"the New Calvinist movement" is bound already to raise certain questions and critiques. Such is the nature of addressing matters that some people (as we will see shortly) have very strong opinions about—whether positive or negative—or are deeply personally invested in, even to the point of attributing these various ministries and leaders to the providential hand of God.

The point here is more modest. There is a religious phenomenon afoot, and this chapter has described the key persons, organizations, and beliefs involved. Of course, merely by describing these players and how they arose over time, this chapter is one kind of causal accounting of the movement.[111] Consider the total weight of, for instance, John Piper and Wayne Grudem cofounding the Council on Biblical Manhood and Womanhood in 1987; their Danvers Statement on complementarian gender roles being published in *Christianity Today* in 1989; Tim Keller and his wife moving to New York City to plant Redeemer in 1989; Al Mohler clearing house at Southern Baptist Theological Seminary in 1993 and the subsequent few years; John Piper along with Jon Bloom beginning Desiring God in 1994; the initial publication of Wayne Grudem's *Systematic Theology* in 1994; Mark Driscoll launching MHC in 1996; the inaugural Passion Conference in 1997 and its expansion after the turn of the century, serving as a platform to expose young people to Piper's preaching; Mark Driscoll with David Nicholas cofounding the Acts 29 Network in 1998; the ESV translation of the Bible initially being published in 2001; Lecrae Moore and Ben Washer cofounding Reach Records in 2004; Mark Dever and others organizing the first Together for the Gospel conference in 2006; Collin Hansen identifying the movement and giving it a moniker in 2006, followed by a book in 2008; Tim Keller and D. A. Carson co-organizing The Gospel Coalition and officially starting it in 2007; and many other events. In fact, this "material cause" approach is the primary way leaders of the New Calvinism have answered the question, "Where did all these Calvinists come from?"[112]

---

[111] Daniel Hirschman and Isaac Ariail Reed, "Formation Stories and Causality in Sociology," *Sociological Theory* 32, no. 4 (2014): 259–282.

[112] See Mark Dever, "Where'd All These Calvinists Come From?" *9Marks*, June 18, 2014 (originally published in 2007 as ten separate posts), https://www.9marks.org/article/whered-all-these-calvinists-come-from/; Tim Challies, "Where Did All These Calvinists Come From? A Visual History," *challies.com*, March 11, 2014, https://www.challies.com/visual-theology/where-did-all-these-calvinists-come-from-a-visual-history/; John Piper, "Where Did All These Calvinists Come From?" *Desiring God*, December 16, 2013, https://www.desiringgod.org/interviews/where-did-all-these-calvinists-come-from; Matt Smethurst, "Where Did All These Calvinists Come From?" *The Gospel Coalition*, October 23, 2013, https://www.thegospelcoalition.org/article/where-did-all-these-calvinists-come-from/; accessed April 27, 2019. These treatments reach further back into Evangelical history than this chapter does, citing formative influences such as Charles Spurgeon, D. Martyn Lloyd-Jones, and the Banner of Truth Trust.

This sort of descriptive, "formation-story" approach to accounting for re-surgent Calvinism is helpful, but the rest of this book moves beyond merely describing the beliefs, persons, and organizations out of which the New Calvinist movement arose. The focus instead from this spot forward is less descriptive and lightly historical but more causally explanatory and sociolog-ical. The task in view is to illuminate the actual sociological relations, strate-gies, conditions, and mechanisms by which the New Calvinism has become the kind of social and religious reality it is—*a resurgence*. The next step, then, is to know more concretely the answer to two related questions: Relative to what and to whom in the big landscape of American Evangelicalism is the Reformed resurgence resurging—and how do those competing religious camps compare regarding their numbers and sociological strength? That is the topic of the next chapter.

3

The Tribes and Their
Comparative Strengths

Having described the New Calvinist movement substantively and analytically, this chapter identifies and details the other "tribes" or "pockets" of American Evangelicalism against which the Reformed resurgence is said to be resurging. These are mainstream American Evangelicalism, neo-Anabaptist Evangelicalism, and progressive or Emergent Evangelicalism. Next, this chapter clarifies a possible confusion about how these three expressions and the New Calvinism relate to the Emerging Church, and then it briefly acknowledges some intermixing and blurring between the four tribes. The latter half of the chapter uses the limited data available to address these tribes' comparative sizes and sociological strengths.

The conclusion is that although the New Calvinism has indeed grown numerically since the late 1990s, the other expressions and tribes of American Evangelicalism either (a) are large enough to match and overshadow the organizational and leadership following of the New Calvinist movement (as with the mainstream of Evangelicalism) or (b) are significantly smaller but have themselves only emerged since the late 1990s and therefore have "resurged" percentage-wise just as much (i.e., neo-Anabaptist and progressive Emergent Evangelicalism). This conclusion sets the stage for an explanatory model of institutional religious strength that relies more on the strategic and conflictual actions of religious leaders to gain symbolic power in and over their field than on simple additive growth—the model of strength based on *strategic action field theory* developed in the next chapter.

Mainstream Evangelicalism

One major category of religious actors within the bigger landscape of American Evangelicalism relative to which the New Calvinist movement is thought to be resurging is (what we might simply call) "mainstream"

Reformed Resurgence. Brad Vermurlen, Oxford University Press (2020). © Oxford University Press.
DOI: 10.1093/oso/9780190073510.001.0001

Evangelicals. I use the word "mainstream" self-consciously to avoid potential confusions with what is customarily called "mainline" Protestantism—that is, those typically more liberal denominations such as the United Methodist Church or the Presbyterian Church (USA). What I mean is not mainline Protestantism but rather mainstream Evangelicalism—the typical American Evangelical. This category is not so much a "pocket" or "tribe" per se in American Evangelicalism (although, for simplicity, I sometimes refer to it as such in the remainder of this book) as it is the broad and diverse background of pastors, churches, seminaries, colleges, publishers, and other institutions that together make up the largest portion of Evangelicalism in the United States. It is what Canadian theologian John Stackhouse has outlined as "generic Evangelicalism."[1] Simply put, by mainstream Evangelicalism and Evangelicals I just mean what most scholars mean when they refer to "Evangelicalism."[2]

Mainstream American Evangelicalism includes several of the approximately 1,600 Protestant megachurches in the United States and the pastors (some of whom enjoy celebrity status) who lead them. Among several others, these at least include Steve Andrews at Kensington Church in Michigan; Mark Batterson of National Community Church around Washington, DC; Mark Beeson at Granger Community Church in Indiana (even though it is a part of the United Methodist Church); Kenton Beshore at Mariners Church in California; Steven Furtick at Elevation Church; Randy Frazee and Max Lucado at Oak Hills Church around San Antonio; Craig Groeschel at LifeChurch.tv; Chris Hodges with Church of the Highlands; and Willow Creek Community Church and its former pastor Bill Hybels.

Other megachurch pastors in mainstream Evangelicalism include Carl Lentz with Hillsong Church in New York City; Robert Morris at Gateway Church; John Ortberg of Menlo Church; Larry Osborne of North Coast Church; Brad Powell with NorthRidge Church in Michigan; Kerry Shook at Woodlands Church in Texas; Judah Smith at The City Church in Seattle; Andy Stanley at North Point Community Church in Atlanta; Dave Stone and Kyle Idleman with Southeast Christian Church based out of Louisville; Greg Surratt at Seacoast Church in South Carolina; Rick Warren at Saddleback Church; Jud Wilhite with Central Christian Church near Las Vegas; Cross

---

[1] John G. Stackhouse, "Generic Evangelicalism," in *Four Views on the Spectrum of Evangelicalism*, ed. Andrew David Naselli and Collin Hansen (Grand Rapids, MI: Zondervan, 2011), 116–142.

[2] For example, Smidt, *American Evangelicals Today*.

Point Church in Nashville until recently led by Pete Wilson; Ed Young with Second Baptist Church in Houston, Texas; and his son commonly known as Ed Young Jr. at Fellowship Church based in Grapevine, Texas.[3]

Aside from these and other megachurches, mainstream Evangelicalism in the United States also includes collegiate ministries such as Campus Crusade for Christ (Cru), Christian Union, InterVarsity Christian Fellowship, Campus Outreach, Reformed University Fellowship (RUF), and The Navigators. It also includes institutions serving a wide range of purposes such as The National Association of Evangelicals (NAE), Billy Graham Evangelistic Association (BGEA), Alliance of Confessing Evangelicals, Focus on the Family, Promise Keepers, Fellowship of Christian Athletes, *Christianity Today*, Leadership Network, The Evangelical Christian Publishers Association (ECPA), and World Vision. It includes youth organizations such as Youth for Christ, Young Life, and Youth With A Mission (YWAM).

Colleges and universities within the mainstream of American Evangelicalism include Wheaton College, Gordon College, Westmont College, Calvin College, Azusa Pacific University, Moody Bible Institute, The King's College, and Biola University, among several others. Mainstream American Evangelicalism's seminaries include Fuller Theological Seminary, Gordon-Conwell Theological Seminary, Talbot School of Theology, George Fox Evangelical Seminary, Reformed Theological Seminary, Moody Theological Seminary, Denver Seminary, and Asbury Theological Seminary—again among many others. Many mainstream Evangelical schools at various levels are connected with the Association of Christian Schools International (ACSI), the Council for Christian Colleges and Universities (CCCU), and The Association of Theological Schools (although not every school connected with those associations is Evangelical). Mainstream Evangelicalism is also deeply formed by publishers, including InterVarsity Press, Zondervan, Eerdmans, Baker Publishing Group (including Bethany House and Brazos Press), NavPress, Moody Publishers, Charisma House, Thomas Nelson Publishers, Tyndale House Publishers, WaterBrook Multnomah, and David C. Cook.

The mainstream of American Evangelicalism is recognizable more by these and other institutions and parachurch organizations than by any particular denominational ties. While much of Evangelicalism is transdenominational

---

[3] Stephen Ellingson, "The Rise of the Megachurches and Changes in Religious Culture: Review Article," *Sociology Compass* 3, no. 1 (2009): 16–30.

or nondenominational, examples of mainstream Evangelical denominations would at least include, among others, The Evangelical Free Church of America (EFCA); much of the Southern Baptist Convention;[4] Pentecostal denominations such as Assemblies of God, Calvary Chapel, and the Vineyard fellowship; and Wesleyan Holiness denominations such as Church of the Nazarene, The Christian and Missionary Alliance (C&MA), and The Salvation Army, to name just a few. Mainstream Evangelicalism encompasses an assortment of Baptists, Presbyterians, Lutherans, Methodists, Holiness denominations, Anglicans, Pentecostals, Charismatics, Restorationists, Congregationalists, and more.[5] In more recent years, some of America's largest Evangelical megachurches have started their own networks that function as quasi-denominations. These include Willow Creek Association (founded in 1992 and tied to Bill Hybels at Willow Creek Community Church)[6] and the Association of Related Churches (founded in 2000 and led by Greg Surratt at Seacoast Church).[7]

None of this is to say Calvinism or Reformed theology (nor the other markers of the New Calvinist movement outlined in the previous chapter, such as social conservatism and complementarianism) is absent among mainstream Evangelicalism in the United States. What I am calling mainstream Evangelicalism includes a diverse array of views on practically every theological issue and therefore includes its fair share of Calvinists (and, for that matter, complementarians and social conservatives).[8] But it also includes Arminians (Wesleyans), semi-Pelagians, and egalitarians—cessationists and charismatics and everything in between. In any event, leaders and organizations in this stream of Evangelicalism who are friendly to Calvinism are not popularly considered by Evangelical leaders to be part of the New Calvinist movement. They all fit squarely into the storyline of the mainstream, postwar "neo-Evangelical" movement.[9] Lastly, it is worth repeating that the

---

[4] Many SBC organizations and leaders (like Rick Warren and Saddleback Church) fit into mainstream Evangelicalism, some (like Matt Chandler and The Village Church) are involved in the New Calvinist movement, and others resemble fundamentalists. See David S. Dockery, ed., *Southern Baptists, Evangelicals, and the Future of Denominationalism* (Nashville, TN: B&H, 2011).

[5] See "Appendix B: Classification of Protestant Denominations," in Pew Research Center's report *America's Changing Religious Landscape*, released online May 12, 2015, especially 103–107.

[6] http://www.willowcreek.com/, now going by the name Global Leadership Network.

[7] https://www.arcchurches.com/

[8] For example, the Alliance of Confessing Evangelicals and Reformed Theological Seminary are both explicitly Reformed and Calvinistic.

[9] See Keith Hunt and Gladys Hunt, *For Christ and the University: The Story of InterVarsity Christian Fellowship of the U.S.A., 1940–1990* (Downers Grove, IL: InterVarsity Press, 1991); George M. Marsden, *Reforming Fundamentalism: Fuller Seminary and the New Evangelicalism*, 2nd ed. (Grand Rapids, MI: William B. Eerdmans, [1987] 1995); Garth M. Rosell, *The Surprising Work of God: Harold*

institutions, megachurches, and leaders listed here do not cohere together, as the word "tribe" would suggest. Rather, they form the massive infrastructural backdrop against which the New Calvinist movement is purportedly resurging.

Neo-Anabaptist Evangelicalism

Counting the New Calvinists, the third identifiable pocket within present-day American Evangelicalism is the neo-Anabaptists. Anabaptists (without the *neo-*) were originally the product of what came to be known as the "Radical Reformation" during the sixteenth century. As reflected in their name ("ana-" being derived from the Greek for "over again"), Anabaptists sought to push the Protestant Reformation of Luther, Calvin, Zwingli, and others even further by arguing Christian believers needed to be *baptized again*, because in their view being baptized as an infant in the Catholic Church was not valid.[10] In this way, one might think of the Anabaptists as the "left wing" of the Protestant Reformation. The Anabaptists are the forbearers to contemporary Baptists, particularly on the issues of baptism and church governance.[11] Other modern Christians are linked more directly to the sixteenth-century "radical reformers" through a handful of small denominations collectively known as the "peace churches," including the Quakers, Brethren, Mennonites, Amish, and Hutterites.[12]

John Ockenga, Billy Graham, and the Rebirth of Evangelicalism (Grand Rapids, MI: Baker Academic, 2008); John G. Turner, *Bill Bright and Campus Crusade for Christ: The Renewal of Evangelicalism in Postwar America* (Chapel Hill: The University of North Carolina Press, 2008).

[10] Lutheran and Calvinist reformers originally used the term "Anabaptists" as a depreciatory label, but in the English-speaking pluralistic religious landscape it is no longer considered pejorative.

[11] Contemporary Baptists, however, are more directly descended from English Puritan Separatists, not Anabaptists. For the connection, see Malcolm B. Yarnell III, ed., *The Anabaptists and Contemporary Baptists: Restoring New Testament Christianity* (Nashville, TN: Broadman & Holman, 2013).

[12] Among a large literature on the history and character of the Anabaptist tradition—much of which is confessional—see, for example, Willem Balke, *Calvin and the Anabaptist Radicals*, trans. William J. Heynen (Grand Rapids, MI: William B. Eerdmans, 1981); Carl F. Bowman, *Brethren Society: The Cultural Transformation of a "Peculiar People"* (Baltimore, MD: The Johns Hopkins University Press, 1995); William R. Estep, *The Anabaptist Story: An Introduction to Sixteenth-Century Anabaptism*, 3rd ed. (Grand Rapids, MI: William B. Eerdmans, [1963] 1996); Thomas N. Finger, *A Contemporary Anabaptist Theology: Biblical, Historical, Constructive* (Downers Grove, IL: InterVarsity Press, 2004); Robert Friedmann, *The Theology of Anabaptism: An Interpretation* (Eugene, OR: Wipf and Stock, 1999); Rod Janzen and Max Stanton, *The Hutterites in North America* (Baltimore, MD: The Johns Hopkins University Press, 2010); Donald B. Kraybill, *Concise Encyclopedia of Amish, Brethren, Hutterites, and Mennonites* (Baltimore, MD: The Johns Hopkins University Press, 2010); Donald B. Kraybill and Carl Desportes Bowman, *On the Backroad to Heaven: Old Order Hutterites, Mennonites,*

Contemporary Anabaptist and neo-Anabaptist Christians commit themselves and their faith communities to a number of lifestyle principles rooted in their reading of the Bible, with special emphasis on the recorded teachings of Jesus himself.[13] These principles include, for instance, an unwavering commitment to nonviolence and pacifism, maintaining critical distance from political power and the State,[14] practices of relational reconciliation (across boundaries of race, gender, nationality, socioeconomic status, etc.), service to the poor and identifying with (and often living among) society's marginalized and oppressed, a subversive posture toward any form of status and hierarchy (often including hierarchy within the governance structure of their own faith communities), the value of "speaking truth to power" (a phrase coined by the Quakers[15]), stewardship of the natural environment, and "simple living," which sometimes entails living communally or vows of poverty. These principles make present-day Anabaptists highly critical of certain features, habits, and pursuits present in contemporary American culture, including war, violence, the death penalty, "Empire," "the powers" of this age and power generally, environmental degradation, the concept of a "Christian nation," political clout, the "American dream," inequality, consumerist capitalism, and excess. The orientation of Anabaptists toward culture and society is generally *passively countercultural*—viewing the Church as a harbinger and sign of God's Kingdom and an alternative community to the kingdom of "the world," while having little hope of transforming the broader culture.

Not all Anabaptists consider themselves "in" Evangelicalism (consider the Amish or Mennonites, for example), but some persons do understand

Amish, and Brethren (Baltimore, MD: The Johns Hopkins University Press, 2001); Donald B. Kraybill, Karen M. Johnson-Weiner, and Steven M. Nolt, *The Amish* (Baltimore, MD: The Johns Hopkins University Press, 2013); Mark Thiessen Nation, *John Howard Yoder: Mennonite Patience, Evangelical Witness, Catholic Convictions* (Grand Rapids, MI: William B. Eerdmans, 2006); C. Arnold Snyder, *Following in the Footsteps of Christ: The Anabaptist Tradition* (Maryknoll, NY: Orbis Books, 2004); and George Huntston Williams, *The Radical Reformation*, 3rd ed. (Kirksville, MO: Truman State University Press, [1962] 1992), along with several books published by Herald Press, a Mennonite Church USA publishing house, including those written by Harold Bender, Cornelius J. Dyck, Walter Klaassen, Donald B. Kraybill, Harry Loewen and Steven M. Nolt, Stuart Murray, Paul Toews, and J. Denny Weaver.

[13] This special emphasis on the recorded teachings of Jesus can be seen in the organization Red Letter Christians, whose name reflects the custom in many Bibles of highlighting Jesus's words in red print.

[14] As James Davison Hunter incisively points out, however, the neo-Anabaptist stance is still paradoxically and profoundly political in nature (Hunter, *To Change the World: The Irony, Tragedy, and Possibility of Christianity in the Late Modern World* (New York: Oxford University Press, 2010), 150–166).

[15] http://www.quaker.org/sttp.html

themselves as both Anabaptist and Evangelical.[16] The "neo-" of "neo-Anabaptists" is therefore used in this case to indicate Christian faith communities and leaders who intentionally cultivate their faith around traditional Anabaptist principles and commitments while also operating within the contemporary Evangelical fold rather than in the traditional "peace churches."[17] Intellectually, neo-Anabaptist Evangelical leaders follow in the footsteps of Mennonite theologian John Howard Yoder (1927–1997) as well as other thinkers whom Yoder has influenced, such as Stanley Hauerwas (even though Hauerwas's influence is not confined only to the Anabaptists). On the ground, key leaders today in neo-Anabaptist Evangelicalism include Tony Campolo, Shane Claiborne, David Fitch, Geoff Holsclaw, Stuart Murray, Kurt Willems, Greg Boyd, Mark Van Steenwyk, Tim Suttle, Jonathan Wilson-Hartgrove, Bruxy Cavey, Neil Cole, and Brian Zahnd, along with others. Leaders with "one foot" in this pocket include Scot McKnight, Ron Sider, and J. R. Woodward.

In addition to the (sometimes quite large) churches in which they are involved, neo-Anabaptist Evangelical leaders connect with one another through a small number of organizations and networks, each of which maintains a notable online presence. Leading among these are Missio Alliance,[18] the Ekklesia Project,[19] Red Letter Christians,[20] and Northern Seminary located just outside of Chicago.[21] It also includes the recently started EVANA Network (the name is a combination of "Evangelical" and "Anabaptist").[22] The neo-Anabaptist pocket would include the small (consistently fewer than nine hundred attendees) outdoor, "almost-annual" PAPA Festival, whose acronym stands for "People Against Poverty and Apathy."[23] The Englewood Review of Books, based in Indianapolis, also has neo-Anabaptist leanings.[24] This pocket of Evangelicalism also encompasses

[16] Jared S. Burkholder and David C. Cramer, *The Activist Impulse: Essays on the Intersection of Evangelicalism and Anabaptism* (Eugene, OR: Pickwick, 2012).

[17] This is also a term and category indigenous to the contemporary American Evangelical field.

[18] http://www.missioalliance.org/

[19] http://www.ekklesiaproject.org/

[20] http://www.redletterchristians.org/

[21] http://www.seminary.edu/. Not to be confused with North Park Theological Seminary.

[22] http://evananetwork.org/

[23] Julia Duin did a nice job capturing the ethos of the PAPA Festival in "PAPA Festival Highlights Christianity, Anarchism, and Community Spirit," *The Washington Post*, September 1, 2011, http://www.washingtonpost.com/lifestyle/magazine/papa-festival-highlights-christianity-anarchism-and-community-spirit/2011/08/03/gIQAFYGmuJ_story.html (last accessed April 8, 2015).

[24] http://erb.kingdomnow.org/

the "New Monasticism"[25]—the moniker applied to the practice among some Christians committed to basic Anabaptist principles to live together in "intentional communities" or other arrangements of proximate housing in order to "relocat[e] to the abandoned places of Empire," to "shar[e] economic resources with fellow community members and the needy among us," and to show "hospitality to the stranger," among other values.[26] Shane Claiborne and his small organization The Simple Way[27] (also known as the Potter Street Community) in Philadelphia is the most widely known leader of the New Monasticism, although there are several dozen similar monastic communities across the United States.[28]

When it comes to the beliefs and convictions New Calvinist leaders are invested in, neo-Anabaptist leaders are unabashedly *not Calvinists* and *not gender complementarians*, but *are missional*. Beyond this, however, its leaders embody a diverse range of perspectives and ideas, which are not always easy to pin down. Some, like David Fitch and Geoff Holsclaw, are hard to distinguish from mainstream Evangelicals other than by their commitments to basic Anabaptist principles. At the same time, Fitch has multiple criticisms of mainstream American Evangelicalism (especially today's megachurches)[29] and often draws insights about Christian faith from Slovenian philosopher and cultural critic Slavoj Žižek. Others, like Mark Van Steenwyk, identify as "Jesus radicals"[30]; Van Steenwyk is passionate about exploring and living out the intersection of Christianity and Anarchism, which is focused on practical, radical ways to challenge social hierarchies and systems of oppression.[31] He told me he does not believe Hell exists but he does believe in "some kind of resurrection from the dead," and he identifies as "a far-leftist who has a mystical relationship with Jesus." Calvinism, he said, "utilitizes" Jesus and makes his teachings "like the setup to a bad joke."

[25] Markofski, *New Monasticism*; Will Samson, "The New Monasticism," in Brian Steensland and Philip Goff, eds., *The New Evangelical Social Engagement* (New York: Oxford University Press, 2014), 94–108.

[26] http://www.thesimpleway.org/about/12-marks-of-new-monasticism/

[27] http://www.thesimpleway.org/

[28] A map and directory of such intentional communities throughout the United States is available at http://www.communityofcommunities.info/

[29] David E. Fitch, *The Great Giveaway: Reclaiming the Mission of the Church from Big Business, Parachurch Organizations, Psychotherapy, Consumer Capitalism, and Other Modern Maladies* (Grand Rapids, MI: Baker Books, 2005); David E. Fitch, *The End of Evangelicalism? Discerning a New Faithfulness for Mission, Towards an Evangelical Political Theology* (Eugene, OR: Cascade Books, 2011).

[30] http://www.jesusradicals.com/

[31] Van Steenwyk told me in an interview that for his undergraduate education he "earned a B.S. in ministry, which I think is quite fitting."

Greg Boyd is known among Evangelicals for holding to open theism, which says God chooses not to predetermine or settle the future, but instead the future is ontologically composed of a set of multiple genuine possibilities. Boyd told me in an interview he understands open theism, including as it relates to soteriology, as "logically consistent Arminianism." When I interviewed Shane Claiborne, he affirmed a few mainstream Evangelical themes while also continually coming back to the importance of "orthopraxy" and "preaching a good sermon with our lives." He mentioned several times how Catholic ways of thinking had informed his faith. Many neo-Anabaptists, because of their belief in a nonviolent and noncoercive God, interpret Jesus's crucifixion as primarily giving the world a good moral example of how to live (*Christus Exemplar*) or as Jesus establishing cosmic victory over "the powers" of evil and darkness (*Christus Victor*),[32] rather than as a blood-bought penal substitution—the emphasis of Calvinism. More generally, as one neo-Anabaptist leader told me in an interview, neo-Anabaptists tend to see conversations about nuances of doctrines and theology as "a nonstarter" and instead are centrally interested in whether they are following Jesus, living in community, and being peaceful.

In sum, these leaders, organizations, networks, and commitments together form the core of the third socio-religious faction in the American Evangelical landscape today.

Progressive Evangelicalism

It might seem odd at first to speak about "progressive Evangelicals" since in the sociology of religion (and among journalists) Evangelicalism has been categorized and defined nearly synonymously with "conservative Protestants." Historically there is much truth to such a label, but the reality nowadays proves far more complicated. While much of American Evangelicalism (including the New Calvinist movement) is clearly conservative—both theologically and on social issues—since the late 1990s a network of theological and social liberals has staked out its own claim to the "Evangelical" label.[33]

---

[32] See, e.g., J. Denny Weaver, *The Nonviolent Atonement*, 2nd ed. (Grand Rapids, MI: William B. Eerdmans, [2001] 2011).

[33] As poet Michael Toy put it: "We kind of resent having to add the word 'progressive' to the label, but feel that in order to be part of a story which is good news to the world, we kind of have to. At the same time, we don't want to stop being 'Evangelicals,' we are post 'post.' We are who we are." Quoted by Doug Pagitt in a post on FaithStreet.com, online at http://www.faithstreet.com/onfaith/2015/

The politically progressive Evangelical Left has been around since the 1970s,[34] and liberal sensibilities and commitments have been powerful in other traditions of Christianity before that.[35] The pocket of American Evangelicalism considered here has inherited this legacy from earlier decades, but it has its own distinct, albeit shorter, history. And they are less politically oriented generally. The distinct pocket referred to here as progressive Evangelicals emerged *only in the late 1990s*, though it was in some ways a reaction to other Evangelical trends that came just before it, such as the pragmatism of the "seeker sensitive" movement. By the mid-1990s, postmodernism and postmodernity had finally entered mainstream American Evangelical discourse (this was in part an outgrowth of now somewhat embarrassing talk about "Gen-X ministry"). And Christian leaders were grappling with how to interact with this "new paradigm" and a "new cultural reality."[36]

The most visible among such leaders were a small group of young Evangelical pastors and thinkers known as the Young Leaders Network—and later, the Terra Nova Project.[37] A mainstream Evangelical organization based in Texas called Leadership Network brought this group together in 1997.[38] This small group of young church leaders included Tony Jones, Doug Pagitt, Chris Seay, Andrew Jones, Dan Kimball, Mark Driscoll, and later Brian McLaren. (Mark Driscoll, of the New Calvinists, quickly cut ties with the nascent network due to what he perceived to be its leftward trajectory on theological and moral matters.) This network of men traveled the country giving

02/19/10-things-i-wish-everyone-knew-about-progressive-evangelicals/36195, accessed February 20, 2015.

[34] See David R. Swartz, *Moral Minority: The Evangelical Left in an Age of Conservatism* (Philadelphia: University of Pennsylvania Press, 2012); Hunter, *To Change the World*, 132–149.

[35] Such as liberation theology, the Social Gospel movement, and mainline liberal Protestantism.

[36] See David S. Dockery, ed., *The Challenge of Postmodernism: An Evangelical Engagement* (Grand Rapids, MI: Baker Books, 1998); Millard J. Erickson, *The Evangelical Left: Encountering Postconservative Evangelical Theology* (Grand Rapids, MI: Baker Books, 1997); Millard J. Erickson, *Postmodernizing the Faith: Evangelical Responses to the Challenge of Postmodernism* (Grand Rapids, MI: Baker Books, 1998); Stanley J. Grenz, *A Primer on Postmodernism* (Grand Rapids, MI: William B. Eerdmans, 1996); Douglas Groothuis, *Truth Decay: Defending Christianity Against the Challenges of Postmodernism* (Downers Grove, IL: InterVarsity Press, 2000); Donald E. Miller, *Reinventing American Protestantism: Christianity in the New Millennium* (Berkeley: University of California Press, 1997); Thomas C. Oden, *After Modernity . . . What? Agenda for Theology* (Grand Rapids, MI: Zondervan, 1990); Robert E. Webber, *Ancient-Future Faith: Rethinking Evangelicalism for a Postmodern World* (Grand Rapids, MI: Baker Books, 1999).

[37] For an insider's history, see Tony Jones, *The New Christians: Dispatches from the Emergent Frontier* (San Francisco: Jossey-Bass, 2008). For a sociological analysis, see Marti and Ganiel, *The Deconstructed Church*.

[38] http://leadnet.org/

talks at conferences and churches about how Christian leaders should navigate postmodernism and the cultural shifts associated with it. Together, they saw their collective task as "re-envisioning" and revising the received ways of thinking about God and truth (theology) as well as expressions and practices of church life (ecclesiology).[39] Brian McLaren, for example, has argued that the new cultural terrain of postmodernism necessitates nothing less than "a new kind of Christian" and "a new kind of Christianity" altogether.[40] It was mainly from this small cadre of young Christian practitioners that progressive Emergent Evangelicalism, as the term is meant and applied throughout this book, emerged.[41]

The animating values for progressive Evangelicalism—as for the Left generally—are equity, inclusion, and justice. And these commitments and standards are worked out in all areas of their view of Christianity. For instance, many in this pocket are universalists, holding that all people will be in the Kingdom of Heaven. Several renarrate Christianity to be a storyline not primarily about creation, fall, and atonement, but instead about liberation, peace, and inclusion. Others attempt to integrate beliefs from other religions. Leaders like Brian McLaren and Rob Bell view human consciousness as it relates to spiritual matters as nested in increasingly complex and inclusive levels—with progressives at a higher, more enlightened level and with mainstream Evangelicals (and certainly the New Calvinist movement) stuck back at a less developed stage. These levels are even color-coded which allows for progressives to refer to entire strata of people as, say, "stuck back at level blue."[42] Many identify themselves as "mystics," focusing on the internal and subjective experience of God rather than on external authority structures or dogmas. On the matter of doctrine and truth, several progressive Evangelicals

---

[39] This ambition reflects the "fierce egoism" of the emergent progressives. Marti and Ganiel, *The Deconstructed Church*, 176.

[40] Brian D. McLaren, *A New Kind of Christian: A Tale of Two Friends on a Spiritual Journey (Book 1)* (San Francisco, CA: Jossey-Bass, 2001); Brian D. McLaren, *A New Kind of Christianity: Ten Questions That Are Transforming the Faith* (New York: HarperCollins, 2010).

[41] Some readers will recognize this is also where most histories of the Emerging/Emergent Church begin. That is not a coincidence. However, now that a decade has passed since the height of talk in Evangelical circles about the Emerging Church—and since not all streams of the Emerging Church were progressive as described in this section—I have severed "progressive Evangelicals" from the "Emerging Church" moniker. The residual effects of the Emerging/ent Conversation are clarified in the next section.

[42] Books used by progressive leaders to argue for this "integral" approach to spirituality and consciousness include, for example, Don Edward Beck and Christopher C. Cowan, *Spiral Dynamics: Mastering Values, Leadership, and Change* (Malden, MA: Blackwell, 1996); Ken Wilber, *A Theory of Everything: An Integral Vision for Business, Politics, Science, and Spirituality* (Boston: Shambhala, 2000); Ken Wilber, *The Integral Vision: A Very Short Introduction to the Revolutionary Integral Approach to Life, God, the Universe, and Everything* (Boston: Shambhala, 2007).

embrace a kind of epistemic relativism and try to shy away from holding definitive positions. As one progressive pastor told me: "I like to hold possibilities, not positions."

On social and cultural issues, progressive Evangelical leaders, not surprisingly, are considerably to the left of American Evangelical leaders more generally. Their social consciousness is bent toward justice and care for the systemically disadvantaged and oppressed, such as LGBTQ persons, women, racial and ethnic minorities, immigrants, and the poor. Attention is also given to promoting peace (and resisting war), practices of reconciliation, and caring for the Earth's natural environment. Progressive Evangelicals are uniformly egalitarian on gender issues and support women serving in all offices of church life, including as pastors. Nearly all in this pocket support redefining marriage to include lesbian and gay couples. Furthermore, most do not think it is immoral to have sex outside of (heterosexual) marriage, with gay and lesbian sexual encounters especially celebrated. Most in this camp are pro-life,[43] but they also tend to be suspicious of recent discourse from their conservative peers for preserving religious freedom related to marriage, abortion, and contraception.

Although Mark Driscoll, Dan Kimball, and Chris Seay transitioned away from the leftward trajectory of the early Young Leaders Network (becoming either New Calvinists in the case of Driscoll or mainstream Evangelicals in the case of Kimball and Seay), the progressive Evangelicalism that "emerged" from those conversations has since added new leadership. In addition to Jones, Pagitt, and McLaren, leaders among this pocket today include former megachurch pastor Rob Bell, Jay Bakker (son of televangelists Jim and Tammy Faye Bakker), Mike Morrell, Peter Rollins, Nadia Bolz-Weber, Christian Piatt, Brandan Robertson, Eric Elnes, John Shore, Diana Butler-Bass, the late Phyllis Tickle,[44] as well as the late feminist blogger and author Rachel Held Evans,[45] among several others. These can be thought of as the

---

[43] See Daniel K. Williams, "Prolifers of the Left: Progressive Evangelicals' Campaign Against Abortion," in *The New Evangelical Social Engagement*, ed. Brian Steensland and Philip Goff (New York: Oxford University Press, 2014), 200–220.

[44] Phyllis Tickle passed away in September 2015 at age eighty-one. See Tony Jones, ed., *Phyllis Tickle: Evangelist of the Future* (Brewster, MA: Paraclete Press, 2014); Phyllis Tickle, *The Great Emergence: How Christianity Is Changing and Why* (Grand Rapids, MI: Baker Books, 2008); Phyllis Tickle, *Emergence Christianity: What It Is, Where It Is Going, and Why It Matters* (Grand Rapids, MI: Baker Books, 2012).

[45] Rachel Held Evans passed away in May 2019 at age thirty-seven. See Rachel Held Evans, *Faith Unraveled: How a Girl Who Knew All the Answers Learned to Ask Questions* (Grand Rapids, MI: Zondervan, 2010).

newest iteration of a previous generation of Evangelical progressives, such as Jim Wallis (of Sojourners), Ron Sider, Tony Campolo, and others, although their progressivism was more narrowly *political* and less theological.

Progressive Evangelicalism in the United States is loosely organized into a small number of far-reaching organizations, events, and networks. One such event is the Wild Goose Festival,[46] the main event of which is an annual four-day outdoor festival each summer in North Carolina. Its website explains that Wild Goose is "a Celtic spirituality metaphor that evokes unpredictability, beauty, and grace." The events were inspired by Greenbelt, an outdoor music festival in England "with spiritual and justice-oriented undertones." In addition, the CANA Initiative—led by Brian McLaren, Doug Pagitt, and Episcopalian priest Stephanie Spellers—is a new effort "to build a movement-building collaborative," as McLaren put it, among progressive American Christians.[47] In a similar vein, Eric Elnes and other progressives have organized the Convergence Network,[48] which aims to bring together "forward-thinking Catholics, Evangelicals, and mainline Protestants, along with ethnic and peace churches and other willing colleagues, in a growing movement-building collaborative."[49] Lastly, on a smaller scale, Doug Pagitt organized Christianity 21 in 2009 and 2014 as a series of "gatherings" and discussion groups for participants to share their visions for what Christianity could and should look like in the twenty-first century.[50]

Together, this blend of progressive Christian leaders, organizations, events, and networks constitutes the fourth identifiable tribe within American Evangelicalism today.

What about the Emerging Church?

With the general landscape of Evangelical tribes laid out, a possible point of disorientation needs to be addressed.[51] What has this typology done with the Emerging Church movement? The "Emerging Church" (with an *-ing*) is an umbrella term for the conversation that arose within American

---

[46] https://wildgoosefestival.org/
[47] http://www.patheos.com/blogs/christianpiatt/2013/10/what-is-the-cana-initiative-an-interview-with-mclaren-spellers-and-pagitt/
[48] https://convergenceus.org/
[49] http://www.convergenceus.org/about.html
[50] http://c21.thejopagroup.com/
[51] Multiple conversations at academic conferences brought this confusion to my attention.

Evangelicalism (along with related expressions in the United Kingdom, Australia, and New Zealand) during the late 1990s about how exactly Christian pastors and other leaders should respond to the (supposed) "paradigm shift" from modernity to postmodernity. The Emerging Church, then, was not so much a religious movement as it was a multifaceted conversation among (usually white male) church leaders, with plenty of interested observers and laypersons listening in. With the recent advent of the Internet and a willing Evangelical subcultural publishing industry, talk about the Emerging Church and postmodernism really took off among Evangelicals after the turn of the millennium and reached its height of popularity from 2005 to 2009.

Unsurprisingly, leaders involved in this extended conversation eventually arrived at differing answers. Some, like Mark Driscoll and Dan Kimball, were not particularly interested in rethinking their views on theology or morality. They were, however, quite interested in thinking about and implementing new styles, strategies, and methods for church. A stereotype emerged from this answer that the Emerging Church amounted to little more than louder music, dimmer lights, and more candles. Others such as Frank Viola, George Barna, Neil Cole, and Shane Claiborne concluded that the most faithful move would be for Christians to get rid of hierarchical church structures, replace them with democratic "organic churches" or "house churches," focus on living simple Christ-like lives, and maybe even live communally. Still others, like Brian McLaren and Doug Pagitt, drank deeply from the well of postmodernist philosophy and mixed it with classic liberal commitments to inclusion and social justice. As a result, this last stream of the Emerging Church re-envisioned new theologies, renarrated the Christian story, and rallied around an organization, formed in 2001, called Emergent Village (with an -ent).

In sum, what started as the Emerging Church conversation eventually coalesced into multiple streams with differing answers for how Christian leaders should respond to the shift to postmodernity. Importantly, specific leaders ended up settling into each of the four major tribes of American Evangelicalism—that is, New Calvinist (Driscoll), neo-Anabaptist (Claiborne), progressive (McLaren, Pagitt), and mainstream (Kimball). Granted, the most theologically progressive stream—Emergent Village— quickly became the most visible and controversial part of the conversation. But this led some observers (mistakenly) to equate the Emergent Church (McLaren, Pagitt, et al.) with the Emerging Church in general. Multiple insiders during the peak years would even identify themselves as "Emerging but not Emergent."

All this to say three things: (1) First, although the Emerging Church conversation has by now mostly lost its energy, throughout the first decade of the new millennium it in effect functioned as a sifter or sorter for what the American Evangelical landscape would be like in the second decade. That is, the conversation served to create and reinforce the four major expressions we now see. (2) Secondly, the progressive Evangelical tribe can be understood as in large part what developed out of the Emergent stream of the Emerging Church. When this investigation uses the word "Emergent," it is referring to this tribe of postmodern progressives. (3) Finally, the present book is not about the Emerging Church broadly nor about particular emerging churches. The New Calvinism is not the Emerging Church, nor a division of the Emerging Church. The Emerging Church conversation influenced the New Calvinism (especially Driscoll and Chandler) to the extent that some—certainly not all—of its leaders use avant-garde styles and methods to reach younger "postmodern" people. Nevertheless, to equate the New Calvinism to the Emerging Church or even to a continuation of one expression of the Emerging Church is a confusion of categories.[52]

Intermixing between Tribes

None of what has been said on previous pages should be taken to suggest the four Evangelical tribes or expressions are completely cordoned off from one another in an absolute sense, without any social overlap or blurring of boundaries. As with any social typology, there are cases—specific persons and organizations—that straddle or move back and forth between these four "realist-typical" categories. Most American Evangelical leaders, it appears, do fit definitively into one or the other of the four tribes, but our picture of the American Evangelical field would be incomplete without recognizing some intermixing.

For instance, Rick Warren, pastor of the 22,000-person Saddleback Church in Lake Forest, California, and author of *The Purpose Driven Life*,[53] is by all accounts a mainstream American Evangelical. And yet he is very friendly

---

[52] See James S. Bielo, *Emerging Evangelicals: Faith, Modernity, and the Desire for Authenticity* (New York: New York University Press, 2011); Josh Packard, *The Emerging Church: Religion at the Margins* (Boulder, CO: Lynne Rienner, 2012); Marti and Ganiel, *The Deconstructed Church*.

[53] Rick Warren, *The Purpose Driven Life: What on Earth Am I Here For?* (Grand Rapids, MI: Zondervan, 2002).

with the New Calvinist movement. Warren was a keynote speaker at both the 2012 and 2013 Resurgence Conferences, organized and hosted by Mark Driscoll's Mars Hill Church (MHC). In the days preceding the 2012 conference, the pushback online reached the point that Driscoll and MHC made a video justifying why they had invited Warren to speak at the conference.[54] Warren and Driscoll have also preached the weekend services at each other's megachurches on multiple occasions, including Warren delivering the last sermon at MHC via video before the organization dissolved at the turn of 2015.[55] Earlier, Rick Warren had gone through a similar experience with John Piper. Piper invited Warren to speak at his 2010 Desiring God National Conference (on "the life of the mind and the love of God") and due to heavy criticism likewise released a video online beforehand defending Warren as theologically sound—and dissuading his followers from falling into the fundamentalist mindset of "double separation."[56] The next spring, in May 2011, Rick Warren sat down with John Piper for an almost two-hour interview on Warren's doctrinal commitments,[57] during which Warren affirmed the five solae of the Protestant Reformation *as well as the five points of Calvinism.* Warren stated that he does not call himself a Calvinist, but only because of the negative connotations the label sometimes carries in American Christianity, not because of any of its doctrinal content. Through these social interactions and other doctrinal stances (including his view of the Bible as inerrant, Christ's atonement as penal and substitutionary, righteousness as imputed, gender roles as complementary, etc.), Rick Warren is an example of a leader who straddles both mainstream American Evangelicalism and the neo-Reformed tribe.[58]

Another, less obvious, example is Preston Sprinkle, who represents a rare blend of both neo-Reformed and neo-Anabaptist religious beliefs.

---

[54] Despite now being nonoperational, the YouTube channel belonging to The Resurgence still displays that video: https://www.youtube.com/watch?v=GmepJiYzj_0, accessed November 30, 2015.

[55] Alex Murashko, "Rick Warren to Deliver Mars Hill Church's Final Sermon via Video; Seattle-Based Megachurch Closes Its Doors at Year's End," *The Christian Post*, December 29, 2014, http://www.christianpost.com/news/rick-warren-to-deliver-mars-hill-churchs-final-sermon-via-video-seattle-based-megachurch-closes-its-doors-at-years-end-131628/, accessed November 30, 2015. The sermon is online on Mars Hill Church's YouTube channel here: https://www.youtube.com/watch?v=HAcegtdWCRA.

[56] https://www.youtube.com/watch?v=RlxRKLXk1WE, accessed November 30, 2015.

[57] John Piper, "John Piper Interviews Rick Warren on Doctrine," *Desiring God*, May 27, 2011, http://www.desiringgod.org/articles/john-piper-interviews-rick-warren-on-doctrine, accessed November 25, 2015.

[58] Still, not every New Calvinist leader was convinced that Warren belonged in the New Calvinist fold. For example, Tim Challies, "Thinking about Rick Warren and John Piper," May 31, 2011, http://www.challies.com/articles/thinking-about-rick-warren-john-piper, accessed November 30, 2015.

Continuing an interest rooted in his dissertation research at Aberdeen University on Leviticus 18:5, Sprinkle wrote a follow-up book with InterVarsity Press evaluating the roles of divine agency versus human agency in salvation, particularly comparing the theology of the Apostle Paul with that of the Dead Sea Scrolls.[59] That work offers a scholarly corrective to "the new perspective on Paul" and concludes that Paul's soteriology was monergistic. So he is friendly to Calvinism. Sprinkle also coauthored a book with Calvinist pastor Francis Chan defending the reality of a literal Hell, although more recently he has begun to lean toward a form of annihilationism instead of an eternal Hell.[60] Additionally, his book celebrating God's grace included a foreword from former Presbyterian megachurch pastor Tullian Tchividjian.[61] On his Patheos blog, he said he "side[s] with [John Piper] on most theological points." At the same time, Sprinkle wrote a different book making "a Christian case for nonviolence,"[62] which has garnered admiration from neo-Anabaptist Evangelicals. Shane Claiborne provided that book's foreword. In short, Preston Sprinkle stands in the rare position of blurring the boundaries between neo-Anabaptism and the New Calvinism.[63]

Some Order of Magnitude

Up to this point no discussion has been given regarding the proportion of these Evangelical pockets relative to one another. For example, which has more followers—the New Calvinist movement or the neo-Anabaptists? And what about the New Calvinism versus the progressive Emergent faction? Are they comparable movements? And how does all this compare, in terms

---

[59] Preston Sprinkle, *Paul and Judaism Revisited: A Study of Divine and Human Agency in Salvation* (Downers Grove, IL: InterVarsity Press, 2013).

[60] Francis Chan and Preston Sprinkle, *Erasing Hell: What God Said About Eternity, and the Things We've Made Up* (Colorado Springs, CO: David C. Cook, 2011). Since the publication of that book, Sprinkle has instead begun to favor "conditional immortality" or "terminal punishment," the view that a literal Hell exists and people do go there but is likely not eternal. See "How can a loving God send people to Hell?" September 8, 2015, https://www.youtube.com/watch?v=nyDsa-dGhW0, accessed November 30, 2015.

[61] Preston Sprinkle, *Charis: God's Scandalous Grace for Us* (Colorado Springs, CO: David C. Cook, 2014).

[62] Preston Sprinkle, *Fight: A Christian Case for Nonviolence* (Colorado Springs, CO: David C. Cook, 2013).

[63] Even rarer than Evangelical leaders who straddle two socio-theological tribes are leaders who do not fit well into any. Although he is somewhat orthogonal to the American Evangelical field, British scholar and retired Anglican bishop N. T. Wright and his "new perspective on Paul" is an example.

of attracting a widespread numerical following, to perhaps more familiar aspects of popular American culture? Those questions are taken up here.

To answer them, I gathered information on the number of Twitter followers for significant leaders and organizations in the New Calvinist movement, in mainstream American Evangelicalism, neo-Anabaptist Evangelicalism, progressive Evangelicalism, and popular American culture. Appendix C displays these figures in six separate tables. (There is an extra table because I separated out leaders who minister at the intersection of Pentecostalism and "prosperity theology," although I still refer to them as "mainstream.") I compiled these data over the course of just a few days in order to get a "snapshot" at a single time, allowing for meaningful comparisons across the six categories. It should be recognized that there are notable limitations to relying on Twitter followers for determining the numerical size of any American religious movement. For one, not every person who follows a leader or organization is on Twitter, and not everyone who *is* on Twitter and likes a given religious leader or organization actually selects to "follow" them on Twitter. Additionally, the audience on Twitter is global, not strictly limited to the United States, although nearly all of the actors listed in Appendix C are based in the United States and (except for the sixth table on popular culture) help to constitute the *American* Evangelical field. For these reasons, it must be borne in mind that one's number of followers on Twitter is not (necessarily) an accurate numerical count of one's actual followers "in real life." Nevertheless, these numbers are measuring something. Based on my own knowledge of both American Evangelicalism and popular American culture, the ordered lists shown in Appendix C appear to align remarkably well with each person's and organization's real following and popularity *relative to the other actors*, even across (not just within) the six categories.[64] Thus, while Twitter followers cannot give us precise counts, they can help us tap into and compare the *order of magnitude*. So, what do these numbers reveal?

First consider the New Calvinism. The leader in this pocket with the most Twitter followers is hip-hop artist Lecrae, with just over a million followers. This makes sense given Lecrae's status as a Grammy-winning, Billboard chart–topping rapper who has appeared twice on *The Tonight Show Starring Jimmy Fallon*. Probably more telling of the comparative order of magnitude for the New Calvinist movement, then, are the next three most followed leaders: John Piper (792,000), Mark Driscoll (502,000), and Matt Chandler

---

[64] That is, relying on Twitter followers to measure relative following enjoys "face validity."

(350,000). Just behind Matt Chandler is Desiring God (349,000), John Piper's online ministry. Trip Lee and Tim Keller are next, both in the ballpark of about a quarter-million Twitter followers. At least six actors in the New Calvinism have between 100,000 and 200,000 followers on Twitter, including four people and two organizations. The rest of the New Calvinist actors have fewer than 90,000 Twitter followers, but many have more than 20,000 followers. Interestingly, Bethlehem Baptist Church has less than 1 percent of the Twitter followers (4,800) of its long-time lead pastor, John Piper.

How does this compare to mainstream American Evangelicalism? It is evident immediately that the numbers get bigger, and even when the numbers are about the same (in the ballpark of 20,000 to 90,000) there are more of them. The leading Twitter stars of mainstream American Evangelicalism are those teachers and leaders who have their own television programs: Joel Osteen (4.09 million), Joyce Meyer (3.81 million), and T. D. Jakes (2.03 million).[65] Three additional mainstream Evangelical actors have more than 1 million followers on Twitter: Rick Warren (1.74 million), pastor and popular author Max Lucado (1.22 million), and Australian megachurch worship band Hillsong United (1.04 million). From there, it was easy to find twenty-five Evangelical accounts with at least 200,000 (but fewer than 1 million) followers. These included Chris Tomlin, Dave Ramsey, Beth Moore, Ed Young, World Vision U.S.A., Andy Stanley, David Crowder, Judah Smith, Steven Furtick, *Christianity Today*, Bill Hybels, *Relevant Magazine*, and Ravi Zacharias, among others. Several mainstream Evangelical leaders and organizations are on Twitter with between 10,000 and 200,000 followers; sixty of them are displayed in Appendix C.

Next, it is clear that at least when it comes to enjoying a following on social media, neo-Anabaptist Evangelicalism is operating on a much smaller scale. Its leaders' Twitter accounts have gained a following one order of magnitude (i.e., 10x) lower than that of both the New Calvinist movement and mainstream American Evangelicalism. Stated differently, if one added a zero to their number of Twitter followers (multiplied them each by 10), the numbers would look very much like the online audience for the New Calvinism and mainstream Evangelicalism. For example, the neo-Anabaptist leader with the biggest social media following, Shane Claiborne, has about 62,000 followers

---

[65] More than a little theological controversy surrounds these three preachers, even in what I am calling mainstream American Evangelicalism. In Appendix C they are therefore listed in a separate table with other leaders who minister in the world of Pentecostalism and the "Word of Faith" movement.

on Twitter. This is approximately one-tenth of the following for mainstream Evangelical leaders such as Ed Young ("Jr."), Beth Moore, and Dave Ramsey; it is likewise roughly one-tenth of the following of New Calvinist leaders like John Piper and Mark Driscoll (although the relatively smaller scope of the New Calvinism compared to mainstream Evangelicalism makes the Twitter air thinner at that level). After Claiborne, there are at least six other neo-Anabaptist Evangelical figures with over 20,000 Twitter followers.

With the exception of Rob Bell (and possibly also Sojourners[66]), progressive Emergent Evangelicalism in the United States operates on roughly the same order of magnitude as neo-Anabaptist Evangelicalism. That is, they both operate on a scale approximately ten times smaller than both the New Calvinists and mainstream Evangelicals. Rob Bell stands out among Emergent Evangelicals as uniquely popular on Twitter,[67] with more than 150,000 followers, although this may be explained in part by the fact that he tours nationwide with Oprah Winfrey.[68] Sojourners and Rachel Held Evans come next with around 91,000 and 82,000 Twitter followers, respectively. The remaining progressive Evangelical leaders and organizations have fewer than 50,000 Twitter followers each.

For the sake of comparisons of scale, Appendix C also displays followers for a convenience sample of figures constituting popular American culture. Not surprisingly, this reveals that in terms of gaining a following on social media, popular American culture exists on an order of magnitude (10x) above both the New Calvinist movement and mainstream American Evangelicalism—and two orders of magnitude (100x) above neo-Anabaptist and progressive Emergent Christianity. Some comparisons between categories help to put the scope of the American Evangelical field into perspective. For instance, John Piper has approximately as many Twitter followers as actress Cobie Smulders and soft rock band Nickelback. Mark Driscoll sits right between journalist Ta-Nehisi Coates and Billy Crystal. Al Mohler has about as many Twitter followers as do Jaleel White and Jeff Foxworthy. Unlike the case for all four tribes of American Evangelicalism, for popular culture it was difficult to find Twitter accounts operated by persons or organizations with

---

[66] As mentioned earlier, Sojourners is an important organization in the Evangelical Left, but if compared to Emergent leaders its progressivism is more narrowly political rather than theological.

[67] James K. Wellman Jr., *Rob Bell and a New American Christianity* (Nashville, TN: The United Methodist Publishing House, 2012).

[68] See Kathryn Lofton, *Oprah: The Gospel of an Icon* (Berkeley: University of California Press, 2011).

nationwide name recognition but also with fewer than 100,000 followers—examples include Carrot Top, David Brooks, and Mateen Cleaves.[69]

From what Twitter accounts can tell us, it appears that mainstream American Evangelicalism enjoys the most populous following on social media, and the New Calvinism has a smaller following but is "in the same ballpark" in terms of order of magnitude. In contrast, neo-Anabaptist and progressive or "Emergent" expressions of American Christianity have a noticeably smaller following on Twitter, gaining numbers roughly an order of magnitude lower. And viewed through a wider lens, all four camps of Evangelicalism pale in comparison to the kind of numerical following popular culture gets in America.

How Big Is the New Calvinism?

How large is the New Calvinist movement in the United States? That is, how many American adults are involved in it? Not surprisingly, that turns out to be very difficult to answer. As a grassroots, decentralized Christian movement, there is no membership list or registry. No precise number will be provided here, because no precise answer can be given, short of administering a nationally representative survey of American adults and asking them whether they have been affected positively in their religious lives by leaders like Piper, Driscoll, Keller, Chandler, Mohler, Grudem, and so on. (The percentage of the sample answering affirmatively could then be applied to the whole adult population in order to arrive at a number.[70]) And even a nationwide survey that asked American adults if they affiliated with a Reformed or Presbyterian denomination (in the Evangelical, not mainline, tradition),[71] or with the Southern Baptist Convention,[72] would be measuring the wrong thing, since the New Calvinism is not coterminous with those denominations.

---

[69] The numbers in the section were accurate as of mid-November 2015. Many accounts have gone up, and some down, in the intervening years, but I think it makes sense analytically to leave this snapshot of 2015.

[70] Even this ideal method would be statistically problematic, given that percentage would certainly be very small.

[71] Pew Research Center's Religious Landscape Study contains this kind of data.

[72] The Southern Baptist Convention has collected its own survey data on its pastors' evaluations of Calvinism and their perceptions of their own congregations' leanings (toward Calvinism or Arminianism), but no survey data exist to my knowledge from SBC congregants themselves. See Russ Rankin, "SBC Pastors Polled on Calvinism and Its Effects," *LifeWay*, June 19, 2012, http://www. lifeway.com/Article/research-sbc-pastors-polled-on-calvinism-affect-on-convention,   accessed December 2, 2015.

According to Pew's recent Religious Landscape Study, which surveyed more than 35,000 American adults, about one-quarter (25.4 percent) of the adult population in the United States fits within Evangelicalism. This means there are roughly 60 million Evangelical Protestants in the United States, excluding both those under age eighteen and Americans in historically black denominations.[73] If in the 1950s and 1960s, as George Marsden put it, an Evangelical was "anyone who likes Billy Graham,"[74] then today a New Calvinist may be said to be "anyone who likes John Piper."[75] Piper's nearly 800,000 followers on Twitter give us a hint regarding his popularity, but for the reasons just outlined in the previous section such a number does not tell us much in terms of this religious movement's actual headcount. In the end, however, as will be developed further in the next chapter, whether the New Calvinist movement constitutes, say, 5 percent of American Evangelicalism (3 million people), or 15 percent (9 million people), or anywhere in between, is ironically the least important dimension of this movement. What is more significant for understanding it is the cultural struggle going on in the Evangelicalism field for symbolic capital and symbolic power.

A Barna Survey and Leaders' Reactions

The only attempt to measure the New Calvinism quantitatively has been from Evangelical pollster, the Barna Group. The firm released a study online in mid-November 2010 purporting to show whether or not there is "a 'Reformed' movement in American churches."[76] On four occasions between 2000 and 2010, they surveyed a random sample of six hundred Protestant pastors (a different sample each time), both Evangelical and mainline, across the United States. During these surveys, the terms "Calvinist or Reformed" and "Wesleyan or Arminian" were left undefined, leaving these categories up to each pastor's interpretation. For what it is worth, the study found that 3 in 10 Protestant clergy across the United States describe their congregation as

---

[73] See Pew Research Center's report *America's Changing Religious Landscape*, released online May 12, 2015, especially 3–4, 9.

[74] Marsden, *Understanding Fundamentalism and Evangelicalism*, 6.

[75] This idea is taken from Flynn Cratty's forthcoming chapter on the New Calvinism.

[76] Barna Group, "Is There a 'Reformed' Movement in American Churches?" *Barna*, November 15, 2010, https://www.barna.org/barna-update/faith-spirituality/447-reformed-movement-in-american-churches#.Vl5GbHsnhRk, accessed December 1, 2015.

Reformed, and that this is statistically unchanged since the year 2000. David Kinnaman, president of Barna Group, concluded:

> There is no discernable evidence from this research that there is a Reformed shift among U.S. congregation leaders over the last decade. Whatever momentum surrounds Reformed churches and the related leaders, events, and associations has not gone much outside traditional boundaries or affected the allegiances of most of today's church leaders.

Reflecting on the Barna study, missiologist Ed Stetzer commented:

> Most Evangelicals underestimate the number of churches and the diversity of churches in the United States. For example, there are 10,000 ELCA (mainline Lutheran) churches in the United States, and they are part of any Protestant sample. The fact that 7,000 Calvinists can meet in Louisville, and many of those same Calvinists show up at many other conferences, does not make as big a dent in the 300,000+ churches in the United States. All that to say, I think there *is* a resurgence of Calvinism (particularly within Evangelicalism), but since it is younger, and a subset of a very large pool of pastors (for polling purposes), it is not evident via the research. (emphasis in the original)[77]

On the Reformation 21 website, operated by the (Calvinistic) Alliance of Confessing Evangelicals, Ligon Duncan dismissed the survey as unimportant:[78]

> I'm not sure that the way [George Barna] has conducted this research actually tells us or can tell us much about the theological tendencies afoot today in the churches (especially in the evangelical neck of the woods). For instance, he speaks of the mainline church responses in the summary, but most of what is going on (in my experience of the YRR movement) is outside of those spheres. At any rate, his conclusion is: "Move along. Nothing

---

[77] Ed Stetzer, "Barna's Research on the Reformed Resurgence," *Christianity Today*, November 15, 2010, http://www.christianitytoday.com/edstetzer/2010/november/barnas-research-on-reformed-resurgence.html, accessed December 1, 2015.

[78] Ligon Duncan, "Arminians Can Breathe a Sigh of Relief: Barna Says There Is No Reformed Resurgence," *Reformation 21*, November 15, 2010, http://www.reformation21.org/blog/2010/11/arminians-can-brief-a-sigh-of.php, accessed December 1, 2015.

to see here" [. . .] And I think our response (from the Calvinist neighbor-hood) ought to be "fine, whatever."

Roger Olson, among other criticisms, argued that the New Calvinism is mostly a religious movement among youth (teens and twenty-somethings) and likely has not yet affected many churches, and therefore the survey took the wrong approach:[79]

> The thrust of the report seems to belittle claims that a Reformed movement is growing in American Protestantism. But I would argue that movement is not growing (yet) among pastors and churches. It is growing among largely unchurched young people—especially college and university students. Ask any youth or college pastor of any Baptist church in America and he or she will tell you that many of the older youths are steeped in the writings of John Piper and the podcasts of Mark Driscoll, Matt Chandler, et al. The "new Calvinism" is a grassroots movement bound eventually to trans-form churches and denominations; it is not yet a widespread movement of pastors and churches. Many pastors I have talked with hardly know an-ything about it (except youth and college pastors). So, I'm skeptical of the report.

James K. A. Smith also offered multiple criticism of this Barna survey. Among them was this (which, with its emphasis on qualitative over quan-titative strength, anticipates the field-theoretic model developed in the next chapter):[80]

> This report is utterly naive about what constitutes cultural significance. It falls prey to what James Davison Hunter has criticized as the "grassroots" naïveté of evangelicalism: the idea that there's power in numbers. So if "the numbers" don't show growth, then there's no significant shift—there's no significant "Reformed movement." But as Hunter shows, it's not populist numbers that change culture: it's the leadership power of "elites." So even if

---

[79] Roger Olson, "Comments on the Barna Survey Report 'Is There a "Reformed" Movement . . . ?'" *Roger E. Olson*, November 17, 2010, http://www.patheos.com/blogs/rogereolson/2010/11/comments-on-the-barna-survey-report-is-there-a-reformed-movement/, accessed December 1, 2015.

[80] James K. A. Smith, "Barna Report on the 'New Calvinism,'" *Fors Clavigera*, November 16, 2010, http://forsclavigera.blogspot.com/2010/11/barna-report-on-new-calvinism.html, accessed December 1, 2015.

there weren't a groundswell of "new Calvinists" in the pews, there only has to be an upsurge of Calvinists in strategic positions of influence and leadership in order for it to make an impact on American evangelicalism. The Barna Report comes nowhere close to being able to measure something like that.

Further reactions were reported in *The Christian Post*, including similar qualms from PCA pastor Kevin DeYoung.[81] These publicly available reactions all have merit and might reinforce concerns among professional sociologists of religion about Barna Group statistics, critiques voiced this time by Evangelical leaders themselves.[82] Despite this Barna survey's considerable flaws, the study and these critical reactions together point in the right direction—namely, that if one is trying to "find" the Reformed resurgence, then broad-scale numerical growth is not the best place to look. Other, more qualitative and relational social dynamics are at work.

Comparable Leaders and Organizations

What would it mean for the New Calvinist movement to be a resurgence in the straightforward, numerical sense? The answer is that it would need to display not merely growth over time in absolute terms (that is, more adherents), and not even just growth percentage-wise. To be a resurgence, understood sociologically in linear and numerical terms, the religious convictions and actors described in the previous chapter would need to experience *significant percentage growth (over a defined period of time) compared to the percentage growth (over that same time) of the other tribes and expressions of American Evangelicalism*. Even if the New Calvinism were growing numerically (and by all accounts it is), it would not be a resurgence if the other tribes of American Evangelicalism were growing just as much.

To determine this empirically, one would need two large surveys— one fielded in the mid-1990s and the other fielded in the mid-2010s— both of which would need to give a nationally representative sample of

[81] Lillian Kwon, "Resurgence of Calvinism Is Real Despite Survey, Pastors Say," *The Christian Post*, November 17, 2010, http://www.christianpost.com/news/resurgence-of-calvinism-is-real-despite-survey-pastors-say-47678/, accessed December 1, 2015.

[82] See Christian Smith, "Evangelicals Behaving Badly with Statistics," *Books and Culture*, Jan/Feb (2007): 11.

American Evangelical laypersons. And both of those surveys would need to ask respondents whether they are Calvinists or Reformed (as opposed to Lutheran, Wesleyan, Pentecostal, "just Christian," and so on).[83] Incidentally, those surveys *do* exist. The first is Christian Smith's 1996 survey that formed the basis of his book *American Evangelicalism: Embattled and Thriving*;[84] and the second is Pew Research Center's 2014 Religious Landscape Study.[85] But here again we run into the knotty issue that the New Calvinist movement is crucially not coterminous with Reformed denominations, nor even with general adherence to Calvinism or the Reformed tradition among laypersons more broadly.

In light of this difficulty in measuring the New Calvinism, the point Ed Stetzer made in the previous section is worth drawing out, because it strikes at the heart of thinking about the Reformed resurgence in terms of a numerical increase over time. There is a tendency to look at a large, well-attended conference or megachurch and infer that it must represent a major development, a milestone event or "the next big thing," in American Evangelicalism. But while some event or organization may be much loved and even life transforming for those involved, and perhaps constitute for its participants its own "small world," it is helpful to remember that other coreligionists or observers may have never even heard of it. Persons' scope of vision is usually quite small. The Evangelical world is far bigger and more diverse than most people have experienced. What is missed are the other conferences and churches in other pockets and expressions of Evangelicalism—organizations and leaders which are often not on one's "radar screen." The polished 10,000-member megachurch across town may seem like the epicenter of the American Evangelical movement, but even a conservative count reveals that there are at least eighty Protestant churches in the United States with 10,000 or more congregants.[86]

The sheer institutional size of mainstream Evangelicalism in the United States means that for every big-name megachurch, conference, network, or leader constituting the New Calvinist movement, it is not difficult to locate a

---

[83] Again here, even with this ideal method there would be problems, since my work suggests at least one-quarter of congregants involved in New Calvinist churches do not know what Calvinism is, let alone identity as a Calvinist. See the section on "under-informed congregants" in chapter 5.

[84] Christian Smith with Michael Emerson, Sally Gallagher, Paul Kennedy, and David Sikkink, *American Evangelicalism: Embattled and Thriving* (Chicago: The University of Chicago Press, 1998).

[85] Pew conducted a very similar survey in 2007, which forms the basis of Smidt's 2013 book *American Evangelicals Today*.

[86] See http://hirr.hartsem.edu/megachurch/database.html, accessed January 5, 2016. Eighty is a conservative count, given that the Hartford database lists ninety-three such churches.

match with comparable following and growth. For every Mark Driscoll, for example, there is an Ed Young, Jr. or Brian Houston or Kerry Shook; for every Tim Keller, there is a Ravi Zacharias or Andy Stanley or Josh McDowell; for every John Piper, there is a Chuck Swindoll or Jack Graham or Lee Strobel. For every Michael Horton, there is a Roger Olson. Organizationally, MHC's explosive growth has likewise been experienced since the late 1990s at more than a few (non–New Calvinist) multisite Evangelical megachurches, including Elevation Church (founded in 2006 by Steven Furtick),[87] NewSpring Church (founded in 2000 by Perry Noble),[88] Church of the Highlands (founded in 2001 by Chris Hodges),[89] and Celebration Church (founded in 1998 by Stovall Weems).[90] The Acts 29 Network is more than matched with the Willow Creek Association. James MacDonald's Harvest Bible Fellowship (now dissolved and reorganized as Great Commission Collective) can be compared to Greg Surratt's (gender egalitarian) Association of Related Churches. When thinking about the Passion conferences, one might also consider the Hillsong conferences[91] or InterVarsity's Urbana conferences,[92] for instance. To go with Together for the Gospel (T4G), there is likewise The New Room Network[93] and its annual New Room Conference—"a decisively, unapologetically, creatively, Wesleyan gathering."[94] The Southern Baptist Theological Seminary is matched numerically by any number of mainstream non–New Calvinist Evangelical seminaries—say, Asbury, Fuller, Denver, Phoenix, Seattle Pacific, or George Fox (if not in isolation, then certainly together). The Council on Biblical Manhood and Womanhood stands in relation to its gender egalitarian counterpart, Christians for Biblical Equality, and its conferences.[95] With Crossway one also finds InterVarsity Press, Zondervan, Eerdmans, Baker, NavPress, Moody, and Thomas Nelson, among others. As mainstream Evangelical alternatives to the ESV, one might pick up the NIV, TNIV, NLT, CSB, NASB, or The Message. And so on. Mainstream

[87] http://elevationchurch.org/

[88] https://newspring.cc/

[89] https://www.churchofthehighlands.com/

[90] http://www.celebration.org/

[91] http://hillsong.com/conference/

[92] https://urbana.org/

[93] http://newroom.network/

[94] http://newroom.seedbed.com/. The organizers of The New Room Conference recognize their speakers are not the big names one usually finds at Christian conferences, saying: "We just don't have the pantheon of celebrities enjoyed by our Reformed brethren, but how are we ever going to establish new prominent voices unless we take some risks with our invitations and attention." They add: "And we will do well to remember, Jesus was not famous."

[95] http://www.cbeinternational.org/

American Evangelicalism, in short, is large enough—and thriving numerically enough—to more than match the organizations and leaders of the New Calvinism.[96]

The neo-Anabaptist and progressive Emergent tribes of American Evangelicalism, as discussed earlier, operate on an order of magnitude lower than the New Calvinist movement and mainstream Evangelicalism. Despite smaller followings in absolute terms, however, *in terms of percentage growth since the late 1990s*, these two expressions of American Evangelicalism have "resurged" at least as much as the New Calvinism, and arguably more. As noted earlier, politically, economically, and socially progressive Evangelical leaders have enjoyed notable influence in the United States since at least the 1970s (Wallis, Campolo, Sider, et al.).[97] But the particular pockets of neo-Anabaptist and progressive Emergent Evangelicals discussed in this analysis represent a new generation of leaders and organizations who have gained followers and founded organizations only since the late 1990s, largely as part of (and then as the residual of) the Emerging Church "conversation."[98] For instance, even though monasticism is quite old, the "New Monasticism" as a viable Evangelical option emerged only in the late 1990s.[99] Shane Claiborne cofounded The Simple Way in 1998, and Jonathan Wilson-Hartgrove cofounded the Rutba House in 2003; Red Letter Christians was organized in 2006. The main gathering place for neo-Anabaptist Evangelical leaders, Missio Alliance, was founded only in 2011. And the progressive Evangelical pocket—to the extent it is the "Emergent stream of the Emerging Church"— came into existence entirely since the late 1990s. If resurgence is conceptualized in a simple additive sense, then it must be concluded that while the New Calvinist movement has expanded since the 1990s, the neo-Anabaptist and progressive Emergent tribes have grown just as much.

---

[96] Not to mention the wildly popular lineup of Charismatic/Pentecostal televangelists, many of whom preach "prosperity theology," such as Kenneth Copeland, Jesse Duplantis, Joel Osteen, Benny Hinn, Joyce Meyer, Creflo Dollar, Paula White, T. D. Jakes, John Hagee, Rod Parsley, and Keith Moore. See Milmon F. Harrison, *Righteous Riches: The Word of Faith Movement in Contemporary African American Religion* (New York: Oxford University Press, 2005); Shayne Lee and Phillip Luke Sinitiere, *Holy Mavericks: Evangelical Innovators and the Spiritual Marketplace* (New York: New York University Press, 2009). See Appendix C for how their numbers of Twitter followers compare with those of the New Calvinists.

[97] Swartz, *Moral Minority*; Hunter, *To Change the World*, 132–149.

[98] Bielo, *Emerging Evangelicals*; Marti and Ganiel, *The Deconstructed Church*; Packard, *The Emerging Church*.

[99] Jonathan R. Wilson, *Living Faithfully in a Fragmented World: Lessons for the Church from MacIntyre's After Virtue* (Harrisburg, PA: Trinity Press International, 1997); Markofski, *New Monasticism*.

Strength beyond Numbers

Roger Olson says, "I don't know anyone who thinks [Calvinism] is not on the rise. As a teacher of theology in three Christian universities over the last thirty-one years, I've definitely seen it on the rise. It's a phenomenon. It's a movement."[100] Calvinism in American Evangelicalism is strong and, yes, growing numerically; any person who has been involved in the annual meetings of the Evangelical Theological Society for a couple decades or more will have noticed its comeback, at least among America's theological scholars. Theologian (and open theist) Clark Pinnock wrote in 1989: "It is my strong impression, confirmed to me even by those not pleased by it, that Augustinian thinking is losing its hold on present-day Christians. [. . .] It is hard to find a Calvinist theologian willing to defend Reformed theology, including the views of both Calvin and Luther, in all its rigorous particulars now that Gordon Clark is no longer with us and John Gerstner is retired. Few have the stomach to tolerate Calvinian [sic] theology in its logical purity."[101] This is certainly not the institutional situation presently.

But notice what Pinnock can also say about Calvinists on the next page:

> At the same time, however, the Calvinists continue to be major players in the Evangelical coalition, even though their dominance has lessened. They pretty well control the teaching of theology in the large Evangelical seminaries; they own and operate the largest book-publishing houses; and in large part they manage the inerrancy movement. *This means they are strong where it counts*—in the area of intellectual leadership and property. Thus one comes to expect Evangelical systematic theology to be Reformed as it usually is. (Emphasis added)[102]

Here, writing in 1989, Pinnock helpfully points out that there are ways for religious groups and movements to have institutional strength aside from only numerical adherence and growth. What are those ways? Pinnock names a

---

[100] https://www.youtube.com/watch?v=JsTAwysSfUY, accessed April 21, 2020.

[101] Clark H. Pinnock, "From Augustine to Arminius: A Pilgrimage in Theology," in *The Grace of God, The Will of Man: A Case for Arminianism*, ed. Clark H. Pinnock (Grand Rapids, MI: Zondervan, 1989), 26. Quoted partially in Horton, *For Calvinism*, 197. Other Calvinist theologians writing in the 1980s included J. I. Packer, Roger Nicole, David F. Wells, R. C. Sproul, Richard Gaffin, Jr., and D. A. Carson, among others. See, for example, R. C. Sproul, *Chosen by God*, revised and updated (Carol Stream, IL: Tyndale House, [1986] 2011); David F. Wells, ed., *Reformed Theology in America: A History of Its Modern Development*, 3rd ed. (Grand Rapids, MI: William B. Eerdmans, [1985] 2009).

[102] Pinnock, "From Augustine to Arminius," 27.

few, but as we will see throughout the rest of this project, there are several others. And it is not just Arminian and open theist Evangelicals—or neo-Anabaptists or progressives—who recognize these social and institutional dynamics going on. New Calvinist leaders themselves recognize this, too. As Tim Keller recently wrote: "[T]he Reformed evangelical world, though numerically small, has an outsized impact on the broader evangelical community through its educational institutions and publications."[103] But, again, it is not only educational institutions and publications that grant Reformed Evangelicalism its "outsized impact."

More than just having more young Calvinists around today than there were twenty years ago, the New Calvinism's strength as a resurgence in its field has also been *fought for and won*—it has been actively constructed and maintained via strategic action and conflict with the competing tribes and expressions of American Evangelicalism detailed in this chapter. The next chapter turns more directly to sociological theory and the sociology of religion to develop a causally explanatory model of the social conditions, mechanisms, and processes by which the Reformed resurgence has been accomplished. It does so using field theory.

---

[103] Keller, *Center Church*, 188. Keller reiterated this to me in an interview, when he said the New Calvinism has "had a powerful impact, especially among younger people to whom the Internet is an outsized reality. Younger people tend to see the Internet as reality, so that if there's a huge online presence you feel like there's a huge presence, but I'm not sure it is. I don't know that it is as big as it seems to be."

4

A Field-Theoretic Model
of Religious Strength

The task at hand is to explain how the New Calvinist movement can constitute a sociological resurgence when the other tribes and expressions of American Evangelicalism—mainstream, neo-Anabaptist, and progressive Emergent—in recent decades have grown just as much. It was suggested at the end of the previous chapter that the New Calvinism or Reformed resurgence enjoys "strength beyond numbers," and that its strength has been "fought for and won" through strategic action and conflict with its competitors in the Evangelical field.

The present chapter systematically develops a theoretical and causal model that explains how this has happened. The goal is to illuminate the sociological relations, motivations, strategies, conditions, and mechanisms by which the New Calvinist movement has become the kind of social and religious reality it is—*a resurgence*. The theoretical and causal model developed in this chapter, as we will see, hinges on Fligstein and McAdam's recent framework of strategic action fields[1]; therefore, it is referred to as "a field-theoretic model of religious strength." The crucial insight from strategic action field theory that explains the New Calvinism is that *through social processes of game-like contestation, leaders of movements and organizations strategically battle and vie with their competitors for a more advantageous position in and over their field, which is defined by possession of symbolic capital and power.*[2]

Of all the chapters, this one is the most demanding in terms of engaging with sociological theory as well as theoretical frameworks in the sociology of religion, but the work done in this chapter is the very core of the book's argument. After working through the theory, this chapter ends with

---

[1] Fligstein and McAdam, *A Theory of Fields*.
[2] If this language of "contestation" and "power" seems off-putting or foreign to the actual thinking of church leaders, see the section later in this chapter on "A Culturalist Field Theory," which suggests the motivations at work are both competitive *and* genuinely about religious beliefs, convictions, and concerns.

Reformed Resurgence. Brad Vermurlen, Oxford University Press (2020). © Oxford University Press.
DOI: 10.1093/oso/9780190073510.001.0001

a systematization of the theory/model, in which seventeen general social mechanisms are specified as causes that together produced the Reformed resurgence. From there, the rest of the book is an unpacking and expounding of these mechanisms and processes.

The Question of Religious Strength

The Reformed resurgence in contemporary Evangelicalism speaks to the question of the sociological strength—or lack thereof—of traditional or conservative religion in the hypermodern world. The question is: Do certain features of our current, modern times cause problems for traditional forms of religion? And, if so, how exactly? In this case, can conservative Evangelical religion survive and even flourish in a hypermodern American cultural context defined largely by pluralism, epistemic relativism, consumerism, scientific rationalism, moral and political gridlock, and liberal assumptions about individual autonomy and freedom?

This is the old question of secularization.[3] From Hume and d'Holbach to Marx and Freud to Dawkins and Dennett, the received orthodoxy throughout much of the modern era up through the 1980s has been that religion is on its way out—if not out of existence, then at least out of intellectual plausibility and out of the public sphere.[4] And many scholars still think that is basically right. Since the 1980s, however, several scholars (including Peter Berger, who was one of the principal architects of secularization theory in the late 1960s) have noted the conspicuous presence of religion both in persons' everyday lives and in global affairs. These scholars write of the "re-enchantment of the world," a "resurgence" of religion, and our day as a "post-secular age."[5] To say

---

[3] Steve Bruce, ed., *Religion and Modernization: Sociologists and Historians Debate the Secularization Thesis* (New York: Oxford University Press, 1992); William H. Swatos Jr. and Daniel V. A. Olson, eds., *The Secularization Debate* (Lanham, MD: Rowman and Littlefield, 2000).

[4] See, for example, Peter L. Berger, *The Sacred Canopy: Elements of a Sociological Theory of Religion* (Garden City, NY: Doubleday, 1967); Steve Bruce, *God Is Dead: Secularization in the West* (Malden, MA: Blackwell, 2002); Steve Bruce, *Secularization: In Defence of an Unfashionable Theory* (New York: Oxford University Press, 2011); Mark Chaves, "Secularization as Declining Religious Authority," *Social Forces* 72, no. 3 (1994): 749–774; Mary Eberstadt, *How the West Really Lost God: A New Theory of Secularization* (West Conshohocken, PA: Templeton Press, 2013); Marcel Gauchet, *The Disenchantment of the World: A Political History of Religion*, trans. Oscar Burge (Princeton, NJ: Princeton University Press, 1997); Brad S. Gregory, *The Unintended Reformation: How a Religious Revolution Secularized Society* (Cambridge, MA: Harvard University Press, 2012); Christian Smith, ed., *The Secular Revolution: Power, Interests, and Conflict in the Secularization of American Public Life* (Berkeley: University of California Press, 2003).

[5] Nancy T. Ammerman, ed., *Everyday Religion: Observing Modern Religious Lives* (New York: Oxford University Press, 2007); Nancy Tatom Ammerman, *Sacred Stories, Spiritual*

the least, the possibility of strong and vital religion in the modern world has proven to be a perennial question.

If the New Calvinism really is a resurgence of early-modern (almost Puritan-esque), socially conservative Calvinistic beliefs among a new generation of twenty- and thirty-something Americans, certainly that should tell us something important about questions of secularization and religious strength in our hypermodern world. But as we have seen in the previous chapter, leveraging the best evidence available gives us little reason to think that, when viewed proportionately, the sociological substance of the Reformed resurgence rests in its numerical growth (although there appears to have been some growth). Why all this talk then, both in Evangelicalism and in the national secular media, about a Reformed resurgence? What is going on here? There undoubtedly is a real phenomenon "out in the world" that social analysts and religion observers can see and experience as a strong and vital Christian movement. (I did this for four years in the process of gathering data for this book.) The sociological question then becomes: What kind of strength is this? In what way is the New Calvinist movement even really "a thing," let alone a resurgence? Field theory helps us answer that question.

The next step in getting there, however, is first to review the five major theoretical frameworks offered over recent years in the social sciences for conceptualizing and explaining religious strength.

Frameworks Currently on Offer

With the "return of religion" in the social sciences (which was really more a return of academic *attention to* religion), scholars had to grapple with the

Tribes: Finding Religion in Everyday Life (New York: Oxford University Press, 2014); Peter L. Berger, ed., *The Desecularization of the World: Resurgent Religion and World Politics* (Grand Rapids, MI: William B. Eerdmans, 1999); Philip S. Gorski and Ates Altınordu, "After Secularization?" *Annual Review of Sociology* 34 (2008): 55–85; Philip S. Gorski, David Kyuman Kim, John Torpey, and Jonathan VanAntwerpen, eds., *The Post-Secular in Question: Religion in Contemporary Society* (New York: New York University Press, 2012); Jeffrey K. Hadden, "Toward Desacralizing Secularization Theory," *Social Forces* 65, no. 3 (1987): 587–611; John Micklethwait and Adrian Wooldridge, *God Is Back: How the Global Revival of Faith Is Changing the World* (New York: The Penguin Press, 2009); James K. A. Smith, ed., *After Modernity? Secularity, Globalization, and the Re-enchantment of the World* (Waco, TX: Baylor University Press, 2008); Rodney Stark, "Secularization, RIP," *Sociology of Religion* 60, no. 3 (1999): 249–273; Scott M. Thomas, *The Global Resurgence of Religion and the Transformation of International Relations: The Struggle for the Soul of the Twenty-First Century* (New York: Palgrave Macmillan, 2005). The point about Berger's reversal and "principal architect" are from Gorski and Altınordu, "After Secularization?," 56.

reality that—despite the predictions of secularization theory—traditional and conservative religion had not withered away in the harsh winds of modernity. In fact, with the rise throughout the 1980s of right-wing, politically focused Christian organizations like Jerry Falwell's Moral Majority and Pat Robertson's Christian Coalition, religion appeared not only to have not withered but indeed to be "flexing its muscles" on the American scene, at least in the political sphere. These and other observations of seemingly vital, active religion (such as tens of millions of American adults still attending religious services on a regular basis) called out for a new theoretical framework to explain how religion and modernity could coexist or even, as some argued, reinforce one another. And in short time sociologists proposed a handful of precisely that kind of framework, offering multiple alternatives to the thesis of inevitable secularization.[6]

One such theory is what Smith et al. called *sheltered enclave theory*. This view built on Berger's understanding of religion as a shared sacred moral order which in order to be sustained needs to be "sheltered" socially, intellectually, and culturally from the (hypothesized-to-be) corrosive effects of the modern world.[7] Hunter, a former graduate student of Berger's at Rutgers, developed and applied this perspective most forcefully in his writings in the 1980s on American Evangelicalism.[8] On this model, it is the religious traditions and movements that "hunker down," so to speak, and distance themselves culturally from the features and forces of modernity—urbanization, scientific rationalism, higher education, cultural pluralism—that are most likely to flourish. Stated differently, if we observe a religious group thriving, then we should expect to find them systematically avoiding the attributes of modernity more so than less thriving groups. It is noteworthy, however, that in his more recent work Hunter himself has proposed a theory close to the opposite: that if religious traditions (Christians, in Hunter's particular case) hope to thrive sociologically, they should pursue "faithful presence" in all the domains and institutions of the pluralistic modern world.[9]

---

[6] The rest of this section follows closely Smith et al., *American Evangelicalism*, 67–119.

[7] Berger, *The Sacred Canopy*.

[8] James Davison Hunter, *American Evangelicalism: Conservative Religion and the Quandary of Modernity* (New Brunswick, NJ: Rutgers University Press, 1983); James Davison Hunter, *Evangelicalism: The Coming Generation* (Chicago: The University of Chicago Press, 1987).

[9] Hunter, *To Change the World: The Irony, Tragedy, and Possibility of Christianity in the Late Modern World* (New York: Oxford University Press, 2010). In an interesting case of (academic) theory meeting (religious) practice, Hunter, I am told, is a close friend of Tim Keller's, the senior pastor at Redeemer Presbyterian Church in Manhattan, and in recent years they have worked through this issue together.

Another explanation for religious strength is *status discontent theory*. On this model, religious groups and traditions will be stronger, or at least will "rally the troops" and mobilize their resources in a concerted effort to become stronger, when they sense a threat to or a notable loss of the group's social status, privilege, and power. Such status discontentment may be in regard to either economics or culture, the former expressed in the group's potential for security and success in the current economic climate and the latter in a perceived devaluation by the broader dominant culture of the group's values and lifestyle.[10] Either way, this theory says religious groups facing some form of decreased status will "fight for a seat at the table"—engaging in "status politics" in order to reassert themselves and their interests within the relevant social context or arena. And during such reassertions of status and respectability, this framework suggests, "religious identities become more salient, religious commitments more firm, religious practices more consistent, and religious resources more easily mobilized for activism."[11]

A third theory on offer is *strict church theory*. The earliest articulation of this theory claimed religious groups and denominations that place high demands on their members—in terms of time, money, behavioral expectations, conservative convictions, and the like—will be stronger sociologically precisely because they produce in and for their adherents the most substantial meanings and commitments. High cost and demand, in short, yield high commitment and therefore strength.[12] In another, later expression of this framework, economist Laurence Iannaccone likewise argued that strict, demanding religious groups and denominations will tend to be stronger but for a somewhat different reason—one based on rational cost-benefit analysis rather than on meaning production. On his view, stricter religious groups will tend toward strength because they root out "free-riders"—persons who want to benefit from the various collective goods of religious communities while not "pulling their own weight" with investments of time, money, and energy. With such persons screened out by the demanding requirements of

[10] Louise J. Lorentzen, "Evangelical Life Style Concerns Expressed in Political Action," *Sociological Analysis* 41, no. 2 (1980): 144–154; Kenneth D. Wald, Dennis E. Owen, and Samuel S. Hill, Jr., "Evangelical Politics and Status Issues," *Journal for the Scientific Study of Religion* 28, no. 1 (1989): 1–16.

[11] Smith et al., *American Evangelicalism*, 70.

[12] Dean Kelley, *Why Conservative Churches Are Growing* (New York: Harper and Row, 1972); Dean Kelley, "Why Conservative Churches Are Still Growing," *Journal for the Scientific Study of Religion* 17, no. 2 (1978): 165–172.

the group, the group flourishes with a high proportion of the most invested adherents.[13]

Zooming out to a more ecological level of analysis, the *religious economies* or *supply-side* framework treats religion like any other mass consumer good and argues that overall levels of religious practice in a society are subject to economic principles of supply and demand.[14] From this view, religious organizations and groups (particularly in the United States) operate within an unregulated, open market system such that higher levels of market competition (i.e., religious pluralism) cause entrepreneurs (i.e., religious leaders) to make and market stronger products (religious messages and experiences) and a wider range of options to suit the needs and wants of religious consumers. Contra early Berger, then, religious and cultural pluralism in a society on this approach is thought to promote robust religious beliefs and practice on a societal scale, not to undermine it. And *within* a competitive, pluralistic religious economy it is the religious groups, traditions, and organizations which market themselves most skillfully to consumers that enjoy higher rates of participation and commitment. In societal contexts like Europe where religious beliefs and practices are remarkably lower, this theory argues the reason is not low levels of religious demand in the populace but instead an insufficient level of religious supply and competition. With its use of macroeconomic principles to explain religious strength, this theory was long celebrated as a "new paradigm" for the sociology of religion.[15]

[13] Laurence Iannaccone, "Sacrifice and Stigma: Reducing Free-Riding in Cults, Communes, and Other Collectives," *Journal of Political Economy* 100, no. 2 (1992): 271–292; Laurence Iannaccone, "Why Strict Churches Are Strong," *American Journal of Sociology* 99, no. 5 (1994): 1180–1212; Daniel V. A. Olson and Paul Perl, "Variations in Strictness and Religious Commitment within and among Five Denominations," *Journal for the Scientific Study of Religion* 40, no. 4 (2001): 757–764; Daniel V. A. Olson and Paul Perl, "Free and Cheap Riding in Strict, Conservative Churches," *Journal for the Scientific Study of Religion* 44, no. 2 (2005): 123–142.

[14] Examples include Roger Finke, Avery M. Guest, and Rodney Stark, "Mobilizing Local Religious Markets: Religious Pluralism in the Empire State, 1855 to 1865," *American Sociological Review* 61, no. 2 (1996): 203–218; Roger Finke and Laurence R. Iannaccone, "Supply-Side Explanations for Religious Change," *Annals of the American Academy of Political and Social Science* 527 (1993): 27–39; Roger Finke and Rodney Stark, "Religious Economies and Sacred Canopies: Religious Mobilization in American Cities, 1906," *American Sociological Review* 53, no. 1 (1988): 41–49; Roger Finke and Rodney Stark, *The Churching of America, 1776–2005: Winners and Losers in Our Religious Economy* (New Brunswick, NJ: Rutgers University Press, [1992] 2005); Paul Perl and Daniel V. A. Olson, "Religious Market Share and Intensity of Church Involvement in Five Denominations," *Journal for the Scientific Study of Religion* 39, no. 1 (2000): 12–31; Rodney Stark and Roger Finke, *Acts of Faith: Explaining the Human Side of Religion* (Berkeley: University of California Press, 2000); Rodney Stark and James C. McCann, "Market Forces and Catholic Commitment: Exploring the New Paradigm," *Journal for the Scientific Study of Religion* 32, no. 2 (1993): 111–124; see also Mara Einstein, *Brands of Faith: Marketing Religion in a Commercial Age* (New York: Routledge, 2008).

[15] R. Stephen Warner, "Work in Progress toward a New Paradigm for the Sociological Study of Religion in the United States," *American Journal of Sociology* 98, no. 5 (1993): 1044–1093. But as

Most recently, Christian Smith and colleagues developed a *subcultural identity theory* of religious strength and vitality. This framework argues modernity need not undermine strong, flourishing religious beliefs and practice as long as a religious group or tradition sustains a meaningful, morally orienting subculture and collective identity.[16] At first blush, that might sound a lot like Hunter's sheltered enclave theory. But unlike Hunter's early framework, subcultural identity theory argues that the posture toward the broader modern world most likely to foster vitality is not distance and isolation but rather active conflict, contestation, and tension. "In a pluralistic society, those religious groups will be relatively stronger which better possess and employ the cultural tools needed to create both clear distinction from and significant engagement and tension with other relevant out-groups."[17] American Evangelicalism was strong during the mid-1990s, Smith argued, because the movement typified this cultural posture of "distinction-with-engagement." On Smith's theory, American Evangelicals are not "beaten down" sociologically by their struggles and conflicts with the modern world; indeed, they thrive on them.

The Need for a New Theory

The five frameworks just summarized offer differing explanations and emphases for how and why precisely, against the assumptions of secularization theory, traditional religion can be strong sociologically in modern contexts. Some of the theories are compatible with one another; others of them make opposing claims and so cannot both be entirely right. Each of them, however, as we would expect, contains some "nugget of truth," however small, that can help to make sense of the New Calvinist movement as a resurgent force within contemporary American Evangelicalism. Despite what is helpful in them, each of these five theories is ill suited or at least incomplete in various ways for explaining the New Calvinist movement as a

Chaves and Gorski together note, Warner was actually referring to a broader pushback against the received wisdom of Berger, not to the stronger claims of the religious economies approach. Mark Chaves and Philip S. Gorski, "Religious Pluralism and Religious Participation," *Annual Review of Sociology* 27 (2001): 261–281.

[16] Smith et al., *American Evangelicalism*. The authors initially framed this theory as an extension of the religious economies framework, although doing so seems unnecessary for understanding it best.
[17] Smith et al., *American Evangelicalism*, 118–119.

religious and cultural phenomenon. Before proceeding to construct a field-theoretic model of religious strength in hypermodernity, this section therefore states what is helpful from each theory but also how each theory falls short of offering a full, satisfying account of this movement.

First, sheltered enclave theory rightly maintains *the importance of meaning and the need for some degree of critical distance from the attributes and assumptions of the modern world*. However, as Smith and his colleagues showed regarding American Evangelicals in the mid-1990s and as an organization like Redeemer Presbyterian Church in Manhattan demonstrates even today, thriving conservative religious groups might in fact not be any more isolated or shielded from modernity than are less thriving groups. So while some critical distance from the modern world is needed (the "distinction" part of Smith's "distinction-with-engagement"), being completely sheltered and protected from it is not required. Moreover, living in a sheltered enclave altogether detached and avoidant of the modern world is also a strange conceptualization of sociological vitality to begin with. In any event, Hunter himself no longer holds this theory, and Smith's subcultural identity theory and Kelley's strict church theory both provide these two helpful elements—meaning and critical distance from modernity—and do so within frameworks more up to the task.[18]

Second, status discontent theory correctly suggests that religious groups *can and sometimes do mobilize themselves to reassert their status and strength*. But beyond this singular insight, the framework provides little analytical leverage as an explanation for religious strength and vitality. In fact, the theory easily falls into tautology. It says little more than that, when religious groups or traditions are (or perceive themselves as) becoming relatively weaker in terms of their social, cultural, or economic standing in the broader society, they become strong instead by mobilizing to become strong.[19] We can

---

[18] Nevertheless, since 2013, a version of sheltered enclave theory has reentered the conversation among some Evangelical leaders in the form of "the Benedict Option." See Rod Dreher, *The Benedict Option: A Strategy for Christians in a Post-Christian Nation* (New York: Sentinel, 2017); Emma Green, "The Christian Retreat from Public Life," *The Atlantic*, February 22, 2017, https://www.theatlantic.com/politics/archive/2017/02/benedict-option/517290/; Elizabeth Bruenig, "City of Rod," *Democracy: A Journal of Ideas*, March 1, 2017, http://democracyjournal.org/magazine/city-of-rod/; Joshua Rothman, "Rod Dreher's Monastic Vision," *The New Yorker*, May 1, 2017, http://www.newyorker.com/magazine/2017/05/01/rod-drehers-monastic-vision; Laura Turner, "What Happens When the 'Moral Majority' Becomes a Minority?" *The Atlantic*, September 27, 2015, https://www.theatlantic.com/politics/archive/2015/09/end-of-moral-majority/407359/, all accessed August 24, 2017.

[19] This is especially problematic if religious strength is conceptualized, as it is in this project, not as a vigor and energy internal to the group but as relationally constructed recognition, status, and power.

therefore bear the issue of status discontent in mind as potentially important for our case while not expecting it to serve as a stand-alone explanatory
theory of religious strength.

Third, strict church theory is correct that *strict and demanding religious
groups provide something meaningful and attractive to many people.* Some
churchgoers attend the (strict, conservative) congregation they do precisely because, among other reasons, "our pastor doesn't back down from
teaching the hard truths." Nevertheless, the logical and methodological
problems associated with (especially Iannaccone's version of) strict church
theory have been well documented.[20] Even Kelley's version, which rightly
taps into the way hard, demanding religious teachings can fulfill a human
craving for meaning, loses much of its analytical leverage as soon as the analyst recognizes that the teachings and behavioral expectations must not be
too strict (to the point of being ill-mannered, outlandish, radical, or cultish).
If that is the case, then strict church theory, too, begins to sound tautolog-
ical: like the porridge that was not too hot and not too cold, this theory claims
many people like the teachings and expectations that are "just right."[21] Put
this way, the theory is both true and unsatisfactory as an explanation.[22]

For its part, the religious economies framework correctly notes *the importance of religious competition, marketing, branding, and entrepreneur-
ship.* With this theory, the personal agency and strategic organizational
capacity of religious leaders were effectively recognized. Nevertheless, its
economistic, rational-choice meta-theoretical underpinnings—which
bracketed factors like culture, identities, emotions, and morality—all but
guaranteed that even if the theory functioned as a fitting model to predict
and explain some religious reality, the model itself wouldn't reflect the actual
"texture" and full meanings of that reality.[23] Additionally, it turned out that

[20] Gerald Marwell, "We Still Don't Know If Strict Churches Are Strong, Much Less Why: Comment
on Iannaccone," *American Journal of Sociology* 101, no. 4 (1996): 1097–1103.

[21] Todd W. Ferguson, "The Optimal Level of Strictness and Congregational Growth," *Religions* 5,
no. 3 (2014): 703–719.

[22] Smith et al., *American Evangelicalism*, 151–152, suggest that whatever is insightful in strict
church theory may be subsumed within their theory of subcultural distinction, engagement, collective identity, and tension.

[23] See Margaret S. Archer and Jonathan Q. Tritter, eds., *Rational Choice Theory: Resisting
Colonization* (New York: Routledge, 2000); Joseph M. Bryant, "Cost-Benefit Accounting and the
Piety Business: Is *Homo Religiosus*, at Bottom, a *Homo Economicus*?" *Method and Theory in the Study
of Religion* 12, no. 4 (2000): 520–548; Colin Jerolmack and Douglas Porpora, "Religion, Rationality,
and Experience: A Response to the New Rational Choice Theory of Religion," *Sociological Theory* 22,
no. 1 (2004): 140–160; Uskali Mäki, ed., *Fact and Fiction in Economics: Models, Realism, and Social
Construction* (Cambridge: Cambridge University Press, 2002).

even the framework's empirical statistical adequacy was less than a homerun. In 2001 and 2002, a pair of articles in two of sociology's top journals dealt a devastating one-two blow to the religious economies framework, showing convincingly that more than a decade of quantitative research on the relationship between religious pluralism and religious participation had resulted in "no compelling evidence that religious pluralism has any effect on religious participation."[24] Hence, the central empirical implication of the framework had amounted to naught, suggesting—if not that the framework itself was faulty—at least that it does not enjoy nearly the empirical support previously thought.

Finally, Smith's subcultural identity theory rightly emphasizes *the critical role of culture, collective identity, in-group vs. out-group conflict, and symbolic boundaries* for religious strength. This theory has a great deal to offer and gets us a long way toward understanding the New Calvinist movement. The new theory developed in what follows in fact is intended to extend and complement rather than to refute or replace Smith et al.'s contributions. Nevertheless, subcultural identity theory cannot simply be adopted and applied wholesale as a satisfying explanation of the New Calvinism. For one thing, Smith's theory and analysis are cast at the analytic level of ordinary religious laypersons, not that of religious leaders and their organizations. That is not a flaw in Smith's theory, but it does leave open the opportunity to apply the subcultural identity theory at the level of religious leaders and organizations—an incompleteness that the authors themselves recognized.[25] Additionally, Smith's project (like most of sociology) treated American Evangelicalism as a diverse but more or less unified religious movement and therefore it overlooked the infighting, tribalism, and contestation that in recent decades have become ever-present for American Evangelicalism writ large.[26] Another way subcultural identity theory does not fit the present case is that the original theory conceptualized and measured religious strength in linear and comparative terms. That is, it analyzed different religious traditions "side by side," and

---

[24] Chaves and Gorski, "Religious Pluralism and Religious Participation"; David Voas, Alasdair Crockett, and Daniel V. A. Olson, "Religious Pluralism and Participation: Why Previous Research Is Wrong," *American Sociological Review* 67, no. 2 (2002): 212–230. Quotation is from Voas et al., p. 212.

[25] Smith et al., *American Evangelicalism*, 21, 86.

[26] Smith et al., *American Evangelicalism*, 13–15, used a field-metaphor to explain the emergence of a distinct neo-Evangelical identity in the broader field of American Protestantism, situated analytically and socially between fundamentalists and liberals. The present study develops more systematically a field-theoretic model of religious strength by explaining the rise of the New Calvinist movement and treating American Evangelicalism itself—not American religion or Protestantism generally—as the contested social field.

whichever tradition had higher scores on certain positive features (like adherence to the right beliefs, salience of faith, confidence and assurance in
beliefs, group participation rates, commitment to the mission, and the reten-
tion and recruitment of members) was said to be stronger. While this clearly
is a helpful approach, it also neglects the relational, symbolic, and interactive aspects of sociological strength, such as which traditions or groups have
power, symbolic capital, or even "buzz" in relation to others.

Even though subcultural identity theory *measured and established religious strength* primarily in linear and comparative terms, the *theory itself—*
with a focus on distinction, engagement, tension, "embattlement," reference
groups, and symbolic boundaries—is actually highly relational and interactive (without being overly formalistic).[27] Of the five frameworks currently on
offer, it is certainly the most relational. Because of this, subcultural identity
theory is easily amenable to the kind of field analysis conducted in this book
to explain the neo-Reformed movement. To subcultural identity theory,
we can add the emphasis from the religious economies framework on religious leadership, organizations, and branding, yet without being ensnared
by its economistic rational choice assumptions. From (Kelley's version of)
strict church theory, we might watch for the role that strict, demanding religious beliefs and practices embedded in organizational contexts may play in
making Calvinism meaningful and attractive to many—but clearly not all—
Evangelical leaders and their followers. Status discontent theory, moreover,
reminds us to watch out for how the leaders of the Calvinistic (and conservative, complementarian) expression of American Evangelicalism, when they
felt that their previously enjoyed standing was slipping away, mobilized to
reassert their status and strength in the relevant arena.

There is, admittedly, quite a bit going on here sociologically, but in terms
of theoretical coherence no aspect of this synthesizing outlook necessarily

---

[27] As "pure," "relational," or "transactional" sociology tends to be, which is to say formalist
approaches focus on social structural arrangements and processes *at the expense of* accounting
for real, concrete entities and "substances" with important properties (such as persons and religious beliefs). As French cubist artist Georges Braque put it, "I do not believe in things; I believe
only in their relationship." See Donald Black, "Dreams of Pure Sociology," *Sociological Theory* 18,
no. 3 (2000): 343–367; Black, "The Purification of Sociology," *Contemporary Sociology* 29, no. 5
(2000): 704–709; Mustafa Emirbayer, "Manifesto for a Relational Sociology," *American Journal of
Sociology* 103, no. 2 (1997): 281–317. Harrison C. White, *Identity and Control: A Structural Theory
of Social Action* (Princeton, NJ: Princeton University Press, 1992). Relevant here, Omar Lizardo
pointed out that *field theory* is "the only theoretical position that can be considered a true hybrid of
both formalism and behavioral-realism currently extant," in "Formalism, Behavioral Realism, and
the Interdisciplinary Challenge in Sociological Theory," *Journal for the Theory of Social Behaviour* 39,
no. 1 (2009): 39–79. The quotation is from p. 57.

contradicts the other parts. The various "nuggets of truth" from each existing framework hold together, it seems. From here, this chapter shows how field theory—and specifically a slightly revised version of strategic action field theory—can wrap these all together to explain the Reformed resurgence.

Field Theory

The New Calvinist movement—as a sociological resurgence in relation to the mainstream, progressive Emergent, and neo-Anabaptist expressions of Evangelicalism in the United States—raises theoretical and empirical puzzles that the standard toolbox of the sociology of religion (especially on the question of religious strength) is ill-equipped to solve satisfactorily. The movement is (and is perceived by several Evangelical leaders and the national news media to be) strong and influential in Evangelicalism. But although the New Calvinism has developed and expanded numerically over the last twenty years, we saw in chapter 3 that other expressions of Evangelicalism have developed and grown just as much. This calls out for a new model of religious strength—a model that can account for symbolic and qualitative vitality which is intersubjectively felt and experienced by both movement insiders and socially nearby parties. A model of religious strength built on the principles of field theory offers that.

Field theory in sociology is a bit unwieldy. This is because since its entrance into the social sciences (as an import from the physical sciences during the 1930s[28]) field theory has developed over time into a multifaceted framework with multiple expressions, variations, and applications. Therefore, the next step in constructing a field-theoretic model of religious strength is to get some bearings, even if only in an outline form, about (what I will call) field theory's two key *dimensions* (namely, fields of *forces* and fields of *contestation*) and sociological field theory's three main *streams* (neo-institutionalism, bourdieusian cultural analysis, and strategic action fields). To give away the punchline upfront, all three major streams of field theory, despite their notable differences in emphases, share four key insights in common: "(1) fields are meso-level social orders, in which (2) actors have a shared orientation to

---

[28] Kurt Koffka, *Principles of Gestalt Psychology* (New York: Harcourt, Brace, 1935); Wolfgang Köhler, *The Place of Value in a World of Facts* (New York: Liveright, 1938); Kurt Lewin, *Principles of Topological Psychology*, trans. Fritz Heider and Grace M. Heider (New York: McGraw Hill, 1936).

the field but heterogeneous self or normative interests within it, which (3) are dependent on their location in [the] field, causing (4) variation in strategies to achieve dominance, power or control through the procurement of structural, physical, financial, or symbolic status and resources."[29]

To disentangle this, the first dimension is fields as meso-level orders constituted by patterned *forces*. Much like the lines of force in a gravitational field or an electromagnetic field along which objects in the field "feel" compelled to move in patterned directions (depending on their position in the field), so in *social* fields social actors (whether persons, groups, or organizations) likewise feel compelled to move in patterned directions depending on their relative positions in the field. In social fields, human actors feel "pulled" (i.e., are qualitatively attracted) toward or away from certain cultural objects and experiences (like classical music, punk rock, going to a top-tier university, garden gnomes, being a Calvinist, etc.). According to field theory, in other words, objects and experiences have real "valences," "affordances," or "demand characters" that "call out" to field actors,[30] telling them what they ought to do. For human actors there is "a vectoral interpretation to experience"; "we actually feel in the environment a push to do or be something."[31] Field theoretic perspectives treat arenas of human action as *vector fields*, again, as in magnetism and gravitation. These gravity-like impulsions—that is, dispositions or habits—are "neither identical nor randomly distributed"[32] across positions and actors in a field; instead, they depend on and systematically vary with the positions each actor occupies within a field relative to the other relevant actors. One's "place" or "standing" in a field (*position*) corresponds to patterned, differentiated action imperatives (*dispositions*) that generate in field actors a sense of "what is to be done"—of which types of cultural objects and experiences are "for me" versus "not for me."[33] These impulsions

[29] C. Clayton Childress, "Regionalism and the Publishing Class: Conflicted Isomorphism and Negotiated Identity in a Nested Field of American Publishing," *Cultural Sociology* 9, no. 3 (2015): 364–381, quoted from p. 369.

[30] John Levi Martin, *The Explanation of Social Action* (New York: Oxford University Press, 2011), 246.

[31] Martin, *The Explanation of Social Action*, 244.

[32] Martin, *The Explanation of Social Action*, 272. A nexus of such predispositions and habits, acquired and developed over time based on one's past lived experiences as movements through a field, is one's *habitus*. A habitus may include everything from one's taste in music to one's hard-won virtues.

[33] Omar Lizardo, "Taste and the Logic of Practice in Distinction," *Czech Sociological Review* 50, no. 3 (2014): 335–364. Demonstrating the intrinsic connection between practice theory and bourdieusian field theory (via the centrality of habitus in both), Lizardo calls this field process Bourdieu's "genetic" (or generative) theory of aesthetic judgments and classifications, that is, the origination of persons' differing cultural tastes. Each person's habitus (as dispositions and competences) is tightly attuned to—because it is the product of—one's early material and cultural "conditions of existence" and one's "social trajectory." Hence, by "making a virtue of necessity," one's habitus "guarantees that

are very often routinized, nondiscursive, and even embodied, but they might also occasionally be consciously articulated and cultivated (especially if the actor is aware of how these social dynamics operate).[34]

The second dimension of field theory is that fields are typically characterized by *contestation*. This means the actors in a given field (consider the field of politics) vie, fight, and jockey with one another in a struggle over legitimation and power in and over the field. A social field, in this sense, is also an arena of conflict, a "battlefield." (Actors can be defined as "in" any given field if they are relevant to, involved in, this contest.) The objective for actors in a field contest is, by definition, to move from their current position in the field to a better, more advantageous position. Winning or losing, success or defeat, is measured in terms of each actor's relative share, both the distributions and the overall volume, of certain valued forms of resources—economic capital, social capital, cultural capital, and symbolic capital. Importantly, it is this last form, symbolic capital—which is best thought of as social prestige, recognition, or esteem—that serves as the basis for *symbolic power*. And it is such symbolic power, the power to impose on others a legitimate vision of the social world and its groupings, that allows for power in and over any given field.[35]

As John Levi Martin states, these two dimensions of social fields—that they are *forcefields and battlefields*—might seem to have little to do with each other, other than as "a set of overlapping metaphors."[36] However, both dimensions of field theory come together in an explanatory construct built around a single overarching metaphor: that of a *game*.[37]

It is not difficult to grasp, once a game is in mind (say, soccer), how a localized, vectoral interpretation of what is to be done based on one's position in the field of play (the first dimension of field theory) can go along with a contest for dominance in the field (the second dimension of field theory). On a soccer field, a goalie experiences different felt action imperatives ("stop this ball!") than a forward does ("get a clear shot!"), but the objective for both

---

what persons 'prefer' is precisely that which they have already acquired the skills to consume in the first place." Quotation is from p. 349.

[34] Vanina Leschziner and Adam Isaiah Green, "Thinking about Food and Sex: Deliberate Cognition in the Routine Practices of a Field," *Sociological Theory* 31, no. 2 (2013): 116–144.

[35] Pierre Bourdieu, "Social Space and Symbolic Power," *Sociological Theory* 7, no. 1 (1989): 14–25.

[36] Martin, *The Explanation of Social Action*, 292.

[37] Using a game as a metaphor for social phenomena in a field should not be seen as suggesting the sense of triviality that the word "game" often carries.

players is to win the game. This game metaphor injects into field theory the crucial vocabulary of *rules* and *strategies*. And it insists both of these are not settled or pregiven but instead are "up for grabs," that is, endogenous to the system. As Martin shows, there is a blurry line between "constitutive rules" (what the game is) and "regulative rules" (how the game ought to be played); it is often strategic and worth the penalty to break a regulative rule (such as fouling one's opponent in the closing minute of a basketball game). Martin likewise shows the introduction of new strategies into a game can change the nature of the game, and thus the kind of play and player that comes to dominate it, without ever changing or breaking the rules.[38] Social rules, after all, Martin suggests, "are themselves subjectively understood patterns of alignment" of neighboring vectors.[39] When vectors or action imperatives (what is to be done) are patterned but vary across a field, the game itself becomes a strategic struggle over the rules, which in turn defines what the game even *is* and what kind of players will dominate it.[40] And with a game that lacks any agreed-upon authoritative referees, the battle over the rules and character of the game, the field itself, is all the more intense.[41]

As to the three streams of field theory in sociology today—neo-institutionalism, bourdieusian cultural analysis, and strategic action fields—they share the feature of explaining human social life at the level of meso-level orders in which action imperatives are linked to spatio-analytic positions (based on resources, legitimacy, etc.) relative to other actors in the field. Beyond this basic commonality, however, each framework has distinctive emphases and puts differing weight on the two key dimensions of field theory. Neo-institutionalism has focused on social fields in which the actors are not persons but instead organizations, and it asks why organizations in a given sector or industry tend to look and behave so much alike. This version of field theory tended to emphasize isomorphic pressures (as forces) toward standardization across a field, but at least in its original formulations paid very little attention to active contestation and conflict over the field.[42]

---

[38] The 2011 film *Moneyball* depicts an example from Major League Baseball of precisely this.

[39] Martin, *The Explanation of Social Action*, 305; with field theory, what our folk theories call our "values" are recast as valances that in a localized area of a field are oriented in roughly the same direction.

[40] Martin, *The Explanation of Social Action*, 293–307.

[41] Benjamin DiCicco-Bloom and David R. Gibson, "More Than a Game: Sociological Theory from the Theories of Games," *Sociological Theory* 28, no. 3 (2010): 247–271.

[42] Paul J. DiMaggio and Walter W. Powell, "The Iron Cage Revisited: Institutional Isomorphism and Collective Rationality in Organizational Fields," *American Sociological Review* 48, no. 2 (1983): 147–160; Walter W. Powell and Paul J. DiMaggio, eds., *The New Institutionalism in Organizational Analysis* (Chicago: The University of Chicago Press, 1991); John W. Meyer and Brian Rowan, "Institutionalized

More recent forms of institutional research, however, are far more attentive to human agency, contestation, and multiple competing "logics," and thus are in many ways hard to distinguish from strategic action fields.[43] Pierre Bourdieu's field theory, in contrast, focused for the most part on individual rather than collective actors or organizations, but they were always analyzed in reference to groups and socioeconomic classes. Of the three streams of field theory in sociology, the bourdieusian approach most consistently held together and applied the two dimensions of fields—both contestations and dispositional impulsions.[44]

The most recent articulation of field theory, Fligstein and McAdam's "strategic action fields," is an attempt to synthesize what the authors saw as common threads in the study of organizations and social movements.[45] Compared to the other two streams, this version of sociological field theory pays much more attention to field contestation than to prediscursive and dispositional action (although there is no principled reason the dispositional element of fields cannot be included). Because of its focus on organizations, movements, leaders, and jockeying for a more advantageous position in and over a given field, this third stream of field theory—with only a couple minor

Organizations: Formal Structure as Myth and Ceremony," *American Journal of Sociology* 83, no. 2 (1977): 340–363; Roland L. Warren, "The Interorganizational Field as a Focus for Investigation," *Administrative Science Quarterly* 12, no. 3 (1967): 396–419.

[43] For newer work in the institutionalist tradition that has more in common with Fligstein and McAdam's framework of "strategic action fields" (discussed later), see, for example, Mary B. Dunn and Candace Jones, "Institutional Logics and Institutional Pluralism: The Contestation of Care and Science Logics in Medical Education, 1967–2005," *Administrative Science Quarterly* 55, no. 1 (2010): 114–149; Royston Greenwood, Amalia Magán Díaz, Stan Xiao Li, and José Céspedes Lorente, "The Multiplicity of Institutional Logics and the Heterogeneity of Organizational Responses," *Organization Science* 21, no. 2 (2010): 521–539; Michael Lounsbury, "A Tale of Two Cities: Competing Logics and Practice Variation in the Professionalizing of Mutual Funds," *Academy of Management Journal*, 50, no. 2 (2007): 289–307; Patricia H. Thornton, William Ocasio, and Michael Lounsbury, *The Institutional Logics Perspective: A New Approach to Culture, Structure, and Process* (New York: Oxford University Press, 2012); Kyoung-Hee Yu, "Institutional Pluralism, Organizations, and Actors: A Review," *Sociology Compass* 9, no. 6 (2015): 464–476; W. Richard Scott, "Approaching Adulthood: The Maturing of Institutional Theory," *Theory and Society* 37, no. 5 (2008): 427–442, especially pp. 434–435 on field-level approaches and pp. 437–438 on conflict and change. Because of advances in organizational and institutional research since the early 1990s that better account for activeness, conflict, interests, and change, Fligstein called original neo-institutionalism "the old new institutionalism" and his own, more recent theoretical framework with Doug McAdam (strategic action fields) "the new new institutionalism." See Fligstein, "The 'Old' New Institutionalism versus the 'New' New Institutionalism," *OrgTheory.net*, August 23, 2012, https://orgtheory.wordpress.com/2012/08/23/the-old-new-institutionalism-versus-the-new-new-institutionalism/, accessed June 12, 2015.

[44] Among many options, see Pierre Bourdieu, *Distinction: A Social Critique of the Judgment of Taste*, trans. Richard Nice (Cambridge, MA: Harvard University Press, [1979] 1984); David Swartz, *Culture and Power: The Sociology of Pierre Bourdieu* (Chicago: The University of Chicago Press, 1997).

[45] Fligstein and McAdam, *A Theory of Fields*.

revisions, explained shortly—serves as the main organizing framework for the strength and resurgence of the New Calvinist movement in American Evangelicalism over the last couple of decades. This newer framework, outlined in greater detail in following pages, picks up on and can incorporate the best of what the previous explanations of religious strength offered, while avoiding their theoretical and empirical shortcomings.

Religious Organizations as Social Movement Organizations

In various social science literatures, religious organizations—especially religious congregations and especially congregations in a pluralistic, "open market" system like the United States—have typically been understood as one among many kinds of voluntary associations. Despite whatever else goes on in religious organizations involving theology or spiritual formation, the general view within sociology is that such organizations are ultimately not much unlike one's favorite local hobby group or country club.[46] When the scholarly literature does record religious leaders mobilizing their organizations and followers and dedicating their (sometimes abundant) resources toward some cause worth pursuing, it is nearly always a social or political cause the energy and impetus for which have already been generated and sustained outside of the context of collective religious life. Thus, regardless of whether the issue examined aligns with left-leaning or right-leaning politics, the explanatory model is that of religious leaders, religious people, and religious organizations having been successfully "co-opted" by a movement or campaign external to them.[47] In the rare instances sociologists analyze religious organizations' involvement in a movement as being genuinely self-motivated

[46] For a review, see Ram A. Cnaan and Daniel W. Curtis, "Religious Congregations as Voluntary Associations: An Overview," *Nonprofit and Voluntary Sector Quarterly* 42, no. 1 (2013): 7–33.

[47] Examples include Pierrette Hondagneu-Sotelo, *God's Heart Has No Borders: How Religious Activists Are Working for Immigrant Rights* (Berkeley: University of California Press, 2008); Charles Kurzman, "Organizational Opportunity and Social Movement Mobilization: A Comparative Analysis of Four Religious Movements," *Mobilization* 3, no. 1 (1998): 23–49; Charles Kurzman, *The Unthinkable Revolution in Iran* (Cambridge, MA: Harvard University Press, 2004); Eric L. McDaniel, *Politics in the Pews: The Political Mobilization of Black Churches* (Ann Arbor: University of Michigan Press, 2008); Rory McVeigh, *The Rise of the Ku Klux Klan: Right-Wing Movements and National Politics* (Minneapolis: University of Minnesota Press, 2009); Ziad W. Munson, *The Making of Pro-Life Activists: How Social Movement Mobilization Works* (Chicago: The University of Chicago Press, 2008); Adam D. Reich, *With God on Our Side: The Struggle for Workers' Rights in a Catholic Hospital* (Ithaca, NY: Cornell University Press, 2012).

because of the actors' faith-based convictions—sometimes labeled as "religious movements"—the collective activity is still at the service of some issue movement, usually a political one.[48]

To rightly apply the framework of strategic action fields to the study of resurgent Calvinism in the field of American Evangelicalism, however, it is important to view religious organizations not just as voluntary associations and not merely as organizations sometimes at the service of some (mostly externally sustained) issue movement. Instead, the field-theoretic model of strength constructed in this chapter insists at least some religious organizations, at least some of the time, are most fruitfully viewed and analyzed as being themselves social movement organizations (SMOs).[49] To this end, I adopt the more colloquial notion of a religious movement as *large-scale collective activity directed toward the goal of shared devoted religious belief and practice for its own sake.* Therefore, religious organizations—whether they are multisite churches, publishers, regularly occurring conferences, formalized networks, educational bodies, or auxiliary councils—may be SMOs in the straightforward sense that they are organizations striving toward that goal: shared devoted religious belief and practice for its own sake. Such organizations might also be called SMOs in the sense that they are fighting against some perceived cultural authority (secularism, feminism, relativism, expressive individualism, etc.),[50] but what is essential here are not extrinsic social and political issues so much as the intrinsic *religious mission* of the organizations—making disciples, planting churches, baptizing new members, growing in religious maturity, and the like.[51] Seeing religious organizations, at least the ones that "fit the bill," as SMOs in this way crucially opens up the full range of literature on organizations and movements for understanding collective religious life.

---

[48] Anna Grzymala-Busse, *Nations under God: How Churches Use Moral Authority to Influence Policy* (Princeton, NJ: Princeton University Press, 2015); Christian Smith, *Resisting Reagan: The U.S. Central America Peace Movement* (Chicago: The University of Chicago Press, 1996); Christian Smith, ed., *Disruptive Religion: The Force of Faith in Social Movement Activism* (New York: Routledge, 1996); Richard L. Wood, *Faith in Action: Religion, Race, and Democratic Organizing in America* (Chicago: The University of Chicago Press, 2002).

[49] Gerald F. Davis, Doug McAdam, W. Richard Scott, and Mayer N. Zald, eds., *Social Movements and Organization Theory* (Cambridge: Cambridge University Press, 2005); Mayer N. Zald and John D. McCarthy, eds., *Social Movements in an Organizational Society: Collected Essays* (New Brunswick, NJ: Transaction, 1987).

[50] David A. Snow, "Social Movements as Challenges to Authority: Resistance to an Emerging Conceptual Hegemony," *Research in Social Movements, Conflicts, and Change* 25 (2004): 3–25.

[51] See, for example, J. R. Woodward and Dan White Jr., *The Church as Movement: Starting and Sustaining Missional-Incarnational Communities* (Downers Grove, IL: InterVarsity Press, 2016).

Strategic Action Fields

Much of the best theorizing on organizations, social movements, leadership, and field theory has been thoughtfully integrated into Fligstein and McAdam's framework of strategic action fields. The chief insight of this newer framework is that both movements and organizations, in the final analysis, are instances of a more generalized kind of social structural phenomenon—namely, *collective strategic action in a social field*. Fligstein and McAdam define a strategic action field as a "meso-level social order in which actors (who can be individual or collective) are attuned to and interact with one another on the basis of shared (which is not to say consensual) understandings about the purposes of the field, the relationships to others in the field (including who has power and why), and the rules governing legitimate action in the field."[52] With only a couple revisions regarding the authors' views of strategy and opportunity, this new framework sheds much analytic insight on American Evangelicalism and the New Calvinist movement within it.

Following a distinction made by William Gamson and long repeated in the literature on social movements, Fligstein and McAdam emphasize the contentious nature of strategic action fields by classifying actors (or tribes of actors) into either incumbents or challengers.[53] Incumbents, they explain, hold a privileged position in their field and wield disproportionate influence if not dominance within it. As such, the "rules of the game" are bent in incumbents' favor and reflect their interests and ideas. In contrast, challengers stand in a less privileged position in a field and typically have little influence over the field's nature and operation. Nevertheless, challengers "can usually articulate an alternative vision of the field"[54] and what their new positions in it would be. There is not always a clear distinction between incumbents and challengers. Fligstein and McAdam claim that conflict is highest when relative power is more equalized. In this kind of social structural arrangement, then, personal and collective actors—while being attuned to one another—vie for an improved, more advantageous social position in and over the field.

Fligstein and McAdam describe the way this kind of contention and jockeying in a field comes about. It begins when a notable change—whether originating from within the field or from the wider structural or cultural environment—destabilizes the field, creating a "shock" or "turbulence" in the

---

[52] Fligstein and McAdam, *A Theory of Fields*, 9.
[53] William A. Gamson, *The Strategy of Social Protest* (Homewood, IL: Dorsey Press, 1975).
[54] Fligstein and McAdam, *A Theory of Fields*, 13.

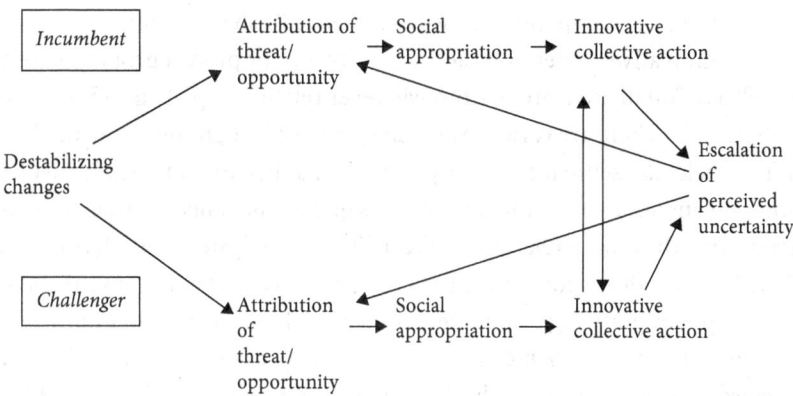

Figure 4.1 The onset of contention.

field. From there, a series of three contingent mechanisms work together to bring about a period of contention. First, actors in the field have to interpret the destabilizing turbulence "as posing a serious threat to, or opportunity for, the realization of collective interests."[55] Second, the field actors perceiving the new threat or opportunity must appropriate the tools and resources, usually based in organizations, needed to mobilize and sustain their actions. And finally, the field actors engage in "heightened interaction involving the use of innovative and previously prohibited forms of collective action."[56] These processes together precipitate an "episode of contention," which Fligstein and McAdam define as "a period of emergent, sustained contentious interaction between . . . [field] actors utilizing new and innovative forms of action vis-à-vis one another."[57] These processes are modeled in Figure 4.1.

During an episode of contention, the relevant players in a given field become embattled with one another in a game-like contest for power and control over the field. An episode of contention is characterized by the escalation of perceived uncertainty about the rules of the field and the power-relations governing the field. Because of heightened uncertainty, there is a generalized sense of disorder and chaos among the collective actors. The field along with its rules and organization are "up for grabs." As the new threat or opportunity

---

[55] Fligstein and McAdam, *A Theory of Fields*, 20.

[56] Fligstein and McAdam, *A Theory of Fields*, 21.

[57] Fligstein and McAdam, *A Theory of Fields*, 21, quoted from Doug McAdam, "Legacies of Anti-Americanism: A Sociological Perspective," in *Anti-Americanisms in World Politics*, ed. Peter J. Katzenstein and Robert O. Keohane (Ithaca, NY: Cornell University Press, 2007), 251–269. Quotation is from p. 253.

is reacted to, the competing parties experience "a shared motivation to engage in innovative contentious action to advance or protect group interests"
as well as a "qualitative break from whatever relationship, if any, they shared
in the past."[58] There are various ways an episode of infighting can wind down
and the field can settle into a new period of stability, but it typically involves
either the incumbents restoring the status quo or challengers successfully re-
structuring the power-relations of the field. But as Fligstein and McAdam explain, "an episode [of contention] can be expected to last as long as the shared
sense of uncertainty regarding the structure and dominant order of the field
persists."[59] (The case of American Evangelicalism, in my estimation, is still in
an episode of contention, so this book pays less attention to the issue of field
settlement than does Fligstein and McAdam's model.)[60]

Strategy as Positioning

The field-theoretic model of religious strength developed here adopts
Fligstein and McAdam's general model while revising their conception of
what strategic action is. They equate strategic action with social skill, and
they conceptualize social skill as the distinctive capacity of leaders to intersubjectively take upon themselves others' ways of viewing the world in order
to get those others to do or believe what the leaders want (or "securing their
cooperation").[61] This is accomplished, they explain, largely by fashioning attractive "existential packages" for others consisting of shared meanings and
identities.

Fligstein and McAdam's conception of social skill is important and has obvious connections to Weber's notion of charismatic leadership and authority.
And charisma and intersubjectivity are factors that can help make sense of
how leaders initiate and organize persons for collective action. However, if

---

[58] McAdam, "Legacies of Anti-Americanism," 253.

[59] Fligstein and McAdam, *A Theory of Fields*, 21.

[60] Many of the published reviews and my own conversations suggest *A Theory of Fields* is neither
"a theory" nor "of fields," and that in terms of its theoretical ambitions the book seeks to do far too
much while somehow also doing very little. Nonetheless, I use "strategic action fields" as the guiding
framework for this project, because the main elements of the framework—that is, positions, power,
strategy, uncertainty, agency, and conflict—together go a long way in explaining contemporary
American Evangelicalism well and yet are underutilized (as a package) in the subfield of the sociology of religion.

[61] Fligstein and McAdam, *A Theory of Fields*, 16–18. See also Neil Fligstein, "Social Skill and the
Theory of Fields," *Sociological Theory* 19, no. 2 (2001): 105–125.

the goal is to understand how a social movement organization (or any other kind of collective or coalition) and its leaders strive to advance to a better, more privileged position in their field, then Fligstein and McAdam's conceptualization of strategy overlooks a more obvious choice: business strategy. An understanding of strategy on loan from the literature on business management fits better for two reasons: what it explains and what it emphasizes. First, business strategy explains competitive advantage in a field rather than explaining how leaders secure the cooperation of followers; and secondly, it emphasizes positioning relative to competitors rather than fashioning shared meanings and identities. In both of these ways, the understanding of strategy in business management is *more field-theoretic* than Fligstein and McAdam's original formulation of strategic action.

For these reasons, the present model replaces Fligstein and McAdam's conception of "social skill"—which they use interchangeably with "strategic action"—with the dominant conception of strategy from the business management literature, that of Harvard Business School professor Michael Porter.[62] Porter's theory of strategy begins by making a distinction between "operational effectiveness" (what I call "tactics") and strategy. Tactics, for Porter, are things organizations do—and that any organization *can* do—to maximize effectiveness and get things done; tactics are "best practices" and are easily imitated by different organizations across a field. Therefore, the use of good, effective tactics leads to improvements for several if not all actors in a field while leading to relative advantage for none.[63] In contrast, strategy is fundamentally about taking and occupying a position in a field that sets one apart in relation to one's field competitors. The essence of strategy, this means, is deliberately doing things differently than rivals do. If "operational effectiveness means performing similar activities *better* than rivals perform them," strategic positioning, in contrast, "means performing *different* activities from rivals or performing similar activities in *different ways*."[64] And marking out for one's organization a unique, niche position in the

---

[62] Michael E. Porter, "What Is Strategy?" *Harvard Business Review* 74, no. 6 (1996): 61–78; see also Porter, *Competitive Strategy: Techniques for Analyzing Industries and Competitors* (New York: The Free Press, 1980); Michael E. Porter, *Competitive Advantage: Creating and Sustaining Superior Performance* (New York: The Free Press, 1985).

[63] Among contemporary Evangelical churches in the United States, maintaining an attractive, polished, intuitive website containing important information would be an example of a tactic in this sense.

[64] Porter, "What Is Strategy," 62, emphasis in the original.

field—based on the activities and character of the organization itself—can result in a real competitive advantage.[65]

Joan Magretta, formerly of Harvard Business School and the author of *Understanding Michael Porter*, provides ten basic, bullet-point insights about Porter's theory of competitive organizational strategy. Thinking about these points not with for-profit companies in mind but rather with free-market religious organizations and the potential adherents they are trying to reach, it is easy to see how attending to strategy as relational positioning in a social field can help to develop a field-theoretic model of religious strength. Her insights were as follows:[66] "(1) Competitive advantage is not about beating rivals; it's about creating unique value for customers [. . .]; (2) No strategy is meaningful unless it makes clear what the organization will not do. Making trade-offs is the linchpin that makes competitive advantage possible and sustainable; (3) There is no honor in size or growth if those are [success]-less. Competition is about [achieving real organizational success], not market share;[67] (4) Don't overestimate or underestimate the importance of good execution. It's unlikely to be a source of a sustainable advantage, but without it even the most brilliant strategy will fail to produce superior performance; (5) Good strategies depend on many choices, not one, and on the connections among them. A core competence alone will rarely produce a sustainable competitive advantage." And furthermore, "(6) Flexibility in the face of uncertainty may sound like a good idea, but it means that your organization will never stand for anything or become good at anything. Too much change can be just as disastrous for strategy as too little; (7) Committing to a strategy does not require heroic predictions about the future. Making that commitment actually improves your ability to innovate and to adapt to turbulence; (8) Vying to be the best [within your field] is an intuitive but self-destructive approach to competition; (9) . . . [S]trategy is more than marketing. If your [organization's] value proposition doesn't require a specifically tailored [set of organizational activities] to deliver it, it will have no strategic relevance;

---

[65] With this revision, Fligstein and McAdam's concept of social skill may be recast, in part, as contributing to an entrepreneur's insight and ability to see and stake out a strategic position in one's field.

[66] The rest of this paragraph is quoted from Joan Magretta, "Strategy Essentials You Ignore at Your Peril," *Harvard Business Review*, December 22, 2011, https://hbr.org/2011/12/strategy-essentials-you-ignore, accessed February 24, 2015. See also Joan Magretta, *Understanding Michael Porter: The Essential Guide to Competition and Strategy* (Boston: Harvard Business Review Press, 2012).

[67] Because I am suggesting these strategy principles apply to religious organizations, I replaced "profit" with the more generally applicable target of "success" and "achieving real organizational success."

(10) Don't feel you have to 'delight' every possible customer out there. The sign of a good strategy is that it deliberately makes some customers unhappy."

In short, rethinking the strategy component of strategic action fields—as relational position-takings within a field—is both more field-theoretic (than Fligstein and McAdam's concept of social skill) and analytically helpful for understanding the efforts of religious leaders and their organizations for establishing a sustainable competitive advantage in their field.[68]

Discursive Opportunity

Fligstein and McAdam's original formulation of strategic action fields conceives of opportunities for collective mobilization toward a cause using the now-classic social movement theory concept of "political opportunity structure."[69] This concept provides a partial explanation of mobilization by reference to contextual factors and conditions in the broader political environment that may facilitate good chances for success (or at least the *perception* of good chances for movement success, which then might turn out to be wrong or become a self-fulfilling prophecy). There are several ways a given political environment might serve as facilitating conditions ripe for movement mobilization and success, having to do in various ways with infrastructural weakness, instability, conflict, and change. Fligstein and McAdam

---

[68] Although the present analysis uses Fligstein and McAdam's stream of field theory, not Bourdieu's stream, the following reflections on Bourdieu's take on human action in fields are illuminating in the context of gleaning sociological insights about (organizational) strategy from the world of business. As Swartz noted ("Bridging the Study of Culture and Religion: Pierre Bourdieu's Political Economy of Symbolic Power," *Sociology of Religion* 57, no. 1 (1996): 71–85, quoted from p. 76), "Bourdieu's theory of human action as suggested by his concept of *habitus* does not share the anthropological assumptions of a rational actor perspective. Bourdieu's actors pursue strategies but not as conscious maximizers of limited means to achieve desired ends. Their 'choices' are tacit, practical, and dispositional, reflecting the encounter between their accumulated capital and corresponding dispositions from past socialization and the present opportunities and constraints of fields where they act." And as Bourdieu described it: "[T]he principle of . . . strategies is not cynical calculation, the conscious pursuit of maximum specific profit, but an unconscious relationship between a *habitus* and a field" (Pierre Bourdieu, "Some Properties of Fields," in *Sociology in Question*, trans. Richard Nice (Thousand Oaks, CA: Sage, [1984] 1993), 72–77, quoted from p. 76). Thus, with field theory, strategy need not imply rational cost-benefit calculation or instrumental utilitarianism; rather, strategies as position-takings can be dispositional, prediscursive, and tacit.

[69] See Hanspeter Kriesi, "Political Context and Opportunity," in *The Blackwell Companion to Social Movements*, ed. David A. Snow, Sarah A. Soule, and Hanspeter Kriesi (Malden, MA: Blackwell, 2004), 67–90; Doug McAdam, *Political Process and the Development of Black Insurgency, 1930–1970*, 2nd ed. (Chicago: The University of Chicago Press, [1982] 1999); David S. Meyer, "Protest and Political Opportunities," *Annual Review of Sociology* 30 (2004): 125–145; David S. Meyer and Debra C. Minkoff, "Conceptualizing Political Opportunity," *Social Forces* 82, no. 4 (2004): 1457–1492.

reinforce this traditional tack with their heavy accent on the role of the state as key player in, and often the target of, collective political action.

But the New Calvinism is a religious movement (as defined previously), not mainly a political or protest movement, and—owing in part to the separation of church and state in the United States—governmental politics and the state are peripheral to this case.[70] The second revision to the strategic action fields framework therefore is to replace its emphasis on political opportunity structure with the related, newer concept of *discursive* opportunity structure.[71] Like its older, better-known counterpart, the concept of discursive opportunity structure directs the focus of attention to facilitating conditions external to the movement itself that affect the likelihood of mobilization and success. Unlike political opportunity structure, however, this concept looks at the broader *cultural and discursive environment* to understand the conditions in which a movement arises and seeks to advance its interests. By emphasizing discourse rather than politics, the focus turns to which ideas, assumptions, questions, and beliefs are legitimate, salient, or plausible (and which are not) in the bigger context of movement emergence.[72] With this shift, the model of religious strength developed in this study takes into account the surrounding cultural and ideational elements that allow movement leaders to have a "space to speak" into the broader institutional context in which the New Calvinism attempts to advance its worldview.[73]

An Analogy from Physics

Seeing as field theory as a framework was first introduced to the social sciences as a metaphor from physics (i.e., as scientists used such theories to map

---

[70] Nevertheless, each subsequent chapter touches in spots on the posture toward politics in the New Calvinist movement, which is usually to minimize its ultimate importance.

[71] Myra Marx Ferree, William A. Gamson, Jürgen Gerhards, and Dieter Rucht, *Shaping Abortion Discourse: Democracy and the Public Sphere in Germany and the United States* (Cambridge: Cambridge University Press, 2002); Ruud Koopmans and Susan Olzak, "Discursive Opportunities and the Evolution of Right-Wing Violence in Germany," *American Journal of Sociology* 110, no. 1 (2004): 198–230; Mattias Wahlström and Abby Peterson, "Between the State and the Market: Expanding the Concept of 'Political Opportunity Structure,'" *Acta Sociologica* 49, no. 4 (2006): 363–377; Holly J. McCammon, "Discursive Opportunity Structure," in *The Wiley-Blackwell Encyclopedia of Social and Political Movements*, ed. David A. Snow, Donatella Della Porta, Bert Klandermans, and Doug McAdam (Malden, MA: Blackwell, 2013).

[72] The concept also harkens back to Peter Berger's older concept of "plausibility structure" in the sociology of religion.

[73] Robert Wuthnow, *Communities of Discourse: Ideology and Social Structure in the Reformation, the Enlightenment, and European Socialism* (Cambridge, MA: Harvard University Press, 1989).

out the dynamics of phenomena such as magnetism and gravitation),[74] perhaps it should not be surprising that a new analogy from physics can likewise assist us at this point in coming to a firmer understanding of the model of religious strength proposed in this chapter.

In addition to the dispositional attraction or repulsion an object experiences in a magnetic field (sociological field theory's original metaphor from physics), Newton's second law of motion in classical mechanics tells us that the net force of a body in motion in some direction is equal to the product of its mass and its acceleration (F = ma), and that acceleration itself is the change in velocity over (i.e., divided by) the span from time-1 to time-2 (a = $\Delta v / \Delta t$). Stated plainly, the force of some object in motion is the result of two factors together: mass and acceleration. In terms of this physics analogy, then, this project is interested in the net force of the New Calvinism as a body in motion through the field of American Evangelicalism; it asks how this religious movement's "force"—its sociological strength—came about over time.

The suggestion is that the New Calvinism's "force" is best explained not by measuring out its mass (i.e., the number of persons and organizations involved in it) but instead by its *acceleration*—its change in "velocity," so to speak, over the last twenty years. By "acceleration" and "velocity" here, I do not mean anything overly technical; I am using them heuristically to indicate a complex of other, more symbolic factors besides "the hard numbers" (mass) that has propelled the New Calvinism as a "social object" through its field. Crucially, religious actors in any social field possess something that iron filings dropped into a magnetic field do not: purposive agency. The leaders of the New Calvinism therefore have the capacity to position themselves strategically in various ways to propel their movement forward, thereby generating "social acceleration" that when combined with its (relatively modest) mass gives this movement its impressive force.[75]

---

[74] See Mary B. Hesse, *Forces and Fields: The Concept of Action at a Distance in the History of Physics* (New York: Dover, [1961] 2005).

[75] Brad Vermurlen, "How Leaders Create Momentum: Rethinking Religious Strength in a Strategic Action Field," paper presented at the annual meeting of the Society for the Scientific Study of Religion, Phoenix, Arizona, November 9–11, 2012.

A Culturalist Field Theory

Largely due to the legacy of Bourdieu, sociological field theory sometimes gets pegged as being insufficiently culturalist[76]—that is, for being overly deterministic (not being able to account well for contingency and change) and for reducing the full range of human motivations for action merely to self-interested maximization of power and status (thus neglecting motivations rooted in beliefs, norms, morality, and so on). There is an abundance of secondary work debating these issues, so these will not be taken up at length here, especially since the field theory applied in this study is not primarily of the bourdieusian "stream." Suffice it to say the field-theoretic model of religious strength developed here is a self-consciously culturalist one, resisting both the charges of determinism and of relying on a fundamentally economistic theory of action.

Take, for instance, the charge of economism and the fact that the story developed throughout this book acknowledges power struggles in and over the field of Evangelicalism. All this language about symbolic power and social domination can understandably leave the impression the leaders of the neo-Reformed movement are at bottom a bunch of ideological bullies self-interestedly trying to commandeer the broad Evangelical tent only for themselves and to ruthlessly squash all dissenting voices, that it is power and status "all the way down." And indeed, many of the neo-Anabaptist and progressive Emergent Evangelicals interviewed for this study made it clear they think this is precisely what is happening. Bourdieu's general theoretical project, as well, would easily lead one to conclude the legitimacy, prominence, and recognition of the New Calvinists as a class of "religious specialists"—that is, the Reformed resurgence itself—is based on constructing and maintaining a more fundamental "misrecognition" or denial of their own self-interest in economic and political domination (over the field of American Evangelicalism). Symbolic capital is, after all, for Bourdieu, denied capital. A fully bourdieusian analysis would try to show that New Calvinist leaders

---

[76] The degree to which (bourdieusian) field theory is really *cultural* depends on what one means by "culture" and for Bourdieu ultimately was inseparable from his theory of cognition and practice. The issues of determinism and economism noted in this section are arguably rooted in *misreadings* of Bourdieu, but are addressed here due to their persistence as questions and critiques. For some conceptual clarity, see Omar Lizardo, "Pierre Bourdieu as a Post-cultural Theorist," *Cultural Sociology* 5, no. 1 (2011): 25–44.

are, despite what they may say, actually only interested in symbolic power and domination.[77]

But the reality is more complex than that. Granted, there *is* a real power struggle going on in and over American Evangelicalism. We do see game-like contestation and jockeying for position within the field. There are books to sell, institutions to be run, and money to be earned. Bourdieu's "political economy of religion" is not altogether incorrect, then. But it is incomplete to the extent it imputes only pernicious and self-interested motivations, disguised as disinterest, to any religious leaders seeing their stock go up. Some of that does happen. But significant portions of the Evangelical infighting we see in the rest of this book are caused just as much by cohesive groups of ambitious, high-functioning leaders with genuine, consequential disagreements with one another. Leaders from *each tribe* believe their positions are correct and those of the other tribes are more or less wrong. Several of the more conservative, Calvinistic leaders are genuinely worried leaders in other groups are mistaken on such important matters that those others are leading people away from Christ, further from faithfulness, and ultimately to eternal damnation in Hell. These are *cultural* differences with *cultural* motivations, animated by beliefs and narratives—not entirely reducible to nothing but self-interested power grabs. So, while recognizing the important role of symbolic power and the battle over which kind of players will dominate the field of Evangelicalism, we must also view the real motivations at work in this case as much more of a mixed bag.[78]

In this light, Figure 4.2 situates the field-theoretic model of religious strength in relation to existing models. Like the religious economies model, the model developed here casts its analytic focus at the level of religious leaders and entrepreneurs (and keeps its attendant emphasis on religious competition), but does so while explicitly rejecting the economistic, rational-choice assumptions that undergirded that paradigm. Likewise, the present model builds on Smith's subcultural identity theory's culturalist commitments in the broad (and not so technical) sense that it takes seriously beliefs, collective identity, symbolic

---

[77] Pierre Bourdieu, "Legitimation and Structured Interests in Weber's Sociology of Religion," trans. Chris Turner, in *Max Weber, Rationality and Modernity*, ed. Sam Whimster and Scott Lash (London: Allen and Unwin, 1987), 119–136; Pierre Bourdieu, "Genesis and Structure of the Religious Field," *Comparative Social Research* 13 ([1971] 1991): 1–44; Terry Rey, *Bourdieu on Religion: Imposing Faith and Legitimacy* (New York: Routledge, 2014); David Swartz, "Bridging the Study of Culture and Religion: Pierre Bourdieu's Political Economy of Symbolic Power," *Sociology of Religion* 57, no. 1 (1996): 71–85.

[78] See Christian Smith, *Moral, Believing Animals: Human Personhood and Culture* (New York: Oxford University Press, 2003), especially pp. 128–133.

		Level of Inquiry	
		Laypersons	Leadership
Assumptions	Economistic	Iannaccone's Strict Church Theory	Religious Economies Theory
	Cultural	Subcultural Identity Theory	Strategic Action Field Theory

Figure 4.2 Situating the theory.

boundaries, meanings, and discourse. But it extends that model by examining religious strength at the level of leaders and the organizations they lead, not just ordinary laypersons. Importantly (though not represented in the figure), the present view also reconceptualizes religious strength in relational and symbolic terms (such as which groups have power and recognition relative to others) instead of the comparative and linear approach that has dominated the sociology of religion. The field-theoretic model of religious strength is thus situated uniquely among alternative, existing frameworks for religion in modernity (contra the secularization perspective) by simultaneously being a *cultural* sociology of religion cast at the analytic level of religious *leadership*.[79]

A Systematization

With all the parts in place, it is now possible to present a more fully systematized field-theoretic model of religious strength in hypermodernity. This presentation takes the form of a series of social causal mechanisms, spanning the micro, meso, and macro levels of social reality. Some of the mechanisms are broken down into subsidiary causal mechanisms, which should be understood as more specific expressions of the operation in reality of the more general, abstracted mechanisms. Crucially, these statements are not meant as hypotheses to be tested, derived deductively from the theory presented on previous pages (as with the hypothetico-deductive model of social scientific inquiry). Rather, these are (verbal descriptions of) the causal mechanisms that sociological theory and the empirical evidence together, over time, have

[79] Penny Edgell, "A Cultural Sociology of Religion: New Directions," *Annual Review of Sociology* 38 (2012): 247–265.

led me to theorize as the most important (sociological) causal forces operative in bringing about and explaining the Reformed resurgence.[80] As Smith has stressed, "The explication of the complex of causes that produced the result *is* itself the explanation."[81] In the case of the New Calvinism, that complex of sociological causes is as follows:

Micro-Personal-Level Causal Mechanisms

1. Religious leaders, individually and corporately, motivated to pursue their subjectively defined religious and moral interests, acting on their genuine beliefs and convictions.[82]
2. Religious leaders leveraging media attention originating from outside their own field in order to legitimate and celebrate their own beliefs, interests, and organizations.
3. Religious leaders rightly perceiving and taking advantage of various macro-structural opportunities to make their beliefs more widely visible and attractive to others.
4. Religious adherents, who are not fully aware of (and may not agree with) the actual beliefs and convictions advocated by their own congregations and the conferences they attend, constitute the substance of a movement for those very convictions.
5. Religious leaders' personal characteristics (style, articulateness, likeability, etc.) grant them charismatic authority, which helps these leaders attract and maintain followers.

Meso-Field-Level Causal Mechanisms

6. Religious leaders acting (whether thoughtfully or unreflexively) in ways such that their message and demeanor fit ecologically with their cities and geographic regions, thereby partly facilitating their own success.

---

[80] Philip S. Gorski, "The Poverty of Deductivism: A Constructive Realist Model of Sociological Explanation," *Sociological Methodology* 34, no. 1 (2004): 1–33.

[81] Christian Smith, *To Flourish or Destruct* (Chicago: The University of Chicago Press, 2015), 271.

[82] Examples include organizing conferences, writing books, giving sermons, critiquing opponents, and so forth. Notice that this first, most basic mechanism is a more specified expression in the context of religious leaders of the general mechanism: *persons acting on their beliefs*. Smith, *To Flourish or Destruct*.

7. Religious leaders, both incumbents and challengers, collectively perceiving changes in the field as significant threats to the realization of their collective interests.

   7a. For religious incumbents, progressive changes and challengers are perceived as threats to the established "orthodoxy" (status quo) of the field.[83]

   7b. For religious challengers, conservative reactions and incumbent leaders are perceived as threats to advancing new, alternative visions of the field.

8. Differing personalities, starting points, and dispositions among field actors as religious leaders generate and reinforce heterogeneous positions and interests in their field.

9. Incumbent religious leaders strategically positioning themselves (in various ways) relative to their competitors in the field in order to gain a competitive advantage.

   These various ways include strategically positioning themselves:

   9a. as having clear, compelling, "black and white" answers to pressing ethical, social, existential, and doctrinal questions (especially to young persons).

   Possibly among others, these at least include:

   9a.i.   promoting traditional, conservative gender roles for both men and women, especially in light of feminism and the gender revolution.

   9a.ii.   offering the weight of historical rootedness within a centuries-old tradition, especially in light of modernity as a "rootless world."[84]

   9a.iii. de-emphasizing autonomous self-direction and individual free will, especially in light of the modern-day emphasis on the same.

   9b. as if they were taking consensually valued elements and topics (such as the Bible, God, and theology) more seriously than do their field competitors.

---

[83] Brophy, "Orthodoxy as Project."
[84] Lynn Davidman, *Tradition in a Rootless World: Women Turn to Orthodox Judaism* (Berkeley: University of California Press, 1991).

9c. physically in culturally "upstream" urban centers and global cities in order most effectively to influence and produce mainstream national culture.

9d. as being apolitical, not committed to any political candidate or party.

9e. as the rightful gatekeepers of the field's established "orthodoxy," as if they had real authority to claim which players are "in" and "out" of the field.

10. Incumbent religious leaders actively policing, drawing symbolic boundaries, and trying to enforce the field's established "orthodoxy" based on the "rules of the game."

One important expression of this is:

10a. publicly critiquing and rejecting the beliefs and ideas of their opponents in the field, especially in written media such as blogposts and books.

11. Religious leaders as challengers in the field challenging and "pushing back against" incumbent leaders as self-appointed gatekeepers of the field's "true orthodoxy."

12. Incumbent religious leaders publicly presenting themselves—and being perceived by challengers and the media—as a significant new movement for orthodoxy.

An important variant of this is:

12a. writing about and documenting themselves, including giving themselves a moniker, so as to construct and present themselves as an identifiable tribe.

13. Incumbent religious leaders' symbolic capital (recognition or esteem) translates into symbolic power as the authority to define legitimacy and membership in the field. (Symbolic capital is relationally constructed and symbolic power is contested.)

Macro-Structural-Level Causal Mechanisms

14. Cultural features and assumptions of American culture infuse the religious field and for some actors bring into question older, received "orthodoxies." This decreases consensus and destabilizes the field.

These include:

14a. the gender and sexual revolutions since the 1960s.

14b. a high degree of cultural and religious pluralism.

14c. "the triumph of the therapeutic" in American culture.[85]

15. Contingent events and developments external to the field facilitated new discursive opportunities for religious leaders to "speak into their field" and make their interests heard.

These include:

15a. the invention and widespread use of the Internet and digital media.

15b. the coordinated terrorist attacks that occurred on September 11, 2001.

15c. the increasing felt need to reckon with postmodernist philosophy and postmodernity as a cultural condition, as seen in the Emerging Church.

16. The multivocality and polysemy of belief-informing texts in an arena with no agreed-upon authority to adjudicate between divergent interpretations leads to intractable conflicts over which beliefs and interpretations ought to be held and allowed.

And in the end

17. Intractable conflict and divergent institutional logics lead over time (and despite pockets of relative strength) to overall field weakness and fragmentation.[86]

These seventeen mechanisms as social processes together causally explain the New Calvinist movement and the battle happening in the field of American Evangelicalism. Clearly these causal mechanisms do not operate in isolation, "indifferent" to one another, but instead play off and build on one another in complex interactive ways. For instance, 1 is a fundamental social causal mechanism—a specific expression in the religious field of persons simply acting on their beliefs—upon which most (but not all) of the others rely. In a different way, mechanisms 2 and 12 are symbiotic with one another. So are mechanisms 3 and 15. Mechanism 15a (the invention

[85] Philip Rieff, *The Triumph of the Therapeutic: Uses of Faith after Freud* (Chicago: The University of Chicago Press, [1966] 1987).

[86] Jeff A. Larson and Omar Lizardo, "An Institutional Logics Approach to the Analysis of Social Movement Fields," *Social Currents* 2, no. 1 (2015): 58–80.

and widespread use of the Internet and digital media) facilitates and amplifies mechanism 5 (charismatic authority helping religious leaders gain followers). Mechanism 12 feeds into and serves to facilitate mechanism 13. Mechanisms 7 and 10 together start to approximate the basic point of status discontent theory. To the extent that strategic position takings in field theory are actually prediscursive and dispositional (rather than mainly reflexive and rational), mechanism 8 plays a role in the operation of social mechanism 9, in all its various forms. Mechanism 9e, in particular, is a precursor to mechanism 10 operating with any punch. Mechanism 17—field fragmentation—in many ways is the natural outworking of several causal mechanisms that come before it, both analytically and temporally. And so on. In the end, this model of symbolic, field-based religious strength (and overall weakness) is necessarily complex, or perhaps even "messy," because so is the social and religious reality it explains. Complex models are needed to model complex realities. Even so, the hope is that laying out this series of causal processes and mechanisms adds some intuitive accessibility to the Reformed resurgence as a social phenomenon and the internal battle over American Evangelicalism.

The big thing to notice—and this is reiterated near the end of chapter 6—is the New Calvinism as a resurgent movement is *real* precisely in the sense that it is socially, relationally constructed. The movement is simultaneously real (and strong) and socially constructed because it is a collectively produced, *ontologically emergent* religious phenomenon at the level of "the social"[87]—specifically within the social field of American Evangelicalism. That is, the various Christian leaders and organizations described in chapters 2 and 3, motivated by their corresponding beliefs and convictions, acted and interacted over time through the causal mechanisms and processes just outlined. And all of this, together, *made something new—the New Calvinism—emerge into existence* at a "higher" level of social organization, stronger than and irreducible to any simple additive mixture of the parts at the "lower" level from which it emerged. As a religious phenomenon and institutional fact, the whole is more than the sum of its parts.

---

[87] On ontological emergence, see Philip Clayton and Paul Davies, eds., *The Re-Emergence of Emergence: The Emergentist Hypothesis from Science to Religion* (New York: Oxford University

Conclusion

The following two chapters demonstrate this field-theoretic model of religious strength empirically using the data introduced in chapter 1 (and detailed in Appendix A.). In the next chapter, Part I focuses on those social mechanisms and processes which precipitated the rise of the New Calvinist movement. In chapter 6, Part II focuses on mechanisms of strategic positioning and game-like contestation in, and over, Evangelicalism. Along the way, the presentation sticks closely to the aforementioned seventeen social mechanisms as guideposts, which are italicized in the text. The concluding chapter focuses specifically on mechanism 17 and what that tells us about the state of American Evangelicalism in our current hypermodern world.

Press, 2006); Geoffrey M. Hodgson, "The Concept of Emergence in Social Science: Its History and Importance," *Emergence* 2, no. 4 (2000): 65–77; John Mingers, *Systems Thinking, Critical Realism, and Philosophy: A Confluence of Ideas* (New York: Routledge, 2014); Stephen Pratten, "Critical Realism and the Process Account of Emergence," *Journal for the Theory of Social Behaviour* 43, no. 3 (2013): 251–279.

5

Demonstration of the Model, Part I

Precipitating Causes

The Cultural Backdrop

Any analysis that hopes to understand and explain the New Calvinist movement and Evangelicalism in the United States more generally needs first to come to some basic familiarity with the cultural "backdrop" of the broader American society, in which all expressions of religion in America are embedded. The idea is not just how American Evangelicals—laypersons but especially leaders—have reacted and defined themselves over against certain aspects of American culture. That by now is common knowledge. At the same time that many Evangelicals have reacted against what they see as problematic, immoral, or misguided aspects of American culture, some *cultural features, values, and assumptions of American culture have infused the Evangelical field and for some leaders brought into question older, received "orthodoxies."* And as more and more Evangelical leaders have accepted those cultural mores, this process has *decreased consensus* among Evangelical leaders and organizations on cultural questions and *destabilized the field.*

The following three subsections highlight three of those pieces of the cultural backdrop, namely, the gender and sexual revolutions, religious pluralism, and therapeutic culture.

The Gender and Sexual Revolutions

One significant piece of the cultural backdrop is *the gender and sexual revolutions in the United States since the 1960s.* Throughout the 1960s and into subsequent decades, the sexual revolution upended traditional sexual norms and sought to replace them with a more open, progressive vision of sexual liberation. Running in parallel and in many ways overlapping, the gender revolution worked to problematize traditional views and norms

Reformed Resurgence. Brad Vermurlen, Oxford University Press (2020). © Oxford University Press.
DOI: 10.1093/oso/9780190073510.001.0001

regarding gender, marriage, and "the nuclear family" (that is, a married man and woman and their children). Over only a few decades, these two "liberation" movements worked themselves out in American culture and legal policy in multiple ways, including a marked increase in, and the normalization of, sex outside of marriage;[1] categories like "second-wave" feminism and "women's liberation"; various legal victories for contraception, first for married couples and shortly thereafter for unmarried persons; the FDA approval and rapid expansion of "the pill" as a choice of birth control; the Stonewall riots in 1969 in Manhattan; the spread of "no-fault" divorce laws since 1970; the nationwide legalization of abortion with *Roe v. Wade* in 1973; the removal of homosexuality (as such) from the American Psychiatric Association's official manual for mental disorders in 1973; women entering the paid labor force in record numbers; gay pride marches and parades; and the rise in age of first marriage for both men and women. Later, with the 1990s, came queer theory; "third-wave" feminism; the "problematization" of binary gender codes; a renewed focus on transgender issues (along with the invention of "cisgender" as a label for nontransgender individuals); the entry of "LGBTQ" into the popular American vocabulary; the steady increase in childbirths outside of marriage; the critique of "heteronormativity"; and the mainstreaming of gay and lesbian identities and sex, especially in popular media. In 2015, the *Obergefell v. Hodges* ruling redefined marriage nationwide to include gay and lesbian couples, in many ways a continuation of both of these cultural revolutions.[2]

[1] See Lawrence B. Finer, "Trends in Premarital Sex in the United States, 1954–2003," *Public Health Reports* 122, no. 1 (2007): 73–78; David J. Harding and Christopher Jencks, "Changing Attitudes Toward Premarital Sex: Cohort, Period, and Aging Effects," *The Public Opinion Quarterly* 67, no. 2 (2003): 211–226; Mark Regnerus and Jeremy Uecker, *Premarital Sex in America: How Young Americans Meet, Mate, and Think about Marrying* (New York: Oxford University Press, 2011); Judith Treas, "How Cohorts, Education, and Ideology Shaped a New Sexual Revolution on American Attitudes Toward Nonmarital Sex, 1972–1998," *Sociological Perspectives* 45, no. 3 (2002): 267–283.

[2] Across several literatures (including both exemplars and analyses), see Judith Butler, *Undoing Gender* (New York: Routledge, 2004); Mary Eberstadt, *Adam and Eve after the Pill: Paradoxes of the Sexual Revolution* (San Francisco, CA: Ignatius Press, 2012); Kathryn Edin and Maria Kefalas, *Promises I Can Keep: Why Poor Women Put Motherhood before Marriage* (Berkeley: University of California Press, 2005); Lillian Faderman, *The Gay Revolution: The Story of the Struggle* (New York: Simon and Schuster, 2015); Shulamith Firestone, *The Dialectic of Sex: The Case for Feminist Revolution* (New York: Farrar, Straus, and Giroux, [1970] 2003); Kathleen Gerson, *The Unfinished Revolution: Coming of Age in a New Era of Gender, Work, and Family* (New York: Oxford University Press, 2010); Lori B. Girshick, *Transgender Voices: Beyond Women and Men* (Lebanon, NH: University Press of New England, 2008); Arlie Hochschild with Anne Machung, *The Second Shift: Working Families and the Revolution at Home*, revised edition (New York: Penguin Books, [1989] 2012); J. Jack Halberstam, *Gaga Feminism: Sex, Gender, and the End of Normal* (Boston: Beacon Press, 2012); Kristin Luker, *Abortion and the Politics of Motherhood* (Berkeley: University of California Press, 1984); Steven Seidman, "Queer-ing Sociology, Sociologizing Queer Theory: An Introduction,"

Contrary to popular assumption, the response from Evangelical leaders to all of this has not been uniform criticism and rejection. Certainly, conservatives and traditionalists—especially leaders who are convinced gender complementarians and social conservatives—do reject practically all of it. (The most likely exception being a broad acceptance of contraception use, *legally* for all adults and *morally* by heterosexual married couples.) Others have more mixed or nuanced reactions. And some leaders are on board with much of it. (The most pronounced exception on this end of the spectrum is that several of the most progressive Evangelical leaders still view abortion as morally problematic.[3]) Sparing the reader a long series of quotations saying the same thing, suffice it to say that many of the Evangelical leaders I interviewed for this book, particularly those in the progressive Emergent pocket, are sympathetic to many of the values, assumptions, and commitments of the gender and sexual revolutions. Regarding gender, many American Evangelical leaders clearly rejected (and passionately so!) the traditional or complementarian ideas of masculinity and femininity as essentialist, oppressive, damaging, and unbiblical. On the sexuality side, many progressive Christian leaders I interviewed did not see anything morally wrong with gay and lesbian sexual relationships and enthusiastically supported the legalization of gay marriage. In these ways, these two moral revolutions have *decreased consensus and destabilized the American Evangelical field.*

Religious Pluralism and Fluidity

The second piece of the American cultural backdrop is *a high degree of cultural and especially religious pluralism and fluidity.* Compared with other nations (especially nations in Asia), on the most surface level of religious affiliations the United States is actually not that religiously *diverse.* As the most recent Pew data show, 94 percent of the US adult population is either Christian (including not only Evangelical Protestants but also Catholics, Mormons, "mainline" Protestants, and historically black denominations) or religiously unaffiliated. All other religions combined account for only

---

Sociological Theory 12, no. 2 (1994): 166–177; Nikki Sullivan, *A Critical Introduction to Queer Theory* (New York: New York University Press, 2003).

[3] Williams, "Prolifers of the Left."

6 percent of Americans.[4] Despite a moderate degree of objective religious diversity, the United States exhibits a remarkable degree of cultural and religious pluralism in the sense of valuing tolerance and inclusivism.[5] This cultural assumption is what Putnam and Campbell smartly called "American grace."[6] As they summarized their survey results: "[M]ost of the American population—save a small but intensely religious segment—are reluctant to assign a unique status to any religion as 'true,' even their own. A majority of Americans believe that members of other faiths can go to heaven."[7] As a deeply believed-in principle of contemporary American culture, this openness, inclusivism, and tolerance regarding the possibility of multiple truths and who ends up "in Heaven" has infused the American Evangelical field, not only among Evangelical laypersons[8] but among its leaders as well.

An example from my data is illustrative. One progressive Christian leader and writer I interviewed explained to me several ways that over the years he had "reimagined" what Christianity is. He self-identified as "a mystic" and a universalist (i.e., everyone goes to Heaven), and he preferred not to hold views on the resurrection or the Trinity. He rejected "atonement theory" altogether and emphasized "the coexistence of multiple truths." He said he had worked hard to integrate his Christian faith with insights from Buddhism and Confucianism, and he wore a Buddhist ohm around his neck instead of a cross, seeing the cross as "an instrument of violence." Near the close of our time together, I asked him if he could explain to me the difference between his kind of Christianity and simply Buddhism. He couldn't. Buddhism and his approach to the Christian faith, he told me, "have sort of mutually informed each other for an awfully long time to the point that it's hard for me to separate them out in my own way of thinking. [. . .] I've spent so much time

---

[4] Alan Cooperman and Michael Lipka, "U.S. Doesn't Rank High in Religious Diversity," *Pew Research Center*, April 4, 2014, http://www.pewresearch.org/fact-tank/2014/04/04/u-s-doesnt-rank-high-in-religious-diversity/, accessed January 30, 2016. See also Charles L. Cohen and Ronald L. Numbers, eds., *Gods in America: Religious Pluralism in the United States* (New York: Oxford University Press, 2013); Stephen Prothero, ed., *A Nation of Religions: The Politics of Pluralism in Multireligious America* (Chapel Hill: The University of North Carolina Press, 2006); Robert Wuthnow, *America and the Challenges of Religious Diversity* (Princeton, NJ: Princeton University Press, 2005).

[5] Alan Wolfe, *One Nation, After All* (New York: Penguin Books, 1998).

[6] Robert D. Putnam and David E. Campbell, *American Grace: How Religion Divides and Unites Us* (New York: Simon and Schuster, 2010), especially pp. 516–550.

[7] Ibid., 517. Putnam and Campbell ground their findings in the substantive significance of interreligious social contact, but that is not essential to the point here.

[8] In Putnam and Campbell's nationally representative survey, 54 percent of Evangelical adults said people from non-Christian faiths can go to Heaven (*American Grace*, 534–537). Likewise, see Pew's report, "Many Americans Say Other Faiths Can Lead to Eternal Life," *Pew Research Center*, December 18, 2008, http://www.pewforum.org/2008/12/18/many-americans-say-other-faiths-can-lead-to-eternal-life/, accessed January 30, 2016.

finding the synergy between the two that I haven't focused too much on the distinctions between them. Ultimately, my goal is to live a Christianity that any Buddhist would be willing to embrace and to live an understanding of Buddhism that any Christian can embrace." Here then is a Christian leader for whom religious pluralism in the form of exposure to Eastern spirituality has deeply influenced his approach to faith. This kind of inclusive pluralism and fluidity, too, although not always as pronounced as with this man, has *decreased consensus and destabilized the Evangelical field*.

The Triumph of the Therapeutic

The third piece of the cultural backdrop that has infused the Evangelical field is *"the triumph of the therapeutic" in American culture*.[9] Observed by social scientists since the 1960s, therapeuticism is a deeply rooted, rarely articulated cultural assumption in the United States which gives an answer to the fundamental questions: What am I here for? What is the purpose of life? Therapeuticism's answer, in brief, is that the right goal of each individual human life is ultimately to feel good about oneself, to have a good handle on one's life problems, and to make steps toward self-fulfillment. On this vision of life's purpose, whatever is "internal" and subjective takes precedent for guiding one's life over anything "external" or objective—like traditions, "organized religion," or any loci of authority other than oneself. "Being true to myself" is a nonnegotiable good, not to be questioned. On issues of truth and morality, feelings rule the day. In this context, "the traditional authority and functions of priests, pastors, parents, and lawmakers are largely displaced by a new authoritative class of professional and popular psychologists, psychiatrists, social workers, and other therapeutic counselors, authors, talk show hosts, and advice givers."[10] "Where once the self was to be surrendered,

---

[9] On America's therapeutic culture, see Timothy Aubry and Trysh Travis, eds., *Rethinking Therapeutic Culture* (Chicago: The University of Chicago Press, 2015); Robert N. Bellah, Richard Madsen, William M. Sullivan, Ann Swidler, and Steven M. Tipton, *Habits of the Heart: Individualism and Commitment in American Life*, 3rd ed. (Berkeley: University of California Press, [1985] 2008); Jonathan B. Imber, ed., *Therapeutic Culture: Triumph and Defeat* (New Brunswick, NJ: Transaction, 2004); Mike W. Martin, *From Morality to Mental Health: Virtue and Vice in a Therapeutic Culture* (New York: Oxford University Press, 2006); Philip Rieff, *The Triumph of the Therapeutic: Uses of Faith after Freud* (Chicago: The University of Chicago Press, [1966] 1987); Christian Smith with Melinda Lundquist Denton, *Soul Searching: The Religious and Spiritual Lives of American Teenagers* (New York: Oxford University Press, 2005).

[10] Smith with Denton, *Soul Searching*, 173. They also rightly emphasized that a tacit commitment to *autonomous individualism* is in many ways inseparable from the cultural ethos of therapeuticism.

denied, sacrificed, and died to, now the self is to be esteemed, actualized, affirmed, and unfettered."[11] Serious struggles, hardships, and tragedies in human life, when they come, get treated as objects of analysis to be overcome by a combination of inspiration, therapy, and good advice.

This therapeutic ethos has not just *displaced* religious leaders, however; as multiple studies of American religion have already observed, it has influenced many of those leaders and shaped their messages, oftentimes only subtly and incompletely.[12] In mainstream megachurches today, it is common to hear sermons on topics such as avoiding burnout, finding work-life balance, being a good parent, overcoming anxiety, being a better husband or wife, managing your finances, persevering through failure, having enough energy, trying something new, beating addiction, decreasing drama, resolving conflicts, making new friends, getting physically fit, dating, getting enough rest, challenging yourself, making good choices, letting God work in your life, finding hope for the future, controlling your impulses, battling discontentment, finding inner peace, dealing with disappointments, feeling significant, having meaning in life, being a hospitable neighbor, discovering your true identity, receiving favor and blessings, opening up opportunities, not getting bogged down by your past, changing your attitude, working through frustrations, overcoming insecurity, living in wholeness, or, of course, "whatever you're going through."[13] Often a keyboard played in the background on stage adds to the moment. While such a therapeutic tenor is at the center of much mainstream Evangelical preaching and book publishing (especially among megachurches), other Evangelical leaders (in the New Calvinism, for example) recognize this therapeutic impulse and resist it. In sum, to the extent this sort of therapeuticism is a dominant feature and assumption of several, but not all, Evangelical ministries, it further serves to accentuate difference and *decrease consensus in the religious field.*

---

[11] James Nolan, *The Therapeutic State: Justifying Government at Century's End* (New York: New York University Press, 1998), 3. Quoted in Smith with Denton, *Soul Searching*, 173.

[12] Todd M. Brenneman, *Homespun Gospel: The Triumph of Sentimentality in Contemporary American Evangelicalism* (New York: Oxford University Press, 2014); Kathleen E. Jenkins, *Sacred Divorce: Religion, Therapeutic Culture, and Ending Life Partnerships* (New Brunswick, NJ: Rutgers University Press, 2014); Joel James Shuman and Keith G. Meador, *Heal Thyself: Spirituality, Medicine, and the Distortion of Christianity* (New York: Oxford University Press, 2003); Marsha G. Witten, *All Is Forgiven: The Secular Message in American Protestantism* (Princeton, NJ: Princeton University Press, 1993).

[13] All of these were topics addressed in weekend sermons over a two-year span at one randomly selected mainstream American Evangelical megachurch.

Three Discursive Opportunities

As shown in chapter 2, the organizational "raw material" out of which the New Calvinist movement would eventually arise had already begun to foment as early as the 1980s (as with John Piper taking the helm at Bethlehem Baptist Church in 1980, for instance, or with the founding of the Council on Biblical Manhood and Womanhood in 1987). But for the more "mechanismic" and sociological explanation of the Reformed resurgence, the story begins in the mid-1990s with three major cultural developments that together set the stage for this new movement's emergence and strength. Starting at that time, *contingent events and developments external to the American Evangelical field facilitated new opportunities for Evangelical leaders to "speak into their field" and to make their interests heard.* As outlined in the previous chapter, these include (a) the invention and expansion of digital media, especially the Internet; (b) the coordinated terrorist attacks of September 11, 2001, and its cultural outworking; and (c) the felt pressure to reckon with postmodernist philosophy and postmodernity as a new, "emerging" cultural condition.

Novel objective conditions and circumstances, as opportunities, would have little practical effect on the field apart from actual people socially located to recognize and leverage those new conditions. Therefore, the aforementioned three macro-structural opportunities must be understood in conjunction with *Evangelical leaders rightly perceiving and taking advantage of those new discursive opportunities in order to make their beliefs, commitments, and interests more widely visible and attractive to others.* The following three subsections detail these causes, which further destabilized the field and sparked the onset of contention.[14]

The Internet as a Tool

The first essential part of the discursive opportunity structure that explains the New Calvinist movement is *the emergence and widespread use of the*

---

[14] If one wanted to follow the questionable trend of conceptualizing new forms of capital to fit into whichever field is under investigation (as has been done recently with "sexual capital" and "spiritual capital"), then complementarian Calvinism might be thought of as having *zeitgeist capital*. As a conservative and highly formalized early-modern religious worldview, it is uniquely suited to offer something distinctive in light of the current, relativistic, hypermodern "spirit of the age." In light of new discursive opportunities and aspects of the broader cultural backdrop infusing the field, the New Calvinism and its accompanying commitments may be considered "an idea whose time has come."

Internet and other digital media as a tool for religious practice and communication. It has become something of a banal observation to point out that the Internet and social media have made—and continue to make—a remarkable difference in innumerable ways for religion in the United States (not to mention other cultural and religious realities globally).[15] But the obviousness of this claim is itself likely a symptom of the degree to which the digital media revolution has come to dominate the daily lives of most Americans, especially younger ones. Stated differently, the indispensable role of the Internet in the story of the neo-Reformed movement is ironically both fairly "soft-hitting" and hugely important. Any sociological attempt to make sense of the New Calvinism in its broader social structural context would simply be incomplete without accounting for the significant communication and organizing capacities that the Internet has provided.

The significance of the Internet and social media in precipitating and facilitating the New Calvinism is evident in multiple ways. Personal websites and blogging platforms host innumerable conversations and comments on Christian ideas. Hours and hours of sermons, interviews, conference presentations, and other events are available for viewing at any time and free of charge on YouTube and Vimeo. Anything that can be condensed to 140 (and now 280) characters or less, including (importantly) links to other content located elsewhere on the Internet, is posted and circulated on Twitter. All sorts of Christian music—from classical hymns to indie-folk rock and Calvinist hip-hop—are available on Pandora and Spotify, with accompanying music videos also on YouTube and Vimeo. Large collections of lectures, music, podcasts, interviews, and sermons are downloadable en

---

[15] Among the literature on religion and the Internet, see Heidi A. Campbell, *Exploring Religious Community Online: We Are One in the Network* (New York: Peter Lang, 2005); Heidi A. Campbell, *When Religion Meets New Media* (New York: Routledge, 2010); Heidi A. Campbell, ed., *Digital Religion: Understanding Religious Practice in New Media Worlds* (New York: Routledge, 2013); Pauline Hope Cheong, Peter Fischer-Nielsen, Stefan Gelfgren, and Charles Ess, eds., *Digital Religion, Social Media, and Culture: Perspectives, Practices, and Futures* (New York: Peter Lang, 2012); Lorne L. Dawson and Douglas E. Cowan, eds., *Religion Online: Finding Faith on the Internet* (New York: Routledge, 2004); Morten T. Hojsgaard and Margit Warburg, eds., *Religion and Cyberspace* (New York: Routledge, 2005); Stewart M. Hoover, *Religion in the Media Age* (New York: Routledge, 2006); Stewart M. Hoover and Lynn Schofield Clark, eds., *Practicing Religion in the Age of the Media: Explorations in Media, Religion, and Culture* (New York: Columbia University Press, 2002); Robert Glenn Howard, *Digital Jesus: The Making of a New Christian Fundamentalist Community on the Internet* (New York: New York University Press, 2011); Rachel Wagner, *Godwired: Religion, Ritual, and Virtual Reality* (New York: Routledge, 2012). To the extent that the New Calvinism is moreover a religious *movement* in a broader strategic action field, see also, for example, Manuel Castells, *Networks of Outrage and Hope: Social Movements in the Internet Age* (Malden, MA: Polity Press, 2012); Jennifer Earl and Katrina Kimport, *Digitally Enabled Social Change: Activism in the Internet Age* (Cambridge, MA: The MIT Press, 2011).

masse onto one's iTunes library. Evangelical books—old and new—can be sifted through, previewed, and purchased with ease on Amazon. Facebook serves as a central gathering place, the city commons, for all of this. Through Facebook, much of one's social network exists in digital form and is accessible all at once. Similar to Twitter, Facebook provides a constant stream of updates and links from one's "weak ties" regarding anything about which the user is interested enough to connect with others.[16] Moreover, many churches constituting the New Calvinism have adopted a Facebook-like social media tool known as The City[17] for organizing and scheduling their own congregational lives. Churches, seminaries, and other organizations, of course, each have their own web homes. So do the most important leaders. The Internet ushers the New Calvinist movement along in other ways, too. John Piper, for example, has made nearly all of his many books downloadable free of cost on the Desiring God website. Some Calvinist churches, including Piper's Bethlehem Baptist Church, offer the option to simulcast a weekend service rather than attending in person. Major Calvinistic conferences, such as The Resurgence or The Gospel Coalition conferences, are viewable online via a live broadcast. And the various social media accounts featuring popular Calvinist leaders bring them into the digital lives of Internet users in a way that makes them "omnipresent" and free to operate apart from their own geographical areas and limitations.[18]

All of these various expressions of the Internet as a tool for religious strength might be categorized into three ways that it contributes to the New Calvinist movement: diffusion, cohesion, and presence. First, the Internet and social media facilitated the rise of the New Calvinist movement by providing an avenue for the *diffusion* of information, an expansive digital stream through which massive amounts of Calvinistic information could flow. Second, the Internet and especially social media helped to produce the New Calvinist movement by providing the platforms and spaces—like Facebook and blogs—for trans-local social *cohesion*. Of course, trans-local, cohesive communities centered on common interests and beliefs were possible prior to the Internet with the help of things like "snail mail," automobiles, and telephones. But it was far more difficult and far less efficient. The Internet

---

[16] Mark S. Granovetter, "The Strength of Weak Ties," *American Journal of Sociology* 78, no. 6 (1973): 1360–1380.

[17] http://www.onthecity.org/

[18] Clay Shirky, *Here Comes Everybody: The Power of Organizing without Organizations* (New York: The Penguin Press, 2008).

and digital media revolution were the technological catalyst that acceler-
ated modern-day conservative Calvinists initially in finding one another and
later in introducing other people to their worldview, whether across town or
across an ocean. Third, the Internet has precipitated the New Calvinism by
making it possible for it and its leaders to be *present*—even highly visible, if
one wanted—in the daily lives (online) of religious persons. This is not just
the first point, the diffusion of information, framed differently. In a very real
way, the Internet lets Calvinistic teachers and friends into the lives of a new
generation of Americans for whom what happens online is "an outsized reality."[19] If the New Calvinism as a religious phenomenon was going to coalesce at all and make headway institutionally into the religious landscape, it
needed to *be there*—online.

The New Calvinist movement is not the only expression of American
Evangelicalism to leverage the Internet and social media as tools for institutional strength. Mainstream, progressive Emergent, and neo-Anabaptist
Evangelical leaders and organizations have their websites, YouTube channels,
Twitter handles, and podcasts, too. The Internet and the powerful capacities it provides is not a causal factor *only for* a sociological explanation of
resurgent Calvinism, but it is an indispensable factor nevertheless. Moreover,
even if using the Internet as a tool is not a unique causal factor for the New
Calvinism, several interviewees (and especially the non-Calvinists observing
the New Calvinism from the outside) noted that the New Calvinism seems
to be uniquely *skilled at it*. Leaders within the movement, too, are well aware
of the strategic role of the Internet. Tim Challies, for example, has pointed it
out and written a book on the topic.[20] It is not a stretch to say that the New
Calvinism is at least as much an "online movement" as it is a flesh-and-blood
movement made up of buildings and pews, parking lots and conference halls.
In these ways, it is a distinctly twenty-first-century religious phenomenon.
It simply would not have emerged as it did without the Internet. In large
part created and sustained by new media, it is a movement only possible in a
world with the Internet. Stated differently, the Internet is a big part of the discursive opportunity structure that made the New Calvinism possible.

---

[19] Tim Keller stressed this to me in his interview.
[20] Tim Challies, "Where Did the New Calvinism Come from?" *challies.com*, August 29, 2012,
http://www.challies.com/articles/where-did-the-new-calvinism-come-from, accessed February
15, 2016; Tim Challies, *The Next Story: Life and Faith after the Digital Explosion* (Grand Rapids,
MI: Zondervan, 2011).

September 11, 2001

Some leaders of the New Calvinism have emphasized the ways *the terrorist attacks on 9/11* have contributed to the increasing prominence, popularity, and strength of Calvinism. For instance, Trevin Wax, who blogs for The Gospel Coalition, said while he doubts that many of the young people in the movement would explicitly point to 9/11 as a reason for their turn to Calvinism, he also thinks that 9/11 and its outworking over the decade to follow changed "the cultural air that we breathe" in a way that made Calvinism more attractive.[21] More specifically, he said, the events of 9/11 made "a wide segment of evangelicalism [begin] entertaining questions that didn't seem as pressing before." Wax suggested three ways.

First, he suggested, "September 11 forced 'the problem of evil' to the forefront of theological reflection." Before 9/11, Wax said, American society had an aversion to the words "evil" and "sin." But afterward, "terrorism brought the concept of 'evil' back from a purgatory of positive thinking and practical theology. Politicians started using the term again. Preachers began sermon series on the reality of evil and suffering." During that time, many young persons, including himself, "began working through questions related to God's sovereignty and human responsibility. The classic problem of evil ('If God is good and all-powerful, why does evil exist?') came roaring back as a topic of intense discussion." In his own mind, the standard response to that question based on the reality of human free will no longer seemed compelling. "Having witnessed the carnage of the terrorist attacks," he wrote, "I questioned whether free will was worth the trouble." Wax suggested that 9/11 raised the question of theodicy for a new generation of Americans.

Second, "September 11 created an environment in which the easy answers of pop evangelicalism were no longer satisfying." Wax recalled some of the ways Evangelical adults in the United States responded to the evil and suffering unveiled on 9/11: mostly a combination of kitschy "God moments" circulated around email inboxes and sentimentalized answers regarding "God being present" in all the heroic acts of that day, in the firefighters who lost their lives, in the rescue workers treating people on the scene, and in the volunteers who spent days trying to rescue people from the rubble. But

---

[21] Trevin Wax, "September 11 and the Rise of New Calvinism," *The Gospel Coalition*, September 6, 2011, http://blogs.thegospelcoalition.org/trevinwax/2011/09/06/september-11-and-the-rise-of-new-calvinism/, accessed February 15, 2016.

these responses, Wax explained, skirted around the real issues and appeared increasingly inadequate. "The vision of God put forth by many evangelicals was that of a doting grandfather who arrived too late to stop the tragedy, but in time to help us put the pieces back together again," Wax argued.

Third, "the post 9/11 culture was ripe for a generation of young people to dig into the Bible for answers to some of life's most perplexing questions." In reaction to the typical, sentimental Evangelical responses to evil and human suffering, "many younger evangelicals," Wax argued, "started questioning things we had always assumed. Many of us started digging deep. We wanted answers. And Reformed theology didn't shy away from the hard questions." As an anecdote, Wax recalled when his brother returned from the war in Iraq, his brother told about seeing his fellow soldiers reading books by men like John Piper and R. C. Sproul. "Reformed theology gave a younger generation a vision of a God who is big enough to have unknown reasons for allowing evil acts to take place *and* big enough to defeat evil for good. The doctrine of God's sovereignty wasn't about scoring debate points with theological nerds, but a haven of rest and assurance in the midst of turbulent times." For some, Calvinist theology scratched the cultural itch.

On the fifteenth anniversary of 9/11, Owen Strachan similarly reflected on how that day opened up an opportunity for conservative Evangelicals to speak anew with a powerful and compelling voice to religious and moral issues. He called 9/11 "the day postmodernism died," by which he meant that many ordinary Americans suddenly came to see that in the end they did not live in a world where good and evil, right and wrong, were merely personally and culturally relative. Instead, pressing questions about justice, morality, evil, truth, and even virtue and heroism were forced back into the conversation. Strachan then explained how Evangelicals can speak into the gap created by 9/11:

We can do several things. Grieve the dead. Honor the virtuous. Pray for justice and the end of a war against terrorism that continues today. (This is truly the long war.) But we can also step into the gap, a gap created by 9/11, and speak of absolute truth, and ultimate reality, and the Christ whose very existence underwrites pure goodness, and whose personal death defeated evil, once and for all.[22]

---

[22] https://www.facebook.com/ostrachan/posts/906637334397, accessed September 12, 2016.

The connection between 9/11 and the New Calvinism is evident most directly in the impact it had on Redeemer Presbyterian Church in Manhattan. Just before 9/11, about 2,900 persons attended Redeemer. The Sunday after the terrorist attacks, 5,700 persons showed up. At its Upper East Side congregation at Hunter College, Redeemer staff were so overwhelmed with the unexpected crowds that Tim Keller announced spontaneously that he would hold a second service for anyone who came back in two hours. About 800 people returned. Of course, churches all across New York City (and the nation) saw an uptick in attendance in the weeks following 9/11. But, Keller said, "Every other church I know—because I checked it out—over about another month, slowly the numbers went down to where they were before." Attendance at Redeemer never went back under 3,700 people.[23] For the next five years, Keller said, whenever he asked congregants when they started coming to Redeemer, their response more often than not was, "right after 9/11."[24]

It is difficult to determine empirically if, and how precisely, September 11th and its cultural out-workings may have contributed to the rise of the New Calvinism. The philosophical and ethical puzzles that 9/11 brought to the fore certainly did not lead large swaths of Americans, or even the majority of American Evangelicals, to Calvinism. One need only consider that the years immediately following 9/11 also dawned the rise among American Evangelicals of open theism, Joel Osteen, and the Emergent Church. Even so, 9/11 and the existential questions it rose, perhaps especially for younger people, constituted a significant "exogenous shock" to the discursive opportunity structure for American religion, a shock that Calvinist leaders could speak into.[25] As Wax concluded: "It's interesting to note that in the 1990s, there was a Reformed rumbling. But only after September 11 was there a Reformed resurgence."

[23] Bachelder, "God Isn't Dead in Gotham."
[24] Luo, "Preaching the Word and Quoting the Voice."
[25] Nancy Foner, ed., *Wounded City: The Social Impact of 9/11* (New York: Russell Sage Foundation, 2005); Tom Pyszczynski, Sheldon Solomon, and Jeff Greenberg, *In the Wake of 9/11: The Psychology of Terror* (Washington, DC: American Psychological Association, 2003).

Postmodernism and the Emerging Church

The third and final part of the discursive opportunity structure that sparked the New Calvinist movement was *the increasing felt pressure to reckon with postmodernist philosophy and postmodernity as a new cultural condition.* Among Evangelical leaders in the United States (along with leaders in the United Kingdom, Australia, and New Zealand), this felt pressure worked itself out primarily in the context of the Emerging Church conversation.[26] Chapter 3 briefly addressed the Emerging Church as the popular, multifaceted "conversation"—which occurred largely online and in book form—among (mostly white and male) Evangelical leaders as they wrestled together with the "paradigm shift" from modernity to postmodernity. Those details need not be repeated here. The important thing to notice, in the context of thinking about discursive opportunities, is that Evangelicals' attention to and serious engagement with postmodernism/-ity in the form of the Emerging Church conversation also produced the cultural moment out of which the New Calvinism could coalesce as a more conservative, less accommodative alternative. Simply put, the New Calvinism arose largely as a conservative reaction to the Emerging Church, and especially in reaction against the progressive Emergent stream of the conversation.[27]

This is evidenced most clearly in the way Collin Hansen has talked and written about the main impetus for first writing about the New Calvinism as a young journalist, fresh out of college, working at *Christianity Today*. In all three of his major statements on the phenomenon—his 2006 cover story for *Christianity Today*, his 2008 book with Crossway, and a retrospective interview in 2013 with Desiring God—Hansen framed and justified his focus on the resurgence of Calvinistic theology as providing a needed counterbalance to widespread journalistic attention, particularly among American Evangelical publishers, to the Emerging Church. The fervor at the time about all things "emerging" and "postmodern," he explained, just did not resonate with his experiences "on the ground" as a young Evangelical in college and what he and his friends in Campus Crusade for Christ at Northwestern

---

[26] See Bielo, *Emerging Evangelicals*; Marti and Ganiel, *The Deconstructed Church*; Packard, *The Emerging Church*.

[27] Although not the same thing as the New Calvinists, see the chapter on Christian "Resisters" to postmodernism and the Emerging Church in Richard Flory and Donald E. Miller, *Finding Faith: The Spiritual Quest of the Post-Boomer Generation* (New Brunswick, NJ: Rutgers University Press, 2008), 84–123.

University were actually interested in and influenced by. During the 2013 interview with Desiring God, Hansen reflected on these matters:

> The origins [of my observations about the New Calvinism] had to do with a lot of things that were swirling in the air in the early to mid-2000s, which was a time that was shortly after I had graduated from college. So I was very much thinking about trends among younger believers, very much against [the backdrop of] my experience of going to a private non-Christian university, outside of Chicago. What I was thinking was, you know, I keep hearing about all these books and all these conferences and all these speakers in this "Emergent" phenomenon. People were talking about Brian McLaren, Tony Jones, Doug Pagitt, people like that. And this was part of what we were always talking about at *Christianity Today*: What does this mean, sort of, re-envisioning Christian theology for a postmodern era and reaching young people who were not persuaded by the old methods and the old theories and the old way of doing church. The problem for me, though, is when I kept hearing about all these trends in the air, I just thought, this doesn't resonate with my experience as a young Christian; this doesn't resonate with the experience of my friends who are young Christians. These were people who were excited when [Christian Book Distributors] would put a big sale on John Calvin's entire commentaries on the Bible, or Charles Spurgeon's sermons, or they were looking forward to George Marsden publishing his biography of Jonathan Edwards,[28] or they were listening to John Piper at Passion Conferences and reading [Piper's signature book] *Desiring God*,[29] and all of that. So, it just didn't add up for me. [. . .] It seemed to me that, and so I wanted to investigate as a journalist if] instead of people wanting to reshape and re-envision and re-imagine Christian theology for a postmodern era, that they would actually want to reinvigorate an Evangelical belief on the authority of Scripture in continuity with the history of Christian thought from the Reformation, well, and before the Reformation, on.

The New Calvinism, therefore, can be understood as both a reaction against and an alternative to the Emerging Church, and especially the progressive

---

[28] George M. Marsden, *Jonathan Edwards: A Life* (New Haven, CT: Yale University Press, 2003).

[29] John Piper, *Desiring God: Meditations of a Christian Hedonist*, revised edition (Colorado Springs, CO: Multnomah Books, 2011 [1986]).

Emergent pocket of the Emerging Church. In this way, "all this talk" after the turn of the millennium among American Evangelical leaders and journalists about postmodernism, postmodernity, and the Emerging Church as a "new conversation" provided a clear discursive opportunity for Calvinists to speak into the field with a different, more conservative theological voice.

The Onset of Contention, 1997–2007

The social and cultural developments described to this point together created "the perfect storm" for the New Calvinist movement to emerge. The first set of factors—the sexual and gender revolutions, religious pluralism and inclusivism, and therapeuticism—infused the American Evangelical field, decreased consensus, and functioned as destabilizing changes. The second set of factors—the Internet, social media, blogging, September 11th, (increased Evangelical attention to) postmodernism, and the Emerging Church—opened up the discursive opportunity structure for conservative, complementarian, Calvinist leaders to speak into their field in new ways.[30] But the New Calvinism did not just arise as a religious phenomenon and then stay put, enjoying its newfound recognition as one among multiple plausible expressions of Christianity in the United States. The reality is far more dynamic. Instead, the birth of the Reformed resurgence (in 2006) itself sparked an episode of contention in the field of American Evangelicalism—a series of Evangelical infighting that, as we will learn, unintentionally strengthened and fortified the New Calvinism. Previous pages have already noted the importance of *religious leaders rightly perceiving these macro-structural developments as opportunities to make their religious interests more widely visible and attractive to others.* On the other side, *leaders in the field, both incumbents and challengers, interpreted various aspects of this destabilizing turbulence as serious threats to the realization of those same religious interests.*

In the language of strategic action field theory, the aforementioned factors precipitated an (ongoing) episode of contention in and over the field of American Evangelicalism, during which competing religious tribes and camps (the New Calvinism plus those detailed in chapter 3) jockey or vie for an improved, more advantageous position in their field. *This*, more than

---

[30] The line between these two sets of factors is blurry analytically. The Emerging Church, for example, could be considered both a destabilizing change and a new discursive opportunity.

any linear or additive growth of Calvinism, is the sociological substance of the Reformed resurgence. All the factors listed earlier served as destabilizing changes to the religious field (mainly as "exogenous shocks" from the broader structural and cultural environment), which disrupted the established, standard mode of operation. Evangelical leaders in each of the major pockets and expressions of Evangelicalism perceived those same features variously as either threats to or opportunities for the advancement of their (symbolic or ideological) interests.[31] The evaluations were different depending on the tribe. For instance, the New Calvinists (as a conservative, incumbent influence in the Evangelical field) interpreted the infusion into their field of the sexual and gender revolutions, religious pluralism and inclusivism, therapeuticism, postmodernism, and the embodiment of several of these values in the (progressive stream of the) Emerging Church as *threats to the established "orthodoxy" (status quo) of the field.*[32] The Internet, social media, and 9/11, in contrast, were not seen as threats but as new discursive opportunities for speaking into their field.

For the progressive Emergent leaders, in contrast, the values of the sexual and gender revolutions, pluralism and inclusivism, and postmodernism were viewed as *new opportunities to advance a new, alternative vision of the field, whereas it was precisely the conservative reaction—including the strong reaction of New Calvinists—that was perceived as threatening.* (As for therapeuticism, some progressive and neo-Anabaptist leaders, along with the New Calvinists, have been critical of the therapeutic and sentimental bent of mainstream megachurch Evangelicalism.[33]) As Fligstein and McAdam's strategic action field framework tells us to expect, these collective attributions of various threats to and opportunities for the realization of group interests and beliefs corresponded in time with the establishment of new organizations. The clearest examples for the New Calvinism include the founding of Together for the Gospel in 2006 and The Gospel Coalition in 2007, at the height of the Emerging Church.

Fligstein and McAdam draw a distinction between the "onset of contention" in a social field and an "episode of contention," which is needed here. The former precedes the latter, both analytically and temporally. In this case, the onset of the present battle over American Evangelicalism stems

---

[31] On symbolic interests as opposed to material interests, see Swartz, *Culture and Power*, 66–73.

[32] See Ryan P. Burge and Paul A. Djupe, "An Emergent Threat: Christian Clergy Perceptions of the Emerging Church Movement," *Journal for the Scientific Study of Religion* 56, no. 1 (2017): 26–32.

[33] For example Fitch, *The Great Giveaway*, 181–200.

from the development and infusion into the field of the factors described earlier, as destabilizing pressures and "turbulence." Among those factors, therapeuticism, postmodernism (in academia, at least), and the sexual and gender revolutions stretch back to the 1960s. But it was only during the mid- to late 1990s that American Evangelical leaders started publicly interacting with (e.g., publishing books about) postmodernism/-ity and when the Internet became a viable tool for Evangelical organizations. And it was only after the turn of the new millennium that we saw 9/11, the Emerging Church as a widely recognized conversation, and popular Evangelical leaders reconsidering their views on same-sex marriage and sexuality. (John Shore gets the timing right when he writes of himself on the "about" section of his website, "When, in 2007, John began using the platform of his blog to advocate for the full and equal acceptance of LGBT people within Christianity, no other Christian blogger, 'progressive,' 'emergent,' or otherwise . . . would step up and help him fight for the cause of LGBT equality.") So, while recognizing that in many ways these precipitating factors reach back to the 1960s,[34] we can say roughly that the *onset of contention* spanned from 1997 to 2007. It is only within this somewhat longer time horizon and institutional context that the current *episode of contention* can fully make sense.[35]

Positions and Dispositions

Why are there such divergent visions among leaders in the current Evangelical field about which principles, beliefs, and values they should hold (and teach to their followers), and which ought to be rejected? Why the differing pictures of what Christianity even is and the grand story about humans and the world it tells? Why have so many leaders landed in such different places on the ideological "map" on nearly every issue imaginable, not only on arguably peripheral issues like whether or not infants should be baptized or the nature of the end-times millennium, but also on more fundamental questions about what salvation is, how it happens, what God is like, and what it looks like for human persons to live morally good lives?[36]

---

[34] See Richard Lints, *Progressive and Conservative Religious Ideologies: The Tumultuous Decade of the 1960s* (Burlington, VT: Ashgate, 2010).

[35] Fligstein and McAdam, *A Theory of Fields*, 18–22.

[36] For a catalogue of such un-agreed-upon issues, see, for example, Gregory A. Boyd and Paul R. Eddy, *Across the Spectrum: Understanding Issues in Evangelical Theology*, 2nd ed. (Grand Rapids, MI: Baker Academic, [2002] 2009).

To address those questions, the analysis hits pause on viewing social fields foremost as fields of contestation and infighting (as Fligstein and McAdam's framework does), and instead considers the other main dimension of sociological field theory—namely, fields as meso-level orders constituted by patterned forces which generate in field actors differing dispositional senses of what it is they should do, and of what they perceive as *attractive* or *repulsive*. Whether it is Calvinism, gender complementarianism, female pastors, the death penalty, free market capitalism, penal substitutionary atonement, gay and lesbian relationships, Hell as eternal conscious torment, the legalization of gay marriage, the role of the therapeutic, how best to serve the poor, or any number of other issues, we have already observed that Evangelical leaders in the United States are "all over the map." The suggestion in this section is that for American Evangelical leaders, their positions in the field correspond with their dispositions. As part of the model developed in the previous chapter, the social causal mechanism here is that *differing personalities, starting points, and dispositions among Evangelical leaders generate and reinforce heterogeneous positions and interests within their field.*[37]

First, we should get some clarity about positions. There are two main approaches to conceptualizing positions in any social field, including American Evangelicalism. The first focuses on objective or analytic positions in the particular field—such as dominant/dominated or incumbent/challenger, and the actors who occupy those positions (at any given time). Which field actors—as "players" in the game—are in dominant or dominated positions is structured by their relative possession of various forms

---

[37] The relation between this dispositional dimension of field theory and causal mechanisms is a debated subject among some social theorists, and I believe I can shed some light on it. The social causal mechanism described in the main text is a general field process that operates at the field level, but one might wonder how that actually works one level "deeper." How, exactly, do dispositional impulses develop in or inscribe upon human actors? And how do those dispositional impulses guide human actions? Some field theorists, I have gathered, find field theory useful precisely because they think this process—the "field effect"—doesn't involve any causal mechanisms. However, if causal mechanisms in social life are understood in a right, nonmechan*istic* way, then that turns out to be mistaken. The first step in recasting the field effect in terms of social causal mechanisms is to accept a basic insight from Gestalt psychology about how humans perceive and physically navigate through the world; this is the observation that things (objects, experiences, etc.) possess real "affordances" or "valences" that "call out" to actors, suggesting to them what they should do. Once that idea is understood, the field effect is easily translatable into two causal mechanisms working in conjunction, namely: (1) *cognitively light internalization*: persons become socialized from early in life based on their particular "conditions of existence" and life trajectories, but what is internalized is not "cognitively heavy" information but mostly cognitively light (often embodied and prediscursive) competences and habits. In short, a habitus develops; and (2) *making a virtue of necessity*: persons will tend to prefer and pursue things they already have the skills or competences to acquire and enjoy in the first place.

of power-infused resources (i.e., economic capital, social capital, cultural capital, symbolic capital, etc.). The second approach, which usually can be mapped back onto the first, focuses on the substantive positions on specific issues that matter in the field in question. In this case, examples would include an organization's or a leader's position on soteriology, or position on the miraculous gifts of the Holy Spirit, or position on gender issues.[38] ("Positions *in*" versus "positions *on*" might be a helpful way to keep this distinction clear in one's own mind.) The four main expressions of American Evangelicalism (i.e., the New Calvinist movement, mainstream, neo-Anabaptist, and progressive Emergent) each occupy different objective positions *in* their field as well as hold differing positions *on* very many issues, topics, and questions that matter to actors who are invested in the field.

The substantive positions of these four pockets have already been described at length in chapters 2 and 3 and need not be repeated here. One possible way to summarize those substantive positions is by employing the familiar conservative-liberal or right-left ideological continuum. Such a summary might seem somewhat forced. As Smith and his colleagues suggested, "Rather than conceptualizing religious positions as values on a continuous variable (for example, church-sect, conservative-liberal), we think it is more accurate and fruitful to conceptualize religious positions as categorical variables, whose 'values' reflect distinct qualities not reducible to placement on a single scale."[39] But for a first blush, it is helpful to see that the New Calvinism is holding the conservative pole on practically every issue in American Evangelicalism, short of slipping into a reactionary, narrow fundamentalism. Mainstream Evangelicalism, in the aggregate, is slightly less conservative than the New Calvinism. The neo-Anabaptists, who are nearly across-the-board pacifists and gender egalitarians (and considering their frequent critique of "Empire" and capitalism), are "to the left" of both New Calvinism and mainstream Evangelicalism.[40] And progressive Emergent Evangelicalism lands on the "far left" end of the spectrum of Evangelicalism on theological, moral, and social issues.[41]

---

[38] This is the distinction in field theory between (objective or analytic) positions and (subjective, or better, substantive) "position-takings"—although I opt not to take up that language here.

[39] Smith et al., *American Evangelicalism*, 153n10.

[40] Markofski, *New Monasticism*.

[41] Ironically, Pew classifies "Emergent Church" ideologically as part of the mainline (liberal) Protestant tradition. See "Appendix B: Classification of Protestant Denominations," in Pew's report, *America's Changing Religious Landscape*, released online May 12, 2015, pp. 107–108.

The tribes' substantive positions *on* issues and questions that matter in their field map onto each tribe's standing *in* the field, as incumbents (dominant) or challengers (the dominated). Mainstream American Evangelicalism, perhaps especially megachurch Evangelicalism, almost by definition, is incumbent and dominant in its field. The New Calvinist movement, given its "newness" (the category did not exist prior to 2006) and its relatively circumscribed institutional scope, might at first seem to be an up-and-coming challenger in the Evangelical field. But it is not. Despite only being one "corner" of American Evangelicalism, the New Calvinism's celebrity star-power, publishing and media prowess, and (especially) its conservative positioning in relation to the mainstream of its field put it decisively in a dominant and incumbent position. When New Calvinist leaders act In and on the Evangelical field, as we will see in the next chapter, it is always to *conserve* the established vision of field orthodoxy and the "rules of the game"— never to revise them. The New Calvinists, therefore, are in an incumbent position. In contrast, neo-Anabaptist and progressive Emergent Evangelical leaders stand in a less privileged, challenger position in the field. In particular, they are trying to advance a new, alternative vision of their field while also possessing relatively less social and economic capital.[42]

For however much hard work and thought goes into piecing together and honing one's religious positions (which for American Evangelical leaders, compared with the ordinary American layperson, is off the charts), we also know from cognitive psychology (and related disciplines interested in human cognition) that the majority of what people choose is guided not by reflexive, deliberative thought but hums along at a "deeper" level of prediscursive habits, intuitions, and dispositions.[43] What about that? Are Evangelical

---

[42] Markofski, *New Monasticism*, 81–87, offers a more detailed breakdown of dominant and dominated positions in the contemporary American Evangelical field using somewhat different categories than I do throughout this work. Unfortunately, his analysis does not include the New Calvinism at all.

[43] Among a large literature, see, for example, Charles Camic, "The Matter of Habit," *American Journal of Sociology* 91, no. 5 (1986): 1039–1087; Roy G. D'Andrade, *The Development of Cognitive Anthropology* (Cambridge: Cambridge University Press, 1995); Jonathan St. B. T. Evans, "Dual-Processing Accounts of Reasoning, Judgment, and Social Cognition," *Annual Review of Psychology* 59 (2008): 255–278; Malcolm Gladwell, *Blink: The Power of Thinking Without Thinking* (New York: Little, Brown and Company, 2005); Jonathan Haidt, "The Emotional Dog and Its Rational Tail: A Social Intuitionist Approach to Moral Judgment," *Psychological Review* 108, no. 4 (2001): 814–834; Jonathan Haidt, *The Righteous Mind: Why Good People Are Divided by Politics and Religion* (New York: Pantheon Books, 2012); Daniel Kahneman, *Thinking, Fast and Slow* (New York: Farrar, Straus and Giroux, 2011); Norbert Schwarz, "Warmer and More Social: Recent Developments in Cognitive Social Psychology," *Annual Review of Sociology* 24 (1998): 239–264; Stephen Vaisey, "Motivation and Justification: A Dual-Process Model of Culture in Action," *American Journal of Sociology* 114, no. 6 (2009): 1675–1715. Incidentally, acknowledging the powerful formative effects of what is habitual and latent is also *Augustinian*.

leaders' beliefs and commitments, or even their careful interpretations of what the Bible says, subconsciously guided and formed by their own underlying, tacit dispositions? It seems so. The differing positions that leaders hold on all sorts of issues in the Evangelical field, I suggest, can be roughly mapped onto just a few, deep, almost always unspoken dispositions for how they approach their faith. Heuristically, we can call this their "first foot forward in their Christian walk." With this phrase, I want to capture the fact that, as with walking, one's "first foot forward" is not the *only* thing involved, but it is still the *dominant* thing. It is what one *leads with*, even if only subconsciously. In the rest of this section, I suggest four basic, dominant dispositions—one for each of the four tribes or expressions of American Evangelicalism today. Obviously, just as the tribes themselves are not clear-cut and uniform, the dispositions undergirding each of them is not a catch-all principle for every leader in each tribe. There are exceptions. Nevertheless, on average, it taps into tendencies that are real and analytically illuminating. As something less than a "rock-solid" case but more than just a tentative proposal, I suggest that the following four basic dispositions correspond to the four major positions today in the American Evangelical field.

For New Calvinist leaders, their first foot forward tends to be *ontology*. Their basic disposition toward their faith and moral and theological issues tends to be centrally concerned with the nature, structure, and order of what is real. What *is* comes first, and what and how humans can know about what is, though still key questions, come somewhere down the line. This disposition is evidenced, for example, in New Calvinists' ease of talking about things like the character of God, the existence of Heaven and Hell as literal realities, the essential nature of masculinity and femininity, objective moral truths built into the fabric of reality (and themselves grounded in the character of God), as well as being born-again (regeneration) and imputed righteousness both as very real, ontological changes in a person when they become a Christian. For New Calvinists, what and how humans can know (*epistemology*), what is morally right and wrong or good and bad (*ethics*), and how they should make their way through the world (*pragmatics*) all flow from the order and nature of reality itself (*ontology*)—their views of which they have interpreted from the Bible.[44] New Calvinists are not the only Evangelical leaders who believe these things or make claims about these things—but

---

[44] See, for example, D. A. Carson, *The God Who Is There: Finding Your Place in God's Story* (Grand Rapids, MI: Baker Books, 2010).

especially when compared to the other three main expressions of American Evangelicalism today, putting ontology first sets them apart.

For progressive Emergent leaders, in contrast, their first foot forward tends to be concerns regarding *epistemology*—the limits, means, and possibilities of what and how humans can know. In effect, for every truth claim about the deep nature and order of reality made by the New Calvinists, the progressive Emergent question inevitably comes forth, "But how can you be so sure?" Instead of viewing the 2,000-year Christian tradition as something to be *received* or *conserved*, Emergent Evangelical leaders interpret it as something to be *progressed* in new and creative directions. Answers, certainty, and "positions" go out the window; questions, uncertainty, skepticism, doubt, possibilities, and creative reinvention are instead held up as intellectual and spiritual virtues. Peter Rollins's persistent invitation in multiple books, lectures, and videos for people to embrace unknowing, doubt, and ambiguity is perhaps the clearest example.[45] "Old" Christianity is "deconstructed" and "a new kind of Christianity" is constructed and fervently promoted as where Christianity needs to go.[46]

Every progressive Emergent leader I interviewed chose, without any leading on my end, to frame his or her personal faith journey in terms of reacting against or questioning and eventually growing beyond early-life encounters with conservative and often fundamentalist Protestantism. Doug Pagitt, for example, shared with me his experience growing up in a poor, intentionally irreligious household entirely cut off from all forms of religion, and encountering Christianity for the first time as a junior in high school. Backstage after a Passion play, someone went through a Gospel tract with him and right away he had a visceral, negative reaction: "I started internally arguing with that presentation of Christianity my first five minutes into the faith. And I now know it was all this Calvinist shit—and not just Calvinists, I mean, really deeply Augustinian, frankly. So it's just been a long process of trying to unravel the Christianity I was introduced to."

Unlike Pagitt's secular upbringing and brief encounter with conservative faith, most of the progressive leaders I interviewed were themselves raised in conservative or fundamentalist Christian homes.[47] In those cases, their faith

---

[45] Peter Rollins, *The Fidelity of Betrayal: Towards a Church beyond Belief* (Brewster, MA: Paraclete Press, 2008); Peter Rollins, *Insurrection: To Believe Is Human, To Doubt, Divine* (New York: Howard Books, 2011); Peter Rollins, *The Idolatry of God: Breaking Our Addiction to Certainty and Satisfaction* (New York: Howard Books, 2012).

[46] Marti and Ganiel, *The Deconstructed Church*; McLaren, *A New Kind of Christianity*; Pagitt, *A Christianity Worth Believing*; Tickle, *The Great Emergence*.

[47] One prominent example is Rachel Held Evans, *Faith Unraveled*.

journeys were even more of a personal, oftentimes painful, epistemological journey of questioning and "unlearning" conservative Protestantism. As progressive leader Tony Jones told me, the progressive tribe is full of "a lot of people who are wounded by Evangelicalism."[48] Some of the more intriguing examples of the epistemic disposition come from current leaders who are the grown children of previous generations of nationally recognized conservative Evangelical leaders. For instance, I interviewed both Jay Bakker and Frank Schaeffer. Jay, the pastor of a small church in Minneapolis, is the son of 1980s televangelists Jim and Tammy Faye Bakker, who hosted *The PTL Club* television program (PTL is "Praise the Lord") until a sex scandal and revelations of accounting fraud led to divorce and Jim's imprisonment. Jay has since written about his religious doubts and process of searching that led him to a more progressive, inclusive faith.[49] Similarly, Frank, who writes literary nonfiction and blogs for the "progressive Christian channel" on Patheos, is the son of Francis Schaeffer, the late conservative Presbyterian theologian, philosopher, and writer. While there was no scandal in the manner of the Bakker family, Frank's faith, too, has evolved and changed over the years and now is guided by what he calls "a theology of unknowing." No longer considering himself an Evangelical, Frank's religious life has been a process of doubting and questioning the epistemic grounding of the conservative faith of his upbringing.[50]

In contrast to both the New Calvinists and progressive Emergents, American neo-Anabaptist leaders' "first foot forward" tends to be *ethics*— that is, a primary concern, even if only tacitly, for what is good and bad, just and unjust, and how they ought to live as Christians in the world. The root question for them is not about ontology or epistemology but instead is,

[48] For his part, Jones emphasized the role of postmodern epistemology in the development of his progressive faith. He told me that while working on his M.Div. at Fuller he was shaped by Nancey Murphy's work on postmodernism and religion. Jones realized Christianity could be recast in a postfoundationalist (instead of modernist) epistemology and called this realization his own "conversion experience." Murphy, Jones said, "was the most influential on me. And she was teaching kind of like an Anglo-American version of postmodern philosophy, and I just had this like complete epiphany and awakening that Christianity could somehow live and thrive in a non-foundationalist epistemology. Like, that was my conversion experience in seminary. I came into my own intellectually." See Nancey Murphy, *Beyond Liberalism and Fundamentalism: How Modern and Postmodern Philosophy Set the Theological Agenda* (Harrisburg, PA: Trinity Press International, 1996); Nancey Murphy, *Anglo-American Postmodernity: Philosophical Perspectives on Science, Religion, and Ethics* (Boulder, CO: Westview Press, 1997).

[49] See Jay Bakker with Linden Gross, *Son of a Preacher Man: My Search for Grace in the Shadows* (New York: HarperCollins, 2001); Jay Bakker with Andy Meisenheimer, *Faith, Doubt, and Other Lines I've Crossed: Walking with the Unknown God* (New York: Jericho Books, 2013).

[50] Frank Schaeffer, *Crazy for God: How I Grew Up as One of the Elect, Helped Found the Religious Right, and Lived to Take All (or Almost All) of It Back* (Cambridge, MA: Da Capo Press, 2007).

"How does Jesus want us to live?" While by no means neglecting theology, theology for neo-Anabaptists is viewed ultimately as in the service of being a faithful follower of Christ and demonstrating this with one's life. In this sense, neo-Anabaptists' dispositional priority of ethics is about being a good, faithful *disciple* and *representative* of Christ. Being Christ-like (gentle, pacifistic, meek, loving, humble, etc.) is of central importance. Also valued are commitments to nonviolence, social justice, gender equality, welcoming "the stranger," community development, racial reconciliation, loving one's neighbor, "simple living," service to the poor, resisting "Empire" and militarism, living in community, "speaking truth to power," caring for the natural environment, eschewing entanglements with political power, critiquing consumerism and excess, identifying with society's marginalized and oppressed, and so on. All of this comes *first*, as essential to what it means to be Christ-like in the modern world. As Shane Claiborne often states, it is about "preaching a good sermon with our lives." Claiborne evinced this primary disposition of ethics again in our interview, where he posited: "They're not going to know that we're Christians by our doctrinal statements; they're going to know that we're Christians by our love. [. . .] The problem is that a lot of Evangelicals, especially in the past 30 years, we've had a lot to say with our mouths but very little to show of God's love with our lives."

Finally, the "first foot forward" for mainstream American Evangelical leaders is often *pragmatism*—that is, a basic disposition favoring solutions that work to problems that matter. By this I mean a tacit prioritization of application, practicality, and results over the specific principles, assumptions, or messages that one communicates in order to get there. The ends justify the means.[51] This tendency ranges from borderline deceptive methods of evangelism ("Do you have time to fill out this short survey about student life on campus?") to the topics addressed in sermons (which itself is inseparable from the "triumph of the therapeutic"). Mainstream Evangelical "seeker-sensitive" churches can be thought of as a combination of therapeuticism with pragmatism. The pragmatic disposition can be found strongly in much

---

[51] Some Calvinistic leaders have critiqued this pragmatic disposition in the mainstream of American Evangelicalism. See, for example, Travis Allen, "You Might Be a Pragmatist," *Grace to You*, October 17, 2011, http://www.gty.org/blog/B111017/you-might-be-a-pragmatist, accessed February 12, 2016; Andy Johnson, "Pragmatism, Pragmatism Everywhere!" *9Marks*, February 26, 2010, http://9marks.org/article/pragmatism-pragmatism-everywhere/, accessed February 12, 2016; Jonathan Leeman, "Long-Term Consequences of Pragmatism in the Church," *9Marks*, August 22, 2014, http://9marks.org/article/long-term-consequences-of-pragmatism-in-the-church/, accessed February 12, 2016.

of the published literature on church growth, as suggested by titles from Evangelical presses (despite whatever wise advice they may include) such as *Effective Church Growth Strategies; How to Spark Immediate Growth in Your Church; Five Keys to Building a Small Group Culture;* and *Seven Practices of Effective Ministry.* Even more clearly, this pragmatic disposition of mainstream, and especially megachurch, Evangelicalism is seen in pastoral and devotional books with titles and subtitles such as *How to Get from Where You Are to Where You Want to Be; Cure for the Common Life; How to Survive and Thrive When Opportunity Roars; Seven Steps to Living at Your Full Potential; Two Words That Will Change Your Life Today; Forty Days to a Healthier Life; Living Your Promised Land Life Now; Eight Undeniable Qualities of a Winner; Becoming God's Best Version of You; Leaving Behind Behaviors and Dependencies That Hold You Back; The Life You've Always Wanted;* and so on. The general ethos of these actual book titles, I am suggesting, is also the basic, tacit disposition of much of mainstream American Evangelical proselytizing, preaching, and publishing, and perhaps especially among mainstream megachurches.[52]

[52] When I asked Frank Schaeffer why he thought some Evangelical megachurch pastors have such a massive following, he responded by de-emphasizing any religious element and emphasizing it as a general phenomenon of mainstream culture, while also giving one of the more impressive monologues in my interview data: "America is a market-oriented society and we live in an entertainment culture of spectacle, and they provide a good spectacle. Plus, we're in a culture of lonely individuals who are looking for community, and so even if the price of that community is a harsh, top-down directive, empire-building, grand-standing, whatever—[the mistake is] to break religion out as if it's a separate subject from American culture. That's like asking why does Beyoncé have a following on Twitter, or why do people care about Jack Nicholson going to rehab. It's all one culture. So, you have celebrity figures within the Evangelical world who have a good delivery, or through a series of circumstances got placed in a position of leadership. It's like saying, why are some people rock gods and other people never got out of the garage band. Well, you can look at individual biographies, but the phenomenon is simple; if you want to understand any of these guys you don't want to be reading theology. You want to be reading *Amusing Ourselves to Death* by Neil Postman, written in the '80s. What succeeds is going to be based on the entertainment value of it, and these guys are very good at this (some of them, and some of them not so much). But if you combine lonely individuals looking for community, failed lives, all the parameters having been either moved or abolished in our culture sexually and culturally—obviously, leaders will emerge that border on cult leaders who are going to have massive followings. The same reason [some popular Evangelical leaders] have a following is the same reason Deepak Chopra has a following or Oprah has a following. [. . .] But we're living in a culture of celebrity and entertainment values, and people want a safe haven; they want to follow somebody with a label. So I think that's much more part of the story of this and in a way the actual theology is just peripheral. The dynamic is part of mainstream American culture. It's not like there's NFL stars and football having become a sport in colleges that they're funding to the detriment of their academic community and then *over here* you've got this religious phenomenon. It's all the same phenomenon. [. . .] As fashions in the culture change fashions in religion will change. This idea that religion is a separate subject is completely wrong. It's just part of mainstream American culture. And that includes its idiosyncrasies and its oddness, because part of mainstream American culture is you've got all these people who are NASCAR fans who really just *live* and *breathe* by cars turning left, cars turning left, cars turning left—or whatever it is—and that's a thing. But the very fact we've got all these little microcosms and all these little tiny empires within themselves—we tend to get bound up in our own

These four root dispositions are analytically illuminating in themselves, and the fact that (as the ingredients of any worldview) they map so tightly onto the four primary tribes or expressions of Evangelicalism in the United States today might explain some of the theological, cultural, and social rifts between each of them. But the point here, not to be lost from view, has to do with how these corresponding positions and dispositions precipitate conflict in the Evangelical field. Which ideas, beliefs, and commitments differing leaders find *attractive* or *repulsive* on all sorts of issues (predestination, gender, empire, capitalism, and so on) seems to be guided in large part by their underlying dispositions—whether their "first foot forward" is ontology, epistemology, ethics, or pragmatism—and not just by conscious evaluation and thought. The social mechanism operative here, to reiterate, is that *differing personalities, starting points, and dispositions among Evangelical leaders generate and reinforce heterogeneous positions and interests within their field.*[53]

The Multivocality of the Bible

A neo-Reformed leader at this point might protest, "Our privileged position in American Evangelicalism has less to do with our dispositions or personalities and much more to do with the simple fact that our interpretation of the Bible is closest to the truth" (if not simply *the* Truth). That might be.[54] Such a protest would be correct that the divergent and even contradictory views among Evangelical leaders today are not attributable entirely to their different dispositions and starting points. Something else is going on; that is true. But taking a step back and viewing the matters of biblical interpretation and truth claims from a more removed, sociological standpoint,

---

little worlds, but the overriding principle is that America is always generating these microcosms because people are looking for community and leadership."

[53] Collin Hansen has tapped into these same dispositions in American Evangelicalism in his book *Blind Spots: Becoming a Courageous, Compassionate, and Commissioned Church* (Wheaton, IL: Crossway, 2015). From my view, the "courageous" maps onto the New Calvinists who put order and conviction first, "compassionate" maps onto the neo-Anabaptists for whom ethics is the first foot forward, and "commissioned" aligns with mainstream Evangelicalism with its eye toward pragmatic effectiveness.

[54] Even here, one might consider the issues and questions on which even New Calvinist leaders disagree, such as modes of baptism, views of the millennium, and proper church governance.

two facts complicate this picture and help us further to see why American Evangelicalism today is such a deeply contested arena.

The first fact is that very many presumably well-intentioned readers and even scholars of the Bible (even if we are just limiting ourselves to American readers over the last few decades) arrive at differing and sometimes outright contradictory conclusions and convictions about what the Bible teaches— on nearly every issue under the sun. This is what Christian Smith so thoroughly documented and named "pervasive interpretive pluralism."[55] Now, by observing that readers interpret the Bible in innumerable ways, I do not want to enter the debate—if there is one—about whether this situation says more about the Bible or about the reader. I am not interested for present purposes in getting into various theologies of the Bible.[56] One does not need to take one side or the other in the ensuing Smith–DeYoung exchange[57] to appreciate what should be an uncontroversial point—namely, the empirical fact that in actual practice, the Bible lends itself to many, many differing and divergent interpretations. And, of course, nearly all interpreters hold some level of confidence that their interpretation is actually right.

The second fact is that American Evangelicalism—as a trans-denominational, decentralized hodgepodge of an array of churches, leaders, colleges, associations, conferences, networks, ministries, publishers, and parachurch organizations—has no final or definitive mechanism for establishing which interpretations are within the bounds of Evangelical religion and which are not. There are no bodies or boards, not even the National Association of Evangelicals or The Gospel Coalition, which have any real institutional authority to declare who is "in" and who is "out." As DeYoung put it in our interview, "No Church council has decreed what 'Evangelical' means." Even if American Evangelicalism has an identifiable center, or, more likely, multiple coexisting centers, the boundaries and edges shade off. (See the concluding chapter on "bounded set" vs. "centered set.") These two facts, when viewed together, add another layer of understanding to American Evangelicalism as a hotly contested religious field. Stated as a causal

---

[55] Smith, *The Bible Made Impossible*.

[56] See Justin S. Holcomb, ed., *Christian Theologies of Scripture: A Comparative Introduction* (New York: New York University Press, 2006); Kevin J. Vanhoozer, *Is There a Meaning in This Text? The Bible, the Reader, and the Morality of Literary Knowledge* (Grand Rapids, MI: Zondervan, [1998] 2009).

[57] Kevin DeYoung, "Christian Smith Makes the Bible Impossible," *DeYoung, Restless, Reformed*, August 2, 2011, http://blogs.thegospelcoalition.org/kevindeyoung/2011/08/02/christian-smith-makes-the-bible-impossible/comment-page-3/#comments, accessed February 7, 2016.

mechanism, *the multivocality and polysemy of the Bible as a belief-informing text in an arena with no agreed-upon authority to adjudicate between divergent interpretations leads to intractable conflicts over which beliefs and interpretations ought to be held and allowed.*

Underinformed Congregants

Another, more mundane cause that has facilitated the New Calvinist movement operates at the lower "micro" level—in short, not everyone who attends a New Calvinist church or participates in a Calvinistic conference is a Calvinist or even knows enough about Calvinism to have formed an opinion about it. But this simple fact on the "micro" level, when multiplied several times over across the United States, means that a significant component of the New Calvinism includes laypersons who are, in reality, not Calvinists and may not agree with some of the other beliefs that tend to accompany it, such as gender complementarianism. That is, *religious adherents, who are not fully aware of (and might not agree with) the actual beliefs and convictions advocated by their own congregations and the conferences they attend, constitute the substance of a religious movement for those very convictions.*

My participant observation taught me that some congregants were unaware that their own church—or the religious conference they were attending—was Calvinistic. For instance, at a two-day conference on the five solae of the Protestant Reformation (i.e., grace alone, faith alone, Christ alone, Scripture alone, glory to God alone), I overheard on the second day a young woman asking her pastor on the walk to lunch, "Now, this might be a silly question, but what is the Reformation? I've never heard so many references to being 'Reformed' and 'the Reformation.'" The speakers at this conference included such prominent Calvinistic pastors and theologians as John Piper, Matt Chandler, Al Mohler, and Kevin DeYoung. And this young woman was a frequent attendee at a local Calvinist-leaning megachurch, which had co-organized the conference. Still, she appeared to be unaware that the particular doctrines being taught as central to orthodox Christian belief, and the men delivering the messages from the stage, represented just one pocket of the broader world of Evangelical belief. The New Calvinism, to her, simply *was* Christianity.

This same phenomenon was evident at each of the three Calvinist megachurches I spent time at, and especially at Keller's Redeemer Presbyterian Church. At each church, the congregants with whom I interacted (oftentimes in their twenties) would often ask me what my research project was about. Not wanting to dive into highly specialized concepts like field theory and the state of conservative religion in modernity, I would typically just respond (at first) simply by asking, "Do you know what Calvinism is?" Roughly a quarter of the time, the answer was "no." And it is likely that among attendees at smaller or lesser-known Calvinist churches across the United States—where their lead pastor does not function as a figurehead of the New Calvinist movement—the proportion would be even higher. Granted, these theologically unacquainted congregants were a minority. Based on my experiences in the field, an observer would be at least as likely to meet a person reading through the selected writings of Jonathan Edwards or Spurgeon's *Lectures to My Students* as to find a person who had never heard of Calvinism. Most congregants at these churches landed somewhere in between. But for an accurate sociological account of the New Calvinism, it must be recognized that a significant minority of laypersons are not aware that they are swimming in the Calvinist stream of American Evangelicalism.

The Christian Right

Another precipitating factor in the rise and success of the New Calvinism, if only indirectly, is the well-known set of conservative Christian leaders who, beginning in the late 1970s, spearheaded an organized nationwide effort to get Evangelicals and fundamentalists more deeply involved in the political process—specifically, on the side of the Republican Party. Known as the "Christian Right" or "Religious Right," these political activists took public stands, with an eye toward rallying their Christian constituencies, in favor of social traditionalism and family values (and, centrally, against abortion) in an attempt to "take back America" from the policy influence of liberals, feminists, and secular humanists. With the help of Catholic political activists such as Paul Weyrich and Richard Viguerie, the team of key Protestant leaders and organizations came to include Jerry Falwell and the Moral Majority; Pat Robertson along with *The 700 Club*, the Christian Coalition, and the Christian Broadcasting Network; Robert Grant and Christian Voice; and Ed McAteer and his Religious Roundtable; among others.[58]

[58] Darren Dochuk, *From Bible Belt to Sunbelt: Plain-Folk Religion, Grassroots Politics, and the Rise of Evangelical Conservatism* (New York: W. W. Norton and Company, 2011); Susan Friend Harding,

Despite seeing limited success in the political realm—including Pat Robertson's failed bid at becoming the Republican presidential candidate for the 1988 election—the Christian Right largely succeeded in functionally wedding theologically conservative Evangelicalism in the United States to the Republican Party.[59] Notable for the story in this book, the association between (white) Evangelicals and Republican Party politics solidified not just in voting booths but also in the popular American imagination *outside* of the Evangelical field. That is, due to the efforts of the Christian Right throughout the 1980s and well into the 1990s, in many non-Evangelicals' minds the word "Evangelical" is practically synonymous with "Republican." And although the Christian Right's influence today is past its prime and hardly, if at all, salient in the religious "life-worlds" of today's younger Evangelicals,[60] the residual link between white Evangelicalism and conservative politics continues to help along the disaffection of younger Americans from religion altogether.[61]

This familiar narrative of the rise of the Christian Right and the popular pushback, especially beginning around the year 1990, among younger Americans to the entanglements of Evangelical religion with Republican Party politics is important for understanding the New Calvinism today. Even though New Calvinist leaders share many of the same religious, moral, and even political views as did leaders of the 1980s Christian Right, New Calvinists do not share the Christian Right's ambitions to exert power in the political sphere or to "take back America for Christ." As will be demonstrated in the next chapter, presenting oneself and one's organization and message as *nonpartisan and apolitical* is a significant way New Calvinist leaders strategically position themselves to gain a hearing among a Millennial generation

The Book of Jerry Falwell: Fundamentalist Language and Politics (Princeton, NJ: Princeton University Press, 2000); Michael Lienesch, *Redeeming America: Piety and Politics in the New Christian Right* (Chapel Hill: The University of North Carolina Press, 1993); William Martin, *With God on Our Side: The Rise of the Religious Right in America* (New York: Broadway Books, 1996); Matthew Avery Sutton, *Jerry Falwell and the Rise of the Religious Right: A Brief History with Documents* (New York: Bedford/St. Martin's Press, 2013); Clyde Wilcox and Carin Robinson, *Onward Christian Soldiers? The Religious Right in American Politics* (Boulder, CO: Westview Press, 2011); Daniel K. Williams, *God's Own Party: The Making of the Christian Right* (New York: Oxford University Press, 2010).

[59] James L. Guth, John C. Green, Corwin E. Smidt, Lyman A. Kellstedt, and Margaret M. Poloma, *The Bully Pulpit: The Politics of Protestant Clergy* (Lawrence: University Press of Kansas, 1997).

[60] See Markofski, *New Monasticism*, 130–133, on the process of "social aging" in the American Evangelical field.

[61] Michael Hout and Claude S. Fischer, "Explaining Why More Americans Have No Religious Preference: Political Backlash and Generational Succession, 1987–2012," *Sociological Science* 1 (2014): 423–447. See also Putnam and Campbell, *American Grace*, 91–133.

weary of a Christianity that finds its energy in being at the service of the Republican Party and its policy goals. The Christian Right is a precipitating cause of the New Calvinism, then, (despite both being conservative, theologically and socially) largely as a negative reference group, to which movement leaders can point and make clear, "That is not what we're about."

The Rules of the Game

Lastly, to finish setting the stage for the strategic positioning and game-like contestation in the next chapter, we must identify the rules around which the Evangelical field has been organized. This step is equal parts analytical and empirical; specifying the field rules grants greater analytical insight into what the field even is and what precisely is "at stake" within it, and therefore those rules must be based on empirical evidence gathered from the field and not merely imposed a priori by the analyst. Fortunately, Scottish historian David Bebbington has already provided an accurate way to make sense of the most significant organizing principles of Evangelicalism in a way that is both supported by the data and already widely accepted.[62] His four-point schematic description, commonly known as the Bebbington Quadrilateral, consists of the following features or rules:

1. *Crucicentrism*: The centrality of Jesus Christ's atoning death on the cross. One might also add to this rule Jesus's sinless life and bodily resurrection.
2. *Biblicism*: The sixty-six books of the Old and New Testaments—together being God's special revelation to humanity—are important, sufficiently clear, and authoritative for informing what Christians believe and how Christians ought to live.
3. *Activism*: An activist orientation toward the broader social and cultural world, including spreading the Christian message (evangelism) and possibly involvement in social or political causes.
4. *Conversionism*: An emphasis on a supernatural, life-directing conversion, that is, being "born again." This might be sudden or gradual but either way it involves a decisive break from one's past spiritual condition.

---

[62] David W. Bebbington, *Evangelicalism in Modern Britain: A History from the 1730s to the 1980s* (London: Unwin Hyman, 1989), 2–17.

Given that Bebbington first identified these four principles as the characteristic features of Evangelicalism in 1989, one might wonder if they are now being unjustifiably imposed onto the contemporary American field. They are not. The interviews for this book clearly revealed that Bebbington's four principles not only still enjoy analytical traction, but over the intervening years have also become a common way that American Evangelical leaders *make sense of themselves* as Evangelicals. Bebbington's four marks were not included in the interview guide (they probably should have been), but almost one-quarter of the leaders interviewed for this investigation nevertheless brought them up explicitly when I asked them what it means to be an Evangelical. DeYoung told me, "In broad categories, I find the Bebbington Quadrilateral helpful." He said he has explained these four principles to his congregation, although in doing so he tried to avoid the jargon. Similarly, Joe Rigney, a professor at John Piper's college and seminary in Minneapolis, told me, "I'm a fan of Bebbington's Quadrilateral, which I never tell anybody who doesn't have a clue what that means. [. . .] So those four, for me, do a pretty good job of identifying Evangelicalism." Or again, when asked what makes someone an Evangelical, one president of a major multiuniversity ministry told me, "I guess the classic Bebbington definition of it, those four elements"—although he was quick to add he shies away from applying the label to himself, preferring instead to identify simply as a "conservative, historic Christian." The former president of Fuller Theological Seminary, Richard Mouw, told me that while the organizing principles (or "rules") of Evangelicalism have been a topic of scholarly debate for decades, he (and he included his friends George Marsden and Mark Noll) now thinks "the Bebbington Quadrilateral, that's roughly it, those four characteristics." Tim Keller, too, has used the Bebbington Quadrilateral to outline Evangelicalism in various public speeches, and he reiterated it when I interviewed him, but he added that one critique of the Bebbington approach is that "being cross-centered and Bible-centered could mean a lot of things."

It was not only the Calvinist interviewees who brought up Bebbington. For example, Andy Crouch, a self-described Wesleyan and former executive editor at *Christianity Today*, explained his Evangelical faith to me by naming and spelling out the Bebbington Quadrilateral. Likewise, mainstream non-Calvinist pastor Austin Fischer, when I asked him if he would consider himself an Evangelical, answered "yeah," and then brought up Bebbington: "Bebbington's Quadrilateral for the most part is fine. I know people have picked on it, but I think it lays out some pretty fair parameters for what I would identity with Evangelical faith, and those are things I would hold to. [. . .] I do think those things describe me well." Additionally, on their website—under the subheading "What is an Evangelical?"—the National Association of Evangelicals (NAE) names and lays out the four principles of the Bebbington Quadrilateral.[63] Furthermore, the interviews for this book included many Evangelical leaders who, without naming Bebbington as the person who first put them together, mentioned the centrality of Jesus's crucifixion, the truth and authority of the Bible, the need for personal conversion (or being "born again"), and/or having a public and evangelistic faith as the basic principles of being an Evangelical.

Synthesizing these four field rules into a more overarching principle is also an illuminating way to understand the rules of American Evangelicalism. The interviews showed that American Evangelical leaders commonly use the Bebbington Quadrilateral to articulate field rules (i.e., what Evangelicalism is all about, or what makes someone an Evangelical). But the interviews further suggested that these four specific features were not intended to be standalone values, but instead were often used *in order to "get at" the contours of an even larger, more all-encompassing field rule*. Fittingly, that bigger rule can be thought of as encoded within the etymological origins of the word "Evangelical" itself. The term "Evangelical" is derived from the Greek εὐαγγέλιον (evangelion), which is a combination of eu- ("good") and -angelion ("message"). Technically, then, the word "Evangelical" means "a good message," or "good news." In Old English, "good news" was represented using the word "gōdspel," which in time evolved into "Gospel."

Through this lens, Evangelicalism is, at bottom, about the Gospel, and therefore the Gospel is the most foundational rule of the field. As is the nature of rules in a contested social field, however, there is practically no consensus today—at least between the four main expressions of American Evangelicalism—regarding what precisely the Gospel is and what it entails. If the Gospel is conceptualized in a traditional, mainstream Evangelical way, then Bebbington's four features can be employed as "pieces of the puzzle" that speak to the "good news" that Jesus's sinless life and sacrificial death on the cross (crucicentrism) have made it possible for people to be "born again" by grace (conversionism) and are now invited to participate in what God is doing in the world, including missions and acts of mercy (activism)—all of

---

[63] http://www.nae.net/church-and-faith-partners/what-is-an-evangelical

this having been authoritatively revealed from God with sufficient clarity in the Bible (biblicism).

But so as not to commit itself uncritically to the incumbents' vision of the rules, this analysis requires a conceptualization of "the Gospel" as the over-arching rule of Evangelicalism that also acknowledges the content of the Gospel is contested in the field. Therefore, a way to conceptualize this over-arching rule without attaching it to the "mainstream" content is simply to say a focus on the Gospel means *Christianity has a message, and that message (whatever that is) is both true and fundamentally "good news" for the world.* This orientation makes sense of the interview I did with Doug Pagitt, a progressive Emergent leader. Pagitt told me that even though he thinks the "mainstream" Gospel is wildly off-track, he still considers himself not just an Evangelical but also a leader among other Evangelicals because he believes his version of Christianity is "good news" (and, in fact, better news).[64] In sum, the four parts of the Bebbington Quadrilateral provide the "building-block" rules of the field but are tied a bit too closely (for present purposes) to the traditional Evangelical understanding of the Gospel. Once that message is the very thing being contested in the field, it becomes clear that for Evangelicals it is typically not "activism" or "conversionism" but *the Gospel* that is ultimately "at stake."[65]

As with any field, there are also identifiable norms and expectations that would cause problems if broken but which do not encapsulate the nature of the field itself. For instance, one could reasonably note "don't be an obnoxious jerk" and "don't be brazenly immoral" as field rules (of a sort) for Evangelicalism. And certainly, generic social "rules" such as these are sometimes violated in American Evangelicalism (as evaluated from the perspectives of others in the field) and do cause conflicts and problems.

---

[64] Pagitt rejects the historic Christian storyline that took shape at least from St. Augustine on-ward, including "the fall," "original sin," and "atonement theory as a whole," he told me. Instead, he understands the true biblical narrative basically to be a combination of Pelagianism (humans freely choosing to live in harmony with God) and Girardian scapegoat theory (which Pagitt summed up by saying that Jesus Christ's death on the cross was a scene that shows us what humans can do to the righteous when power and groupthink goes unchecked). However, Pagitt was quick to add he does not want to think about his own religious beliefs as "downstream" from other thinkers within church history, because that "is all a part of the kind of power structures that the Gospel wants to ex-plode." Instead, "Pelagius was an early Pagittian," he told me. See Doug Pagitt, *A Christianity Worth Believing* (San Francisco, CA: Jossey-Bass, 2008); René Girard, *The Scapegoat*, trans. Yvonne Freccero (Baltimore, MD: Johns Hopkins University Press, 1986).

[65] From the New Calvinist view, see, for example, Matt Chandler with Jared Wilson, *The Explicit Gospel* (Wheaton, IL: Crossway, 2012); Greg Gilbert, *What Is the Gospel?* (Wheaton, IL: Crossway, 2010).

However, these more generic "rules," and other norms and expectations like them, do not provide any analytic leverage on the animating principles of the field of American Evangelicalism qua Evangelicalism. These therefore are not considered relevant rules worthy of focus in the contestation addressed in the next chapter.[66]

Conclusion

To this point, the analysis has demonstrated not quite half of the social causal mechanisms identified near the end of the previous chapter—namely, those mechanisms which most powerfully precipitated the rise of the New Calvinist movement. The next chapter, which forms Part II of the demonstration of a field-theoretic model of religious strength, unpacks several more of the relevant social processes and mechanisms, focusing on strategic positioning and game-like contestation among American Evangelical leaders. In other words, the attention shifts at this point from the onset of contention within the American Evangelical field to a more direct look at the episode of contention over the field itself.[67] It is through these strategic and conflictual actions among leaders that we will see the Reformed resurgence most clearly emerge, gain significant recognition, and become fortified as a religious and social reality.

[66] However, field actors might interpret such breaches of generic rules as indicative of a flippant or deviant posture toward other, more constitutive rules. On which kind of rules are relevant to a field analysis, and which are not, see Martin, *The Explanation of Social Action*, 291–307.

[67] See Doug McAdam, Sidney Tarrow, and Charles Tilly, "Methods for Measuring Mechanisms of Contention," *Qualitative Sociology* 31, no. 4 (2008): 307–331.

6

Demonstration of the Model, Part II

Game-Like Contestation

Everything in Its Place

In areas of life such as family, marriage, gender, sexuality, vocation, technology, the economy, healthcare, global affairs, and morality—not to mention questions about theology and God—the Western world today exists in an unprecedented era of openness, uncertainty, skepticism, doubt, choice, and sometimes fear.[1] While most American adults move through life from day to day well enough,[2] at the "higher" sociological level of culture and institutions it seems Americans are living in "liquid times."[3] And due to the unique combination of life course, cohort, and period effects, such unsettledness, instability, and flux are likely felt most acutely today by younger Americans—those who constitute the Millennial generation and who, now as old as thirty-seven, are currently in (or have only recently graduated out of) that stage of life called "emerging adulthood."[4] In light of this reality, a crucial and multifaceted social cause of the Reformed resurgence is that *New Calvinist leaders strategically position themselves as having clear, compelling, "black and white" answers to pressing ethical, social, existential, and doctrinal questions, and especially to young persons.* For those invested in it, the New Calvinist movement offers a new generation firm moral, theological, and

---

[1] Robert Wuthnow, *Be Very Afraid: The Cultural Response to Terror, Pandemics, Environmental Devastation, Nuclear Annihilation, and Other Threats* (New York: Oxford University Press, 2010).

[2] See Smith et al., *American Evangelicalism*, 106–107, on the functional impossibility of persons living every day in a social world characterized by a constant looming threat of disorder and anomie.

[3] Zygmunt Bauman, *Liquid Times: Living in an Age of Uncertainty* (Malden, MA: Polity Press, 2007).

[4] Jeffrey Jensen Arnett, *Emerging Adulthood: The Winding Road from the Late Teens through the Twenties*, 2nd ed. (New York: Oxford University Press, [2004] 2015); Carolyn McNamara Barry and Mona M. Abo-Zena, eds., *Emerging Adults' Religiousness and Spirituality: Meaning-Making in an Age of Transition* (New York: Oxford University Press, 2014); Christian Smith with Patricia Snell, *Souls in Transition: The Religious and Spiritual Lives of Emerging Adults* (New York: Oxford University Press, 2009).

Reformed Resurgence. Brad Vermurlen, Oxford University Press (2020). © Oxford University Press.
DOI: 10.1093/oso/9780190073510.001.0001

intellectual ground on which to stand amid the tectonic shifts of the post-1960s cultural and institutional environment in which they live.[5]

Several of the non-Calvinist leaders I interviewed pointed to this as a reason why Calvinism appeals to a lot of young Americans today. As one neo-Anabaptist pastor stated in our interview, "With the neo-Reformed there is a very strong confident sense of getting something right, of getting the Gospel right. [...] I think New Calvinism is so popular mostly because of its sense of certainty, and of being right about things, and being 'black and white.'" Similarly, Tony Campolo, after explaining to me that he believes women should serve as pastors even though, as he put it, he does not have any good arguments from either the Bible or Church history to support it, said to me: "That's the problem with Calvinism—everything is answered, everything is tied up. There's no question they can't answer." In our interview, Emergent leader Doug Pagitt opined: "I think that version of Christianity doesn't make sense, but if you get plugged into a system that forces it on you ... This is why Reformed theology people have to become so well-educated in Reformed theology, in my view, because it only makes sense as an insular system." Or again, Rachel Held Evans stated, "There's an appeal about how it supposedly answers every question. It has this cohesiveness about it that I think is really appealing. When you're young, you kind of want and long for an answer to everything. You want to find somebody who has the entire world figured out, everything's 'black and white,' no room for gray. I think the neo-Calvinist movement is beautiful at presenting people with that." Greg Boyd put it more simply: "Folks who don't like loose ends—these are tough times for them." Statements like these came up repeatedly among non-Calvinist Evangelical leaders.

A number of my interviewees tied this same explanation of the New Calvinism to postmodernism (as a style of thinking) and postmodernity (as a socio-cultural condition) in American culture and society today. During our interview, for example, progressive Emergent leader Tony Jones said:

> [The New Calvinist movement is] an honest hermeneutical and theological response to the postmodern situation. Piper believes that he is within a theological system that is perfectly enclosed and has no loopholes. And in a

---

[5] For a broader contrastive account, including how younger Americans merely "tinker" with religion, see Robert Wuthnow, *After the Baby Boomers: How Twenty- and Thirty-Somethings Are Shaping the Future of American Religion* (Princeton, NJ: Princeton University Press, 2007), especially pp. 1–19.

time of radical pluralism, certain people—and it may be as much a personality thing as anything else—look for ideological systems that provide them
with all of the answer[s] and, you know, that's what that version of Jonathan
Edwards Calvinism does.

Andy Crouch, at the time executive editor at *Christianity Today* (and not
a Calvinist), had a similar theory. He said he thinks the Emergent Church
conversation possessed "the right diagnosis" at the turn of the millennium
in terms of the need to respond to relativism, postmodernism, and post-
Christendom, but it was the New Calvinism that had "the right prescription." "The new Reformed movement," Crouch explained, "responds to the
anxieties of life in a postmodern environment in very compelling ways for
people. Now, whether or not I may think those are adequate philosophically,
theologically, or whatever, the point is they work for people to anchor them
in what feels like a very adrift world."

Austin Fischer, a young Evangelical pastor, made a similar observation:[6]

[M]any young evangelicals carry around the shrapnel of postmodernism.
They feel crushed and battered by skepticism, cynicism, and nihilism, and
are looking for a remedy. I think the new young, restless, Reformed movement offers a strong remedy to postmodern refugees because once you
sign off on the dotted line, you're like a wandering vagabond who steps
inside this clean, ordered house and for the first time in a long time, you
feel a sense of structure and clarity. From a sociological perspective, I think
the spike in Calvinist theology is rooted in its ability to provide a sturdy
"postmodernism-fallout shelter," replacing the barrage of grey with some
strong accents of black and white.

This frequent observation ties back to the discussion in the previous
chapter on the various positions and underlying dispositions of Evangelical
leaders. New Calvinists prioritize order and structure over disorder and
ambiguity. And while such an approach to religion and life more generally is attractive for some young (and some not so young) Americans,
other Evangelical leaders—especially the Emergent progressives and

---

[6] Jonathan Merritt, "Author Says Calvinism Can't Make Sense of the Cross," *Religion News Service*,
April 3, 2014, http://jonathanmerritt.religionnews.com/2014/04/03/author-says-calvinism-cant-
make-sense-cross/, accessed January 4, 2016.

neo-Anabaptists—criticize it for offering simple, stark answers when what is needed is to wrestle with mystery, nuance, and uncertainty. For instance, poststructuralist theologian Peter Rollins says the "true conflict" that separates people from one another is between persons who do not know truth but "embrace unknowing," on one hand, and, on the other, "those who do not know but who refuse to accept it; those who turn away from that, and pretend that they have the answers, because they are too frightened to look at the terror of the unknowing and the mystery that we are immersed in."[7] The New Calvinism offers a lot of answers and "knowing" on several questions, which turns out to be quite a strategic position in today's broader field of American Evangelicalism.

This same general social mechanism expresses itself in multiple ways.

Teaching Boys To Be Men

One prominent expression of providing clear, compelling, "black and white" answers to young people has to do specifically with gender, with masculinity and femininity. New Calvinist leaders stake out a strategic position within the American Evangelical field by *promoting traditional, conservative gender roles for both men and women, especially in light of feminism and the gender revolution.*[8] In particular, one significant focus is on training, challenging, and instructing men with a specific, traditional—and they would say biblical—vision of what it looks like to be a man. Ideally, due to "the privilege of youth" in American Evangelicalism,[9] the preferred focus is on younger "guys" during their transition into adulthood, in their twenties and thirties. The roots of this dynamic have been laid out in previous chapters—specifically the gender and sexual revolutions taking hold since the 1960s, the New Calvinism's unswerving commitment to gender complementarianism, and the integral role of the Council on Biblical Manhood and Womanhood as an organization. These factors together point toward the New Calvinism's

---

[7] http://vimeo.com/35083246, accessed February 22, 2016.

[8] This mechanism could be seen as three related social processes wrapped up into one, those being: (1) promoting a traditional, conservative vision of complementarity between the sexes; and within that (2) teaching and challenging young guys to "man up" in light of a perceived problem of "extended adolescence"; and (3) encouraging women to lean into their distinctly feminine nature, especially in the roles of wives and mothers. In this section, I elected to focus on the second of those three, since for a causal explanation of the New Calvinist movement within a strategic action field it is the most causally efficacious and pronounced of the three.

[9] Markofski, *New Monasticism*, 133–136.

emphasis on conservative prescriptions for gender, especially as an alternative to contemporary liberal sensibilities of self-invention, egalitarianism, and gender fluidity in American culture and society.

This is not new. From the "muscular Christianity" of the mid- to late 1800s[10] to the Promise Keepers rallies throughout the 1990s,[11] American Evangelicalism has long been a cultural force for conservative gender roles and gender expression, with particular zeal regarding the men. However, with the rise in recent decades of a clearly articulated and vigorously defended egalitarianism *within American Evangelicalism* (for example, Christians for Biblical Equality[12]), promoting a conservative picture of manhood and womanhood no longer serves merely to distinguish incumbent Evangelical leaders from their secular (liberal, feminist) surroundings; now it *also* sets them apart from *challenger* organizations and leaders from inside the American Evangelical field itself. Thus, even though it is a story that has been told many times, admonishing young guys to "man up," take responsibility, and lead their families well is nonetheless a powerful social causal mechanism by which New Calvinist leaders secure a competitive advantage in their field.

The clearest voice in this regard has been Mark Driscoll. In a 2013 interview with Glenn Beck, Driscoll reflected on what he saw as the dire state of young men in the United States and their need for clear, compelling direction in how to put their lives together:

Say you're a 25-year-old guy, living in a city. You have no idea what to be or do. Where do you go? Like, what door do you go knock on? What organization do you check out, to just ask, "How do I get a job? How do I marry a woman? How do I raise a kid? How do I buy a house? How do I pay off my debt? Like, what am I doing?" [They would say about themselves] "I'm

---

[10] See Donald E. Hall, ed., *Muscular Christianity: Embodying the Victorian Age* (Cambridge: Cambridge University Press, 1994); Clifford Putney, *Muscular Christianity: Manhood and Sports in Protestant America, 1880–1920* (Cambridge, MA: Harvard University Press, 2001).

[11] See Michael Armato and William Marsiglio, "Self-Structure, Identity, and Commitment: Promise Keepers' Godly Man Project," *Symbolic Interaction* 25, no. 1 (2002): 41–65; John P. Bartkowski, *The Promise Keepers: Servants, Soldiers, and Godly Men* (New Brunswick, NJ: Rutgers University Press, 2004); Brian Donovan, "Political Consequences of Private Authority: Promise Keepers and the Transformation of Hegemonic Masculinity," *Theory and Society* 27, no. 6 (1998): 817–843; Rhys H. Williams, ed., *Promise Keepers and the New Masculinity: Private Lives and Public Morality* (Lanham, MD: Lexington Books, 2001).

[12] http://www.cbeinternational.org/

good at collecting Bitcoins[13] and finding free porn. But beyond that, I really haven't put my life together."[14]

When Beck asked Driscoll how he attracts so many young single "guys" to his church, Driscoll responded:

> You gotta tell them that they're wrong—that they're absolutely wrong and that they have no idea what they're doing. And that the culture has sold them a bunch of products and it's just trying to make them addicted to porn, and pot, and substances, and to take all the money out of their wallet, and to get some out of their mom's wallet, and rip them off—because the fools' parade just keeps going to the ATM and handing away their future. I mean, guys just don't think about anything other than a good time and it's about thinking about good legacy . . .
>
> It's boys who can shave, man. It's just a joke. Nobody looks at these guys and says, "You didn't have a dad; you're addicted to porn; you don't have a clue; you don't have a plan; you're part of the problem; stop smiling 'cuz you're the joke." I mean, nobody just tells them like that, but that's exactly what they need. And if they had a good dad, that's what he would have told them.[15]

Beck countered:

> And so, I'm trying to think how you get people to walk into your church.

Driscoll replied:

> You punch a guy, he goes and gets two friends, 'cuz nobody has ever punched him. It's countercultural. It's revolutionary. Who right now [in the broader American cultural and religious landscape] is in the business of offending people? I mean, you do that and all of a sudden, you're unique.

---

[13] Bitcoin is a recently invented alternative, digital currency.

[14] https://www.youtube.com/watch?v=slaCP4mK4_8

[15] Tony Jones reflected on how Driscoll's megachurch had "this super masculine vibe—like even the paint color on the walls and all the interior decoration, but it's also this strangely homoerotic kind of place. And you can just see how a young metro-sexual 24-year-old guy who's kind of still shaping his nascent identity and personality would be drawn to Driscoll telling him, 'You're not gay, you only like this kind of women, this is how we read the Bible'—like 'boom, boom, boom.' He just lays it out and he's so fucking confident about it. There's just like not an iota of doubt or caveat."

All of a sudden, you're the rebel, you're the lawbreaker, you're the punk-rocker, because you're the one who's standing up against the majority by telling people that God's not okay with certain behavior, and that Jesus died and rose, and Hell's hot, forever's a long time, and they better pay attention. And it's saying it just like that.[16]

Evident here are the basic principles of strict church theory, except in this case we see it from the perspective of a strategizing Evangelical leader. Driscoll continued:

No one else is doing [this]. I mean, the world is just filled with noise and if you can cut against the grain, say something in a different tone with different content, something they've never heard—initially you're offended by it. You're like, "I have never heard that, but now I'm interested, because maybe—maybe—I've been lied to."[17]

Mark Driscoll is the most widely recognized face of this strong masculine bent to the New Calvinism. But other leaders of the movement often strike the same note, even if in a somewhat less rousing way. One example is the writing and ministry of Darrin Patrick, formerly at The Journey in St. Louis. His 2014 book *The Dude's Guide to Manhood: Finding True Manliness in a World of Counterfeits*[18] instructs "men without maps" how to be a determined, coachable, disciplined, working, content, socially connected, forgiven, devoted family man.[19] Elsewhere, Patrick has spoken about the problem in American culture of what he calls the "ban"—that is, the guy who is stuck between being a boy and being a man and who wants to avoid responsibility and to prolong his adolescence indefinitely.[20] "I have a church full of those kind of guys," he explained. "And I kept seeing that over and over again. Most of these guys did not have dads. They did not learn how to be men." Darrin Patrick hopes churches like The Journey can work toward reversing that trend: "The reason we have a societal crisis with men is because we do not have strong churches that draw out, train, equip, empower, and challenge

---

[16] https://www.youtube.com/watch?v=38BBsfL3Fkg, accessed January 20, 2016.

[17] Ibid.

[18] Darrin Patrick, *The Dude's Guide to Manhood: Finding True Manliness in a World of Counterfeits* (Nashville, TN: Thomas Nelson, 2014).

[19] These adjectives form some of the chapter titles of Patrick's book.

[20] Michael Kimmel, *Guyland: The Perilous World Where Boys Become Men* (New York: HarperColl ins, 2008).

men."[21] In an episode of the Acts 29 podcast, Patrick talked further about the need for men to live in the balance between, in his words, "chauvinism and cowardice"—not falling into either vice. He stated that apart from the expected resistance from "the progressive mafia that always wants to take shots in the blogosphere," he was surprised most people have been receptive to his persistent message championing a robust, biblical manhood.

Institutionally, the New Calvinism also includes a series of men's conferences that were launched in the fall of 2013 named Act Like Men.[22] Spearheaded by James MacDonald (at the time) of Harvest Bible Chapel in Chicago, the two-day conferences have featured other Evangelical Calvinistic preachers such as Matt Chandler, Eric Mason, Greg Laurie, and, of course, Mark Driscoll. The first season of conferences in 2013 included events in Long Beach, California; Hamilton, Ontario; and Indianapolis, Indiana. In 2015 additional conferences were held in Dallas and Chicago. As Chandler explained it, "What we're not talking about is some sort of false bravado, overly masculine type of man." MacDonald emphasized this, too: "I don't want some narrow, crazy view of manhood that doesn't make room for the different ways that God has made all of us."[23] Instead, the focus at these conferences tends to be more about character issues such as being sacrificial, loving, responsible, and simultaneously "tough and tender." Two of the conference speakers have recently written books on biblical manhood—namely, James MacDonald's book *Act Like Men*[24] and Eric Mason's 2013 book *Manhood Restored.*[25]

A less typical example of the New Calvinist emphasis on manhood is Calvinist hip-hop artist Lecrae and his involvement with the Obama administration's *This Is Fatherhood* initiative, which launched to the public on May 1, 2013. Lecrae joined a team along with NBA star Dwayne Wade, mainstream rapper Jay-Z, and Joshua DuBois (the former director of the Office of Faith-based and Neighborhood Partnerships) to promote responsible, present fatherhood among (especially younger) men in the United States. The fact that these four men are black might also imply that the

---

[21] https://www.youtube.com/watch?v=phf6r6Zmilk, accessed January 21, 2016.

[22] http://actlikemen.com/. While the name seems blunt, it is a reference to Paul's words in 1 Corinthians 16: 13–14, which reads: "Be watchful, stand firm in the faith, act like men, be strong. Let all that you do be done in love."

[23] In one forty-eight-minute sermon, MacDonald outlined what it means to "act like a man" in three parts as "don't act like a *woman*, don't act like an *animal*, and don't act like a *boy*."

[24] James MacDonald, *Act Like Men: 40 Days to Biblical Manhood* (Chicago: Moody, 2014).

[25] Eric Mason, *Manhood Restored: How the Gospel Makes Men Whole* (Nashville, TN: B&H, 2013).

initiative was intended to reach black men. The initiative included Public Service Announcements and a nationwide contest in which men were asked to express what fatherhood means to them in the form of a song, video, essay, or photograph. In one Public Service Announcement, Lecrae shared some of his own experience of struggling to grow up without a father: "Being raised without my biological father made me question a lot of my significance. What does it mean to be a man? And how do I know if I've lived up to that?"[26] Here, we get a glimpse of how New Calvinist visions of manhood overlap with broader, more widely held national values.[27]

What do the women think of all this? Outside of conservative expressions of American Evangelicalism, and especially in the progressive Emergent pocket, one finds several female (and male) *religious leaders as challengers in the field actively "pushing back against"* this conservative prescription of gender. Rachel Held Evans and Sarah Bessey stand out as dominant voices making the argument that there is actually no such thing as biblical manhood or biblical womanhood—that there is only (gender-neutral) biblical character.[28]

Within the New Calvinism, however, the dominant reaction from the women is *gratitude*. They are thankful for churches that challenge men to be distinctly masculine, not feminine, to take responsibility and to lead. One young, unmarried female leader at Mars Hill Church whom I interviewed was representative of this sentiment:

I know that people look at [Mars Hill] and they think that women are just seen as second class, almost, at the church. [But] I feel like it would be so much harder to be the guy, because they're put under so much responsibility. [...] I feel protected there. [...] Women are loved on there and cared for and seen as precious gifts—that's why it's emphasized so much that men need to be leaders. I don't see it as a bad thing.

---

[26] Lecrae's Public Service Announcement is still on the *This Is Fatherhood* YouTube channel here: https://www.youtube.com/watch?v=rd9H65-Iubo, accessed January 25, 2016.

[27] Some New Calvinist leaders pointed out what they saw as a deep contradiction in President Obama's promotion of the essential role of fatherhood while also supporting the redefinition of marriage to include lesbian couples, thus institutionalizing a family arrangement in which fatherhood is inessential.

[28] Rachel Held Evans, *A Year of Biblical Womanhood: How a Liberated Woman Found Herself Sitting on Her Roof, Covering Her Head, and Calling Her Husband Master* (Nashville, TN: Thomas Nelson, 2012); Sarah Bessey, *Jesus Feminist: An Invitation to Revisit the Bible's View of Women* (New York: Howard Books, 2013).

Mars Hill Church, she concluded, has "a really high view of women."
Similarly, I interviewed a twenty-five-year-old female deacon at Mars Hill
who at the time was working toward a doctorate and recently married.
When I asked her what it is like being a woman at Mars Hill, she responded
enthusiastically:

> I think it's wonderful. I know a lot of people disagree with that, but I feel
> loved; I feel respected; I feel supported; I feel encouraged. [. . .] Because the
> men [here] are so strong, it makes it possible for the women to lead the lives
> that God intended for us—to have more of the nurturing roles, more of the
> helper roles, and to let our men lead. [. . .] It's refreshing.

On one level, this is altogether unsurprising. Women involved in the New
Calvinist movement tend to agree with and appreciate its teachings. More
progressive women and men outside of the New Calvinism, in contrast, disagree. More to the point, though, against an assumption that the women in the
New Calvinism begrudgingly go along with its vision of biblical manhood
and womanhood, they tend to believe it is what the Bible teaches and that it is
beneficial both for them and for the men in their lives.

The clear, explicit directive for men to be masculine and women to be feminine, and especially a call targeted toward younger Americans struggling
to figure out what it looks like to be an adult, marks out a strategic position for the New Calvinism. These beliefs are hotly contested—more so
than space allows here—not only in the broader liberal American culture
but also within the American Evangelical field itself. But recall that a field-
theoretic view of strategy says that organizational leaders should not feel like
they "have to 'delight' every possible customer out there. The sign of a good
strategy is that it deliberately makes some customers unhappy."[29] Gender
complementarianism certainly does that; many Americans find their message off-putting or dangerous.[30] Nevertheless, for a lot of American men—
and women—this challenge is precisely what they want to hear.

---

[29] Magretta, "Strategy Essentials You Ignore at Your Peril."
[30] One progressive Christian leader I interviewed, for example, despite emphasizing uncertainty
and "the coexistence of multiple truths," was very sure that gender complementarianism is "wrong
and unbiblical."

Tradition with Innovation

Another way the New Calvinist movement provides clear, compelling answers and thereby gains strength, especially among younger Americans, is by *New Calvinists, as incumbent religious leaders, positioning themselves as offering the weight of historical rootedness within a centuries-old tradition, especially in light of modernity as a "rootless world."*[31] As younger generations of Americans find themselves adrift and "homeless" in a modern world that attempts to cast off all traditions of the past, and which claims autonomous individualism as the only genuine authority,[32] a segment are finding the historical rootedness of the Reformed tradition to be an attractive alternative. Like any strategic position, it is not for everyone, but the New Calvinism's emphasis on history and tradition is an essential aspect of its sociological strength.

In our current era when the therapeutic, pragmatic, and vaguely a-theological ethos of large swaths of Evangelicalism in America means this tradition resembles what Dietrich Bonhoeffer called "Protestantism without the Reformation,"[33] the New Calvinist movement is aiming to retrieve and reclaim conservative American Protestantism's Reformation heritage. The Reformed resurgence offers people—especially young people—a clear religious and moral "home" which includes a historic lineage through which to make sense of themselves, God, the world, and their connection to the past. This Christian lineage goes primarily through the Particular Baptist, Presbyterian, Reformed, and Anglican traditions, including the Puritans, and encompasses historical figures such as Abraham Kuyper (1837–1920), Charles Spurgeon (1834–1892), George Whitefield (1714–1770), and Jonathan Edwards (1703–1758). It includes much of the Protestant Reformation of the sixteenth century, including magisterial Reformers like John Knox (1513–1572), John Calvin (1509–1564), and, less directly, Martin Luther (1483–1546).

Looking even prior to the Reformation, New Calvinists recognize the doctrines of grace in (Catholic) theologians and churchmen such as Johann von Staupitz (c. 1460–1524), Gregory of Rimini (c. 1300–1358), Thomas

---

[31] Davidman, *Tradition in a Rootless World.*

[32] Peter Berger, Brigitte Berger, and Hansfried Kellner, *The Homeless Mind: Modernization and Consciousness* (New York: Random House, 1973).

[33] Dietrich Bonhoeffer, "Protestantism without the Reformation," in *The Collected Works of Dietrich Bonhoeffer, vol. 1, No Rusty Swords: Letters, Lectures and Notes, 1928-1936,* ed. Edwin H. Robertson, trans. Edwin H. Robertson and John Bowden (London: Collins, 1965), 92–118.

Bradwardine (c. 1290–1349), Anselm of Canterbury (c. 1033–1109), Augustine of Hippo (354–430), the Apostle Paul, and ultimately in the words of Jesus Christ Himself as recorded in the New Testament.[34] Emphasizing this long historical continuity, some contemporary Calvinists understand the Reformed confession of the Christian faith as a type of small-c *catholic* Christianity, part of the whole Church spanning two thousand years from the early Church through the medieval period up to the present day; Calvinist leaders who articulate this sort of Reformed catholicity (although some are not typically identified with the New Calvinism of Driscoll and Piper) include R. C. Sproul, Michael Horton, James K. A. Smith, Scott Swain, Michael Allen, Todd Billings, Kevin Vanhoozer, and Derek Rishmawy, among others.[35]

Scholars in the broad orbit of American Calvinism write prolifically in the areas of Church history and historical theology, producing books that young, restless Calvinists can read to learn about and feel at home in the Reformed tradition. Among countless examples, one could pick up Justin Holcomb's book about the creeds and councils;[36] Al Mohler's book on the Apostles' Creed;[37] K. Scott Oliphint's book on Thomas Aquinas;[38] either Matthew Barrett's or Kevin DeYoung's book about the Canons of Dort;[39] John Piper's book about Augustine, Luther, and Calvin;[40] Mark Noll's work on confessions and catechisms of the Reformation and the rise of Evangelicalism;[41] Michael A. G. Haykin's book on the Reformers and Puritans as spiritual mentors;[42] James K. A. Smith's *Letters to a Young Calvinist*;[43] Owen Strachan and Doug Sweeney's book on Jonathan Edwards;[44] Thomas Kidd's book on George

[34] Horton, *For Calvinism*, 19.

[35] Allen and Swain, *Reformed Catholicity*.

[36] Justin S. Holcomb, *Know the Creeds and Councils* (Grand Rapids, MI: Zondervan, 2014).

[37] Albert Mohler, *The Apostles' Creed: Discovering Authentic Christianity in an Age of Counterfeits* (Nashville, TN: Thomas Nelson, 2019).

[38] K. Scott Oliphint, *Thomas Aquinas* (Phillipsburg, NJ: P&R, 2017).

[39] Matthew Barrett, *The Grace of Godliness: An Introduction to Doctrine and Piety in the Canons of Dort* (Kitchener, ON: Joshua Press, 2013); Kevin DeYoung, *Grace Defined and Defended: What a 400-Year-Old Confession Teaches Us about Sin, Salvation, and the Sovereignty of God* (Wheaton, IL: Crossway, 2019).

[40] John Piper, *The Legacy of Sovereign Joy: God's Triumphant Grace in the Lives of Augustine, Luther, and Calvin* (Wheaton, IL: Crossway, 2000).

[41] Mark A. Noll, ed., *Confessions and Catechisms of the Reformation* (Vancouver, BC: Regent College, 2004); Mark A. Noll, *The Rise of Evangelicalism: The Age of Edwards, Whitefield, and the Wesleys* (Downers Grove, IL: InterVarsity Press, 2003).

[42] Michael A. G. Haykin, *The Reformers and Puritans as Spiritual Mentors* (Kitchener, ON: Joshua Press, 2012).

[43] James K. A. Smith, *Letters to a Young Calvinist: An Invitation to the Reformed Tradition* (Grand Rapids, MI: Brazos Press, 2010).

[44] Owen Strachan and Douglas A. Sweeney, *The Essential Jonathan Edwards: An Introduction to the Life and Teaching of America's Greatest Theologian* (Chicago: Moody, 2018).

Whitefield;[45] Michael Reeves's book on Charles Spurgeon;[46] or (as a companion to Wayne Grudem's *Systematic Theology*) Gregg Allison's *Historical Theology*.[47] This abundant literature, which is very easily accessible via websites like Amazon, further reinforces for young New Calvinists the sense that they are living within a significant theological, intellectual, and moral tradition.

The matter of gender complementarianism shows up on this point as well. Among many New Calvinists, their convictions about men and women (natural complementarity, male leadership, no female pastors, and the like) get framed as the traditional, historic, 2,000-year-old Christian perspective on the issue, which for young religious traditionalists is itself enough to make it compelling and attractive. This rootedness in history is another way complementarianism grants the New Calvinists a sustainable competitive advantage in relation to the rest of the field.

Yet it is not theological and moral tradition by itself that gives the New Calvinist movement its strategic position in Evangelicalism; this alone would not be enough. Its emphasis on tradition and history is paired with cultural innovation and "culture making."[48] Unlike Catholic or Anglican churches, which are also steeped in historic tradition, the New Calvinism generally has a more contemporary style. Mars Hill Church, for instance, embraced low-church nondenominationalism and stood out as a leading light in music, video production, and aesthetic design. Although Redeemer Presbyterian Church has a more traditional liturgical style, the church is on the cutting edge in other areas of culture in New York City such as business, public lectures, and theater. One exception is John Piper's church, Bethlehem Baptist Church. In one of my conversations with Mark Driscoll during my time in Seattle, I explained that I saw how Mars Hill was innovating culturally, as well as how in a different way Redeemer is involved in "culture making," but I had trouble seeing how Bethlehem was engaged in similar work; Driscoll responded: "Piper is like the grandfather of the neo-Reformed

---

[45] Thomas S. Kidd, *George Whitefield: America's Spiritual Founding Father* (New Haven, CT: Yale University Press, 2014).

[46] Michael Reeves, *Spurgeon on the Christian Life: Alive in Christ* (Wheaton, IL: Crossway, 2018).

[47] Gregg R. Allison, *Historical Theology: An Introduction to Christian Doctrine* (Grand Rapids, MI: Zondervan, 2011).

[48] Andy Crouch, *Culture Making: Recovering Our Creative Calling* (Downers Grove, IL: InterVarsity Press, 2008). Though himself not a Calvinist, Crouch's book was well-received in the New Calvinist movement.

movement. He doesn't need to be cool. You don't want your grandpa to be cool; you want your grandpa to be wise."

On the whole, though, the New Calvinist movement does a great job holding in tension both theological traditionalism and forward-looking cultural engagement, sometimes even engaging in genuine cultural innovation. That this contributes to the New Calvinism's appeal and strength harkens back to Christian Smith and his colleagues' emphasis on "distinction with engagement" as the optimal posture for religious groups and movements to thrive in our modern, pluralistic world.[49] The current observation is similar to Smith's, except making the turn to "tradition with innovation" adds a crucial temporal and historical dimension to this general social dynamic that Smith and colleagues correctly recognized and articulated years ago.

God Is in Control

In contemporary America, especially among younger Americans with at least a bachelor's degree, self is King. Each individual person, not some divine Being, is ultimately in control of each individual's life and aspirations.[50] A recent report from Pew showed that among younger American adults, ages eighteen to forty-nine, fewer than half claim to *or try to* believe in God "as described in the Bible," and even fewer (around 41 or 42 percent) believe God determines what happens in their lives most or all of the time. Only slightly more than half believe in a God who has the power to direct or change everything that goes on in the world.[51] Additionally, each of these religious beliefs becomes less common among people with higher levels of education.[52] In this environment, yet another way the New Calvinism stakes out a competitive advantage is with *New Calvinists, as incumbent religious leaders, positioning themselves by deemphasizing autonomous self-direction and individual free will, especially in light of the modern-day emphasis on these principles.*

For younger, educated Americans, the New Calvinism offers a distinctive, alternative worldview in which Jesus—not Self—sits on the thrown. It

---

[49] Smith et al., *American Evangelicalism.*

[50] Phillip E. Hammond, *Religion and Personal Autonomy: The Third Disestablishment in America* (Columbia: University of South Carolina Press, 1992); Andrew Delbanco, *The Real American Dream: A Meditation on Hope* (Cambridge, MA: Harvard University Press, 1999), 81–118.

[51] Pew Research Center, *When Americans Say They Believe in God, What Do They Mean?* April 25, 2018, 16, 23, 24, 31.

[52] Pew, *When Americans Say They Believe in God, What Do They Mean?*, 17–18, 23, 24, 31.

is not hard to see why, on a personal level, believing in divine sovereignty is attractive to some people—and repulsive to others. That makes it strategic, which is not to say disingenuous. While many of their less religious, city-dwelling, college-educated peers try—and sometimes really struggle—to build and direct their own lives, young Calvinists place their hope in a sovereign, triu-ne God who works all things together for the good of those who love Him. On such weighty matters as education, career, dating, marriage, and parenthood, young Calvinists believe that while they are responsible for making wise and moral decisions, God is always working in the background.[53] When suffering and hardship come, God is in control. Regarding sexuality and what can be done with and to one's body, you are not your own; you were bought at a price. Various anxieties and insecurities are met with abiding confidence in the providence of God. New Calvinist pastors and theologians, in their preaching and books, present people with this vision, and for many it provides reassurance and structure in areas of life that otherwise would be much too open-ended and overwhelming. For a Calvinist, even on the question of why he or she became a Christian, and thereby is saved, the answer in the final analysis is not personal free will ("I chose to place my faith in Jesus") but God's sovereign grace. In these and other ways, Calvinism offers Americans, especially younger Americans, a radical counternarrative to the predominant modern commitment to autonomy and individual free will. This proves to be quite a strategic position.

"It's Just a Good Hermeneutic"

New Calvinist leaders position themselves strategically in American Evangelicalism by presenting themselves—especially publicly—*as if they were taking consensually valued elements and topics (such as the Bible, God, and theology) more seriously than do their field competitors.* Regarding Calvinism and the belief commitments that come along with it in the Reformed resurgence, such as gender complementarianism and social conservativism, there is a clear matter-of-factness to leaders' speech, both public and private. They give the strong impression that they approach the

---

[53] Garry Friesen with J. Robin Maxson, *Decision Making and the Will of God: A Biblical Alternative to the Traditional View*, revised and updated edition (Colorado Springs, CO: Multnomah Books, [1980] 2004); D. A. Carson, *Divine Sovereignty and Human Responsibility: Biblical Perspectives in Tension*, 2nd ed. (Eugene, OR: Wipf and Stock, [1981] 2002).

Bible, God, and theology with rigor and seriousness, while the other tribes and expressions of Evangelicalism approach these matters somewhat less seriously. The issue sociologically is not whether Calvinism actually is or is not a sound interpretation of the text of the Bible; it is that when New Calvinist leaders present themselves as if their interpretation of the text is simply the best, most accurate, most scholarly reading, this creates for them a competitive advantage in relation to the rest of the Evangelical field.

One of the clearest examples of this dynamic is language of "big-God theology." It is very common for New Calvinist leaders to refer to Reformed theology, the doctrines of grace, as "big-God theology," which refers to a God who is sovereign, mighty, glorious, beautiful, all-knowing, and powerful. The subtext to this is that other approaches to Christian theology that are anything other than Reformed or Calvinistic—whether Arminian, open theistic, therapeutic, or vaguely a-theological—are worshipping a God who is something less than "big."[54]

Aside from "big-God theology," this social mechanism expresses itself in a number of other forms. Most simply, most—probably all—leaders of the New Calvinism believe Calvinism is the most accurate and most rigorous way to read and interpret the Bible. It's just a good hermeneutic. This is not surprising, and other Evangelical leaders who are committed to other, competing positions likewise believe their interpretations are best. But Calvinist leaders are uniquely skilled at making arguments that the Bible, interpreted rightly, teaches Calvinism—and their arguments often come with the sense that their conclusions should be obvious. Jason Meyer told me: "I started with the Bible. I felt like somebody had rewritten my Bible after I began to see the doctrines of grace. I just began to see them everywhere, like, how could I have missed this?" John Piper, in introducing his recent book on the five points of Calvinism, wrote:

> I do not begin as a Calvinist and defend a system. I begin as a Bible-believing Christian who wants to put the Bible above all systems of thought. But over the years—many years of struggle—I have deepened in my conviction that Calvinistic teachings on the five points are biblical and therefore true, and therefore a precious pathway into deeper experiences of God's grace.[55]

---

[54] J. D. Greear, *Not God Enough: Why Your Small God Leads to Big Problems* (Grand Rapids, MI: Zondervan, 2018).

[55] Piper, *Five Points*, 9.

Some Calvinist leaders connected Calvinism to complementarianism, suggesting that both derive from "a high view of Scripture" and proper exegesis. For example, Andy Naselli said it is "really unusual" to find a Calvinist egalitarian today. When I asked him why that is, he answered: "I don't know how to answer that in a way that an egalitarian wouldn't be offended. I think both [positions stem from] a high view of Scripture and a good hermeneutic." Similarly, Joe Rigney explained to me that one can tell which Christian leaders are on their way toward forfeiting biblical authority by looking at the issues of gender and sexuality. "There's folks who would self-describe as Evangelicals but are on their way out the door, and are essentially liberals who haven't quite gotten there yet," he said. "Where you come down on the Bible's teaching on sexuality and manhood and womanhood," he said, is "a better telltale sign" and "one of the key signal issues" for people who have started to give up on biblical authority.

Other leaders contrasted New Calvinism with mainstream American Evangelicalism, contrasting the seriousness and rigor of the New Calvinism with the therapeutic, sentimental, and shallow tendencies of some megachurches. James K. A. Smith suggested the New Calvinism represents "a kind of frustration with the wishy-washiness and namby-pambiness of megachurch Christianity in the 80s." Similarly, Tim Challies told me: "My impression is that the New Calvinism kind of grew out of the church growth movement. You had the Rick Warrens and Bill Hybels doing their thing, kind of the Walmart-church model—everything bigger, everything professionalized—and I think people grew weary of that. And so you ended up with the Reformed movement coming out of it." Even though some New Calvinist churches are "mega," their style and content offers something different from "seeker-sensitive" churches.

Al Mohler argued that, for serious young Evangelicals, the New Calvinism is the only game in town:

> Where else are [young Evangelicals] gonna go? I mean, what options are there? If you're a theologically-minded, deeply convictional, young Evangelical; if you're committed to the Gospel and you want to see the nations rejoice in the name of Christ; if you want to see Gospel-built and -structured and -committed churches—your theology is just going to end up basically being Reformed, basically being something like this New

Calvinism, or you're going to have to invent some other label for what's going to be the same thing. There just are not options out there.[56]

Tim Challies said:

> If you're intellectually inclined, if you just like to think, if you want meat to chew on, I do think you end up gravitating toward this movement. There's just more satisfying truth to be found in Reformed theology than in non-Reformed theology, and in this New Calvinism than in the broader Evangelicalism. Think about systematic theologies. How many solid systematic theologies have been written by those Max Lucado type of authors, right? They're simply not doing it. If you want sound, solid theology, you're almost always ending up toward the conservative wing of the Church, and you're almost always ending up among the Reformed crowd.

Many Calvinist leaders minimize being "a Calvinist" at all, since, as they see it, all John Calvin did was accurately and faithfully expound what the Bible teaches. They don't understand themselves as holding foremost to the theology of John Calvin per se, but to the essential message of the Christian faith as found in the Bible—a message that long predates Calvin but which he correctly taught. This is what Michael Horton has in mind when he writes: "I don't like the term 'Calvinism' very much. In fact, I don't know many Calvinists who do."[57] Similarly, Mark Driscoll in a sermon from 2009 quipped, "I'm not a Calvinist, but I believe in what he taught, and what he taught was the Bible." Driscoll clarified: "Technically, I am a Calvinist, and all John Calvin did was teach the Bible. That's why I don't like to say I'm a Calvinist; I like to say I love the Bible." Examples of this type of strategic discourse—this uneasy tension with the very word "Calvinism" *for this reason*—could easily be multiplied many times over.

This matter-of-factness has a long track record among Calvinists. Consider the nineteenth-century English, Baptist preacher Charles Spurgeon's famous line: "I have my own private opinion that there is no such thing as preaching Christ and Him crucified, unless we preach what nowadays is called Calvinism. It is a nickname to call it Calvinism; Calvinism is the gospel, and

---

[56] https://www.youtube.com/watch?v=jscdlO1BUj0, accessed May 11, 2018.

[57] Horton, *For Calvinism*, 19. To be fair, one page prior, Horton wrote: "It is not only unhelpful but erroneous to suggest that Arminians do not take the Bible seriously or entrust their salvation to God's grace in Christ."

nothing else."[58] Spurgeon's confidence has carried over into present-day New Calvinists. And this public presentation functions as a strategic position-taking, giving Calvinists a significant competitive advantage in relation to the rest of American Evangelicalism today.

Focus on Urban Centers

Moreover, New Calvinist leaders seek to generate their own sociocultural strength by *strategically positioning themselves in culturally "upstream" urban centers and global cities in order to influence and produce mainstream national culture most effectively*. The word "upstream" is the crux of the idea—namely, that large cities are the places from which nearly all of the most consequential things in cultural and political fields (art, music, education, research, fashion, mores, publishing, policy, media, commerce, etc.) originate and in time "flow downstream" to the rest of a nation. What happens in cities, the thinking goes, holds disproportionate "weight" and influence on what happens in out-lying suburban and rural areas. For this reason, New Calvinist leaders have broadly accepted the strategic import of moving into and ministering in in-fluential urban centers.

No leader in the Reformed resurgence has heralded the call to cities as much as Tim Keller, pastor at RPC in Manhattan. Back in 2006, speaking at John Piper's Desiring God conference, Keller argued for the crucial need for what he called "gospel urbanizing."[59] "[T]he cities are disproportion-ately important with respect to culture," Keller later wrote. "As the cities go, so goes society."[60] More recently, Keller has written at length about the stra-tegic importance of urban centers for Evangelical ministry and cultural in-fluence in his 2012 book, *Center Church: Doing Balanced, Gospel-Centered Ministry in Your City*.[61] The middle third of the book falls under the rubric "City"[62]—the other two being "Gospel" and "Movement." In that work, Keller spells out in great detail his vision for doing Evangelical ministry in cities,

---

[58] Charles H. Spurgeon, *A Defense of Calvinism*, accessed online from https://archive.spurgeon.org/calvinis.php

[59] http://www.desiringgod.org/messages/the-supremacy-of-christ-and-the-gospel-in-a-postmodern-world, accessed January 18, 2016. Keller's talk at this conference was adopted into print as "The Gospel and the Supremacy of Christ in a Postmodern World," in *The Supremacy of Christ in a Postmodern World*, ed. John Piper and Justin Taylor (Wheaton, IL: Crossway, 2007), 103–123.

[60] Ibid., 113.

[61] Published by Zondervan, 2012.

[62] Keller, *Center Church*, 87–247, especially 135–180.

contending: "Fruitful ministry in this century must embrace the unavoidable reality of the city. . . . [B]ecause the world is on its way to becoming 70 percent urban, we all need a theological vision that is distinctly urban. Even if you don't go to the city to minister, make no mistake: the city is coming to you."[63]

As Keller sees it, urban ministry provides unparalleled opportunities for reaching four groups of people.[64] The first is *young people*. Keller writes: "The prospects for advancement, the climate of constant innovation and change, the coming together of diverse influences and people—all of these appeal to young adults." "If the church in the West remains, for the most part, in the suburbs of Middle America and neglects the great cities, it risks losing an entire generation of American society's leaders." The second is *cultural elites*. Here Keller focuses on "those who have a disproportionate influence on how human life is lived in a society because they exert power in business, publishing, the media, the academy, and the arts." Third is *accessible but "unreached" people groups*, especially new immigrants. And fourth, urban ministry offers opportunities to serve *the poor*, which, Keller notes, also validates the church's ministry to the professional class.

Al Mohler of SBTS has made a similar observation. Responding on his website to new statistics about global urbanization from the *Financial Times*, he argued:

[T]he cities are where the people are. In the course of less than 300 years, our world will have shifted from one in which only 3 percent of people live in cities, to one in which 80 percent are resident in urban areas. If the Christian church does not learn new modes of urban ministry, we will find ourselves on the outside looking in. The Gospel of Jesus Christ must call a new generation of committed Christians into these teeming cities. As these new numbers make clear, there really is no choice.[65]

---

[63] Ibid., 88. Demonstrating the place of leaders' strategy, savvy, and "social skill" for religious vitality, in one brief section (pp. 173–178) Keller expounds seven features of "a church for the city"—these are "(1) respect for urban sensibility, (2) unusual sensitivity to cultural differences, (3) commitment to neighborhood and justice, (4) integration of faith and work, (5) bias for complex evangelism, (6) preaching that both attracts and challenges urban people, and (7) commitment to artistry and creativity."

[64] Ibid., 160–162.

[65] Al Mohler, "From Megacity to 'Metacity'—The Shape of the Future," *AlbertMohler.com*, April 22, 2010, http://www.albertmohler.com/2010/04/22/from-megacity-to-metacity-the-shape-of-the-future/, accessed January 18, 2016. Mohler struck the same note a few months later on his website when he likewise responded to an issue of the journal *Foreign Policy* on global urbanization: Al Mohler, "Mission and Metropolis: The Church and the City," *AlbertMohler.com*, September 10, 2010, http://www.albertmohler.com/2010/09/10/mission-and-metropolis-the-church-and-the-city/, accessed January 18, 2016.

Mark Driscoll, too, has emphasized the need for Evangelical leaders to focus on cities. In his 2013 interview with conservative media host Glenn Beck, Driscoll said:

> Culture is made "upstream" in the city and then it flows "downstream" into the suburban and rural areas. A lot of people of faith, a lot of conservative families—husbands, wives, kids—they're in the suburbs, they're in the rural areas, because [of factors like] cost of living, education, all the very real variables. Meanwhile, all the single college-educated culture-makers are flooding into the cities[66]—the very places that the churches have tended to flee over the generations prior. And the question [for Evangelical leaders] is, is there an opportunity to plant churches, to go back and to re-evangelize major urban centers, especially young men.[67]

Recent years have seen a handful of shorter devotional and missiological books from neo-Reformed leaders on the call to minister in urban centers. One is *For the City*,[68] coauthored by Matt Carter, pastor at The Austin Stone Community Church in Austin, Texas, and Darrin Patrick. Another is *Why Cities Matter*,[69] coauthored by Stephen Um, who leads Citylife Presbyterian Church (PCA) in Boston, Massachusetts, and Justin Buzzard, senior pastor of Garden City Church in Silicon Valley, California. Yet another example is *Christ + City*,[70] by Jon Dennis at Holy Trinity Church in downtown Chicago—which is a rare case of a nondenominational Evangelical church that also explicitly subscribes to the Westminster Confession of Faith.

Other prominent examples of New Calvinist leaders intentionally ministering in urban centers include John Piper in Minneapolis, James MacDonald in Chicago, and Mark Dever in Washington, DC, to name just a few. Looking beyond the United States, Redeemer City to City is a major engine for planting churches in diverse "global cities" around the world.[71]

---

[66] See Richard Florida, *Cities and the Creative Class* (New York: Routledge, 2005).

[67] https://www.youtube.com/watch?v=38BBsfL3Fkg, accessed January 18, 2016. This was also a reoccurring theme in his preaching at Mars Hill Church.

[68] Darrin Patrick and Matt Carter with Joel A. Lindsey, *For the City: Proclaiming and Living Out the Gospel* (Grand Rapids, MI: Zondervan, 2010).

[69] Stephen T. Um and Justin Buzzard, *Why Cities Matter: To God, the Culture, and the Church* (Wheaton, IL: Crossway, 2013).

[70] Jon M. Dennis, *Christ + City: Why the Greatest Need of the City Is the Greatest News of All* (Wheaton, IL: Crossway, 2013).

[71] Saskia Sassen, *The Global City: New York, London, Tokyo* (Princeton, NJ: Princeton University Press, [1991] 2001); Saskia Sassen, ed., *Global Networks, Linked Cities* (New York: Routledge, 2002).

Worth highlighting is the subtext in all this—namely, not only are neo-Reformed Evangelical leaders not afraid of the supposedly religiously corrosive effects of multiculturalism, rationalization, and (post)modernism in urban settings, as 1960s Bergerian secularization theory would have it.[72] They are convinced that—with a little thought and work—Christians can "hold their own" in cities, intellectually and culturally. More than that, these leaders envision not only existing in community as a thriving Evangelical subculture in the broader urban "ecosystem," but, further, attempt to be an engaged, vital source of betterment for the good of the whole city. And in fact many are currently doing just that. This adds further credence to Christian Smith's argument that urban centers are more than capable of sustaining traditional religious faith.[73] In contrast to conventional secularization theory's view, New Calvinist leaders see that sustaining a vibrant, traditional Evangelical faith in large cities is not only possible—it's *strategic*.[74]

Strategically Apolitical and Nonpartisan

New Calvinist leaders also strategically position themselves and their message as *apolitical and nonpartisan, particularly in light of the negative associations many Americans, and especially Millennials, have with the political ambitions of the Christian Right*. Granted, this positioning on politics is hardly unique today in the American Evangelical field; many Evangelical leaders outside of the New Calvinist movement but who likewise lean in a socially and politically conservative direction similarly choose to present themselves and their Christian message as simply not interested in joining forces with the Republican Party. And others, especially several neo-Anabaptist and progressive Emergent leaders, lean left politically and are genuinely not sympathetic with political conservatism at all. So being nonpartisan offers less of a "competitive advantage" in the field than does, say,

---

[72] Berger, *The Sacred Canopy.*

[73] Smith et al., *American Evangelicalism*, 107–113. See also Claude S. Fischer, "Toward a Subcultural Theory of Urbanism," *American Journal of Sociology* 80, no. 6 (1975): 1319–1341; Claude S. Fischer, *The Urban Experience*, 2nd ed. (New York: Harcourt Brace Jovanovich, [1976] 1984).

[74] On the centrality of urban ministry in the rise of the early Church, see Wayne A. Meeks, *The First Urban Christians: The Social World of the Apostle Paul*, 2nd ed. (New Haven, CT: Yale University Press, [1983] 2003); Rodney Stark, *The Rise of Christianity: How the Obscure, Marginal Jesus Movement Became the Dominant Religious Force in the Western World in a Few Centuries* (Princeton, NJ: Princeton University Press, 1996); Rodney Stark, *Cities of God: The Real Story of How Christianity Became an Urban Movement and Conquered Rome* (New York: HarperCollins, 2006).

gender complementarianism or Calvinism itself. It is closer to a tactic than a strategy, as those were distinguished in chapter 4.

Despite the commonness of this standpoint, it is nevertheless noteworthy because of the long shadow the Christian Right of the 1980s and 1990s still casts over American Evangelicalism—less so among Evangelical leaders themselves but more in the "public mind" and in scholarly (and journalistic) attention to Evangelicalism. There is an unfortunate mismatch today between the extent to which scholars and journalists, on one hand, and present-day Evangelical leaders themselves, on the other, understand Evangelicalism to be in large measure really about political ambitions. Among sociologists who study religion in the United States, "Evangelicalism" and "politics" are more often than not spoken in the same breath, thus mirroring the common perception among religiously unaffiliated Americans more generally.[75] Books on Jerry Falwell, the Moral Majority, culture wars, the Religious Right, and the link between Evangelicalism and conservative politics still proliferate.[76] Even recent books seeking to point out that not all American Evangelical leaders are GOP culture warriors frame their discussion mainly in terms of alternative, less conservative political visions of some Evangelicals.[77] Without detracting from this body of scholarship, the overwhelming impression it gives is nevertheless that American Evangelicalism is of scholarly interest only to the degree that it is a thinly veiled appendage of the American political field.

Partly because of the association between American Evangelicalism and politics, and partly because over the years conservative Evangelical leaders have worked out new, less triumphalist theologies of public engagement,[78] leaders of the New Calvinism do not pin their hopes on success in politics. The standard approach among New Calvinist leaders is to encourage their

[75] Brad Vermurlen, "Perceptions of and Objections to Christianity among Unchurched and Dechurched Adults," *Review of Religious Research* 57, no. 1 (2015): 161–162; David Kinnaman and Gabe Lyons, *UnChristian: What a New Generation Really Thinks about Christianity and Why It Matters* (Grand Rapids, MI: Baker Books, 2007), 153–180.

[76] Among a large literature, see Lydia Bean, *The Politics of Evangelical Identity: Local Churches and Partisan Divides in the United States and Canada* (Princeton, NJ: Princeton University Press, 2014); Tina Fetner, *How the Religious Right Shaped Lesbian and Gay Activism* (Minneapolis: University of Minnesota Press, 2008); Dochuk, *From Bible Belt to Sunbelt*; Harding, *The Book of Jerry Falwell*; Lienesch, *Redeeming America*; Martin, *With God on Our Side*; Sutton, *Jerry Falwell and the Rise of the Religious Right*; Wilcox and Robinson, *Onward Christian Soldiers?*; Williams, *God's Own Party*.

[77] For instance, E. J. Dionne, Jr., *Souled Out: Reclaiming Faith and Politics after the Religious Right* (Princeton, NJ: Princeton University Press, 2008); Wes Markofski, *New Monasticism*.

[78] For example, Hunter, *To Change the World*; Tyler Wigg-Stevenson, *The World Is Not Ours to Save: Finding the Freedom to Do Good* (Downers Grove, IL: InterVarsity Press, 2013).

congregants and other followers to be involved in the political process and (like all Americans who vote do) to vote based on their personal values and convictions; at the same time, one will rarely hear a leader say the only faithful vote is a vote for the Republican Party. Another layer deeper, there is a genuine belief that, as Al Mohler stated it, "the Kingdom of God is never up for a vote in any election. [. . .] As Evangelical Christians, we must engage in political action, not because we believe the conceit that politics is ultimate, but because we must obey our Redeemer when He commanded that we must love our neighbor."[79] There is a sense among New Calvinists that the age of the Moral Majority is a bygone era, that its political focus evinced a peculiar blend of triumphalism and insecurity in the reign of God, and that faithfulness as a Christian does not depend on success in the political sphere.

Talking about what he called "the death of Christendom in the West," Mark Driscoll, during his interview with Glenn Beck, said: "The Religious Right, the Moral Majority—everybody put those T-shirts away. Nobody's wearing 'em."[80] That project, he thinks, has failed.[81] More recently, during a sermon on politics, Driscoll said:

> I'm not highly political. I'm a Bible teacher. [. . .] What the Word of God does is it goes above culture, goes above nations, goes above politics—and says there is a King, whose name is Jesus, and there is a Kingdom that lasts forever. What that gives us is an opportunity to not just look out at the culture but to look up to the Kingdom. [. . .] The Gospel of Jesus Christ and the salvation of Jesus Christ and the transformation of Jesus Christ—it's the only hope for the entire world. What I don't want us to understand is there's two groups out there, let's bring it in here [the Church]. No, no.

---

[79] Al Mohler, "Engaging the City of Man: Christian Faith and Politics," *AlbertMohler.com*, July 13, 2005, http://www.albertmohler.com/2005/07/13/engaging-the-city-of-man-christian-faith-and-politics/, accessed February 25, 2016. The piece about loving one's neighbor shows New Calvinist leaders understand their votes not to be imposing their particular religious and moral ideas on others but as pursuing what is objectively in the best interest of everyone, whether they know it or not: "We are concerned for the culture not because we believe that the culture is ultimate, but because we know that our neighbors must hear the gospel, even as we hope and strive for their good, peace, security, and well-being."

[80] https://www.youtube.com/watch?v=slaCP4mK4_8, accessed February 25, 2016.

[81] Apparently having trouble believing New Calvinist leaders are not interested in advancing a political project, progressive neo-Anabaptist leader Zach Hoag argued that Driscoll was just speaking in "code" and is trying to usher in "a new religious right." See Zach Hoag, "Mark Driscoll on Glenn Beck," *The Huffington Post*, December 6, 2013, http://www.huffingtonpost.com/zach-j-hoag/mark-driscoll-glenn-beck_b_4392602.html?utm_hp_ref=mark-driscoll, accessed February 29, 2016.

There's a third group in here, and we're sent out there. We're sent to invite all people, all races, all cultures, all parties, all tribes, all ideologies, all perspectives to realize that they are the problem, not the solution. That they are by nature an enemy of God, and they are not in the position to judge like God. That they need Jesus and everyone needs Jesus and our answer is always give your sin to Jesus, become a "new man,"[82] join the third way, be part of the Church of Jesus Christ, and love and serve the family, and love and endure with those who disagree with you.

One of the events I attended at Bethlehem Baptist Church, in June 2013, was a well-attended evening seminar at the downtown campus addressing issues related to the recent legal redefinition of marriage in Minnesota to include gay and lesbian couples. The event was titled "Standing Firm in the Evil Day."[83] Thinking back on the event in an interview, one of the panelists, Joe Rigney, told me: "We don't want to be partisans for any kind of political debate. We want to be biblically faithful, which might mean that we look like one political party more than another, but our allegiance isn't to that party. Our allegiance is to God, to Christ."

John Piper made it clear that he has no interest in preaching politics or being co-opted by any political party. In a lecture later uploaded to YouTube,[84] he acknowledged that when the question is how to relate to politics, the answer is different for individual Christians than it is for the Church as an organization or institution. "I do think the role of the Christian and the role of the Church are not the same." Individual Christians, he said, can and should get political, express their political views, vote, and even be involved in political office. The Church, on the other hand, ought to relate to politics in a less direct and more measured way. "As a pastor in the pulpit, I don't want to play any partisan politics, even on issues I'm totally committed to." The reason for this, Piper said, is that being explicitly political would undermine his "prophetic voice"—that is, his credibility to speak influentially to every person, regardless of one's political preferences. Still, like most pastors

---

[82] This is a reference to Ephesians 2, where the Apostle Paul encourages oneness between Jews and Gentiles: "But now in Christ Jesus you who once were far off have been brought near by the blood of Christ. For he himself is our peace, who has made us both one and has broken down in his flesh the dividing wall of hostility by abolishing the law of commandments expressed in ordinances, that he might create in himself one new man in place of the two, so making peace, and might reconcile us both to God in one body through the cross, thereby killing the hostility."

[83] A video of the event is available online at https://www.youtube.com/watch?v=Sklvrh1XHXw, accessed May 16, 2018.

[84] https://www.youtube.com/watch?v=X3tWD1MZrQ8, accessed February 25, 2016.

within the New Calvinist movement, he does address hot-button issues like abortion, gay marriage, poverty, and racial justice. But he tries to address them as moral, theological, practical, and spiritual issues—*not* as political issues. "We're not Democrats; we're not Republicans; we're *Christians*," Piper cried out.

Tim Keller holds a similar view—refusing to align himself publicly with any political party, and drawing a distinction between how individual Christians should be involved in politics versus how the Church as an institution ought to be involved:

> I never tell anybody how I vote. . . . [N]either the Democratic nor the Republican party can capture all of the Christian social ethical points. Catholic social policy and Evangelical Christian social policy are roughly the same. They tend to be more conservative of things like abortion, sex, that sort of thing; they tend to be more liberal on things like the environment, being pro-union. And so I think most thoughtful Christians—Catholic and Protestant—would agree that neither party can just capture the whole Christian social ethical agenda. [. . .]
>
> As a *church*, let's not so much lift up candidates or parties. But as a congregation, what we ought to do is work directly on needs like education, poverty, environmental problems, sex trafficking, whatever. So as a congregation, we try to work directly on issues in our city that have political ramifications, but aren't particularly aligned with one party or the other.
>
> As *individuals*, I say go get involved in parties. Don't stay out of that, but just do it critically. And that's the reason why I don't tell people how I vote. Because then folks in my church would be feeling that one party or another was being made to feel less than welcome. All I have to do as a Senior Pastor is to say "I vote this way or that way," and people from the other party will just feel less welcome. And that's not what I want to do.[85]

The way abortion is typically addressed in the New Calvinism illustrates this further. Every year on Sanctity of Human Life Sunday, the Sunday falling closest to the January 22nd anniversary of the *Roe v. Wade* decision, Matt Chandler at The Village Church preaches a sermon about the sanctity of human life and the problem of abortion. Most years, he prefaces his sermon by saying that for him abortion is not a political issue. In 2015, he prefaced

---

[85] https://www.youtube.com/watch?v=nx0NULq_KRU, accessed February 25, 2016.

his sermon with these words: "This is not a political sermon, as I do not consider myself a political man. Here's what I know from my Bible: all the parties are going to fail me. They cannot be where my hope resides. [. . .] I don't believe this is a political issue. I believe this is a scientific issue and a deeply theological issue. I'm not trying to make political statements."[86] In 2016, near the beginning of his sermon, he said: "Don't think I'm having a political conversation today. I'm kingdom of God party. I've got my Guy. I've watched the debate. I'm not confident that any of those brothers are our savior. I'm fairly certain none of them are. My hope is not in America being great again, although I want to be a good citizen." Chandler continued: "I don't have a Republican agenda here. I'm not bought or owned by any party. I've got my Guy, and my hope is in that Guy, and long after the United States ceases to exist, I'll have my Guy."[87] In 2014, Chandler tackled the issue of voting as it relates to abortion, saying: "This should inform how we vote. I'm not talking Republican, Democrat. I'm saying we can't afford for this issue to not bear weight on who we vote for."[88] He then made the argument that, for Christians, a political candidate who is not pro-life ought to be automatically ruled out as a realistic option.

As described in chapter 2, New Calvinist leaders are uniformly pro-life, against gay marriage, strong on religious liberty, and socially conservative on various other topics. The way they tend to vote is perhaps the most poorly kept secret in American Evangelicalism. Nevertheless, in a contemporary American religious and political landscape historically and culturally "downstream" from the overtly political Christian Right of the 1980s and 1990s, coming across in public as nonpartisan and apolitical is another significant way New Calvinist leaders have found to position themselves to gain a hearing for their religious message.

Excursus: Trump

National politics are only marginally important to leaders of the New Calvinism, especially in contrast with their animating mission to preach and

---

[86] https://www.tvcresources.net/resource-library/sermons/the-sanctity-of-human-life-prayer-2015, accessed May 7, 2019.

[87] https://www.tvcresources.net/resource-library/sermons/the-sanctity-of-human-life--2, accessed May 7, 2019.

[88] https://www.tvcresources.net/resource-library/sermons/the-sanctity-of-human-life, accessed May 7, 2019.

explain their understanding of the Christian message, to evangelize non-Christians, to form mature disciples of Jesus, and to found new, culturally savvy, Gospel-centered churches. Also, data collection for this book wrapped up prior to the 2016 election. Nevertheless, the current link between Evangelicals and Trump begs for further comment. Given that New Calvinist leaders are uniformly pro-life, against same-sex marriage, strong on religious liberty, and socially conservative on various other topics, one might reasonably expect New Calvinists tend to be Trump supporters—or at least to have reluctantly voted for the Trump-Pence ticket. In fact, the opposite is the case. Neo-Reformed leaders, in turns out, are among the most vocal in publicly expressing concerns about Donald Trump's character and temperament, and these leaders significantly help constitute what is now called the "Never Trump" faction of Evangelicalism in the United States.

In other words, leaders of the Reformed resurgence are distinctly and emphatically not like the "court Evangelicals," to use John Fea's term, who in recent years have sought access to and publicly defended President Trump—people such as Robert Jeffress, Jerry Falwell Jr., Franklin Graham, James Dobson, Paula White, Mark Burns, Ralph Reed, and Tony Perkins.[89] My data do not include any special access to how New Calvinist leaders voted, but a general awareness of the New Calvinism strongly suggests they do not fit the stereotype of conservative Evangelical Trump supporters. One need only look at their public comments.

In September 2015, before Trump had clinched the Republican nomination, Russell Moore penned a strongly worded op-ed in *The New York Times* expressing dismay that Evangelicals would support Donald Trump's campaign for the presidency.[90] Moore wrote: "Donald J. Trump stands astride the polls in the Republican presidential race, beating all comers in virtually every demographic of the primary electorate. Most illogical is his support from Evangelicals and other social conservatives. To back Mr. Trump, these voters must repudiate everything they believe." Moore concluded:

> Jesus taught his disciples to "count the cost" of following him. We should know, he said, where we're going and what we're leaving behind. We should

---

[89] John Fea, *Believe Me: The Evangelical Road to Donald Trump* (Grand Rapids, MI: William B. Eerdmans, 2018).

[90] Russell Moore, "Have Evangelicals Who Support Trump Lost Their Values?" *The New York Times*, September 17, 2015, https://www.nytimes.com/2015/09/17/opinion/have-evangelicals-who-support-trump-lost-their-values.html, accessed December 21, 2017.

also count the cost of following Donald Trump. To do so would mean that we've decided to join the other side of the culture war, that image and celebrity and money and power and social Darwinist "winning" trump the conservation of moral principles and a just society.

Likewise, the month before the 2016 election, Collin Hansen, editorial director for The Gospel Coalition, published an op-ed in *The Washington Post* in which he called out the hypocrisy of Evangelical leaders supporting Donald Trump.[91] He wrote that Trump is "beholden to the unholy trinity of money, sex and power," and his campaign for president was marked by "overt and implicit misogyny and racism." Hansen, disturbed by his fellow Evangelicals' willingness to cast their vote for Trump, argued: "The 2016 presidential election will be remembered as the last spasm of energy from the Religious Right before its overdue death." The following year, when approximately 80 percent of white Evangelicals in Alabama voted for Roy Moore, a Christian nationalist accused of pursuing romantic relationships with multiple underaged girls, Hansen said the special election for the Alabama senate seat exposed "the moral and theological rot" in American Evangelicalism. "There will not be a coherent Evangelical movement to emerge from this political season," Hansen concluded.[92] He later sat down for a nearly hour-long interview with ABC News in which he reiterated these concerns.[93]

Also the month before the election, Al Mohler published an op-ed in *The Washington Post* in which he wrote: "This year, the Republican nominee is, in terms of character, the personification of what evangelicals have preached (and voted) against." And "I am among those who see Evangelical support for Trump as a horrifying embarrassment—a price for possible political gain that is simply unthinkable and too high to pay."[94] Two days later, Mohler was on CNN Tonight with Don Lemon and explained why he believed both Trump

[91] Collin Hansen, "This Is the Last Spastic Breath from the Religious Right before Its Overdue Death," *The Washington Post*, October 8, 2016, https://www.washingtonpost.com/news/acts-of-faith/wp/2016/10/08/this-is-the-last-spastic-breath-from-the-religious-right-before-its-overdue-death/, accessed May 3, 2019.

[92] Quoted in Sarah Pulliam Bailey, "'A Spiritual Battle:' How Roy Moore Tested White Evangelical Allegiance to the Republican Party," *The Washington Post*, December 13, 2017, https://www.washingtonpost.com/news/acts-of-faith/wp/2017/12/13/a-spiritual-battle-how-roy-moores-failed-campaign-tested-evangelicals/, accessed May 6, 2019.

[93] Available at https://abcnews.go.com/Politics/evangelical-leader-collin-hansen-believes-live-culture-full/story?id=53370130, accessed May 6, 2019.

[94] Mohler, "Donald Trump Has Created an Excruciating Moment for Evangelicals," *The Washington Post*, October 9, 2016, https://www.washingtonpost.com/news/acts-of-faith/wp/2016/10/09/donald-trump-has-created-an-excruciating-moment-for-evangelicals/, accessed May 6, 2019.

and Hillary Clinton fail "the baseline test of character" needed for the presidency. Mohler commented: "When it comes to Donald Trump, Evangelicals are going to have to ask the huge question: Is it worth destroying our moral credibility to support someone who is beneath the baseline level of human decency for anyone who should deserve our vote?" Trump, Mohler stated, presents himself as "a sexual predator" and his bad behavior is "so far over the line that I think we have to recognize we wouldn't want this man as our next door neighbor much less as the inhabitant of 1600 Pennsylvania Avenue. And long term, I'm afraid people are going to remember Evangelicals in this election for supporting the unsupportable and defending the absolutely indefensible."[95]

On his blog at The Gospel Coalition, the month before the election, Kevin DeYoung revealed: "I will vote for President, but I will not vote for either of the major party candidates. I have been critical of both candidates—more so than in any previous presidential election—because I believe both fail to clear a basic threshold of personal integrity, sound judgment, and trustworthiness."[96] DeYoung continued: "Even if you are a hold-your-noser instead of a NeverTrumper, every Christian should agree that Trump's comments about women and his actions toward women (not to mention the way he has spoken of minorities) have been horrid. We embarrass ourselves when we try to defend the indefensible."

Tim Keller wrote an article for *The New Yorker* with the title "Can Evangelicalism Survive Donald Trump and Roy Moore?"[97] After explaining the history of the label "Evangelical," Keller wrote: "People who once called themselves the 'Moral Majority' are now seemingly willing to vote for anyone, however immoral, who supports their political positions." He went on: "Many younger believers and Christians of color, who had previously identified with Evangelicalism, have also declared their abandonment of the label. 'Evangelical' used to denote people who claimed the high moral ground; now, in popular usage, the word is nearly synonymous with 'hypocrite.'" He suggested an "older, white Evangelicalism" is giving way to a newer form of historic Protestantism that is theologically orthodox, politically

---

[95] https://www.youtube.com/watch?v=exvuCgWiIGk, accessed May 6, 2019.

[96] Kevin DeYoung, "Seeking Clarity in This Confusing Election Season: Ten Thoughts," *DeYoung, Restless, and Reformed,* October 13, 2016, https://www.thegospelcoalition.org/blogs/kevin-deyoung/seeking-clarity-in-this-confusing-election-season-ten-thoughts/, accessed May 8, 2019.

[97] Tim Keller, "Can Evangelicalism Survive Donald Trump and Roy Moore?" *The New Yorker,* December 19, 2017, https://www.newyorker.com/news/news-desk/can-evangelicalism-survive-donald-trump-and-roy-moore, accessed December 21, 2017.

nonpartisan, multiethnic, younger, and socially conscious even if it doesn't use or like the name "Evangelical." About nine months later, a book excerpt from Keller appeared in *The New York Times* and was given the title "How Do Christians Fit into the Two-Party System? They Don't." While the article did not mention President Trump, Roy Moore, or the controversies surrounding them, Keller offered several reasons why, in his estimation, Christian believers "should not identify the Christian church or faith with a political party as the only Christian one."[98]

Justin Taylor of Crossway, writing for The Gospel Coalition, has been a consistent critic of Trump. A week before the election, reflecting on a mass email from Franklin Graham, Taylor wrote: "Graham's manner of talking about the 2016 election perfectly illustrates the problems of the old-style Religious Right, and why so many faithful Evangelicals will *not* be voting for Trump, in spite of the pleading of Graham, Pat Robertson, Jerry Falwell Jr., and others." Taylor highlighted "Trump's record of misogyny, race-baiting, boasting about sexual assault and adultery, and his lack of basic knowledge about all kinds of political matters," but Taylor made clear he also does not advocate voting for Hillary Clinton.[99] In another post, Taylor called Trump "boorish, divisive, and uninformed," and finally concluded: "I remain convinced that no major party has offered us a candidate worthy of evangelicals' support in 2016."[100]

As for Piper, a week before the election he said, "I will vote, but not for these two candidates."[101] On Trump's inauguration day, Piper released a statement at Desiring God titled "How to Live under an Unqualified President,"[102] which opened: "Today we will inaugurate a man to the presidency of the United States who is morally unqualified to be there. This is important to say just now because not to see it and feel it will add to the collapsing vision of leadership that enabled him to be nominated and elected." And

---

[98] Tim Keller, "How Do Christians Fit into the Two-Party System? They Don't," *The New York Times*, September 29, 2018, https://www.nytimes.com/2018/09/29/opinion/sunday/christians-politics-belief.html, accessed May 6, 2019.

[99] Justin Taylor, "Trump Victory: The Beginning of Revival?" *The Gospel Coalition*, November 1, 2016, https://www.thegospelcoalition.org/blogs/evangelical-history/republican-victory-a-sign-of-revival/, accessed May 9, 2019.

[100] Justin Taylor, "The Supreme Court and the Convoluted Case for Trump," *The Gospel Coalition*, September 29, 2016, https://www.thegospelcoalition.org/blogs/evangelical-history/the-supreme-court-and-the-convoluted-case-for-trump/, accessed May 9, 2019.

[101] https://www.youtube.com/watch?v=Ab8x_vrN_K0, accessed May 3, 2019.

[102] John Piper, "How to Live under an Unqualified President," *Desiring God*, January 20, 2017, https://www.desiringgod.org/articles/how-to-live-under-an-unqualified-president, accessed May 7, 2019.

after the election, in the context of growing black-white racial tensions and discussions about "white Evangelicalism," he reiterated that he did not vote for Donald Trump.[103] Public statements such as these capture the overall attitude from New Calvinist leaders regarding Trump and his nationalist politics.

The major exception is Wayne Grudem. Although Grudem didn't support or endorse Trump during the primaries, in July 2016 Grudem posted a 5,300-word essay in which he made his case why, "Now that Trump has won the GOP nomination, I think voting for Trump is a morally good choice."[104] Grudem recognized Trump's many flaws but nevertheless concluded "most of the policies he supports are those that will do the most good for the nation," especially in contrast to a Hillary Clinton presidency. However, a couple months later, immediately following the release of the *Access Hollywood* video from 2005, Grudem retracted his essay and in a new essay wrote: "There is no morally good presidential candidate in this election. I previously called Donald Trump a 'good candidate with flaws' and a 'flawed candidate' but I now regret that I did not more strongly condemn his moral character. I cannot commend Trump's moral character, and I strongly urge him to withdraw from the election."[105] Grudem made clear he was personally torn about what to do if Trump did not withdraw, but he absolutely would not vote for Hillary Clinton. Ten days later, Grudem released a third essay stating he would be voting for Trump despite his objectionable character "not with joy but reluctantly" on the basis of his policies and from a sense of obligation not to help Clinton implement her policies.[106]

---

[103] In a post reflecting on hip-hop artist Lecrae distancing himself from "white Evangelicalism," Piper comments: "John Piper and a few million other supposed natives [to white Evangelicalism] didn't vote for Donald Trump. We don't think unrepentant lechers should be president. We don't think Robert E. Lee is a simple embodiment of nobility. We don't think the confederate flag can fly with impunity. We don't think kneeling for justice desecrates the other flag. We are baffled that Philando Castile's shooter walks free. We are dismayed at the nationwide resurgence of manifest racial antagonism. We don't think 'systemic' is an unintelligible word. And a few of us, believe it or not, are impenitent five-point Calvinists (how else can you survive?). Is that 'white evangelicalism'?" Available at https://www.desiringgod.org/articles/116-been-real, accessed May 3, 2019.

[104] Wayne Grudem, "Why Voting for Donald Trump Is a Morally Good Choice," *Townhall*, July 28, 2016, https://townhall.com/columnists/waynegrudem/2016/07/28/why-voting-for-donald-trump-is-a-morally-good-choice-n2199564, accessed May 7, 2019.

[105] Wayne Grudem, "Trump's Moral Character and the Election," *Townhall*, October 9, 2016, https://townhall.com/columnists/waynegrudem/2016/10/09/trumps-moral-character-and-the-election-n2229846, accessed May 7, 2019.

[106] Wayne Grudem, "If You Don't Like Either Candidate, Then Vote for Trump's Policies," *Townhall*, October 19, 2016, https://townhall.com/columnists/waynegrudem/2016/10/19/if-you-dont-like-either-candidate-then-vote-for-trumps-policies-n2234187, accessed May 7, 2019.

Public comments such as these reflect the overall attitude toward Donald Trump and Trumpism among the New Calvinist movement, at least at the level of pastors, seminary professors, and other leaders. My strong impression without systematic social science data is that most leaders of the New Calvinism did not support Trump in the primaries, were seriously concerned about Trump's character and rhetoric throughout his entire campaign, and in the end did not vote for Trump. Some lesser-known men pastoring smaller churches in the orbit of the New Calvinism likely voted, along with Grudem, for Trump reluctantly and after much searching by focusing on the competing policy visions of the two major parties. Even with little data, it is clear the New Calvinism—at the level of religious leadership—does not fit the popular image of conservative Evangelicals enthusiastically supporting President Trump.

Self-Appointed Gatekeepers

In addition to the ways already described on previous pages, several New Calvinist leaders also strategically position themselves *as the rightful gatekeepers of their field's established "orthodoxy," functioning as if they had real authority to claim which other players are "in" and "out" of the American Evangelical field.*[107] Stated differently, some (though not all) New Calvinist leaders enact their accumulated symbolic power in the American Evangelical field as part of a "classification struggle" over which Christian leaders (in addition to themselves) ought to be classified or categorized as belonging to the field at all. This is accomplished mainly through the force of their public "speech,"[108] especially on the Internet, in which they draw symbolic boundaries marking off "lines" of inclusion and exclusion for being an Evangelical.[109] The concern is: who *really, truly* is an Evangelical Christian, and who, despite what they might say, is not? Which beliefs fit within Evangelicalism and which are out of bounds?

---

[107] Mamadi Corra and David Willer, "The Gatekeeper," *Sociological Theory* 20, no. 2 (2002): 180–207.

[108] Pierre Bourdieu, *Language and Symbolic Power* (Malden, MA: Polity Press, 1991); Loïc Wacquant, "Symbolic Power and Group-making: On Pierre Bourdieu's Reframing of Class," *Journal of Classical Sociology* 13, no. 2 (2013): 274–291.

[109] Michèle Lamont and Virág Molnár, "The Study of Boundaries in the Social Sciences," *Annual Review of Sociology* 28 (2002): 167–195.

This observation is not missed among leaders themselves. Propaganda, a hip-hop and spoken word artist who has moved mostly in Reformed circles, reflected on his experience: "Somehow or another the [R]eformed world centered itself as the sole protector and purveyor of orthodoxy. And I'm still seeing how the depths of how much that ruined my ability to see the absolute grandness of Christ incarnate really is [sic]."[110] Leaders in challenger positions, especially, are aware of this ongoing dynamic of the Evangelical field. As feminist writer Rachel Held Evans told me during her interview, the New Calvinism, in her estimation, is "a movement of gatekeepers, and it seems very focused on keeping the wrong people out and just really strict definitions for what a true Christian is, and [that basic definition] seems to be: Calvinist."[111]

This social dynamic—the strategic positioning of (many) New Calvinist leaders as authoritative gatekeepers of orthodoxy as part of the "classification struggle" over who and what counts as Evangelical—is illustrated in the following two subsections with what were two very public contests: the case of Rob Bell and the case of World Vision-USA. Along with this strategic positioning, a closely related but analytically distinct social causal mechanism we will also see in both examples is *incumbent religious leaders actively policing, drawing symbolic boundaries, and trying to enforce the Evangelical field's established "orthodoxy" based on the "rules of the game"* (as these rules were defined in the previous chapter).[112]

---

[110] https://twitter.com/prophiphop/status/1110975051593973760, accessed March 28, 2019.

[111] She, like several of the more progressive leaders I interviewed, made an exception for Tim Keller, when I asked.

[112] The need for the distinction between strategically positioning oneself as a field gatekeeper (with institutional or historical weight behind it) and the simple action of drawing symbolic boundaries can be seen, for example, with progressive Emergent leader Tony Jones's call on his *Patheos* blog for a "schism" from any church, ministry, publisher, or conference that does not accept the ordination of women. (Tony Jones, "It's Time for a Schism Regarding Women in the Church," *Theoblogy*, November 22, 2013, https://www.patheos.com/blogs/tonyjones/2013/11/22/its-time-for-a-schism-regarding-women-in-the-church/, accessed March 27, 2019) Because Jones was already part of an institutionally disconnected, up-start corner of American Protestantism, his impassioned call for schism was roundly dismissed and mocked by more traditional Christians. See, for example, Rod Dreher, "Oh Dear. We're Losing the Emergents," *The American Conservative*, November 26, 2013, http://www.theamericanconservative.com/dreher/oh-dear-were-losing-the-emergents/.

The Case of Rob Bell and *Love Wins*

One of the clearest examples in recent years of the penchant for contestation and boundary drawing in Evangelicalism is the controversy that surrounded the book *Love Wins*,[113] by Rob Bell, who at the time was the senior pastor at Mars Hill Bible Church[114] in Grandville, Michigan.[115] At the time of the controversy—in March 2011—Bell's Mars Hill was one of the largest and most visible churches in the country, with roughly 10,000 congregants walking through its doors on an average Sunday. Bell, now in his late forties, is nationally known, at least among Evangelicals, for his accessible and artistic books and his teaching role in a series of short Christian films called *Nooma*.[116] His influence in and over American Evangelicalism has been far-reaching. Rob Bell has been described in the mainstream press as being "savvy," "avant-garde," a "hipster," and a "rock star" in the Evangelical subculture. More than these, Bell is also a provocateur among American Evangelicals—communicating in nonlinear, poetic ways, hence often raising more questions than he answers, preferring conversation to clarity, discussions over dogmas.[117] His style embraces mystery and irony. While he does not apply the label to himself, eschewing labels generally, Bell is considered one of the figureheads of the "Emergent Church" (although that phrase has mostly fallen out of use among Evangelicals today).[118]

The controversy began with an online video of Rob Bell,[119] followed by a blog-post from Crossway's Justin Taylor, hosted by The Gospel Coalition,[120]

---

[113] Rob Bell, *Love Wins: A Book about Heaven, Hell, and the Fate of Every Person Who Ever Lived* (New York: HarperCollins, 2011).

[114] A clarification is needed to prevent a likely confusion. The megachurch in Grandville, Michigan, formerly pastored by Rob Bell, is named Mars Hill Bible Church. In contrast, the now-defunct megachurch centered in Seattle, led by Mark Driscoll, was named Mars Hill Church. Both were highly visible, nationally known, Evangelical megachurches, and both go (or went) by the shortened name, "Mars Hill." Despite their similar names, however, these churches were entirely independent of each other and theologically quite different. Their shared name stems from a biblical reference: "Mars Hill" is the transliterated form of the Greek word *Areopagus*, which is the spot in Athens that functioned as the intellectual and judicial hub of the ancient world. This key location is the setting for Acts 17, verses 16–34, in which the Apostle Paul preaches the news of the resurrected Jesus to the aristocracy in Greece.

[115] http://marshill.org/

[116] http://nooma.com/. The name "Nooma" is a phonetic spelling of the Greek word πνευμα (transliterated as "pneuma"), which means "wind," "spirit," or "breath."

[117] See James K. Wellman Jr., *Rob Bell and a New American Christianity* (Nashville, TN: The United Methodist Publishing House, 2012).

[118] This section draws information and quotations from more than thirty sources, which include mostly a combination of journalistic news articles and blog-posts from Evangelical leaders who were involved in the conflict (pastors, seminary professors, etc.). A list of these sources is available by request.

[119] http://vimeo.com/20272585

[120] http://thegospelcoalition.org/blogs/justintaylor/2011/02/26/rob-bell-universalist/

and a subsequent tweet from John Piper on Twitter. For present purposes, the story begins when Justin Taylor published a post on his blog *Between Two Worlds* that brought attention to—and warned about—a promotional video for Rob Bell's (at the time) forthcoming book, *Love Wins*. In the art-themed video trailer, Rob Bell walks through an empty, snow-covered street while addressing the claim that Mahatma Gandhi, a Hindu, is now in Hell, asking:

> Gandhi's in hell? He is? And someone knows this for sure? [. . .] Will only a few select people make it to heaven? And will billions and billions of people burn forever in hell? And if that's the case, how do you become one of the few? [. . .] What we believe about heaven and hell is incredibly important, because it exposes what we believe about who God is and what God is like. What you discover in the Bible is so surprising, unexpected, and beautiful that whatever we've been told or taught, the good news is actually better than that—better than we could ever imagine. The good news is that love wins.

This is hardly a clear theological statement on the afterlife. Nevertheless, Justin Taylor saw the promotional video—along with the publisher's description of the book, which stated that Rob Bell is "arguing that a loving God would never sentence human souls to eternal suffering"[121]—as suggesting that Bell is a universalist. The term "universalism" is theological parlance for the view that everyone, at least eventually, somehow, "goes to heaven," and therefore there either is no hell or hell exists but is, or eventually will be, empty.[122] Such a view runs counter to the more familiar, traditionalist Christian understanding of the afterlife, with only some people going to heaven for eternity and others enduring God's judgment and wrath for eternity in hell. For some, more theologically conservative pastors and theologians, the issue of heaven and hell is serious enough that to promote universalism warrants charges of heresy. Taylor, on his blog, for example,

---

[121] The publisher's description was later changed to say, somewhat awkwardly, that Rob Bell is "arguing, would a loving God send people to eternal torment forever?"

[122] As the choppy structure of this sentence hints, there is more than one kind of universalism. As just one point of variation, Calvin College professor James K. A. Smith (writing in light of the Rob Bell controversy) distinguished between "old" and "new" universalism. Old universalism, Smith argued, is a relativistic, "all-roads-lead-to-God" view that is "generally embarrassed by Christian particularity and any claims to the divinity of Christ." The "new universalism," in contrast, is a distinctively "Christocentric universalism," in which all persons are saved *in Christ*, who is the Victor over all sin and death. Available at http://forsclavigera.blogspot.com/2011/04/can-hope-be-wrong-on-new-universalism.html.

argued, "[T]his video from Bell himself shows that he is moving farther and farther away from anything resembling biblical Christianity." It did not take long for other leaders of the New Calvinism to see Taylor's post and to become aware of Bell's controversial new book. But unexpectedly, the issue of Bell possibly being a universalist "went viral."

The original thrust of the controversy—and its first several hours—happened on Twitter. John Piper tweeted (to his at the time almost half a million followers) a link to Justin Taylor's original post, along with the caption (now infamous among Evangelicals): "Farewell, Rob Bell." This was around 3:00 pm on February 26, 2011. By that evening, the user handle "@RobBell" had become a top-ten worldwide "trending" topic on Twitter.[123] Because of John Piper's tweet, and its rapid expansion on Twitter, there was even some initial confusion over its meaning, with some Twitter users mistakenly thinking that Rob Bell had died. In actuality, John Piper's "Farewell" meant that, according to Piper, Rob Bell was no longer a partaker of Evangelical orthodoxy.[124] When all was said and done, Taylor's debate-igniting post had roughly a quarter-million unique views, had been tweeted more than 4,000 times, and was "recommended" on Facebook by 29,000 users.

But the spectacle was only getting started. From there, Kevin DeYoung quickly shot back with eight reasons that "we need God's wrath" and "the doctrine of eternal punishment." Following that, Al Mohler called Rob Bell's position "a new form of cultural Christianity," claiming that Bell "plays with theology the way a cat plays with a mouse" and is introducing "distortions of the Gospel that deceive the people of God." No matter how the new book turned out, Mohler wrote, "its promotion is the sad equivalent of a theological striptease." Likewise, Douglas Wilson highlighted what he views to be the present, negative effects of denying the reality of an eternal hell.[125]

---

[123] In an odd twist, this was the user name for the incorrect Rob Bell—namely, a relatively non-religious web designer and business consultant living in northern England. But he took the incident in good stride. For an interview with this Rob Bell, see http://rachelheldevans.com/blog/rob-bell-interview.

[124] On this point, Roger Olson wrote: "Another thing I've been wondering is what 'farewell, Rob Bell' means. Is that an attempt to expel him from evangelicalism? Who really has the authority to do that? Are they [John Piper et al.] assuming he [Rob Bell] *is* evangelical in their sense? Does he think he is? Are they assuming they are the person who has the authority to expel someone from something as amorphous as evangelicalism?" See http://www.patheos.com/blogs/rogereolson/2011/03/evangelicals-behaving-badly-and-some-important-footnotes/, accessed February 10, 2015.

[125] Non-Calvinist theologians such as Scot McKnight and Roger Olson argued Evangelical leaders ought to wait to comment until they have actually read Bell's book. DeYoung countered that Reformed leaders were in fact not jumping the gun: "[O]ur deep dismay and the reason for issuing an urgent warning is not based on what [Rob Bell] *might* say in the book. It's based on what he *did* say in the video. [. . .] Whether the sentences end in question marks or not, the force of these sentences is to undermine—nay, to ridicule—the reality of eternal conscious punishment, the wrath of the God, and

Picking up on the Twitter firestorm, CNN summarized the debate. A few days after that, *The New York Times* did likewise. More than a week removed, CNN revisited the online controversy, saying that "the firestorm around Rob Bell has grown considerably in the last week." In light of the anticipation, the book's publisher moved the release date up by two weeks. And, of course, a handful of prominent pastors and bloggers who were given advanced copies quickly posted critical reviews—the one from DeYoung totaling twenty-one pages. The next month, Rob Bell and Evangelical infighting was covered in *TIME Magazine*.

In an interview with Rob Bell the day before *Love Wins* was released to the public,[126] he was asked why the book—and therefore, *he*—had been so controversial and so heavily criticized online, even before the book was released or read. Here is what he said:

> I think that grace and love always rattle people. As soon as you say that perhaps this particular little club of people who have decided they're the orthodox ones—as soon as you say, "I think it might be a little wider than that"—you're threatening whole systems. You're threatening whole ways of thinking. [. . .] Do I think that I am Evangelical and orthodox to the bone? Yes. And I actually think that orthodoxy is a terribly wide, diverse stream. I think that's the real question here, is: the endless religious, sort of, compulsion to say, "we're in, you're out"—to constantly sort of narrow it, and all of that. And I think that vibrant, real, historic Christian faith is wide and leaves lots and lots of room for lots of varying perspectives. [. . .] That's actually part of its strength . . . its life and vibrancy.[127]

The controversy could have ended with that. The damage was done to the place and acceptability of Rob Bell as an orthodox Evangelical—at least in

---

penal substitutionary atonement. [. . .] Questions teach. And only a teacher with stunning naivety or remarkable cowardice would suggest they didn't [. . .] *Love Wins* can be the second coming of Jonathan Edwards and it still doesn't change that what was communicated in the video was untrue to the Scriptures, inconsistent with historic orthodoxy, belittling of the cross, deceiving to unbelievers, and a tragic distortion of God's character. [. . .] We don't have to guess if Bell will say something dreadfully, horribly, disgracefully wrong. He already has." See http://www.thegospelcoalition.org/blogs/kevindeyoung/2011/02/28/bell-brouhaha/.

[126] http://blog.christianitytoday.com/ctliveblog/archives/2011/03/rob_bell_on_uni.html
[127] Elsewhere, in a recent interview with *USA Today*, Rob Bell said: "Jesus spoke of the renewal of all things. He said, 'I have sheep who are not of this flock.' Through him, extraordinary things are happening in the world. If saying that gets you banned from the E-club, so be it." By "banned from the E-club," Bell was referring to Christian leaders who no longer consider him an Evangelical.

the eyes of the New Calvinist movement. After *Love Wins* was released to the public, and a host of highly critical reviews blasted Bell and his beliefs about hell and God, the uproar was as good as settled. The "Rob Bell Brouhaha," as DeYoung called it, calmed to a faint whisper throughout the summer months of 2011. But while the online debate had cooled, the problems were heating up back in Grand Rapids. During the controversy, about 3,000 people left Mars Hill. In previous years, due to the church allowing women to be pastors, another 3,000 people had left.[128] By the end of summer 2011, a thriving "giga-church" that had welcomed more than 10,000 congregants each Sunday had shrunk precipitously to about 3,500 followers. And then, on September 22, 2011, just as Mars Hill seemed to be stabilizing into its drastically smaller size, news broke that Bell would be resigning from Mars Hill that December, in hope of "sharing the message of God's love with a broader audience."[129] Bell now lives with his wife in Orange County, near the ocean, and reportedly surfs nearly every day while working on further projects.

Two years almost to the day after *Love Wins* was published, Rob Bell came out with another book.[130] But this time the collective response from Calvinistic Evangelical leaders was the complete opposite—namely, simply ignoring him. Writing about a month before Bell's new book was published, Denny Burk stated the mindset this way:

> I predict that Bell's book will be greeted largely with a collective yawn from conservative evangelical reviewers. There won't be an outcry like there was last time. Why? Because Bell's reputation as a heterodox theological liberal is now well known. Why belabor the point? That is why I don't expect to see a flood of urgency among evangelicals to critique his new work. [. . .] *Rob Bell is no longer relevant to the larger evangelical theological conversation.* Yes, his book will probably sell a lot of copies. No, *evangelicals by and large won't mistake him for one of their own like they used to.* [Emphases added]

In light of Bell's 2013 book, and in response to Burk's comments, Tim Suttle, pastor of Redemption Church in Olathe, Kansas, argued Evangelicalism might not hold together as a single bloc much longer, if it even does

---

[128] Kelefa Sanneh, "The Hell-Raiser: A Megachurch Pastor's Search for a More Forgiving Faith." *The New Yorker*, November 26, 2012. Available at http://www.newyorker.com/magazine/2012/11/26/the-hell-raiser-3.

[129] Rob Bell eventually ended up going on tour with Oprah.

[130] Rob Bell, *What We Talk about When We Talk about God* (New York: HarperCollins, 2013).

anymore.[131] Noting Burk's dismissive comments on Bell's newest book, Suttle disparagingly called leaders of the New Calvinist movement "the truth-police." Suttle thinks neo-Reformed leaders view themselves as the legitimate gatekeepers of all things Evangelical, especially when it comes to theological truths. But while acknowledging truth is important (because, as he writes, "Truth is a person. Jesus is the Truth"), Suttle also claims: " 'Truth' is not [a] rational abstraction—a concept, doctrine, or idea you can write down—especially not one which *you* conveniently have right and *everyone else* conveniently has wrong." He suggested these kinds of claims to truth and knowledge are "nearly always" more about game-like contestation over power and control.

> [W]e must recognize that the fight for truth is nearly always a fight for *control*. Those who passionately defend the truth are often just grasping for power. It's a game that only those who have never been transformed by the love of God have the stomach for.

In the end, the case of Rob Bell, his book *Love Wins*, and the resistance it elicited from leaders of the neo-Reformed movement is an example of the internal struggles and contestation in and over the broader field of American Evangelicalism. In this case, a thriving megachurch and its (former) "rock star" celebrity pastor were expelled altogether from the ranks of Evangelicals—at least in the minds of New Calvinist leaders. As Bell continues to publish books, tour the country with Oprah, and find a new audience in American religious life, only time will tell whether he truly is no longer "in the game."

The Case of World Vision

If the controversy over Rob Bell and universalism was an instance of intertribal conflict between New Calvinist leaders and the progressive Emergents, the case of World Vision shows intertribal conflict between the New

---

[131] Suttle writes: "Whatever the subject, there's more uncomfortable tension in the evangelical family than a Sacha Baron Cohen movie. This has many evangelicals wondering if we have a future together at all. One thing seems clear: If evangelicalism continues to be defined primarily by a *theological* center, it will crumble—especially if guys like Denny Burk get to decide who's in and who's out." Tim Suttle, "Will Evangelicalism Last?" *The Huffington Post*, April 27, 2013, https://www.huffpost.com/entry/will-evangelicalism-last_b_2727883, accessed September 12, 2019.

Calvinists and mainstream American Evangelicals. World Vision, founded in 1950, is a mainstream Evangelical humanitarian aid organization that focuses on community development and sponsoring disadvantaged children around the globe. As the largest US-based international relief and development organization, World Vision employs more than 40,000 people in nearly one hundred countries.[132]

In March 2014, the Evangelical periodical *Christianity Today* released online an exclusive interview with Richard Stearns,[133] the president of the US branch of World Vision, in which Stearns explained that World Vision-USA was voluntarily changing its conduct policy for employees regarding their sexual activities.[134] World Vision's previous policy required the roughly 1,100 employees of its US branch to restrict their sexual activity to between one man and one woman within marriage, with the expectation that any unmarried employees would abstain from sex entirely. The new conduct policy, Stearns explained, would still require all unmarried employees to abstain from sex, but employment would now be permitted for persons in same-sex sexual relationships as long as they were also in a legally recognized same-sex marriage. Stearns said this policy alteration was intended not as an endorsement of gay marriage, but to promote Christian unity across disagreement by remaining fully neutral on the question of gay marriage and instead leaving the issue of sexual faithfulness up to denominations and local churches.

The online backlash from New Calvinist leaders was quick and severe. Russell Moore, the president of the Ethics and Religious Liberty Commission within the Southern Baptist Convention, unwittingly used field-theoretic-talk about "what is at stake" when he wrote:

> Here's what's at stake. This isn't, as the World Vision statement (incredibly!) puts it, the equivalent of a big tent on baptism, church polity, and so forth. At stake is the Gospel of Jesus Christ. [. . .] We're entering an era where we will see who the evangelicals really are, and by that I mean those who believe in the gospel itself, in all of its truth and all of its grace. And many will shrink back. [. . .] I don't mind people switching sides [on this issue] and

---

[132] Nicholas Kristof, "Learning from the Sin of Sodom," *The New York Times*, February 27, 2010, https://www.nytimes.com/2010/02/28/opinion/28kristof.html, accessed September 12, 2019.

[133] https://www.worldvision.org/about-us/media-contacts/richard-stearns

[134] Celeste Gracey and Jeremy Weber, "World Vision: Why We're Hiring Gay Christians in Same-Sex Marriages," *Christianity Today*, March 24, 2014, https://www.christianitytoday.com/ct/2014/march-web-only/world-vision-why-hiring-gay-christians-same-sex-marriage.html,   accessed September 12, 2019.

standing up for things that they believe in. But just be honest about what you want to do. Don't say "Hath God said?" and then tell us you're doing it to advance the gospel and the unity of the church.[135]

DeYoung, too, was highly critical of the policy change, writing on his blog for The Gospel Coalition that "World Vision's new hiring policy is a profound mistake." He expressed concern that the change was "sacrific[ing] the gospel for a togetherness that will not hold and a shortsighted vision that is sure to fail" and emphasized that "Despite the claims of neutrality, Richard Stearns and World Vision are not neutral." Furthermore:

> The new policy makes no sense if World Vision thinks homosexual behavior is a sin, which is, after all, how it views fornication and adultery. [. . .] We are entering the days and the decade of a great shifting and sifting of Evangelicalism. The capitulation will not happen all at once. [. . .] World Vision has decided that to be a practicing homosexual and a practicing Christian is no contradiction in terms.[136]

Moreover, Al Mohler described World Vision's policy decision as "pointing to disaster" for the broader Evangelical field. The change was "ominous and threatening," he wrote, because of World Vision's size and influence "in the Christian world." "There is no rational sense in claiming that this represents neutrality," Mohler contested. More so than in many of the other conservative reactions, one can see in Mohler's words, quoted next, his palpable sense that the *rules of the Evangelical field* had been violated. Over the course of just a couple paragraphs, Mohler mentioned how World Vision had rejected the Bible's authority and clarity (biblicism), the need for sinners (i.e., everyone) to repent of their sins for salvation (conversionism), and ultimately had violated the Gospel itself.[137]

---

[135] Russell Moore, "On World Vision and the Gospel," *RussellMoore.com*, March 24, 2014, https://www.russellmoore.com/2014/03/24/on-world-vision-and-the-gospel/, accessed September 12, 2019.

[136] Kevin DeYoung, "The Worldliness in World Vision's New Hiring Policy," *DeYoung, Restless, and Reformed*, March 25, 2014, https://www.thegospelcoalition.org/blogs/kevin-deyoung/the-worldliness-in-world-visions-new-hiring-policy/; Kevin DeYoung, "Two More Thoughts on the World Vision Controversy," *DeYoung, Restless, and Reformed*, March 26, 2014, https://www.thegospelcoalition.org/blogs/kevin-deyoung/two-more-thoughts-on-the-world-vision-controversy/, accessed September 12, 2019.

[137] Al Mohler, "Pointing to Disaster—The Flawed Moral Vision of World Vision," *AlbertMohler.com*, March 25, 2014, https://albertmohler.com/2014/03/25/pointing-to-disaster-the-flawed-moral-vision-of-world-vision/, accessed September 12, 2019.

World Vision claims not to have compromised the authority of Scripture, even as its U.S. president basically throws the Bible into a pit of confusion by suggesting that the Bible is not sufficiently clear on the question of the morality of same-sex sexuality. Stearns insists that he is not compromising biblical authority even as he undermines confidence that the church can understand and trust what the Bible reveals about same-sex sexuality. [. . .] The worst aspect of the World Vision U.S. policy shift is the fact that it will mislead the world about the reality of sin and the urgent need of salvation. Willingly recognizing same-sex marriage and validating openly homosexual employees in their homosexuality is a grave and tragic act that confirms sinners in their sin—and that [policy] violates the gospel of Christ.

Likewise, Piper framed his criticism of World Vision in terms of *violating the field "rules" of biblicism and crucicentrism*. On his Desiring God website, he argued World Vision's policy shift "undermine[s] biblical authority" and "trivializes the cross." He called World Vision's claim to be taking only a neutral stance on the issue "fanciful." "Make no mistake," he continued, "this so-called 'neutral' position of World Vision is a position to regard practicing homosexuals (under the guise of an imaginary 'marriage') as following an acceptable Christian lifestyle, on the analogy of choosing infant baptism over believers' baptism." He wrote that with this change, World Vision was undermining their own claims to be serving the poor and marginalized out of authentic Christian care and compassion: "Of course, World Vision does not intend to shipwreck their legacy of compassion for the poor. But that is what they are doing. [. . .] Without care about eternal suffering, care about temporal suffering is a mirage." Piper ended his statement this way: "[W]ithout repentance and change, World Vision will go the way of worldliness and weakness. . . . [T]he Christian soul [of World Vision] will disappear. And who will suffer most? The poor. Therefore, for the sake of Christ and his call to true compassion, World Vision's decision is tragic. I pray they will repent and turn back to their faithful roots."[138]

Denny Burk commented, "The announcement from Stearns is all at once sad and self-contradictory. While claiming not to endorse same-sex

---

[138] John Piper, "World Vision: Adultery No, Homosexual Practice Yes," *Desiring God*, March 25, 2014, https://www.desiringgod.org/articles/world-vision-adultery-no-homosexual-practice-yes, accessed September 12, 2019.

marriage, World Vision has adopted a policy that looks just like the one that would be in place if they had endorsed same-sex marriage." Burk highlighted what he viewed as a serious inconsistency between the revised conduct policy and Stearns's statement that "We are absolutely resolute about every employee being followers of Jesus Christ"—this was inconsistent, Burk insisted, because, "[I]t is impossible to be a 'follower of Christ' while endorsing or participating in a same-sex marriage." The revised conduct policy, Burk argued, "can *only* mean that [Stearns] believes being a 'follower of Jesus Christ' is somehow compatible with being in a same-sex marriage." Like many other conservative critics, Burk contested that, despite what World Vision claimed, its new policy was anything but neutral. If the revised policy were implemented, World Vision and Stearns, he wrote, would be "false teachers." Near the end, he invoked *biblicism*: "Yes, it is true that the issue is greatly debated in our time. But the presence of theological controversy does not mean the absence of biblical clarity."[139] Intentionally harkening back to Piper's famous tweet that ignited the controversy around Rob Bell, Burk added on Twitter, "Farewell, World Vision."

Because of the hullabaloo stirred up around World Vision's policy change about homosexuality and gay marriage, donors cancelled "several thousand" child sponsorships within two days of the announcement, Stearns said. This major hit, along with reactions such as these from Calvinist Evangelicals and others, led World Vision-USA to reverse its decision less than forty-eight hours after it had been announced publicly online.[140] In comments to the press after the reversal, Richard Stearns expressed deep regret for the initial policy change, saying it was "a mistake" and that he should have sought far more consultation from Evangelical leaders before making the change. After the reversal, New Calvinist leaders quickly reaffirmed World Vision as a morally acceptable avenue through which to make charitable donations and expressed heavy relief and thankfulness on social media for World Vision's decision to return to its former policy on sexuality and marriage.[141]

[139] Denny Burk, "The Collapse of Christianity at World Vision," *DennyBurk.com*, March 25, 2014, http://www.dennyburk.com/the-collapse-of-christianity-at-world-vision/, accessed September 12, 2019.

[140] Celeste Gracey and Jeremy Weber, "World Vision Reverses Decision to Hire Christians in Same-Sex Marriages," *Christianity Today*, March 26, 2014, https://www.christianitytoday.com/ct/2014/march-web-only/world-vision-reverses-decision-gay-same-sex-marriage.html; Laurie Goodstein, "Christian Charity Backtracks on Gays," *The New York Times*, March 27, 2014, https://www.nytimes.com/2014/03/28/us/christian-charity-backtracks-on-gays.html, accessed September 12, 2019.

[141] Justin Taylor, "World Vision USA Reverses Its Decision: The Letter and Some Reactions," *Between Two Worlds*, March 26, 2014, https://www.thegospelcoalition.org/blogs/justin-taylor/

As soon as the reversal was announced, *religious leaders as challengers in the Evangelical field "pushed back against" New Calvinist leaders as self-appointed gatekeepers of the field's "true orthodoxy."* Many progressive Evangelicals—who two days earlier had applauded the initial policy change on social media as one step closer to LGBTQ acceptance and inclusion in the Church—expressed dismay at the reversal. For instance, Rachel Held Evans lamented on her website: "This whole situation has left me feeling frustrated, heartbroken, and lost. I don't think I've ever been more angry at the Church, particularly the Evangelical culture in which I was raised and with which I for so long identified."[142] As for the New Calvinist leaders (and others, like Franklin Graham) who had criticized the policy revision, Evans claimed they were "playing the gatekeeper with smug, self-righteous pride."[143] Answering their charge that "the Gospel is at stake," she argued: "The Gospel is at stake only insofar as we make one's position on same-sex marriage a part of it. The Gospel is threatened, not by gay people getting married, but by Christians saying support or opposition to gay marriage is an essential part of the Gospel when it's not."[144] Soon thereafter, Rachel Held Evans cited the World Vision controversy as the final straw, so to speak, that led her to stop "fighting for a seat at the evangelical table" and instead join the (mainline and more socially progressive) Episcopal Church.[145]

In a similar fashion, a few days after the policy reversal, feminist Christian writer Sarah Bessey offered encouragement for anyone now "leaving Evangelicalism." "Maybe this is your time to let go and walk away. I know you're grieving. Let yourself grieve," Bessey wrote. "Your pet evangelical gate-keeper isn't the sole arbitrator of the Christian faith: there is more complexity and beauty and diversity of voices and experiences within followers of the Way than you know. [. . .] A lot of us [are] on the other side of that faith shift, eschewing labels and fear-tactics, boundary markers and tribalist thinking."[146] In an interview, Brian McLaren pointed to the World

---

world-vision-usa-reverses-its-decision-the-letter-and-some-reactions/, accessed September 12, 2019.

[142] Rachel Held Evans, "World Vision Update," *Rachel Held Evans*, March 26, 2014, http://rachelheldevans.com/blog/world-vision-update, accessed March 3, 2016.

[143] Rachel Held Evans, "On the World Vision Reaction," *Rachel Held Evans*, March 25, 2014, http://rachelheldevans.com/blog/world-vision, accessed March 3, 2016.

[144] Ibid.

[145] Rachel Held Evans, "What Now?" *Rachel Held Evans*, April 1, 2014, http://rachelheldevans.com/blog/what-now-world-vision, accessed March 3, 2016.

[146] Sarah Bessey, "For the Ones Leaving Evangelicalism," *Sarah Bessey*, March 29, 2014, http://sarahbessey.com/ones-leaving-evangelicalism/, accessed March 3, 2016.

Vision controversy as an example of how difficult it is within American Evangelicalism "for anyone to make a break from people to their right [. . .] without losing their funding." Neo-Anabaptist pastor Greg Boyd made the same observation as did McLaren during our interview when he mentioned the World Vision dustup to underline the power that the New Calvinist movement wields to influence mainstream American Evangelicalism, especially when matters of funding are involved. Popular writer Kristen Howerton called the conservative response "astounding" and "disheartening." She said World Vision's decision to reverse the policy change "was simply wrong and ungodly and deeply defeating," which left her feeling "angry, discouraged, and a bit betrayed." She encouraged her blog readers to sign up for new child sponsorships in order to offset those that were being dropped. "I am thankful this does not represent all of us," she added.[147]

Benjamin Corey, who writes for the progressive Christian channel on *Patheos*, questioned why World Vision did not also ban employment for professing Christians who smoke, overeat, watch pornography, buy immodest luxury goods, or drink too much alcohol. Corey then emphasized (seven times) the various reasons why he was sad about the reversal of the policy, including: "I lament that one group of people is singled out, but that so many others get a free pass."[148] Tony Jones used the metaphor of battle, expressing confidence that even though conservative Evangelicals had won this particular "battle" over sexuality and gay marriage, they were inevitably going to lose the war. Jones continued, "There are many tragedies about how this all went down, not the least of which is the message that Christianity is a faith that is run by ideological bullies."[149] Furthermore, Christian LGBTQ activist Brandan Robertson, writing for Tony Campolo's *Red Letter Christians* website, said the New Calvinists' reaction to World Vision's new employee conduct policy, and especially the cancelling of child sponsorships, was "shameful," "the height of depravity," and ultimately revealed "the sad

---

[147] Kristen Howerton, "On World Vision, Gay Marriage, and Taking a Stand on the Backs of Starving Children," *Rage Against the Minivan*, March 25, 2014, http://rageagainsttheminivan.com/2014/03/on-world-vision-gay-marriage-and-taking.html; Kristen Howerton, "World Vision, the Reversal of Inclusion, and the Aftermath," *Rage Against the Minivan*, March 28, 2014, http://rageagainsttheminivan.com/2014/03/world-vision-reversal-of-inclusion-and.html, accessed September 12, 2019.

[148] Benjamin L. Corey, "World Vision Announces New, Radically Consistent Employment Standards," March 27, 2014, http://www.patheos.com/blogs/formerlyfundie/world-vision-announces-new-radically-consistent-employment-standards/, accessed April 3, 2015.

[149] Tony Jones, "Let's Talk about What Happened Yesterday at World Vision," *Theoblogy*, March 27, 2014, http://www.patheos.com/blogs/tonyjones/2014/03/27/lets-talk-about-what-happened-yesterday-at-world-vision/, accessed March 3, 2016.

state of American Evangelicalism."[150] Expressions such as these of grief, anger, dismay, sadness, betrayal, and frustration from progressive American Evangelicals at the Calvinist response and World Vision's reversal could be multiplied several times over.

Beyond the (not particularly surprising) contrast between New Calvinist leaders and the Emergent Progressives on this issue, it is informative to hear what Calvinist leaders said World Vision's initial decision to change their policy showed about the current state of *mainstream* Evangelicalism in the United States. World Vision, after all, belongs to neither the Calvinists nor the Progressives, but instead fits squarely into the post–World War II infrastructural mainstream of the American Evangelical field. This dispute would not have been nearly as heated, if there even was a fight at all, if not for World Vision's symbolic status and weightiness as a mainstream institution of American Evangelicalism. New Calvinist leaders would not have so loudly or sharply criticized an organization or leader they had already collectively written off and dismissed as liberal.[151] So, for example, the president of Reformed Theological Seminary in Orlando, Florida, Don Sweeting, told me in an interview that although World Vision quickly reverted to its previous policy, the "tortured reasoning," as Sweeting put it, of their initial decision demonstrated that American Evangelicalism's "edges seem to be fraying. It seems to be broadening, and there are lots of examples of that," he said.

Similarly, a week after the World Vision controversy had mostly settled, Trevin Wax commented: "The World Vision decision was a tremor that warns us of a coming earthquake in which churches and leaders historically identified with evangelicalism will divide along all-too-familiar fault lines."[152] He continued to say:

[T]his particular controversy was about the meaning of *evangelical.* Can an institution with an historic evangelical identity be divided on an issue as central as marriage and family and still be evangelical? Related to this discussion are questions about the authority and interpretation of Scripture, cultural engagement, and institutional power. All sides of the debate

---

[150] Brandan Robertson, "World Vision and the Sad State of American Evangelicalism," *Red Letter Christians,* March 25, 2014, http://www.redletterchristians.org/world-vision-sad-state-american-evangelicalism/, accessed March 3, 2016.

[151] This is why Rob Bell and his books are now all but ignored among New Calvinists.

[152] Trevin Wax, "The Fault Lines before the Evangelical Earthquake," *The Gospel Coalition,* April 2, 2014, https://www.thegospelcoalition.org/blogs/trevin-wax/the-fault-lines-before-the-evangelical-earthquake/, accessed September 12, 2019.

recognize that the definition of evangelical is at stake, which is why some are now publicly casting off the term altogether.[153]

Critiquing Opponents (More) in Books

Robert Wuthnow has commented, "a close reading of the social science literature prior to the 1980s would suggest that religious people rarely spoke and probably were completely mute."[154] The present field-theoretic model of religious strength adds to the large body of work in recent years correcting that omission. In the cases of Rob Bell and World Vision-USA, we have seen *incumbent Evangelical leaders actively policing, drawing symbolic boundaries, and trying to enforce the field's established "orthodoxy" based on the "rules of the game,"* and specifically by *publicly critiquing and rejecting on blogs and other websites the beliefs and ideas of their opponents in the field.* Still today, in the sociology of religion there remains very little recognition (in published scholarship, at least) that religious leaders write books, let alone that they sometimes write books against the positions and beliefs of other, competing religious leaders. This section gives some examples of New Calvinist leaders arguing against their field competitors *in their books.*

One clear example, especially between 2005 and 2009, is published critiques of the progressive Emergent stream of the Emerging Church. D. A. Carson was the first to produce a book-length critical evaluation of the Emerging Church "conversation" with his 2005 book, *Becoming Conversant with the Emerging Church.*[155] Carson concluded: "I have to say, as kindly but as forcefully as I can, that to my mind, if words mean anything, [Emergent leaders] have largely abandoned the Gospel."[156] Likewise, Biola University professor R. Scott Smith wrote *Truth and the New Kind of Christian*, published by Crossway in 2005.[157] Smith focused in part on the writings of Emergent teachers Brian McLaren and Tony Jones to critically

---

[153] Ibid. See also Kathleen T. Talvacchia, Michael F. Pettinger, and Mark Larrimore, eds., *Queer Christianities: Lived Religion in Transgressive Forms* (New York: New York University Press, 2015).

[154] Robert J. Wuthnow, "Taking Talk Seriously: Religious Discourse as Social Practice," *Journal for the Scientific Study of Religion* 50, no. 1 (2011): 1–21. Quoted from p. 1.

[155] D. A. Carson, *Becoming Conversant with the Emerging Church: Understanding a Movement and Its Implications* (Grand Rapids, MI: Zondervan, 2005).

[156] Carson, *Becoming Conversant*, 186; Markofski, *New Monasticism*, 125, also chose this line as an apt summary of the book's conclusion.

[157] R. Scott Smith, *Truth and the New Kind of Christian: The Emerging Effects of Postmodernism in the Church* (Wheaton, IL: Crossway, 2005).

evaluate the postmodernist, subjectivist rejection of both objective truth (especially in matters concerning religion and morality) and humans' ability to know the truth about reality. A few years later, DeYoung and journalist Ted Kluck provided a thorough yet personal critique of progressive Emergent Christianity in their book *Why We're Not Emergent, by Two Guys Who Should Be*.[158] Moreover, although more squarely in the realm of Southern Baptists than New Calvinists, a team of writers collaborated to produce *Evangelicals Engaging Emergent: A Discussion of the Emergent Church Movement*.[159] Additionally, Driscoll's book chapter on the Emerging Church critically evaluated the views of Brian McLaren, Doug Pagitt, and Rob Bell, concluding: "The emergent liberals [. . .] have taken an off-ramp and now are not reaching out to postmoderns but are blazing a new path in search of a new land of postmodern Christianity."[160]

Similarly, Reformed Evangelical leaders have produced a number of books criticizing "open theism," the view that God does not (or cannot) know the future, which has been advanced by Christian thinkers such as Richard Rice, Clark Pinnock, William Hasker, John Sanders, and Greg Boyd, among others. Books by Calvinists critiquing open theism include, for example, John Frame's *No Other God: A Response to Open Theism*; Douglas Wilson's edited volume, *Bound Only Once: The Failure of Open Theism*; and John Piper, Justin Taylor, and Paul Kjoss Helseth's edited volume, *Beyond the Bounds: Open Theism and the Undermining of Biblical Christianity*.[161] Introducing their book, Justin Taylor says: "The essays in this book contend that open theism presents us with a different God—a God compatible, perhaps, with contemporary sentiments, but one who is not the God of the Bible."[162] In his concluding chapter, Piper writes: "I see open theism as theologically ruinous, dishonoring to God, belittling to Christ, and pastorally hurtful. My prayer is that Christian leaders will come to see it this way, and

---

[158] Kevin DeYoung and Ted Kluck, *Why We're Not Emergent (By Two Guys Who Should Be)* (Chicago: Moody, 2008).

[159] William D. Henard and Adam W. Greenway, eds., *Evangelicals Engaging Emergent: A Discussion of the Emergent Church Movement* (Nashville, TN: B&H, 2009).

[160] Mark Driscoll, *Religion Saves and Nine Other Misconceptions* (Wheaton, IL: Crossway, 2009), 209–241, quoted from p. 235; see also Mark Driscoll, "A Pastoral Perspective on the Emergent Church," *Criswell Theological Review* 3, no. 2 (2006): 87–93.

[161] John M. Frame, *No Other God: A Response to Open Theism* (Phillipsburg, NJ: P&R, 2001); Douglas Wilson, ed., *Bound Only Once: The Failure of Open Theism* (Moscow, ID: Canon Press, 2001); John Piper, Justin Taylor, and Paul Kjoss Helseth, eds., *Beyond the Bounds: Open Theism and the Undermining of Biblical Christianity* (Wheaton, IL: Crossway, 2003).

[162] Taylor, "Introduction," in *Beyond the Bounds*, 14.

thus love the church by counting open theism beyond the bounds of orthodox Christian teaching."[163] This book also includes a thirty-page chapter by Wayne Grudem explicitly theorizing "why, when, and for what should we draw new boundaries?"[164] Bruce Ware, a professor at the Southern Baptist Theological Seminary, himself has written multiple books critiquing open theism, including *God's Lesser Glory: The Diminished God of Open Theism; God's Greater Glory: The Exalted God of Scripture and the Christian Faith;* and *Their God Is Too Small: Open Theism and the Undermining of Confidence in God.*[165] Ware writes, "The openness understanding of God belittles his glory and perfection, and its vision of faith leads to despair. We simply cannot stand by idly and allow the advocates of the openness view to influence the next generation of evangelicals unchallenged."[166]

More recently, some New Calvinist leaders have responded in book form to the new acceptance and affirmation of LGBTQ relationships and sexuality among some leaders and writers in the orbit of Evangelicalism—typically progressive Emergents and "post-Evangelicals." When a book appeared by a young, gay LGBTQ activist espousing gay and lesbian sexual relationships as consistent with the Bible and Christianity, Al Mohler and others responded with *God and the Gay Christian? A Response to Matthew Vines.*[167] After dissecting Vines's overall argument, Mohler concluded: "The consequences of accepting his argument would include misleading people about their sin and about their need for Christ, about what obedience to Christ requires and what faithfulness to Christ demands."[168] Subsequent chapters in the book address how Vines misrepresents verses and themes in the Old Testament (James Hamilton), how Vines misrepresents verses and themes in the New Testament (Denny Burk), that Vines proposes to overthrow the unanimous teaching of the broad Christian tradition stretching over nearly 2,000 years (Owen Strachan), and why it is improper to refer to a "gay Christian" at all (Heath Lambert). Other recent books in the realm of the New Calvinism

---

[163] Piper, "Grounds for Dismay: The Error and Injury of Open Theism," in *Beyond the Bounds,* 384.

[164] Wayne Grudem, "Why, When, and for What Should We Draw New Boundaries?" in *Beyond the Bounds,* 339–370.

[165] Bruce A. Ware, *God's Lesser Glory: The Diminished God of Open Theism* (Wheaton, IL: Crossway, 2000); Bruce A. Ware, *God's Greater Glory: The Exalted God of Scripture and the Christian Faith* (Wheaton, IL: Crossway, 2004); Bruce A. Ware, *Their God Is Too Small: Open Theism and the Undermining of Confidence in God* (Wheaton, IL: Crossway, 2003).

[166] Ware, *Their God Is Too Small,* 8.

[167] R. Albert Mohler Jr., ed., *God and the Gay Christian? A Response to Matthew Vines* (Louisville, KY: SBTS Press, 2014).

[168] Mohler, "God, the Gospel and the Gay Challenge: A Response to Matthew Vines," in *God and the Gay Christian?,* 22.

making a case for traditional sexual ethics and against LGBTQ affirmation include Kevin DeYoung's *What Does the Bible Really Teach about Homosexuality?*;[169] David Platt's *Counter Culture*, which includes a chapter on sexual morality;[170] and Denny Burk's *What Is the Meaning of Sex?*[171]

In all these cases, published books serve as yet another avenue—in addition to podcasts, conferences, social media, and online articles—for leaders of the New Calvinism to *draw symbolic boundaries and try to enforce the field's established "orthodoxy" based on the "rules of the game,"* specifically by *publicly critiquing and rejecting the beliefs and ideas of their opponents in the field.*

Charismatic Authority and Affect

There is another social mechanism that is neither a precipitating cause nor a matter of game-like contestation, but nevertheless plays an important causal role in generating and sustaining the Reformed resurgence. That is the issue of charismatic authority. It is evident that *Evangelical leaders' personal characteristics—their style, articulateness, likeability, etc.—give them charismatic authority, which helps these leaders attract and maintain followers.* This is not a strategic position taking in the field of American Evangelicalism because charisma is not unique to the leaders of the New Calvinism. Other leaders in other expressions and tribes have charismatic authority, too. In this way, charisma is closer to a tactic than a strategy.

As with many of the other social and cultural dynamics discussed on previous pages, it was the non-Calvinist leaders who were quick to put this matter into words. For instance, Austin Fischer talked about the importance of good preachers in the New Calvinist movement:

> It is hard to overemphasize the impact that the Passion conferences in particular have had on turning the Young Restless Reformed movement into a juggernaut, and bringing a lot of young Evangelicals into it. Basically, everyone who speaks at those is a Calvinist, and a lot of times it's not really overt. So for young Evangelicals, they don't know what they're getting is

---

[169] Kevin DeYoung, *What Does the Bible Really Teach about Homosexuality?* (Wheaton, IL: Crossway, 2015).

[170] David Platt, *Counter Culture: Following Christ in an Anti-Christian Age*, revised and updated (Carol Stream, IL: Tyndale House, 2017), 159–187.

[171] Denny Burk, *What Is the Meaning of Sex?* (Wheaton, IL: Crossway, 2013).

Calvinism, but they know that they like John Piper's preaching and they like Mark Driscoll's preaching and they like Louie Giglio's preaching—and so these are the people that they're introduced to. Matt Chandler, we could go on here. And for me it's very rare that you consistently listen to someone's preaching and don't end up sharing their theological presuppositions. It doesn't happen like that. So, I think the fact that there are good preachers who have been given really big platforms is a huge reason we're seeing a resurgence in the New Calvinism.

Likewise, Tony Campolo told me:

Mark Driscoll, Tim Keller, John Piper all have the gift—a gift that enables them to communicate with great effectiveness, and I think that young people are being swept into this movement simply by the charisma of these guys. These guys are great speakers, incredible communicators, charismatic in the pulpit, and they have done their job well in sweeping people into the movement.

Tony Jones told me in an interview:

If you do a little bourdieuian analysis on Driscoll, you're like, damn, this guy is like Chris Rock funny, he dresses super sharp, he carries himself in a way that kind of says, "I have cultural capital" and—Piper doesn't so much; Piper is a nerdy dude—but Keller is the same way. [. . .] The neo-Reformed guys, I think part of their success is that they do carry themselves like they're very powerful figures in twenty-first-century America. They wear really sharp clothes, they have expensive haircuts, they speak well, they use technology well, they have a nice aesthetic sense of design. And that just gives everybody the impression that, like, shit, these guys know what they're doing.

The polished style, communication skills, and personal magnetism of many New Calvinist leaders have granted them the unofficial status of being a "celebrity pastor." These leaders are widely known and admired, nationally and sometimes internationally, by their many devout Evangelical followers. In its less intense forms, this influence means Reformed pastors and theologians are household names, their teachings and books discussed with familiarity among friends in home groups and church lobbies. In its more intense forms, some Calvinist laypersons closely identify with or rally around their favorite Reformed pastors and theologians. Recognizing this, one commentator, writing in *First Things*, warned of "the New Calvinism's personality-driven life,"[172] a play on the title of Rick Warren's best-selling book.

A major derivation of this factor is the tactical use of affect—"affective labor"—at megachurches. By "affect" I mean the ability or tendency to "move" someone, often below the level of conscious awareness (emotionally, bodily, etc.) in a way that resonates and appeals, in a way that "grabs" them. While affective labor and affective appeal were less prominent at Bethlehem Baptist Church and Redeemer Presbyterian Church, they were employed skillfully and intentionally at Mars Hill Church.[173] What moves people "to great affect" depends on the target audience, and at Mars Hill the target audience was educated, city-dwelling, tech-savvy men in their twenties and thirties. For this target audience (which I fit), the deployment of affect at Mars Hill Church included the use of warm and arresting colors (especially blood red and graphite gray); well-timed humor and irony; militaristic language and metaphors (for example, preaching was "air war" while community groups were "ground war"); and frank talk about sexuality and masculinity. Notice, again, how gender complementarianism links into the point here.

Other notable aspects of Mars Hill Church that had affective, "grabbing" appeal included productivity, as through book-writing and publicly championed church expansion metrics; articulate, content-packed speech; very impressive music; professional quality video production (including Mark Driscoll's larger-than-life presence on big screens); and even good coffee. At Mars Hill, the tactical use of affect added to and solidified charismatic authority, not merely the authority of Mark Driscoll as a leader but also of the entire Mars Hill "brand."

Beyond the power of charismatic authority itself, this causal dynamic is amplified and reinforced by the Internet, perhaps especially by online videos. Through publicly available videos showing lectures, seminars, sermons, discussions, and interviews, religious practitioners get an added dose of these leaders' style, charm, intelligence, likeability, and articulateness. Calvinist leaders are effortlessly welcomed into one's home and life, readily accessible

[172] Adam Omelianchuk, "The New Calvinism's Personality-Driven Life," *First Things*, April 6, 2010, https://www.firstthings.com/blogs/firstthoughts/2010/04/the-new-calvinisme28099s-personality-driven-life, accessed September 20, 2017.

[173] Jessica Johnson, *Biblical Porn: Affect, Labor, and Pastor Mark Driscoll's Evangelical Empire* (Durham, NC: Duke University Press, 2018).

anytime. It is possible to listen to the weekly sermon by a pastor at a mega-church one has never attended in person. With enough consumption, one may even begin to feel like a favorite charismatic religious leader is an important part of one's life and spiritual formation. By no means do Christians need to be physically in the presence of these leaders to get a sense of their charisma and the compelling power it carries.

Regional Variation and Contextualization

It is well-known that different regions and cities can, to some degree, have differing cultures, values, and ways of doing things. The American South differs culturally from the Midwest, and both differ in various ways from the East Coast, for example. At a smaller level of analysis, cities and metropolitan areas themselves have differing cultures.[174] Because of these regional variations and differences, another factor contributing to the New Calvinism is *religious leaders acting (whether thoughtfully or unreflexively) in ways such that their message and demeanor fit ecologically with their cities and geographic regions, thereby partly facilitating their own success.* In Evangelicalism, these considerations often go under the banner of "contextualization."[175] Like charisma, contextualization is something any Evangelical church or ministry can do and therefore is more a tactic of operational effectiveness than a strategically staked-out position in "social space." Nevertheless, contextualization further demonstrates how religious leaders, with thought and savviness, can help to foster institutional strength.

A big part of contextualization is verbal communication, especially in sermons. New Calvinist leaders know they need to think carefully about which sermon illustrations will make sense and which will not, which jokes will land and which will flop—all depending on the specific audiences one is preaching to.[176] But contextualized communication often goes much deeper than illustrations and jokes, impacting pastors' very talking points and

---

[174] Sharon Zukin, *The Cultures of Cities* (Malden, MA: Blackwell, 1995); Wellman and Corcoran, "Religion and Regional Culture."

[175] See the essays in Matthew Cook, Rob Haskell, Ruth Julian, and Natee Tanchanpongs, eds., *Local Theology for the Global Church: Principles for an Evangelical Approach to Contextualization* (Pasadena, CA: William Carey Library, 2010); Bruce J. Nicholls, *Contextualization: A Theology of Gospel and Culture* (Vancouver: Regent College, [1979] 2003).

[176] https://t4g.org/media/2012/05/contextualization-lost-in-translation-2/, accessed May 17, 2019.

modes of argumentation. Tim Keller, as one example, has written at length about how he uses the beliefs secular Manhattanites already hold and which align with traditional Christianity (like the goodness of genuine community or the reality of human rights) to show them why they should also hold *other* biblical beliefs that ground or pair with their commitments better than a secular worldview does. *Since you believe this, then why don't you also believe that?*[177] He defines "contextualization" not as giving people what they want to hear but "giving people the Bible's answers, which they may not at all want to hear, to questions about life that people in their particular time and place are asking, in language and forms they can comprehend, and through appeals and arguments with force they can feel, even if they reject them."[178] Likewise, Driscoll has argued worship services and sermons should not be "seeker sensitive" but instead "seeker sensible"—that is, not watered-down for non-Christians but conducted in a manner that is clear and removes any unnecessary barriers to understanding the Christian message.[179]

Beyond verbal communication, contextualization also involves everything from programming and service times, to clothes and demeanor, to music and aesthetics—all with the culture and values of a church's local community or target audience in mind. For pastors and other ministry leaders, this means they must not only interpret the biblical text but also "exegete the culture," one will hear. New Calvinists point to the Apostle Paul, who appealed to the Athenians' altar "to the unknown god" and their own poets to explain the Christian message,[180] and who wrote that he became "all things to all people" so by all possible means he might rescue some of them.[181] The goal is to adapt aspects of church to maximize effectiveness in a given locale without compromising "the faith that was once for all delivered to the saints."[182]

This dynamic was noticeable with the three Calvinistic megachurches I visited. At Redeemer Presbyterian Church, contextualization is aligned mostly with smart, cosmopolitan, professional-class Manhattanites, including those who care a lot about justice, their careers, and identities. The venues have a sophisticated feel; the marble and golden hues one

---

[177] Keller, *Center Church*, 123–132; Keller, *Preaching: Communicating Faith in an Age of Skepticism* (New York: Viking, 2015), 93–156.

[178] Keller, *Center Church*, 89—italics removed.

[179] Mark Driscoll and Gerry Breshears, *Doctrine: What Christians Should Believe* (Wheaton, IL: Crossway, 2010), 353.

[180] Acts 17: 16–34.

[181] 1 Corinthians 9: 19–22.

[182] Jude 3.

encounters walking through the doors made it feel, at least to me, like a privilege just to be there. The music is refined. Keller's professorial style and measured tone fit effortlessly with "the city"—or at least the borough of Manhattan.[183] Mars Hill Church was contextualized well for a certain segment of Seattle, with its industrial "hipster" atmosphere and Driscoll's brusque, direct style fitting naturally with the city's broader mood, and especially its young men. Bethlehem Baptist Church is less obviously contextualized to its city context, but the culture of Minneapolis in my estimation (as a lifelong Midwesterner) is also less distinct than the cultures of Manhattan or Seattle, which ironically suggests Bethlehem is still contextualized fairly well. New Calvinists pastoring churches in Dallas-Fort Worth (i.e., Matt Chandler) and Washington, DC (i.e., Mark Dever) have also talked about how they consider the particular cultures of their areas.[184]

Contextualization, for New Calvinists, is a subtle dance that is rarely seen as easy or straightforward. They recognize the dual dangers of either "undercontextualizing" or "overcontextualizing." Undercontextualizing means naively delivering the same Gospel presentation the same way using the same arguments with little or no regard for the cultural narratives, priorities, assumptions, and concerns of the city or people groups one is attempting to reach. The other danger is overcontextualization, which (at best) would mean becoming a "seeker-sensitive" church, which New Calvinists typically perceive as rooted in therapeuticism and pragmatism, delivering a watered-down Gospel and possibly using gimmicks to attract people to Christianity; overcontextualization could also mean (at worst) forfeiting distinctly Christian convictions on theological or moral issues—in other words, becoming a liberal.[185] Even with endless possibilities for subtleties and dangers, contextualizing based on cultural and geographic variations, including resonating ecologically in particular cities, is another way the Reformed resurgence is not a matter of cultural happenstance but has been fought for and won.

---

[183] McMillan, "Contextualization, Big Apple Style."

[184] https://t4g.org/media/2012/05/contextualization-lost-in-translation-2/, accessed May 17, 2019.

[185] On the dual dangers of contextualization, see Keller, *Center Church*, 91–97; Keller, *Preaching*, 102–103.

Critiques of the New Calvinism

Throughout this chapter, we have seen Evangelical leaders from other tribes and expressions of American Evangelicalism as *challengers in the field* "*pushing back against*" the New Calvinism in various ways. This was such a recurring theme that this section documents even more, especially public, criticisms of the New Calvinism.

In June 2012, Ed Young, Jr.—the preaching pastor of a Southern Baptist megachurch of more than 20,000 attendees in Grapevine, Texas—used about a quarter of his sermon to critique Calvinism in Evangelicalism.[186] "There's a huge movement these days in the Christian community called Reformed theology. It's not new; it's old. But now people run around with skinny jeans and v-necks." Calvinism, he claimed, often leads to a "deformed" doctrine of the Church that neglects reaching out to non-Christians. "Most of the Calvinistic churches don't reach anybody," he said. They instead "prey on" and draw in young impressionable people who are already Christians. He warned the young people in his own church: "You are prey for these churches." He said that Calvinism "puts God in a box" by claiming to have figured out the relationship between God's sovereignty and human choice. He continued: "When they say 'Gospel,' they don't mean the same Gospel that we do. It's different. [. . .] Those people prey on believers all over the world, and it's ruining the Church." Calvinism, he said, "uses God" and "pimps out God." In the end, Ed Young concluded, "Most of it leads to intellectual snobbery, meanness, and people who don't give a flying flip about those going to hell."

Evangelical journalist Jonathan Merritt offered a more measured critique on his blog hosted by *Religion News Service*.[187] "[T]here are several troubling trends that must be addressed if this faithful faction hopes to move from a niche Christian cadre to a sustainable and more mainstream movement." As three of the New Calvinism's biggest problems, Merritt named *isolationism* (from other, non-Calvinist Evangelicals), *tribalism* (which he described as "the kinship tendency within a group to protect insiders while combating outsiders"), and *egotism* (or "haughtiness"). Citing John Piper's "Farewell,

---

[186] https://www.youtube.com/watch?v=Vk4d1AiX-G4, accessed February 3, 2016.

[187] Jonathan Merritt, "The Troubling Trends in America's 'Calvinist Revival,'" *Religion News Service*, May 20, 2014, http://jonathanmerritt.religionnews.com/2014/05/20/troubling-trends-americas-calvinist-revival/, accessed January 1, 2016.

Rob Bell" tweet as an example, he wrote: "Sometimes it seems as if Calvinists view themselves as judge, jury, and executioner of the Christian movement at large—determining who is faithful and not, who believes the gospel and who doesn't, who is in and who is out." "If neo-Calvinists don't get a rapid infusion of humility—and quickly—then perceptions of egotism will be an albatross around their necks," he concluded.[188]

Jonathan Merritt also interviewed Austin Fischer, a young Evangelical pastor and the author of *Young, Restless, No Longer Reformed*,[189] a title that plays off Hansen's 2008 book that helped to spark the movement. On Merritt's website, Fischer took a more philosophical approach, arguing that the God of Calvinism would not be a good God:

> I began my journey out of Calvinism when I realized that if I were to be a consistent, honest Calvinist I would have to believe some terrible things about God. I realized I, personally, could not have Calvinism and a *recognizably* good God whose heart was *fully revealed* at the crucifixion of Jesus Christ. I could not have Calvinism and a God who would rather die than give humans what they deserve. For me, the crucifixion of Jesus Christ was something too generous for Calvinism to make sense of. (Emphasis in the original)[190]

Fischer concluded:

> If the God who could die for sinners could also create sinners in order to damn them, then the universe [is] an incoherent place ruled by an enigmatic deity of arbitrary, raw power. It is certainly within God's rights to do such a thing, but if it's within God's heart then we're all in big trouble.[191]

---

[188] More than 21,000 people shared Merritt's article on Facebook.

[189] Austin Fischer, *Young, Restless, No Longer Reformed: Black Holes, Love, and a Journey In and Out of Calvinism* (Eugene, OR: Cascade Books, 2014). On the Reformation 21 website of the Alliance of Confessing Evangelicals (and reposted on The Gospel Coalition's website), Kevin DeYoung reviewed Fischer's book and stated that—while the book is "honest, intelligent, accessible" and "engaging"— he found it "unconvincing—and actually reinforcing for my Calvinist convictions." February 2014, http://www.reformation21.org/articles/young-restless-no-longer-reformed.php, accessed January 4, 2016.

[190] Jonathan Merritt, "Author Says Calvinism Can't Make Sense of the Cross," *Religion News Service*, April 3, 2014, http://jonathanmerritt.religionnews.com/2014/04/03/author-says-calvinism-cant-make-sense-cross/, accessed January 4, 2016.

[191] Ibid. When I interviewed Austin Fischer for this project, he reiterated his theological shift away from Calvinism using almost the exact same phrasing and framing as he did in Merritt's article.

Biblical scholar Peter Enns, reflecting on the contentious departure of Tullian Tchividjian from The Gospel Coalition, focused on the sociological practice by leaders of the movement of "contending for the Gospel" and drawing strong boundaries:

> [T]he resurgence of Reformed theology in American evangelicalism and fundamentalism—commonly referred to as the Neo-Reformed movement—*is* a belligerent movement. This is why it exists—to correct others, not to turn the spotlight inward. There are exceptions within, of course, and I am by no means suggesting everyone who sees him or herself as part of this movement exhibits this tendency. But the "system" is set up to fight. It's what they do.[192]

Scot McKnight has consistently and publicly expressed concern about the New Calvinist movement. On his *Patheos* blog, as just one example, he reposted seven years removed a slightly edited version of two older posts (originally posted back in February 2009).[193] The essence of McKnight's concern was that leaders of the New Calvinism are trying to "capture Evangelicalism, redefine it by some clearly defined doctrines that are Reformed, and kick the rest of us—and there are lots more 'of us' than the Neo-Reformed—off the village green. (Or at least imply that the rest of us are not courageous enough to embrace the truth.)" ". . . [T]hey look down their noses at the non-Reformed" and "they think the only truly faithful Evangelicals are Reformed," he claims. And "they are more than happy to call into question the legitimacy and fidelity of any Evangelical who doesn't believe in classic Reformed doctrines." ". . . [T]here is no official Evangelical gate but there are gatekeepers who approve and disapprove, so I'm talking about recognized Neo-Reformed leaders routinely approving and disapproving the theology of others. These gatekeepers are, to give two examples, the leaders of TGC and T4G." And regarding gender complementarity, McKnight observed, "Some see it as the litmus test of Evangelical orthodoxy these days. This grieves me. Don't we have more significant battles to wage?" He

---

[192] Peter Enns, "Tullian Tchividjian, The Gospel Coalition, and a (Rather Obvious) Theology Problem," *Peter Enns*, May 25, 2014, http://www.patheos.com/blogs/peterenns/2014/05/tullian-tchividjian-the-gospel-coalition-and-a-rather-obvious-theology-problem/, accessed February 29, 2016.

[193] Scot McKnight, "A Return to an Oldie but Goodie: The Neo-Reformed," *Jesus Creed*, March 1, 2016, http://www.patheos.com/blogs/jesuscreed/2016/03/01/a-return-to-an-oldie-but-much-discussed- post-the-neoreformed/, accessed March 1, 2016.

concluded, "We might not be able to agree on theology," but he still believes "there's room for all of us who call ourselves Evangelicals."[194]

Moreover, in response to a video showing Piper defending genocide in the Old Testament as God's will, neo-Anabaptist leader Brian Zahnd, who is pastor of Word of Life Church in St. Joseph, Missouri, critiqued the New Calvinism this way:[195]

> I understand that the disciples of John Calvin feel obligated to defend their ism at all costs, but my, what a cost it is when it requires impugning the character of God! God is revealed in Jesus, not genocide. The perfect image of God is Christ, not Calvin's ism. [...] Once you reduce all that exists or occurs to God's will, you have moved out of the Judeo-Christian understanding of God into Voluntarism or even Pantheism. Was Nietzsche right? Is everything ultimately about the Will to Power? In the kind of absolute determinism that John Piper espouses there is no authentic being, no genuine freedom, only the sheer will of God ...
>
> If your theological system does not allow you to condemn genocide as *always* morally wrong, please pitch it and embrace the revelation of God found in Jesus Christ! Don't begin your theology with Greek philosophical categories; begin with Jesus. And the moment your theology of God begins to not resemble Jesus, retrace your steps until you've found your mistake. Jesus is the doctrine of God. God didn't give us a theological system—he gave us Jesus! And don't let the Old Testament work you into a corner. You don't need to defend the Old Testament to the extent you find it necessary to justify genocide. God forbid![196]

Christian Piatt critiqued the Acts 29 Network for using some of the language and looks common to "emergent" Christianity (he noted the use of "missional" and "network," in particular) while nevertheless adhering to

---

[194] In part two of the original post, but removed from the later reposting, McKnight wrote: "These folks are America's newest religious zealots and they are wounding, perhaps for a generation or two, Evangelicalism."

[195] Brian Zahnd, "John Piper and Allahu Akbar," *BrianZahnd.com*, August 12, 2013, http://brianzahnd.com/2013/08/john-piper-and-allah-akbar/, accessed February 29, 2016.

[196] Reformed leader and seminarian Derek Rishmawy critiqued Zahnd's argument as "crypto-Marcionism," which says the loving God of the New Testament, revealed in Jesus Christ, is different from, and better than, the wrathful deity of the Old Testament. Derek Rishmawy, "The Cure That Killed the Patient (or, Sorry Zahnd, Marcionism Isn't a Better Option)," *Reformedish*, August 21, 2013, http://derekzrishmawy.com/2013/08/21/the-cure-that-killed-the-patient-or-sorry-zahnd-marcionism-isnt-a-better-option/comment-page-1/, accessed February 29, 2016.

conservative Evangelical doctrine.[197] He mentioned Acts 29 "branding" itself with "the coolest new media [and] the hippest looking [. . .] web-based ministry." "But of course," he lamented, "underneath the veneer of something new lies the same old evangelical doctrine." Further, "They even have an entire web page dedicated to outlining their group's doctrine," Piatt noticed. "It seems opportunistic to me, if not disingenuous simply to change the packaging on an old message, just to grab people's attention." Piatt concluded his article with this analysis: "I'm all for congregational and denominational change. But when it's the same old white guys preaching largely the same old agenda, it smacks more of a desperate power grab than a genuine longing to better know and connect with the world around us." For Piatt, conservative Evangelical doctrine expressed in "hip" and "cool" ways—and using words like "missional"—is in reality little more than deception, desperation, and power grabs.

Later, in a post for Tony Campolo's *Red Letter Christians*[198] and then reproduced on *The Huffington Post*,[199] Christian Piatt reasoned that Calvinism (and he highlighted specifically Driscoll and Piper as figureheads) is actually just a thinly veiled ideology that white men can use to perpetuate elitism and racism. The idea that Christians are God's elect and that everyone else is totally depraved, Piatt contended, lends itself to racism.[200] "If you believe humanity ultimately is depraved, and that only a preordained few are to receive God's sovereign grace, this is fertile ground for seeing much of the world as 'less than,'" he wrote. "And what's more, Calvinists can divest themselves of the culpability for such supremacist thinking, because, after all, it's God's will!" Calvinist soteriology, Piatt concluded, "furthers the toxic, violent notion that some are more worthy than others, which in my understanding, is entirely counter to the notion of God's kingdom."[201]

---

[197] Christian Piatt, "Evangelical 2.0: The Deception of Driscoll's Acts 29 Network," *The Huffington Post*, March 1, 2012, http://www.huffingtonpost.com/christian-piatt/evangelical-20-the-decept_b_ 1299486.html, accessed February 29, 2016.

[198] Christian Piatt, "Driscoll, Piper, Calvin, and God's Gift of . . . Racism?" *Red Letter Christians*, November 5, 2012, http://www.redletterchristians.org/driscoll-piper-calvin-and-gods-gift-of-racism/, accessed February 29, 2016.

[199] Christian Piatt, "Driscoll, Piper, Calvin, and God's Gift of . . . Racism?" *The Huffington Post*, November 10, 2012, http://www.huffingtonpost.com/christian-piatt/driscoll-piper-calvin-and-gods-gift-of-racism_b_2050070.html, accessed February 29, 2016.

[200] Piatt's argument only begins to make sense if he thinks global Christianity is a racial group, which of course it is not.

[201] Among innumerable examples from within the New Calvinist movement of leaders decrying the sin of racism, see John Piper, *Bloodlines: Race, Cross, and the Christian* (Wheaton, IL: Crossway, 2011).

Also with *Red Letter Christians*, Wesleyan pastor Jenny Armstrong argued Reformed theology's vision of God turns Calvinists into "control freaks" who are enamored with power and authority, which, she wrote, "is so completely contrary to the way that God revealed himself in Christ."[202] Worshipping a God who has control over everything, she reasoned, creates followers who feel the need to control everything as well. "And what, if anything, does all of this have to do with our own fear of weakness, despisal of vulnerability, and the resurgence of macho Christianity?" Jenny wondered. "This is the point where theology slams into praxis, where philosophy and personality become hard to disentangle." In the end, she urged New Calvinists instead to look toward Jesus, not power.[203]

Cool Fundamentalism?

Another theme that emerged in the data for critics and opponents of the New Calvinism—and especially from neo-Anabaptists and progressives—had to do with what this popular movement should be called. In the Christian blogosphere, a common argument was that instead of "neo-Reformed" or "New Calvinist" (or "neo-Calvinist"), this movement would be more accurately characterized as "neo-Puritanism" or "neo-fundamentalism."

Progressive Christian leader Zach Hoag—who describes himself as a "charismatic Wesleyanabaptist" (a combination of Wesleyan and Anabaptist)—said on his *Patheos* blog that he used to call this movement "neo-Reformed" until he "became sensitive to the fact that the label unnecessarily lumps other Reformed individuals and groups into this rather particular emphasis on a controlling, wrathful God and the practice of keeping women subordinated to men in most areas of life." And that, he saw, was unfair to other Reformed theologians like Barth, Pannenberg, Bosch, Boesak, Newbigin, and Moltmann. And "neo-Calvinist," as shown in chapter 2, already refers to early to mid-twentieth-century Dutch Calvinists of the Kuyperian variety. Hoag reasoned that the most accurate label for the Reformed resurgence was simply "neo-fundamentalists."

---

[202] Jenny Rae Armstrong, "Calvinism, Control Freaks, and the Sovereignty of God," *Red Letter Christians*, May 22, 2014, https://www.redletterchristians.org/calvinism-control-freaks-sovereignty-god/, accessed May 17, 2019.

[203] Recall the issue of being in control.

This movement of conservative/evangelical Calvinistic-Baptist and Presbyterian Christians is most accurately a revival of 1920's fundamentalism, the historic movement led by the likes of B.B. Warfield, J. Gresham Machen, and the Hodge brothers at old Princeton Seminary. This self-proclaimed fundamentalist surge was overwhelmingly Calvinistic and unabashedly devoted to the sovereignty of God in salvation and damnation as the essence of the gospel.[204]

Similarly, neo-Anabaptist pastor and professor David Fitch asked on his personal blog, "Is the New Calvinism a New Fundamentalism?" He said if Christian fundamentalism is characterized by insularity, distrust toward culture, and an "us against them" mentality, then the New Calvinism "is on its way to becoming a fundamentalism, even in its edgier forms." Near the end of his post it became clear that by "edgier forms" Fitch mostly had in mind Mark Driscoll—especially his aesthetic choices (including the way he dressed) and the way Mars Hill Church produced new "indie" worship music. This, Fitch suggested, was merely a naïve and superficial brand of cultural engagement masking what in reality is the onset of fundamentalism. Fitch's blog-post was edited and posted the next day on the website for *Christianity Today*'s Leadership Journal.[205]

Arminian Baptist theologian Roger Olson, too, has made a clear link between New Calvinism and fundamentalism.[206] In 2014, on his personal *Patheos* blog, he wrote:

So what's happened in the [N]ew Calvinism? It's infected with fundamentalist elitism, exclusivism and even, at times, separatism. It's often intolerant of differences about secondary doctrinal matters. Is that unique to the [N]ew Calvinism? Hardly. But that doesn't free it from criticism. My main criticism of the [N]ew Calvinism is that it harbors a fundamentalist ethos. I have never had a quarrel with classical Calvinists, Reformed Christians,

---

[204] Zach Hoag, "Neo-Calvinist, Neo-Reformed, or . . . Neo-Fundamentalist?" *The Apocalypse Review*, June 2, 2014, http://www.patheos.com/blogs/zhoag/2014/06/02/neo-calvinist-neo-reformed-or-neo-fundamentalist/, accessed October 20, 2015.

[205] David Fitch, "Is the New Calvinism a New Fundamentalism?" *Reclaiming the Mission*, November 9, 2010, http://www.reclaimingthemission.com/blog/1505, accessed October 20, 2015; David Fitch, "Is the New Calvinism Really New Fundamentalism?" *Christianity Today*, November 10, 2010, accessed October 20, 2015.

[206] Roger Olson, "Is the Problem Calvinism or Fundamentalism (or the Combination)?" *Roger E. Olson*, February 4, 2014, http://www.patheos.com/blogs/rogereolson/2014/02/is-the-problem-calvinism-or-fundamentalism-or-the-combination/, accessed October 20, 2015.

who value their heritage and their theology but do not imply that those not sharing it are lesser Christians.

Bob Robinson, founder and executive director of Re-integrate, took a different tack and argued the New Calvinist movement should more accurately be called "neo-Puritanism"—because of their admiration of Jonathan Edwards, for example.[207] (On his own blog, Scot McKnight approvingly reposted Robinson's post the next day.[208]) Robinson argued, in short (and correctly), that this new movement should not be called "neo-Calvinism" because that term already designates the tradition of Dutch Calvinists associated with Kuyper, Bavinck, Dooyeweerd, and others (see chapter 2). Neither Robinson nor McKnight made a distinction between "neo-Calvinism" and "New Calvinism"—a simple nuance that would solve the labeling problem. Robinson made it a point to insist "I don't use the term 'Puritan' in any derogatory manner. When this term is used, some hear 'puritanical,' with all the caricatures of staunch religious strictness. That is not what I'm referring to." Even with this caveat, however, the effect and implication was the same as calling them fundamentalists—that these New Calvinists are actually something other and more extreme than what they admit they are.

True, it can be difficult to tell the differences between conservative Evangelicals and fundamentalists. Thus, George Marsden's now famous definition that "a fundamentalist is an evangelical who is angry about something."[209] Or Alvin Plantinga's less famous observation that the word "fundamentalist" seems to mean little more than "stupid sumbitch considerably to the right, theologically speaking, of me and my enlightened friends."[210] But fundamentalists and conservative, complementarian, Calvinistic Evangelicals are not the same.[211] And granted, leaders like Albert

---

[207] Bob Robinson, "So What's Wrong with Neo-Calvinism?" *Re-integrate*, May 27, 2014, http://www.re-integrate.org/2014/05/27/whats-wrong-neocalvinism/, accessed October 23, 2015.

[208] Scot McKnight, "What to Call the So-Called New Calvinists?" *Jesus Creed*, May 28, 2014, http://www.patheos.com/blogs/jesuscreed/2014/05/28/what-to-call-the-so-called-new-calvinists/, accessed October 23, 2015.

[209] Marsden, *Understanding Fundamentalism and Evangelicalism*, 1.

[210] Alvin Plantinga, *Warranted Christian Belief* (New York: Oxford University Press, 2000), 245.

[211] See Gabriel A. Almond, R. Scott Appleby, and Emmanuel Sivan, *Strong Religion: The Rise of Fundamentalisms around the World* (Chicago: The University of Chicago Press, 2003); Nancy Tatom Ammerman, *Bible Believers: Fundamentalists in the Modern World* (New Brunswick, NJ: Rutgers University Press, 1987); Joel A. Carpenter, "Fundamentalist Institutions and the Rise of Evangelical Protestantism, 1929–1942," *Church History: Studies in Christianity and Culture* 49 (1980): 62–75; Joel A. Carpenter, *Revive Us Again: The Reawakening of American Fundamentalism* (New York: Oxford University Press, 1997); Michael O. Emerson and David Hartman, "The Rise of Religious Fundamentalism," *Annual Review of Sociology* 32 (2006): 127–144; Martin E. Marty and R. Scott Appleby, eds., *Fundamentalisms Observed* (Chicago: The University of Chicago Press, 1991); Malise

Mohler and John MacArthur seem to straddle that line more than most do. At the same time, pastors such as Tim Keller and Matt Chandler—leading lights of the New Calvinism—are clearly not fundamentalists. Fundamentalists, almost by definition, are not culturally cool or savvy; if they are, they become Evangelicals. Additionally, one ought not be surprised that (clear cut) fundamentalist Christians have started publishing criticisms of the New Calvinist/neo-Reformed movement, unearthing in it what they perceive as worldliness and compromise. They focus on issues like the New Calvinists' use of contemporary music (Driscoll), openness to evolution (Keller), and continuationism (Mahaney, Piper)[212]—and more recently the charge that the movement is enwrapped in social justice and cultural Marxism.

When I asked Andy Naselli—who grew up a middle-class, self-professed fundamentalist—if the New Calvinism is just neo-fundamentalism, he said: "No, no, no. Do you understand what fundamentalism is?" He went on to explain the origins of the term in the 1920s and the later break with Billy Graham after his New York City crusade in the late 1950s. "The term 'fundamentalist,'" he explained, "connotes people who are affirming a specific view of separation—not just separation from false teachers (which these New Calvinists would affirm) and separation from the world but [also] separation from what's called 'disobedient Christians.'" While he said it is right to disassociate with a "disobedient Christian" *in Christian ministry*, he said, "that right kind of carefulness devolved into a third, fourth, fifth degree of separation. [. . .] The New Calvinism is not about that at all. So that's how they differ from self-professed fundamentalists today."

Altogether, the terms "fundamentalism" and "fundamentalists" float around the institutional context surrounding the New Calvinist movement precisely how one would expect. The more progressive Christian leaders use the term to disparage New Calvinist leaders, suggesting they are little more than the newest expression of anti-intellectual, boorish, reactionary conservatives. And the Calvinist leaders themselves, not surprisingly, consciously deny the label. It may be difficult to tell the difference between fundamentalists and conservative Evangelicals, but it is just as difficult to

Ruthven, *Fundamentalism: A Very Short Introduction* (New York: Oxford University Press, 2007); Robert D. Woodberry and Christian S. Smith, "Fundamentalism et al: Conservative Protestants in America," *Annual Review of Sociology* 24 (1998): 25–56.

[212] See, for example, E. S. Williams, *The New Calvinists: Changing the Gospel* (Oberlin, OH: Wakeman Trust, 2014).

tell the difference between a good-faith effort at lay social analysis and back-handed name-calling. In the end, while there are affinities, brandishing the "fundamentalist" label appears to add more heat than light.

The New Calvinism: More Than the Sum of Its Parts

The Reformed resurgence further constructed its own sociological strength by *religious leaders leveraging media attention originating from outside the Evangelical field in order to legitimate and celebrate their own beliefs, interests, and organizations.* When David Van Biema, writing for *TIME Magazine*, included New Calvinism on a list of "10 Ideas Changing the World Right Now,"[213] some New Calvinist leaders latched onto the brief news story and championed it. The most prominent example was Mark Driscoll writing at The Resurgence. The same day as the *TIME* article, Driscoll published a post linking to the *TIME* article and compared the New Calvinism with "old Calvinism,"[214] and posted a follow-up post in which he wrote: "[T]he fact that Reformed theology has gotten so big that it merits this kind of attention is nothing short of shocking."[215] Likewise, Al Mohler reviewed the list on his website and expressed gratitude that *TIME* was taking theology and world-view seriously.[216] Justin Taylor, too, highlighted the *TIME* story on the website for The Gospel Coalition.[217] J. D. Greear said the inclusion of the New Calvinism on the *TIME* list was a "profoundly positive development," but it also was regrettable "that it is the name of Calvin, rather than the Gospel of Jesus, that has become the defining moniker."[218] By leveraging this media attention, leaders added fuel to the growing New Calvinist fire.

---

[213] David Van Biema, "The New Calvinism," *TIME*, March 12, 2009, http://content.time.com/time/specials/packages/article/0,28804,1884779_1884782_1884760,00.html, accessed December 28, 2015.

[214] Mark Driscoll, "Time Magazine Names New Calvinism 3rd Most Powerful Idea," *The Resurgence*, March 12, 2009, http://theresurgence.com/2009/03/12/time-magazine-names-new-calvinism-3rd-most-powerful-idea, accessed December 20, 2014.

[215] Mark Driscoll, "More Thoughts on Time Magazine and New Calvinism," *The Resurgence*, March 12, 2009, http://theresurgence.com/2009/03/12/more-thoughts-on-time-magazine-and-new-calvinism, accessed December 20, 2014.

[216] Albert Mohler, "TIME Magazine on '10 Ideas Changing the World Right Now,'" *AlbertMohler.com*, March 18, 2009, https://albertmohler.com/2009/03/18/time-magazine-on-10-ideas-changing-the-world-right-now/, accessed June 4, 2018.

[217] Justin Taylor, "Time Magazine: The New Calvinism Is Changing the World," *The Gospel Coalition*, March 12, 2009, https://www.thegospelcoalition.org/blogs/justin-taylor/time-magazine-new-calvinism-is-changing/, accessed June 4, 2018.

[218] J. D. Greear, "Time Magazine and the 'New' Calvinism," *JDGreear.com*, March 14, 2009, https://jdgreear.com/blog/time-magazine-and-the-new-calvinism/, accessed June 4, 2018.

Not every leader in the New Calvinism was excited about *TIME*'s coverage of the movement, though. On his blog with The Gospel Coalition, for instance, black Calvinist pastor Thabiti Anyabwile gave seven reasons "why the TIME magazine trumpeting of New Calvinism is a bad thing."[219] Among his reasons were uncertainty that the New Calvinism is all that "new" and "the potential for making biblical truth a fad." "All fads die," he commented. "If the resurgence of robust biblical theology rides an emotional crest until that superficial, emotional wave dies, so too will interest in robust biblical truth. We're all familiar enough with church history to have seen this several times over." Further, such media attention, Anyabwile wrote, "prompts some unhealthy Reformed/non-Reformed tensions. The potential for playa hatin' is great. Well-informed leaders inside the SBC have been dealing with this enough over recent years, I think. Do we want the attention of secular news outlets stirring the cauldron of Christian disunity?" He also warned against a "false view of success"—"Do we want to define success by media spots? I'm sure we don't. So we probably ought not put too much stock and spill too much ink over this." He concluded: "Is the 'new Calvinism' and its spread a cause for rejoicing? I think so. But there are also some pitfalls that come with loving the applause of men." Anyabwile's hesitancy about the news coverage, however, was the exception.

Relatedly, an additional mechanism contributing to the New Calvinism is *incumbent religious leaders publicly presenting themselves—and being perceived by challengers and the media—as a significant new movement for orthodoxy.* An important variant of this mechanism is *writing about and documenting themselves, including giving themselves a moniker, so as to construct and present themselves as an identifiable tribe.* Clearly the most important version of this is the writings of Collin Hansen—first his 2006 article in *Christianity Today*[220] and later his 2008 book, *Young, Restless, Reformed: A Journalist's Journey with the New Calvinists.*[221] In this manner, Hansen's work is just as much a part of and a milestone for the New Calvinist movement's development and rise to prominence as it is a description of it.

---

[219] Thabiti Anyabwile, "Why the TIME Magazine Trumpeting of New Calvinism Is a Bad Thing," *Pure Church*, March 17, 2009, http://blogs.thegospelcoalition.org/thabitianyabwile/2009/03/17/why-time-magazine-trumpeting-of-new/, accessed June 4, 2018.

[220] Collin Hansen, "Young, Restless, Reformed: Calvinism Is Making a Comeback—And Shaking Up the Church," *Christianity Today*, September 22, 2006, http://www.christianitytoday.com/ct/2006/september/42.32.html, accessed December 28, 2015.

[221] Hansen, *Young, Restless, Reformed.*

Another example is a lecture Mark Driscoll delivered in February 2009 at an Acts 29 boot-camp in Raleigh, North Carolina. The seventy-two-minute lecture was titled "We Are a Movement," and it served to inform and encourage church planters on "what God is in the midst of doing" through the Acts 29 Network. Among the attributes of a Christian movement, Driscoll discussed the importance of young people in their twenties, auxiliary organizations, and cultural production like music and publishing. He also emphasized that Acts 29 is collaborating and networking ("clumping," as he called it) with other like-minded Evangelical organizations and leaders (he mentioned Carson, Keller, Grudem, Akin, Mohler, Mahaney, Dever, Piper, Greear, and the organizations they lead), and how these ministries are coalescing into the larger New Calvinism as "an overarching movement of God." Driscoll also highlighted Hansen's work that identified and named the movement. Later, Driscoll provided a brief history of the Calvary Chapel and Vineyard movements, and pointed out how much more quickly Acts 29 is planting churches than those two movements did. Acts 29, he explained, is intentionally organizationally lean and noninstitutional; he stated: "What holds us together is love and theology and mission." His lecture was bookended by two prayers, the first of which included: "We want to be part of a movement, not simply because we want to have our way, but because we want the Church of Jesus Christ to flourish." And in closing, Driscoll prayed to God, "that You'd keep us from becoming a museum. I pray we would stay a movement."[222] For anyone who saw or heard Driscoll's lecture, whether in-person or online, the point was clear: this expansive, young, urban, culturally savvy, complementarian, Calvinistic energy is a significant, identifiable movement.

Mars Hill Church was particularly good at documenting and publicizing the church's growth and success. Each year, they released a well-designed annual report that included metrics such as average weekly attendance, membership, baptisms, campus expansions, number of community groups, the operating budget, financial giving, the number of new and total Acts 29 churches, sermon downloads, iPhone app users, unique visitors to the church's website, a timeline of the church, personal testimonies, Bibles given away, international work, number of pastors, music albums sold, and more. The annual reports not only informed Mars Hill congregants and those who followed the church from afar, but also functioned to create buzz and

---

[222] The full lecture is viewable online here: https://vimeo.com/9154887.

excitement about Mars Hill, the Acts 29 Network, and the broader New Calvinist resurgence.

In all the ways detailed in this chapter, the sociological strength of the New Calvinist movement is a strategically and relationally constructed strength—a resurgent religious vitality which has been fought for and won via strategic action and game-like contestation with competitors in the Evangelical field. While there does seem to be more Calvinists in the United States today than there were twenty years ago, the "force" of the New Calvinism in its field has more to do with its "acceleration" (i.e., qualitative and symbolic factors) than with its "mass" (the hard numbers). Like any socially constructed phenomenon in human social life, the New Calvinist movement is ontologically emergent.[223] This means the various Evangelical leaders and organizations described in chapters 2 and 3, motivated by their corresponding beliefs and convictions, acted and interacted over time through the causal mechanisms and processes outlined at the end of chapter 4. And all of this, together, *made something new—the New Calvinism—emerge into existence* at a "higher" level of social organization, stronger than and irreducible to any simple additive mixture of the persons, organizations, and beliefs at the "lower" analytic levels from which it emerged. More simply, the whole is more than the sum of its parts. Additionally, that the Reformed resurgence is relationally constructed and ontologically emergent does not mean it isn't real. It is a mistake to think just because something is socially constructed it therefore isn't real. In fact, every organization and institution in human social and political life (families, capitalism, the university system, etc.) is relationally constructed and ontologically emergent, but that does not make such things any less real or powerful. The field-theoretic model of religious strength has shown that the Reformed resurgence is another socially produced, relationally constructed, yet very real aspect of our contemporary social reality.

One more note: Emergent social and cultural phenomena typically "work back" on the parts at the lower analytic levels from which they emerged. Sociologists call this "downward causation." In various ways, the New Calvinism exerts causal force "back down" on the persons, organizations, and beliefs that produce and constitute it. When a staff member with Cru or InterVarsity understands herself as influenced by the New Calvinism and

---

[223] Clayton and Davies, *The Re-Emergence of Emergence*; Hodgson, "The Concept of Emergence in Social Science"; Mingers, *Systems Thinking, Critical Realism, and Philosophy*; Pratten, "Critical Realism and the Process Account of Emergence"; again, the word "emergent" in this context has nothing to do with the progressive Emergent expression of American Christianity.

suggests a book by Piper or Sproul to an undergrad, hoping to influence him to be Reformed and complementarian, this is the New Calvinism exerting downward causation. When neo-Anabaptist and progressive Emergent leaders get worked up on Facebook, Twitter, or their blogs about those pesky neo-Reformed folks, this is the New Calvinism exerting downward causation. When a small-town pastor joins Acts 29 and switches from preaching out of the TNIV to the ESV translation of the Bible mostly because that is what Mark Driscoll and Matt Chandler use, this as well is the New Calvinism exerting downward causation. In all sorts of ways, the causal interplay between "upward" ontological emergence and "downward" causation further strengthens and perpetuates the Reformed resurgence as a real, powerful, and significant Evangelical submovement.

Symbolic Power, Field Unrest

We have observed how the Reformed resurgence makes its own sociological strength through social processes of strategic positioning and game-like contestation within the wider landscape of American Evangelicalism as a field. And even public criticism of and pushback to the New Calvinism from other tribes of Evangelicalism—to the extent people are talking about the New Calvinism ("treating a social fact as a thing," as Durkheim would have it)—strengthens and legitimizes the neo-Reformed movement "as a thing." The New Calvinist movement and its figurehead leaders therefore possess symbolic capital, which means the movement has recognition or esteem or clout, at least among players involved in the Evangelical game. Neither the New Calvinism as a phenomenon nor its symbolic capital is a substantially preexisting entity; both are relationally constructed social products of the Evangelical field.[224]

Built on the possession of symbolic capital is what Pierre Bourdieu called "symbolic power."[225] In this case, *New Calvinist leaders' symbolic capital (recognition or esteem) translates into symbolic power as the authority to define*

---

[224] Pierre Bourdieu, "The Forms of Capital," in *Handbook of Theory and Research for the Sociology of Education*, ed. John G. Richardson and trans. Richard Nice (New York: Greenwood Press, [1983] 1986), 241–258.

[225] Pierre Bourdieu, "Social Space and Symbolic Power," *Sociological Theory* 7, no. 1 (1989): 14–25; Pierre Bourdieu, *Language and Symbolic Power* (Malden, MA: Polity Press, 1991); Loïc Wacquant, "Symbolic Power and Group-making: On Pierre Bourdieu's Reframing of Class," *Journal of Classical Sociology* 13, no. 2 (2013): 274–291.

legitimacy and membership in the field. In a similar fashion as economic capital translates into economic power, symbolic capital translates into symbolic power. "Symbolic power," Bourdieu says, "is the power to make things with words" and its "form par excellence is the power to make groups," especially through the use and manipulation of labels.[226] Like when a University Dean announces you've made the honor roll, or when the Court says you're no longer a free citizen, there is a level of authoritative weight when John Piper or Justin Taylor publicly says you're no longer within the fold of Evangelical orthodoxy. The symbolic power of the New Calvinists in Evangelicalism means their discourse both helped create themselves as an identifiable movement, the Reformed resurgence, and oftentimes attempts to demarcate the broader category of "Evangelical."[227]

As demonstrated, the New Calvinism's symbolic power in the field of American Evangelicalism does not go uncontested. With attempts at classification comes a "classification struggle," during which incumbents and challengers in the field vie to define which players and their views/interests are orthodox versus unorthodox, who is core and who is on the periphery. This chapter has shown American Evangelicalism is by no means a unified religious or theological movement. It is instead a contested social field, a field in a state of unrest—a *battlefield*. The concluding chapter discusses what this means for Evangelicalism in the United States today, highlighting how Calvinism's resurgence in its field also reveals the field's overall weakness, fragmentation, and incoherence. The Reformed resurgence experiences strength within a destabilized religious field in which Evangelical coherence has fallen apart.

---

[226] Bourdieu, "Social Space and Symbolic Power," 22–23.
[227] Bourdieu explains: "Obviously, the construction of groups cannot be a construction *ex nihilo*. It has all the more chance of succeeding the more it is founded in reality, that is, as I indicated, in the objective affinities between the agents who have to be brought together." Ibid., 23.

7

American Evangelicalism in Hypermodernity

Taking Stock

Let's briefly take stock of the storyline up to this point. This book started by laying a foundation of thorough description of the Reformed resurgence—describing the most important organizations, conferences, networks, and leaders constituting the New Calvinism followed by the various beliefs, doctrines, convictions, and other features animating the movement. Beginning the move from description to explanation, two questions were posed: Relative to what and to whom in the larger landscape of American Evangelicalism is the Reformed resurgence resurging—and how do those competing religious camps compare regarding their numbers and sociological strength? Those other major camps or tribes were identified as generic mainstream Evangelicalism, neo-Anabaptist Evangelicalism (including the New Monasticism), and progressive Evangelicalism. However, it turned out that although the New Calvinism has indeed grown numerically since the late 1990s, mainstream Evangelicalism is infrastructurally huge—and certainly large enough to match and overshadow the leaders, networks, and organizations of the New Calvinism. The neo-Anabaptist and progressive Emergent tribes of American Evangelicalism, while significantly smaller than the New Calvinist movement, have themselves both only emerged since the late 1990s and therefore have "resurged" percentage-wise just as much.

It was argued the New Calvinism enjoys "strength beyond numbers"—that is, the Reformed resurgence is in large part a "qualitative" or "symbolic" (as opposed to quantitative and linear) resurgence of institutional religious strength, which has been "fought for and won." Using a slightly modified version of Fligstein and McAdam's recent framework of "strategic action fields," I developed an explanatory model that specified several causal mechanisms and processes by which the New Calvinist movement has become the kind of social and religious reality it is—a *resurgence*. This causal model was

Reformed Resurgence. Brad Vermurlen, Oxford University Press (2020). © Oxford University Press.
DOI: 10.1093/oso/9780190073510.001.0001

demonstrated and expounded at length—including various precipitating causes and factors; the New Calvinism's strategic positionings that granted it a sustainable competitive advantage, especially among college-educated Americans in their twenties and thirties; and lastly outright contestation and conflict with its competitors in the Evangelical field. Through all of this, the New Calvinism is revealed to be less about there simply being more young, restless Calvinists today than there were twenty years ago (although there appears to be), and more a socially produced, relationally constructed, and ontologically emergent—yet nevertheless very real—religious phenomenon.

Where does that leave us? This concluding chapter steps back to discuss what the preceding argument means for Evangelicalism in the United States today. It is also, through this discussion, an unpacking of the final mechanism of the causal model: *Intractable conflict and divergent institutional logics lead over time (and despite pockets of relative strength) to overall field weakness and fragmentation.* This final mechanism is the endpoint of the larger narrative—in many ways the natural outworking, both analytically and temporally, of several causal mechanisms constituting the argument in previous chapters. The basic idea is that Calvinism's resurgence in the Evangelical field, ironically, also reveals the field's overall disorder, weakness, fragmentation, and incoherence. There certainly remain pockets of relative strength—most notably the New Calvinism but also any number of polished, thriving megachurches that did not even enter the story of this book. But even with these pockets of strength, the underlying intractable conflict and divergent institutional logics and interpretations portend rough news for Evangelicalism in the hypermodern era. In fact, as will be shown, the field-theoretic model of religious strength at the core of this book has baked into it a concomitant element of significant overall religious weakness—a new vision of secularization not as *decline* but as *dissolving*.

The State of American Evangelicalism

On the most surface level, Evangelical Christianity in America is doing okay—it is not growing, but at least it isn't declining like the characteristically-more-liberal mainline Protestant tradition. If one looks simply at the percentage of American adults who can be classified as belonging to the Evangelical Protestant tradition, then Evangelicalism has remained remarkably steady. Sociologists Landon Schnabel and Sean Bock, using data from the General

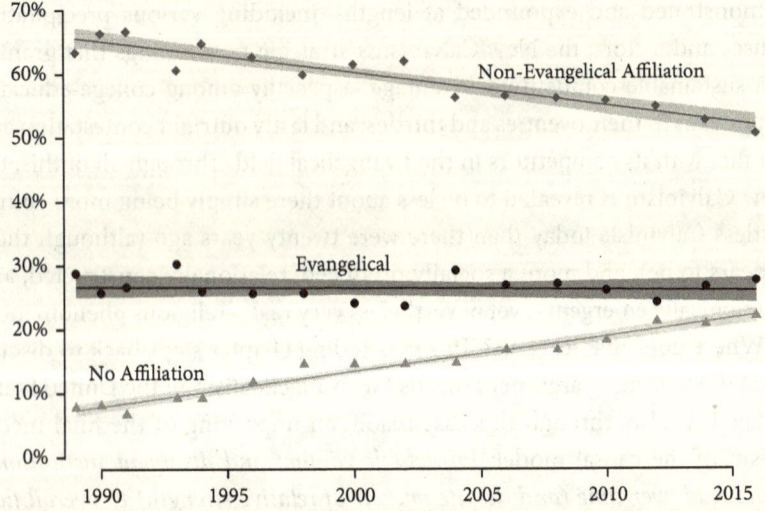

Figure 7.1 Evangelical affiliation has been steady since 1989.

Social Survey, demonstrated that Evangelical affiliation has been steady since 1989, hovering around 28 percent of the adult population. Across the same time span, American adults with no religious affiliation (including atheists, agnostics, and "nothing in particular," collectively known as "the nones") have increased significantly, while all other religious affiliations, if grouped and analyzed together, balance the score chart. These patterns are displayed in Figure 7.1.[1]

Despite its numerical steadiness, previous pages have shown some of the tumult, unrest, conflict, and disorder churning "inside" that straight trend line, particularly among Evangelicalism's leaders. What, then, do Evangelical leaders themselves think about the present state of their own religious tradition, at least within the bounds of the United States? They should offer a telling view. Not surprisingly, their views differ wildly, ranging from those who think Evangelicalism is basically strong to those expecting its demise. Let's hear what some of them have to say.

[1] Landon Schnabel and Sean Bock, "The Persistence and Exceptional Intensity of American Religion: A Response to Recent Research," *Sociological Science* 4 (2017): 686–700. The figure is taken from p. 692. The figure has not been modified and is used here in accordance with https://creativecommons.org/licenses/by/4.0/.

At the extreme pessimistic end of the spectrum, progressive Christian leader and LGBTQ activist Brandan Robertson's message is "R.I.P. Evangelicalism." On his *Patheos* blog, he writes:

> [A]ll hope of rescuing Evangelicalism from its impending demise is in vain. . . . I do not take delight in the fact that Evangelicalism is a "fading reality,"[2] but I also refuse to continue a charade that pretends that there is any hope for [a] sustainable future for the movement. There simply isn't. . . . If the history of religious movements has taught us anything, we must be willing to acknowledge that the Evangelical movement is on its final legs and that all of our attempts to slow or stop its death are futile. . . . [T]he signs clearly indicate that God is bringing a swift end to Evangelicalism and is birthing new forms of Christianity all around.[3]

Other Evangelical leaders perceive American Evangelicalism as strong by any measure. For example, during our interview, Tony Campolo told me: "Do I think American Evangelicalism is in a state of crisis? Definitely not. It's doing well. While mainline churches are dying, these churches like Piper's church are growing leaps and bounds. It's not in a state of crisis by any stretch of the imagination."

A more common response was that American Evangelicalism is strong and weak at the same time in different ways. For example, Geoff Holsclaw told me American Evangelicalism "is in somewhat of decline and crisis, but, along with Churchill, I guess I would say, of all the other options it's the best one still. So I think it is in decline and crisis, but compared to everything else going on in the American Christian landscape, comparatively it's still fairly robust."

When I asked Andy Naselli if he thinks American Evangelicalism is in a state of crisis, he answered:

> Yeah. When there's debate about whether the Bible is God-breathed— really? We're debating that? Or you're debating the nature of the Bible's authority, or debating whether homosexuality is a sin. Just, what have been givens in the history of the Church are now debated. That's a really bad sign.

---

[2] With this phrase, Robertson is making a point about American Evangelicalism writ large using parallel language to the way John Piper in early 2010 described the Emergent Church movement.

[3] Brandan Robertson, "R.I.P. Evangelicalism," *Nomad*, August 2, 2014, http://www.patheos.com/blogs/revangelical/2014/08/02/r-i-p-evangelicalism.html, accessed August 21, 2018.

On the other hand, I look at a movement like the New Calvinism and I'm very encouraged. So I'm simultaneously encouraged and discouraged.

I asked J. I. Packer in a phone interview about the state of Evangelicalism in the United States, its relative strength or weakness. He offered this measured response while at the same time attributing problems within Evangelicalism to the work of Satan:

> It is always the case that Evangelical Christianity—in the States and any-where else in the world—will have marginal difficulties with errors of the mind and errors of beliefs. I believe in the Devil, you see, just as I believe in the Trinity. And I believe that the Devil will see to it that Evangelicalism is always under attack along those lines. So I think, yes, there is a good deal of marginal tension about lots of matters for Evangelicalism in America. But for all that, it is, by the grace of God, strong.

On his blog, Roger Olson made a distinction between the Evangelical ethos, which he thinks is "alive and well," and Evangelicalism as a socio-religious movement:

> [W]hen I identify myself as "evangelical" I'm referring to a particular Christian *ethos* and not a movement. My own judgment as a theological historian is that the American evangelical movement is either dead or hopelessly divided, but the spiritual-theological ethos I call "evangelical" is still alive and well. It pre-dates the "evangelical movement" and will survive its demise.
>
> When I talk about "evangelical" as my spiritual-theological identity I mean the evangelical ethos. The evangelical movement, as a cohesive co-alition, is dead. It has dissolved into competing parties, each with its own expression of the evangelical ethos. To be sure, there still exists "evangeli-calism" as an affinity group, but it is too large and too diverse to call a move-ment. The affinity is its ethos, but the affinity is too weak and admits too much opposition and competition to forge and cement a coherent and co-hesive movement.
>
> According to evangelical historian George Marsden the post-fundamentalist, neo-evangelical movement that came together in the 1940s died out in 1976. I think its last gasps were in the 1990s as the evangel-ical coalition divided over politics, biblical inerrancy, the roles of women

in church and family, God's attributes, Calvinism versus Arminianism and postmodernity. As a historian of evangelicalism I was not surprised by the movement's fragmentation and demise; it was a combustible compound from the beginning.[4]

The argument developed in previous chapters helps to make sense of how each of these perceptions can be right in its own way. If an observer looks *locally*, these "churches like Piper's" and many non-Calvinist megachurches besides are thriving—and Evangelicalism seems strong. But if one looks *globally*—that is, at the whole of American Evangelicalism—one sees fragmentation, division, infighting, disorder, and doctrinal and ethical incoherence. In this sense, there is no "the Evangelical movement"; there is only an Evangelical field, as a field was described in chapter 4. This is also how the New Calvinist movement, the Reformed resurgence, can be strong and vital while Evangelicalism writ large in America is divided. Indeed, as should now be clear, the former cannot be understood or explained rightly apart from the latter.

Two Frequently Asked Questions

Over the course of working on this project, two questions were posed to me repeatedly. These questions were asked mostly by my colleagues in sociology but also, to a lesser extent, by some of the Evangelical leaders I interviewed. While both questions have been broached in previous chapters, and in some ways run in the background of the entire project, here some space is taken to address both questions plainly—giving them the explicit attention they deserve.

What's New about the New Calvinism?

The first question posed to me repeatedly was "What's new about the New Calvinism?" With this question it seems most people meant: What features

---

[4] Roger Olson, "Why I Still Call Myself 'Evangelical' in Spite of Everything," *Roger E. Olson*, October 15, 2015, http://www.patheos.com/blogs/rogereolson/2015/10/why-i-still-call-myself-evangelical-in-spite-of-everything/, accessed August 22, 2018.

or characteristics does this present Calvinist movement have that makes it notably different from other, older expressions of Calvinist Christianity, particularly on the American religious scene? Why even call it "new?" It is a reasonable question. But posed and understood this way, the answer is: not much—except perhaps the movement's strategic and skillful use of the Internet and digital media. In fact, by its nature, the New Calvinist movement has a strong conservative, incumbent impulse and so does not want to change or reinvent this stream of Protestant Christianity. It is a preserving force.

As stated in passing at the end of chapter 2, any focus on the "new" in this movement's name should not be seen as indicating a major *revision* or *alteration* of Calvinism but a *resurgence* of it. This means the newness of the New Calvinism is not about its substantive features or beliefs but instead its prominence and historical situatedness in a post-9/11, digital-age America, especially among a new generation of mostly college-educated persons in their twenties and thirties. It is conservative, complementarian Calvinism in the new millennium. Even here, the New Calvinism is not simply *all of* Calvinism in American Evangelicalism today, but only the energy and comradery among the specific cluster of Calvinistic megachurches, networks, councils, conferences, and well-known pastors described in chapter 2. It is that set of actors' prominence, symbolic capital, and symbolic power in a specific temporal context that makes the New Calvinist movement new.

What Are the Boundaries of the Evangelical Field?

The second question I frequently met—a question that is central to understanding the condition of American Evangelicalism in hypermodernity— was "What are the boundaries of the Evangelical field?" With this inquiry, my interlocutors were asking which markers or viewpoints delineated which leaders and organizations to be properly "in" Evangelicalism and which are "out." In short, who is included in and excluded from Evangelicalism, and why?[5] I heard this question mostly from fellow sociologists near the beginning of my project when I told them I was writing a book on "the field of American Evangelicalism." (Mention any social field among social scientists and the question of boundaries is one of the first to come up.)

---

[5] Jon R. Stone, *On the Boundaries of American Evangelicalism: The Postwar Evangelical Coalition* (New York: St. Martin's Press, 1997).

Now, at the book's end, the answer should already be clear: the boundaries of the Evangelical field are by no means definitive or settled; instead, they are "blurry" and continually contested. But this doesn't mean the Evangelical field is endless. Like a large pile of sand on a beach, there may not be a clear border, but at some point the object of interest has trailed off.

Some might propose self-identification as an Evangelical as a marker for inclusion and exclusion. This method works for "obvious" cases, such as atheists, Muslims, Hindus, or religiously apathetic people, who have no connection to or interest in Protestant religion—but it works *only* for such "obvious" cases. Precisely where a boundary marker is needed most—near the border—self-identity fails as a workable boundary of bona fide Evangelical faith, and it fails in both possible directions. In the first direction, there are Christian leaders who identify as Evangelical (like Rachel Held Evans until very recently or Doug Pagitt or Rob Bell) who leaders in dominant positions in the field say should be excluded. In the other direction, there exist Christian leaders who easily fit the mainstream, dominant category of Evangelical but who, often for reasons related to the political baggage attached to the term and the way it hampers public witness, eschew the label. This is especially the case after the election of Donald Trump and the candidacy of Roy Moore,[6] but my interview data (gathered well before November 2016) likewise revealed multiple theologically, socially, and politically conservative Protestant leaders who shied away from the describing themselves as "Evangelical." If the goal is to get beyond blurry and contested boundaries of this field, then self-identification does not get us anywhere.

Another reasonable-sounding option is that beliefs—whether on doctrine and theology or social and cultural issues, or both—define the boundaries of Evangelicalism. Can someone actually be considered an Evangelical Christian if he or she denies—or, more likely among laypersons, does not know or understand—basic ecumenical orthodoxy such as the triune nature of God, the full divinity and humanity of Jesus Christ, or His bodily resurrection? Regarding other doctrinal views, previous chapters have demonstrated that multiple Evangelical leaders in dominant, incumbent positions will claim a leader isn't an Evangelical if he or she rejects the exclusivity of Christ for salvation, the existence or eternality of Hell, the penal substitution

---

[6] Peter Wehner, "Why I Can No Longer Call Myself an Evangelical Republican," *The New York Times*, December 9, 2017, https://www.nytimes.com/2017/12/09/opinion/sunday/wehner-evangelical-republicans.html, accessed August 22, 2018.

theory of the atonement, the objective and propositional character of truth, the authority and sufficient clarity of the Bible, God's knowledge of a settled future, and more. Regarding social views, several Evangelical leaders believe someone cannot be an Evangelical and affirm same-sex relationships and sexuality, a pro-choice stance on abortion, or the legal redefinition of marriage to include gay and lesbian couples. Some progressive and neo-Anabaptist leaders believe New Calvinists think Evangelical Christianity includes only Calvinists and complementarians (although empirically this doesn't appear to be the case). However, a belief-based set of boundaries fails for at least two reasons: First, there is active disagreement among leaders in the Evangelical field about which beliefs would or should constitute a boundary. And second, even if there were agreement on belief boundaries, no organization, network, or set of leaders has any real institutional authority to enforce such boundaries. A leader who teaches controversial things may get shunned, ignored, or farewelled by other leaders, but he or she cannot be stopped from participating and preaching in the American Evangelical marketplace of ideas (and will almost certainly have followers). All one is left with, again, is ambiguity, blurriness, and contestation.

What Is Evangelicalism Centered On?

Perhaps the better concern is not what Evangelical Protestantism is *bounded by* but instead what it *centers on*. That is, instead of conceiving American Evangelicalism as a bounded set, what would it look like to conceptualize it as a centered set? The common image for understanding bounded set versus centered set is this: A shepherd owns a pasture full of sheep, but he does not have the material to construct a fence around the perimeter of his very large plot of land. So instead of a fence, he places the water and food reservoirs in the center of his land. Because the sheep need water and food, the shepherd can be confident his sheep won't wander too far off. His pasture of sheep, then, is a centered set, not a bounded set. For Evangelicalism in America today, what would be "in the center?" And would this method reveal a clear, more substantive Evangelicalism?[7]

[7] See Jake Meador, "The Evangelical Center after Billy Graham," *Mere Orthodoxy*, March 6, 2018, https://mereorthodoxy.com/evangelical-center-after-billy-graham/, accessed August 24, 2018.

Isn't Evangelicalism centered on the Bible? In a wide-ranging way, yes. But to see the Bible as constituting a substantive, defining center would require a naïve and/or overconfident view of biblical interpretation and hermeneutics, as well as how these factors actually play out empirically "on the ground" among Evangelical groups. Evangelical faith can seem straightforwardly centered on the Bible as long as one's gaze is confined only to Calvinistic Baptists, conservative Presbyterians, and some nondenominational churches, but with a broader lens the picture gets far more complicated. Previous pages have shown there are multiple and sometimes contradicting interpretations on very many issues and concerns within Evangelicalism, both central and peripheral, including the nature of the Bible and how it should be approached and used.[8] The empirical fact of pervasive interpretive pluralism in American Evangelicalism nowadays problematizes any simple claim that the Bible is its center.[9]

Is Evangelicalism centered on Jesus Christ? In a generic way, yes. However, Calvinists would be the first to admit that differing perspectives in the Evangelical field today amount to quite different substantial views of Christ, especially pertaining to His character, purposes, will, abilities, temperament, and desires—including His desires for organizing church and family and what it means to live a morally upright life. Jesus is clearly very important in American Evangelicalism, but as an analytical center Jesus turns out to be quite blurry and contested. What one sees empirically is markedly different conceptions of and beliefs about Jesus Christ broadcasted and proclaimed by big-name Evangelical teachers: I am of Piper. I am of Osteen. I am of Furtick. I am of Bell. I am of Young. I am of Lentz.[10]

Is Evangelicalism "Gospel-centered," as this common phrase has it? In a diverse way, yes. As discussed at the end of chapter 5, "Gospel" means "good message" or "good news"—and most every Evangelical leader, church, and ministry has a message they believe is both true and fundamentally good

---

[8] See J. Merrick and Stephen M. Garrett, eds., *Five Views on Biblical Inerrancy* (Grand Rapids, MI: Zondervan, 2013); Kenton L. Sparks, *God's Word in Human Words: An Evangelical Appropriation of Critical Biblical Scholarship* (Grand Rapids, MI: Baker Academic, 2008); Peter Enns, *The Bible Tells Me So: Why Defending Scripture Has Made Us Unable to Read It* (New York: HarperCollins, 2014); Rob Bell, *What Is the Bible? How an Ancient Library of Poems, Letters, and Stories Can Transform the Way You Think and Feel about Everything* (New York: HarperCollins, 2017); Kern Robert Trembath, *Evangelical Theories of Biblical Inspiration: A Review and Proposal* (New York: Oxford University Press, 1987); Vincent Bacote, Laura C. Miguélez, and Dennis L. Okholm, eds., *Evangelicals and Scripture: Tradition, Authority, and Hermeneutics* (Downers Grove, IL: InterVarsity Press, 2004); Holcomb, ed., *Christian Theologies of Scripture.*

[9] Smith, *The Bible Made Impossible.*

[10] Lee and Sinitiere, *Holy Mavericks.*

news for the world. But as demonstrated, there is no consensus on (and oftentimes outright conflict over) what that message is. For Calvinistic Evangelicals, the good news is that God, by sheer grace, has sovereignly redeemed and secured the eternal salvation of certain individuals through the substitutionary death and bodily resurrection of Jesus. For mainstream Arminian or Wesleyan Evangelicals, the good news is that if you place your faith in Jesus as Lord and Savior, your sins will be forgiven, and you can go to Heaven. For some, the good news is that God is actively making all things new and invites us to participate with Him in His beautiful work advancing mercy and justice in the world, ushering in His Kingdom. For others, the good news is the story of how Jesus was sent by God the Father to become the saving king who now rules forever at His right hand through the sending of the Holy Spirit, fulfilling God's promises in Scripture.[11] For certain Pentecostal Evangelicals, the good news is that God, through His Spirit, is revealing fresh insights and energy and, if you place your faith in Him, will empower or even save your life. For some pragmatic seeker-sensitive Evangelicals, the good news is functionally that with God's help, if you trust Him, you can have a happy family, overcome anxiety and strife, discover your true identity, and enjoy a well-functioning life with Christ. For Evangelicals formed by a therapeutic ethos, the good news is that whatever problem you're going through, God is there for you to comfort, help, and save. For prosperity Evangelicals, the good news is that if you demonstrate strong faith, then God will make you prosper abundantly in health, finances, and relationships, having life to the full. For progressive Evangelicals, the good news is that God isn't out for blood but instead welcomes and affirms everyone in Her unfathomable love and invites people into the mysteries of the Christ event. Hardly a center.

Is mission the center of Evangelicalism? In a muddled way, sure. Most Evangelical pastors and leaders have an activist impulse and evangelistic zeal for their messages and other causes, even if laypersons in practice do not always share their enthusiasm. But given the diverging perspectives on biblical interpretation, Jesus Christ, and the Gospel among leaders of American Evangelicalism, it follows there is also no definitive, unifying, common mission. Specific churches, denominations, networks, and agencies typically have a good idea of their mission, but for American Evangelicalism as a collective whole it is not clear what is trying to be accomplished—and

---

[11] Matthew W. Bates, *Gospel Allegiance: What Faith in Jesus Misses for Salvation in Christ* (Grand Rapids, MI: Brazos Press, 2019), 228.

how and why. Even if one sets aside progressive leaders, prosperity preachers, and other fringe characters, recent books with titles like *Four Views on the Church's Mission* and *The Mission of the Church: Five Views in Conversation* show mission is important, but in empirical reality Evangelical groups today are running in multiple directions.[12]

Is American Evangelicalism centered on politics? Not really. Even at the level of religious leadership, Evangelical Christianity and national politics in America are only somewhat overlapping fields. Most Evangelical leaders hold political beliefs and priorities like other Americans, and presumably many vote. But conservative Evangelical leaders are by no means beholden to or the mouthpiece for the Republican Party. That view, particularly among social scientists, is a holdover from the 1980s and '90s—not based on a contemporary empirical understanding of the Evangelical field. As demonstrated in the previous chapter, neo-Reformed leaders try to be apolitical and nonpartisan, and occasionally teach their congregants not to place too much hope in politics. Interestingly, a leader like Jim Wallis is more wedded to the Democratic Party than a leader like John Piper or Mark Driscoll is wedded to the Republican Party. Too often among sociologists, Evangelicals are mentioned in the same breath as national politics, thus becoming the topic of *Evangelicals-and-politics*, which blocks from their vision other potentially more interesting aspects of Evangelicals. The more immediate point is simply that despite a common (mis)perception in the popular imagination and media and among some scholars, Evangelicalism today is not primarily about politics. It is not close to what Evangelicalism *centers on*.[13]

At this point one might wonder—Do American Evangelical leaders hold anything in common? Certainly there must be some commonality, or in what sense do they constitute a field? In sociological field theory, the concept of *doxa* refers to those ideas, beliefs, or presumptions that are taken for granted, which form the "common sense" of the field. *Doxa* in a field, in other words, is what the orthodox and the heterodox hold in common. *Doxa* is the foundations or very premises of the field, and thus the premises that are not

---

[12] Jason S. Sexton, ed., *Four Views on the Church's Mission* (Grand Rapids, MI: Zondervan, 2017); Craig Ott, ed., *The Mission of the Church: Five Views in Conversation* (Grand Rapids, MI: Baker Academic, 2016); DeYoung and Gilbert, *What Is the Mission of the Church?*

[13] Paul A. Djupe and Ryan L. Claassen, eds., *The Evangelical Crackup? The Future of the Evangelical-Republican Coalition* (Philadelphia, PA: Temple University Press, 2018); see also David D. Kirkpatrick, "The Evangelical Crackup," *The New York Times*, October 28, 2007, http://www.nytimes.com/2007/10/28/magazine/28Evangelicals-t.html, accessed February 23, 2016.

battled over but, as unquestioned and undiscussed, are battled upon.[14] *Doxa* "goes without saying because it comes without saying."[15]

To uncover the *doxa* of American Evangelicalism, consider a thought experiment. Imagine several big-name leaders and organizations, for whatever reason, decide it is finally time to recognize "big tent" Evangelicalism, even if they don't exactly celebrate it. To do this, they set out to organize a national conference, which will include speakers from all the major expressions of American Evangelicalism—Calvinists, generic mainstream Evangelicals, Pentecostals, neo-Anabaptists, and progressive Emergents. The conference will not address or try to resolve the many points of disagreement and conflict among the participants, which they all know they have. The purpose, instead, is to be cooperative and peaceable. In fact, the publicized theme of the conference is "Evangelical Unity: Togetherness and New Hope for the 21st Century." Many noteworthy Evangelical organizations, excited by this vision, decide to bracket their theological and ethical differences and sponsor the conference. These include The Gospel Coalition, Acts 29, *Christianity Today*, the National Association of Evangelicals, Missio Alliance, Red Letter Christians, the CANA Initiative, and a handful of reputable seminaries. This is a big deal. After much anticipation, the speaking lineup is announced. It includes New Calvinist figureheads John Piper and Tim Keller, but also included are Rick Warren, Andy Crouch, Joel Osteen, Brian Zahnd, David Fitch, Greg Boyd, Tony Campolo, Shane Claiborne, Rob Bell, Rachel Held Evans, and Doug Pagitt. To accompany such a milestone conference on Evangelical unity, Greg Boyd suggests this group craft a "statement of belief," which would express the actual "lowest common denominator" of Evangelical faith. Each participant should be able to affirm this statement without reservation. Shane Claiborne, Rob Bell, and Rachel Held Evans each voice deep concern about producing a "statement of belief," but after some persuasion the group settles in and starts brainstorming. What would they come up with? My data suggest they would come up with something very close to the following five principles, and no more:

- The Bible is somehow informative and important.
- Jesus was a real person and divine—and somehow helps people.

---

[14] Pierre Bourdieu, *Outline of a Theory of Practice*, trans. Richard Nice (Cambridge: Cambridge University Press, [1972] 1977), 159–171; Jacques Berlinerblau, "Toward a Sociology of Heresy, Orthodoxy, and Doxa," *History of Religions* 40, no. 4 (2001): 327–351.

[15] Bourdieu, *Outline*, 167.

- There is some kind of special, desirable eternal state.
- Christianity is fundamentally a good message that should be shared and expressed publicly.
- This faith is Christian but not part of Roman Catholicism.[16]

Notice that these five commonalities are chastened, very weakly stated versions of the Bebbington Quadrilateral (biblicism, crucicentrism, conversionism, and activism)—along with the assumption that this field is, essentially, Protestant. As set out near the end of chapter 5, Bebbington's four principles constitute "the rules of the game" in the battle over Evangelicalism in America. They are the rules or terms of the conflict between the incumbent, orthodox religious camp (in this case, the Reformed resurgence) and various challenger, heterodox factions. The Bebbington Quadrilateral makes sense as the conclusive features of Evangelicalism's dominant, mainstream expressions, but in view of the broader field they only function as contested sensitizing concepts. It is their much weaker, more ambiguous articulations which actually define Evangelicalism's *doxic* core. This is not unexpected. As Berlinerblau explained: "*[D]oxic* assumptions shadow, so to speak, the imperatives of orthodox rule," and "[W]e may speculate that *doxic* beliefs are the unseen and unforeseen epistemological residue of an intentional system of domination."[17] Although the orthodox, dominant expressions of Evangelicalism are well-described by the full-flower Bebbington Quadrilateral, the field as a whole can be made sense of only with a much weaker "shadow" and "residue" of its supposedly central characteristics.

Taking Seriously Theological Particularities

One lesson for sociology from this book is that to understand and explain religion and its social influences well sociologists should do better to understand the theological issues and particularities that matter to religious people, and especially to religious elites. Whether the religion under examination is Catholicism, Judaism, Islam, Buddhism, Hinduism, or—in the

---

[16] Nor Eastern Orthodoxy, nor Mormonism. This last point might be phrased "This faith is Protestant," except not all Evangelical leaders conceive of themselves as within the historic stream coming out of the sixteenth-century Reformation—even though, in actuality, they are. Consider the survey category "Just Christian."

[17] Berlinerblau, "Toward a Sociology of Heresy, Orthodoxy, and Doxa," 346–347.

present case—Evangelical Protestant Christianity, there is always a richness and deep complexity to religious traditions, including at the level of ideas, that for social scientists could matter in unexpected ways or motivate creative new research projects.

In the case of Evangelicalism, social scientists would benefit from knowing at least a little about varying contested perspectives in soteriology, theology proper, ecclesiology, missiology, theological ethics, eschatology, and hermeneutics. For the present case, it would not be possible to describe, understand, or explain the Reformed resurgence as a distinctly social and cultural phenomenon without engaging in a "sociology of theologies."[18] Sociology as a discipline, and sociology of religion as a subdiscipline especially, will be more fruitful and more interesting in the long run if it pays more attention to complex theological and religious particularities.

Of course, taking theology seriously looks different for a sociologist than it does for a theologian. Although usually quite abstract in themselves, such ideas have concrete social, cultural, and institutional contexts and consequences of interest to sociologists. Theology intersects in interesting and important ways with conflict, violence, politics, race, class, gender, sexuality, and more. Religion is rarely, if ever, sealed off from these factors. But even while not neglecting such factors, taking religious particularities seriously also opens up a range of possibilities for sociologists to interrogate deeper questions related to modernity, the sacred, and religious life. As Alexander Riley, professor of sociology at Bucknell, recently noted:

> [P]ick up a journal article or book on religion by a contemporary sociologist and you can be reasonably sure that race, class, gender, sexuality, and diversity in one form or another will somehow be *the central theme*. [. . .] Meanwhile, the nature of the sacred, the experiences of the religious *in terms not reducible to the categories of intersectionality*, and the question of what can be expected in a society without the sacred—these topics make *rare appearances in that literature*.[19]

---

[18] Another example is Christian Smith, *The Emergence of Liberation Theology: Radical Religion and Social Movement Theory* (Chicago: The University of Chicago Press, 1991).

[19] Alexander Riley, "A Religion of Activism," *First Things*, April 2019, https://www.firstthings.com/article/2019/04/a-religion-of-activism, accessed March 15, 2019. Italics added.

Secularization as Cultural Entropy

The larger lesson concerns religious strength and weakness in the hypermodern Western world. It is now apparent the field-theoretic model of religious strength—in which religious leaders thoughtfully and strategically vie for strength—also entails a corresponding element of significant religious weakness. The reason for this is deceptively simple: A field-theoretic model of religious strength is premised upon an underlying current of disunity and conflict. As Mark Galli, at the time editor in chief of *Christianity Today*, wrote:

> This is the great strength and weakness of evangelicalism. Its lack of structured authority—with only the Bible and each person's reading of it—has allowed it to be a dynamic movement that shapes the faith attractively to each generation and each culture. But that lack of a central authority inevitably creates arguments and divisions, and therefore in some ways an ongoing crisis.[20]

Even as Evangelicalism in the United States maintains a steady trend line of affiliation, and certain organizations and ministries experience real vitality, Evangelicalism has *turned in on itself*. It has devolved in recent decades into competing and occasionally mutually hostile factions. As Markofski rightly put it, "There is today no 'evangelical point of view' concerning theological, social, or political matters. Rather, there are multiple, distinctive, often contradictory evangelical *points* of view in competition with one another to offer the *legitimate representation of biblical Christianity in the United States*."[21] Evangelicalism in America writ large can no longer properly be considered a unified Christian movement but instead is a heterogeneous arena of conflict and contestation—that is, a *field*. It is not merely *diverse*; it is *divided*.

It should also be recognized that Evangelical leaders themselves have long claimed that their own religious tradition is not merely diverse but deeply divided against itself.[22] Christian Smith, who in the mid to late 1990s saw a

---

[20] Mark Galli, "The Heart of the Evangelical Crisis," *Christianity Today*, May 15, 2019, https://www.christianitytoday.com/ct/2019/may-web-only/elusive-presence-1-heart-of-evangelical-crisis.html, accessed May 20, 2019.

[21] Markofski, *New Monasticism*, 109, emphasis in the original.

[22] For example, Donald W. Dayton and Robert K. Johnston, eds., *The Variety of American Evangelicalism* (Knoxville: The University of Tennessee Press, 1991); D. G. Hart, *Deconstructing Evangelicalism: Conservative Protestantism in the Age of Billy Graham* (Grand Rapids, MI: Baker Academic, 2004); Gerald R. McDermott, "The Emerging Divide in Evangelical Theology," *Journal*

thriving Evangelical religious subculture, now observes: "American evangel-icalism today is increasingly coming apart at the seams. Perceptive evangel-ical leaders know this and have no idea what to do about it."[23] Nevertheless, leaders' observation "from the inside," as correct and illuminating as it is, has yet to gain the attention it deserves among sociologists and other scholars of American religion, most of who still think and write about "the Evangelical movement" as a more or less coherent Christian bloc.

Relatedly, I do not want to give the impression that Evangelicalism in the United States ever enjoyed a unified past, with a clear authoritative center, from which it is now devolving. Molly Worthen, for instance, in her detailed intellectual history of the modern (neo-) Evangelical movement, shows how tensions between Reformed and various non-Reformed Evangelical leaders go back to the very beginning of the neo-Evangelical movement in the 1940s and '50s.[24] As Roger Olson noted, "it was a combustible compound from the beginning." While Evangelicalism in America has always been contested and its boundaries always unsure, the observation at the end of this book is that this tradition is *increasingly* fragmented and incoherent, particularly now "downstream" from the Internet, the sexual and gender revolutions, 9/11, the Emerging Church, and postmodernism. That is, the contestation and inco-herence have *intensified*.

Although the tribalism, fragmentation, infighting, disorder, and incoher-ence evident presently in Evangelicalism at the level of its own leadership is a manifestation of field-level weakness, it does not neatly fit any leading expressions of secularization theory. It is not a case of the religious sphere becoming increasingly autonomous and differentiated from other institu-tional spheres or fields of American society, such as education, the family, or the state.[25] Nor is the present case an example of the most straightforward

---

of the Evangelical Theological Society 56, no. 2 (2013): 355–377; Iain H. Murray, *Evangelicalism Divided: A Record of Crucial Change in the Years 1950 to 2000* (Carlisle, PA: Banner of Truth, 2000); Andrew David Naselli and Collin Hansen, eds., *Four Views on the Spectrum of Evangelicalism* (Grand Rapids, MI: Zondervan, 2011); Kenneth J. Collins, *Power, Politics and the Fragmentation of Evangelicalism: From the Scopes Trial to the Obama Administration* (Downers Grove, IL: InterVarsity Press, 2012).

[23] Smith, "A Preceding Generation in the Quandary of an Accommodating Evangelicalism," *Journal for the Scientific Study of Religion* 58, no. 4 (2019): 913–915. Quoted from p. 914.

[24] Molly Worthen, *Apostles of Reason: The Crisis of Authority in American Evangelicalism* (New York: Oxford University Press, 2014).

[25] Karel Dobbelaere, *Secularization: An Analysis at Three Levels* (Brussels: Peter Lang, 2002); Rudi Laermans, Bryan Wilson, and Jaak Billiet, eds., *Secularization and Social Integration: Papers in Honor of Karel Dobbelaere* (Leuven, Belgium: Leuven University Press, 1998).

and common notion of secularization, based on the sorts of quantitative decline that are easily measured on surveys: declines in religious affiliation (or strength of affiliation); belief in God (or certainty of belief in God); subjective importance of religion; frequency of attendance at religious services;[26] or decreases in "orthodox" beliefs among adherents, which represent declining religious authority.[27] Nor is it exactly "internal secularization," which refers to "the process by which religious organizations undergo internal development toward conformity with the secular world" or "the declining control of religious authority within religious organizations themselves"[28]—such as when entire Protestant denominations liberalize on theological, moral, or social matters. Instead, what one finds are factionalized religious authorities themselves battling seriously over ideas.

The battle over American Evangelicalism, fought at the level of leadership and elites, represents a new understanding of secularization as a meso-level order or entire religious tradition losing its coherence, or "dissolving." The vision of religious weakness suggested by the present case, in other words, is secularization as "cultural entropy." By "cultural entropy" I mean a process in which a meaningful cultural system gradually deteriorates and falls apart over time.[29] And the culture in this phrase does not refer to the surrounding secular culture but rather the meanings, ideas, values, commitments, and beliefs of American Evangelicalism itself—the Evangelical religious culture. This notion of secularization—as cultural entropy—is of necessity somewhat more abstract and qualitative (and perhaps harder to measure empirically) than existing models of secularization focused on decline, and it cannot be fully developed here, but it offers a genuinely new framework for seeing religious weakness in the hypermodern era.[30]

It should be emphasized: Secularization as cultural entropy does not mean Evangelical leaders over time are taking their ideas and commitments less seriously. Quite the opposite. They take their ideas and commitments

---

[26] David Voas and Mark Chaves, "Is the United States a Counterexample to the Secularization Thesis?" *American Journal of Sociology* 121, no. 5 (2016): 1517–1556.

[27] Chaves, "Secularization as Declining Religious Authority."

[28] Mark Chaves, "Intraorganizational Power and Internal Secularization in Protestant Denominations," *American Journal of Sociology* 99, no. 1 (1993): 1–48. Quoted from p. 3.

[29] The idea of cultural entropy is from McDonnell, *Best Laid Plans*.

[30] However, for similarly "qualitative" notions of secularization, start with Charles Taylor, *A Secular Age* (Cambridge, MA: Belknap Press of Harvard University Press, 2007); Brad S. Gregory, *The Unintended Reformation: How a Religious Revolution Secularized Society* (Cambridge, MA: Belknap Press of Harvard University Press, 2012); Hans Joas, *Faith as an Option: Possible Futures for Christianity* (Stanford, CA: Stanford University Press, 2014).

so seriously that those beliefs are worth debating and sometimes possibly even dividing over. Through this process, even while remaining passionately devout in their own respective views, Evangelical leaders have ended up diverging from one another. The shared common substance of their Evangelical faith has faded away or dissolved. In Evangelicalism, the religious authorities themselves have drifted further and further apart from one another regarding their beliefs and dispositions, resulting in a state of disorder.

Moreover, this disordered condition is not the New Calvinists' fault; the Reformed resurgence is best understood as a reaction to, not the cause of, Evangelicalism's troubles in the United States. Instead, cultural entropy of the American Evangelical field is the result of a combination of its internal logic and dynamics along with broader external forces. Those internal factors include Evangelicalism's entrepreneurial character, open market structure, lack of centralized authority, and democratized approach to interpreting the biblical text. The external forces, as discussed in chapter 5, include philosophical postmodernism, the Internet, the triumph of the therapeutic, September 11th, and the gender and sexual revolutions. It is these factors working together which have brought about the entropy and incoherence of Evangelicalism.[31]

A Game Metaphor—Calvinball

Lastly, if Evangelical Protestantism in the United States today is characterized by strategic positionings and game-like contestation, what would be the nature of that game? Does it resemble chess, for instance? Or basketball? As a

---

[31] As far as first-person explanations go in social research, one factor that has been neglected in the secularization question is *Christians' self-understandings about the future of Christianity*. Although the specifics of "end times" doctrine vary widely among Christians, one common theme among conservative and moderate Evangelicals is that the complete disappearance of religion—specifically Christianity—is ultimately not possible. The reasoning relates to Jesus's words in the New Testament when Jesus says He will build His Church "and the gates of Hell shall not prevail against it" (Matthew 16:18). Promised events like Jesus's second coming, the final Day of Judgment, the consummation of all things, and the full realization of the Kingdom of God on Earth are indispensable plot elements of the broader story in which many Christians understand themselves (and in fact all people) to be living. So while religious beliefs, practices, or authorities may decline and religion may be pushed further out of the public sphere, many Evangelical Christians believe in a grand, sweeping story about reality that instills real confidence in them that their religion can never and will never entirely go away.

closing image, I suggest the field resembles a game of Calvinball, a recurring feature in the Calvin and Hobbes comic strips.[32]

In a game of Calvinball, the players compete not within a well-organized or settled system. Instead, the game itself is a struggle over the rules. A game of Calvinball is problematic (and humorous) because each player has the ability to make up a new rule at any time and thereby change the nature of the game in whatever way gives him the best shot at gaining the upper hand. There is, after all, no authoritative referee. When the game itself is a battle over the rules, the game eventually devolves into a state of disorder and chaos.

"Sooner or later, all our games turn into Calvinball," Calvin shouts in one iteration of the comic, as he sprints through his backyard with a badminton racket in-hand, chasing after a volleyball as Hobbes follows him riding on a stick-horse, holding a croquet mallet. "No cheating!" Hobbes declares. Like Calvinball, present-day Evangelicalism in the United States is less a regulated system than a battle with and over the rules of the game—a field contest in which religious players vie to win a game as it becomes an interpretive free-for-all.[33]

* * *

At the T4G conference in 2018, Collin Hansen taught a seminar on "Still Young, Restless, Reformed? The New Calvinists at 10." When asked by an attendee if "Evangelicalism" is a term conservative Protestants should cling to, given its clear tensions and complexity, Hansen commented:[34]

I will mourn if we lose that word because "Evangelical" is just "Gospel-people"—people who talk about the death and resurrection of Christ for sinners. So, we're not going to be able to find a better word [. . . But] I think there's way too much focus on Evangelicalism. [. . .] Evangelicalism in itself is a figment of the imagination of certain historians and journalists and also political mobilizers. So, it's a thing that people talk about, but because there's no centralized authority, there's no discipline, there's no unified

---

[32] The fictional characters Calvin and Hobbes, fittingly, were named after John Calvin and seventeenth-century British philosopher Thomas Hobbes. Hobbes held that without a sufficiently cohesive and directive social contract the alternative by nature would be competing interest parties warring for dominance and power.

[33] "But there are much worse games to play." Suzanne Collins, *Mockingjay* (New York: Scholastic Press, 2010), 390.

[34] https://t4g.org/media/2018/04/still-young-restless-reformed-new-calvinists-10/, accessed April 19, 2019.

purpose to it—it's not a *thing*. There are Evangelical institutions; there are colleges; there are conferences; there are organizations, but there's no *thing* out there. Robert Jeffress doesn't speak for me. Ok? A historian might [call us both Evangelicals], but I don't care what Robert Jeffress says on TV any more than he cares what I say on TV. In that sense, it's a figment of imagination. And that's why I don't believe we need to fight for it, but we fight for the beliefs. We fight for Christ. We fight for His Church.

APPENDIX A
Research Methods

Participant Observation

Event Log

Table A.1 contains the dates, times, and descriptions of the events that I attended for the participant observation portion of data collection.

Personal Interviews

Leaders Interviewed

Table A.2 displays the names, positions, and main organizational affiliations of the Evangelical leaders whom I interviewed for this project. The titles and affiliations listed reflect each interviewee's position at the time the interview took place, not necessarily his or her current position.

Interview Guide

What follows is the interview guide I used during data collection. Respondents were allowed to read over this interview protocol both before and during their interviews. On a number of the questions, the wording closely follows that used in Michael Lindsay's work on Evangelical elites.[1]

Looking back, there are some aspects of the interview guide I would trim down or construct differently. For example, following theoretical insights from Pierre Bourdieu, I sought considerable detail about each leader's upbringing, thinking this background information would give me insights into their habitus and dispositions toward religion and culture. In actuality, that line of questioning proved not as fruitful as I had initially expected.

Also, the middle of the interview guide used a five-point scale from (1) "strongly disagree" to (5) "strongly agree" to inquire about a range of religious beliefs. The thinking was that, in light of well-known findings in cultural sociology about people's common inability to talk about their values and beliefs, providing a simple number scale would make the process easier. Instead, it just made the process tedious. I quickly learned nearly all of my interviewees—several of whom have a PhD in theology or a related field—were fully capable of articulating and explaining their beliefs when asked by a researcher. Thus, after

---

[1] D. Michael Lindsay, *Faith in the Halls of Power: How Evangelicals Joined the American Elite* (New York: Oxford University Press, 2007), 249–251.

Table A.1 Participant Observation Event Log

Date	Event	Time	Church	Ministry Area
Saturday, October 13, 2012	Junior and Senior High, Special Fall Event	3:30 pm–5:30 pm	Mars Hill Church	Shoreline
Sunday, October 14, 2012	Sunday Services (9:00; 11:15; 5:00)	9:00 am–7:00 pm	MHC	Shoreline
Sunday, October 14, 2012	The Post-Funk (after the 5:00 service)	7:00 pm–9:00 pm	MHC	Shoreline
Monday, October 15, 2012	Community Group (at a Deacon's house)	6:00 pm–8:30 pm	MHC	Shoreline
Wednesday, October 17, 2012	Junior and Senior High, Weekly Youth Group	7:00 pm–9:00 pm	MHC	Shoreline
Friday, October 19, 2012	Community Group (at a Deacon's house)	6:00 pm–8:30 pm	MHC	Shoreline
Saturday, October 20, 2012	Men's Training Day	9:00 am–12:00 pm	MHC	Shoreline
Saturday, October 20, 2012	Saturday Service (6:00)	6:00 pm–8:00 pm	MHC	Downtown
Sunday, October 21, 2012	Sunday Services (9:00; 11:15; 5:00)	9:00 am–7:00 pm	MHC	Shoreline
Sunday, October 21, 2012	The Post-Funk (after the 5:00 service)	7:00 pm–9:00 pm	MHC	Shoreline
Wednesday, October 24, 2012	Junior and Senior High, Weekly Youth Group	7:00 pm–9:00 pm	MHC	Shoreline
Sunday, October 28, 2012	Sunday Services (9:00; 11:15; 5:00; 7:15)	9:00 am–9:00 pm	MHC	Downtown
Sunday, October 28, 2012	Post-Service Gathering	9:00 pm–11:00 pm	MHC	Downtown
Wednesday, October 31, 2012	Junior and Senior High, Weekly Youth Group	6:30 pm–9:00 pm	MHC	Shoreline
Sunday, November 4, 2012	Sunday Service (8:00 pm)	8:00 pm–10:00 pm	MHC	U-District
Wednesday, November 7, 2012	Community Group (at a Deacon's house)	6:00 pm–8:30 pm	MHC	Downtown
Sunday, November 11, 2012	Sunday Services (6:00; 8:00 pm)	6:00 pm–10:00 pm	MHC	U-District
Wednesday, November 14, 2012	Junior and Senior High, Weekly Youth Group	7:00 pm–9:00 pm	MHC	Shoreline
Saturday, November 17, 2012	Apologetics Seminar	9:00 am–12:00 pm	MHC	U-District
Saturday, November 17, 2012	Saturday Service (6:00)	6:00 pm–8:00 pm	MHC	Downtown
Sunday, November 18, 2012	Sunday Services (9:00; 11:15; 4:00)	9:00 am–6:00 pm	MHC	Bellevue
Wednesday, November 21, 2012	Thanksgiving Service	7:00 pm–8:30 pm	MHC	Shoreline

Date	Event	Time	Church	Ministry Area
Thursday, November 22, 2012	Thanksgiving Dinner	4:00 pm–6:00 pm	MHC	U-District
Sunday, November 25, 2012	Sunday Services (9:00; 11:15)	9:00 am–2:00 pm	MHC	West Seattle
Wednesday, November 28, 2012	Community Group (at a Deacon's house)	6:00 pm–8:30 pm	MHC	U-District
Sunday, December 2, 2012	Sunday Services (4:00; 7:00)	4:00 pm–9:00 pm	MHC	Ballard
Sunday, December 2, 2012	Drinks with King's Kaleidoscope	9:00 pm–11:00 pm	MHC	Ballard
Saturday, December 8, 2012	Saturday Service (6:00)	6:00 pm–8:00 pm	MHC	Downtown
Sunday, December 9, 2012	Sunday Services (9:15; 11:30)	9:00 am–1:00 pm	MHC	Rainier Valley
Sunday, December 9, 2012	Sunday Services (4:00; 7:00)	4:00 pm–9:00 pm	MHC	Ballard
Tuesday, December 11, 2012	Q School: Training Tomorrow's Preachers	6:00 pm–9:30 pm	MHC	U-District
Sunday, December 16, 2012	Sunday Services (9:00; 11:15)	9:00 am–1:00 pm	MHC	Bellevue
Sunday, December 16, 2012	Sunday Services (4:00; 7:00)	4:00 pm–9:00 pm	MHC	Ballard
Monday, December 17, 2012	Tour of the B50 Building	12:00 pm–2:00 pm	MHC	Production
Tuesday, December 18, 2012	Shadowing at the B50 Building	3:00 pm–4:45 pm	MHC	Production
Sunday, January 27, 2013	Sunday Services (9:15; 11:15; 5:00)	9:15 am–6:20 pm	Redeemer Presbyterian Church	West Side Congregation
Sunday, January 27, 2013	Credibility of Christianity Class	6:30 pm–8:00 pm	RPC	Classes and Training
Monday, January 28, 2013	Writers Group Winter Kickoff Event	7:00 pm–9:30 pm	RPC	Center for Faith and Work
Friday, February 1, 2013	Citywide Worship and Prayer Night	7:00 pm–9:00 pm	Various Evangelical Churches	Ecumenical Efforts
Saturday, February 2, 2013	Don't Walk By, Homeless Outreach	2:30 pm–8:00 pm	RPC	Hope For New York
Saturday, February 2, 2013	Drinks with Redeemer Gotham Fellows	9:00 pm–1:00 am	RPC	Informal Socializing
Sunday, February 3, 2013	Sunday Services (10:30; 6:00)	10:30 am–8:00 pm	RPC	East Side Congregation
Tuesday, February 5, 2013	Community Group	5:00 pm–7:00 pm	RPC	Community Groups
Thursday, February 7, 2013	Ph.D. Student Group, Monthly Gathering	7:00 pm–9:20 pm	RPC	Center for Faith and Work

Date	Event	Time	Church	Ministry Area
Friday, February 8, 2013	Personal Meeting with Director of CTC	3:30 pm–4:30 pm	RPC	Redeemer City to City
Sunday, February 10, 2013	Sunday Services (9:30; 5:00)	9:30 am–7:00 pm	RPC	Downtown Congregation
Sunday, February 10, 2013	Dinner at Chipotle with Laypersons	7:00 pm–9:00 pm	RPC	Downtown Congregation
Thursday, February 14, 2013	Pastors at West 83rd: Gospel Contextualization	1:00 pm–3:30 pm	RPC	Redeemer City to City
Friday, February 15, 2013	Community Group	7:30 pm–9:40 pm	RPC	Downtown Congregation
Sunday, February 17, 2013	Sunday Services (11:15; 5:00; 7:00)	11:15 am–8:40 pm	RPC	West Side Congregation
Friday, February 22, 2013	Social Event with Redeemer Congregants	9:00 pm–12:00 am	RPC	Informal Socializing
Sunday, February 24, 2013	Sunday Services (9:30; 5:00)	9:30 am–6:15 pm	RPC	Downtown Congregation
Sunday, February 24, 2013	Gotham Fellowship Information Session	6:15 pm–7:30 pm	RPC	Center for Faith and Work
Monday, February 25, 2013	The Writing Life—Vocational Group	7:00 pm–9:15 pm	RPC	Center for Faith and Work
Wednesday, February 27, 2013	Ei Business Plan Competition Finals	7:00 pm–9:30 pm	RPC	Center for Faith and Work
Saturday, March 2, 2013	Citilights Praise and Pizza (Redeemer Offices)	7:00 pm–9:00 pm	RPC	Congregational Life
Sunday, March 3, 2013	Sunday Services (10:30; 6:00)	10:30 am–8:00 pm	RPC	East Side Congregation
Sunday, March 3, 2013	Newcomers' Informational Lunch	12:15 pm–2:00 pm	RPC	East Side Congregation
Tuesday, March 5, 2013	"Quarters" 20s Ministry Happy Hour	8:00 pm–11:00 pm	RPC	Congregational Life
Thursday, March 7, 2013	PhD Student Group, Monthly Gathering	7:00 pm–9:00 pm	RPC	Center for Faith and Work
Saturday, March 9, 2013	Twenties Potluck and Game Night	7:00 pm–10:00 pm	RPC	Congregational Life
Sunday, March 10, 2013	Sunday Services (10:30; 6:00)	10:30 am–8:00 pm	RPC	East Side Congregation
Tuesday, March 12, 2013	Hope for New York Information Session	7:00 pm–8:30 pm	RPC	Hope For New York
Thursday, March 14, 2013	Pastors at West 83rd: City Vision	1:00 pm–3:00 pm	RPC	Redeemer City to City
Thursday, March 14, 2013	Gospel and Culture Lecture (on Work)	7:30 pm–9:00 pm	RPC	Center for Faith and Work
Sunday, March 17, 2013	Sunday Services (9:15; 11:15; 5:00)	9:15 am–6:20 pm	RPC	West Side Congregation
Wednesday, March 20, 2013	InterArts Fellowship Lecture	7:00 pm–10:00 pm	RPC	Center for Faith and Work

Date	Event	Time	Church	Ministry Area
Sunday, March 24, 2013	Sunday Services (9:30; 5:00)	9:30 am–7:00 pm	RPC	Downtown Congregation
Monday, March 25, 2013	Writers Vocational Group	7:00 pm–9:00 pm	RPC	Center for Faith and Work
Saturday, June 1, 2013	Saturday Worship Service (5:30)	5:30 pm–7:00 pm	Bethlehem Baptist Church	Downtown Campus
Saturday, June 1, 2013	Evangelism Training: Dinner and Movie Night	7:00 pm–9:00 pm	BBC	Downtown Campus
Sunday, June 2, 2013	Sunday Worship Service (9:00)	9:00 am–11:00 am	BBC	Downtown Campus
Sunday, June 2, 2013	Getting Acquainted with Bethlehem	11:00 am–12:15 pm	BBC	Downtown Campus
Sunday, June 2, 2013	Sunday Night Service (5:00)	5:00 pm–7:00 pm	BBC	Downtown Campus
Sunday, June 2, 2013	Standing Firm in the Evil Day: A Panel Discussion	7:00 pm–8:30 pm	BBC	Downtown Campus
Monday, June 3, 2013	Sanctity of Life Monthly Meeting	6:30 pm–9:30 pm	BBC	Downtown Campus
Wednesday, June 5, 2013	Summer Connection	5:30 pm–7:00 pm	BBC	Downtown Campus
Saturday, June 8, 2013	Saturday Worship Service (5:30)	5:30 pm–7:00 pm	BBC	Downtown Campus
Sunday, June 9, 2013	Sunday Worship Service (9:00)	9:00 am–11:00 am	BBC	Downtown Campus
Sunday, June 9, 2013	Getting Acquainted with Bethlehem	11:00 am–12:30 pm	BBC	Downtown Campus
Sunday, June 9, 2013	Sunday Night Service (5:00)	5:00 pm–7:00 pm	BBC	Downtown Campus
Sunday, June 9, 2013	Shepherd Group Leader Appreciation Dinner	7:00 pm–9:30 pm	BBC	Downtown Campus
Friday, June 14, 2013	Prayer for the Persecuted Church	7:00 pm–9:00 pm	BBC	North Campus
Saturday, June 15, 2013	Saturday Worship Service (5:30)	5:30 pm–7:00 pm	BBC	Downtown Campus
Sunday, June 16, 2013	Sunday Worship Service (9:00)	9:00 am–11:00 am	BBC	Downtown Campus
Sunday, June 16, 2013	Getting Acquainted with Bethlehem	11:00 am–12:30 pm	BBC	Downtown Campus
Sunday, June 16, 2013	Sunday Night Service (5:00)	5:00 pm–7:00 pm	BBC	Downtown Campus
Wednesday, June 19, 2013	Downtown Outdoor Baptism Service	5:30 pm–7:00 pm	BBC	Downtown Campus
Thursday, June 20, 2013	TULIP: The Five Points of Calvinism	6:30 pm–8:30 pm	BBC	The Bethlehem Institute

Date	Event	Time	Church	Ministry Area
Saturday, June 22, 2013	Saturday Worship Service (5:30)	5:30 pm–7:00 pm	BBC	Downtown Campus
Sunday, June 23, 2013	Sunday Worship Services (9:00; 11:00)	9:00 am–1:00 pm	BBC	North Campus
Sunday, June 23, 2013	Sunday Night Service (5:00)	5:00 pm–7:00 pm	BBC	Downtown Campus
Sunday, June 23, 2013	Antioch Moment Q&A with Elder Panel	7:00 pm–8:00 pm	BBC	Downtown Campus
Wednesday, June 26, 2013	Summer Connection	5:30 pm–7:00 pm	BBC	Downtown Campus
Wednesday, July 3, 2013	Summer Connection	5:30 pm–7:00 pm	BBC	Downtown Campus
Saturday, July 6, 2013	Saturday Worship Service (5:30)	5:30 pm–7:00 pm	BBC	Downtown Campus
Sunday, July 7, 2013	Sunday Worship Services (9:00; 11:00)	9:00 am–1:00 pm	BBC	North Campus
Sunday, July 7, 2013	Sunday Night Service (5:00)	5:00 pm–7:00 pm	BBC	Downtown Campus
Thursday, July 11, 2013	TULIP: The Five Points of Calvinism	6:30 pm–8:30 pm	BBC	The Bethlehem Institute
Friday, July 12, 2013	Children's Music Camp Finale	7:00 pm–9:00 pm	BBC	North Campus
Saturday, July 13, 2013	Saturday Worship Service (5:30)	5:30 pm–7:00 pm	BBC	Downtown Campus
Sunday, July 14, 2013	Sunday Worship Service (11:00)	11:00 am–1:00 pm	BBC	North Campus
Sunday, July 14, 2013	Sunday Night Service (5:00)	5:00 pm–7:00 pm	BBC	Downtown Campus
Tuesday, July 16, 2013	Informal Meeting with Pastor	7:30 pm–8:30 pm	Solomon's Porch	Main Building
Wednesday, July 17, 2013	Downtown Outdoor Baptism Service	5:30 pm–7:30 pm	BBC	Downtown Campus
Saturday, July 20, 2013	Missional Roundtable: Paradigms and Practices	8:30 am–2:30 pm	Missio Alliance	Elim Baptist Church
Saturday, July 20, 2013	Saturday Worship Service (5:30)	5:30 pm–7:00 pm	BBC	Downtown Campus
Sunday, July 21, 2013	Sunday Gatherings (10:00; 5:00)	10:00 am–7:00 pm	Solomon's Porch	Main Building
Saturday, July 27, 2013	Saturday Worship Service (5:30)	5:30 pm–7:00 pm	BBC	Downtown Campus
Sunday, July 28, 2013	Sunday Gathering (5:00)	5:00 pm–6:30 pm	Solomon's Porch	Main Building
Sunday, July 28, 2013	All-Church Quarterly Strategy Meeting	7:00 pm–9:00 pm	BBC	Downtown Campus

Date	Event	Time	Church	Ministry Area
Tuesday, November 5, 2013	National Resurgence Conference: Day 1	8:00 am–4:25 pm	Various Reformed Churches	Seattle, Downtown
Wednesday, November 6, 2013	National Resurgence Conference: Day 2	8:00 am–3:30 pm	Various Reformed Churches	Seattle, Downtown
Sunday, November 17, 2013	Can Life Have Meaning Without God?	7:00 pm–8:45 pm	RPC	East Side Congregation
Friday, December 6, 2013	Sola Conference: Sessions 1–3	2:30 pm–9:00 pm	Various Reformed Churches	Lansing, Michigan
Saturday, December 7, 2013	Sola Conference: Sessions 4–8	8:30 am–5:30 pm	Various Reformed Churches	Lansing, Michigan

a handful of interviews, I approached that section in a less methodical way than the guide implies.

I made every effort to address all the questions listed with each interviewee. At times, however, I deviated from the guide when it seemed necessary to probe further, to cut the interview short due to time constraints, or to pursue an unexpected path of conversation. I also made it a habit to ask about particular topics of special interest to whomever I was interviewing—music for musicians, writing for bloggers, and so on—at the close of the interview.

Demographics

(1) Can you start by telling me your name and age? [ALSO NOTE RACE AND GENDER]

Organizational Role

(2) What exactly is your position or title at [ORGANIZATION]?
(3) Can you tell me about what you do in that role?
(4) Are you involved in any other Christian projects, councils, or initiatives?

FIRST I'M GOING TO ASK A LITTLE ABOUT YOU, AND THEN, AFTER THAT, I'LL SWITCH TO QUESTIONS ABOUT [ORGANIZATION] AND YOUR VIEWS ON THE "NEW CALVINIST MOVEMENT" IN AMERICAN EVANGELICALISM.

Background

(5) I'll start with your personal background. What was your upbringing like? For example:

a) Did you grow up in an Evangelical Christian home?

Table A.2 Evangelical Leaders Interviewed

Name	Title and Organization	Location
Danny Akin	President, Southeastern Baptist Theological Seminary	Wake Forest, NC
Jay Bakker	Pastor, Revolution Church	Minneapolis, MN
Matt Bennett	Founder and President, Christian Union	New York City
Debbie Blue	Minister, House of Mercy	St. Paul, MN
Peter Blum	Professor of Philosophy and Culture and Director of the Sociology and Social Thought Program, Hillsdale College	Hillsdale, MI
Greg Boyd	Senior Pastor, Woodland Hills Church	St. Paul, MN
Dave Bruskas	Network Pastor and Executive Elder, Mars Hill Church	Seattle, WA
Nathan Burke	Executive Pastor, Mars Hill Church	Seattle, WA
Tony Campolo	Pastor, author, social activist	St. Davids, PA
Tim Challies	Associate Pastor, Grace Fellowship Church; blogger	Oakville, Ontario
Calvin Chin	Director of the Entrepreneurship Initiative, Redeemer Presbyterian Church	New York City
Shane Claiborne	Author, activist, and speaker	Philadelphia, PA
Sam Crabtree	Executive Pastor, Bethlehem Baptist Church	Minneapolis, MN
Andy Crouch	Executive Editor, Christianity Today	Swarthmore, PA
Colin Day	Creative Director, Mars Hill Church	Seattle, WA
Joe Day	Worship Pastor, Mars Hill Church	Seattle, WA
Mark Dever	Lead Pastor, Capitol Hill Baptist Church; President, 9Marks	Washington, DC
Kevin DeYoung	Lead Pastor, University Reformed Church	East Lansing, MI
Colonel Doner	Chairman, Children's Hunger Relief Fund	Santa Rosa, CA
Alex Early	Lead Pastor, Mars Hill Church	Seattle, WA
Eric Elnes	Senior Minister, Countryside Community Church	Omaha, NE
Austin Fischer	Teaching Pastor, The Vista Community Church	Temple, TX
David Fitch	Founding Pastor, Life on the Vine; Betty R. Lindner Professor of Evangelical Theology, Northern Seminary	Chicago, IL
Chad Gardner	Worship Director, Mars Hill Church	Seattle, WA
Collin Hansen	Editor-at-large, Christianity Today; Editorial Director, The Gospel Coalition	Montvale, NJ
Scott Harris	Executive Director of Ministries, Mars Hill Church	Seattle, WA
Rachel Held Evans	Evangelical Feminist Speaker, Blogger, and Author	Dayton, TN
Omari Hill	Pastor, Redeemer Presbyterian Church	New York City

Name	Title and Organization	Location
Shane Hipps	Former Lead Pastor, Mars Hill Bible Church	Grand Rapids, MI
Geoff Holsclaw	Co-Pastor, Life on the Vine; Affiliate Professor of Ministry, Northern Seminary	Chicago, IL
Matt Johnson	Pastor, Mars Hill Church	Seattle, WA
Tony Jones	Theologian and blogger	Minneapolis, MN
Scott Kauffmann	Executive Director, Redeemer Labs	New York City
Ryan Kearns	Pastor of Leadership Development	Seattle, WA
Keas Keasler	Teaching Pastor, Rhythm Church	Miami, FL
Tim Keller	Lead Pastor, Redeemer Presbyterian Church	New York City
David Kim	Director of the Center for Faith and Work, Redeemer Presbyterian Church	New York City
Zach Lind	Drummer, Jimmy Eat World	Phoenix, AZ
Brian McLaren	Theologian and author	Florida
Jason Meyer	Assistant Professor of New Testament, Bethlehem College and Seminary; Future Successor to John Piper	Minneapolis, MN
Mike Morrell	Promoter, Wild Goose Festival; Publicist and Writer, The David Group International	Raleigh, NC
Richard Mouw	Former President, Fuller Theological Seminary (currently Professor of Faith and Public Life, FTS)	Pasadena, CA
Andy Naselli	Research Manager for D.A. Carson, Trinity Evangelical Divinity School; Assistant Professor, Bethlehem College and Seminary	Minneapolis, MN
Roger Olson	Professor of Theology, Baylor University	Waco, TX
J. I. Packer	Board of Governors' Professor of Theology, Regent College; Executive Editor, Christianity Today	Vancouver, BC
Doug Pagitt	Founder and Lead Pastor, Solomon's Porch; Cofounder, Emergent Village	Minneapolis, MN
Christian Piatt	Blogger and journalist	Pueblo, CO
Paul Poteat	Campus Outreach Regional Director; Downtown Campus Elder, Bethlehem Baptist Church	Minneapolis, MN
Todd Rasmuson	Minister for Global Outreach, Bethlehem Baptist Church	Minneapolis, MN
Joe Rigney	Assistant Professor of Theology and Christian Worldview, Bethlehem College and Seminary	Minneapolis, MN
Frank Schaeffer	Independent writer	Boston, MA
Justin Schaeffer	Biblical Living Pastor, Mars Hill Church	Seattle, WA
Leo R. Schuster III	Lead Pastor, Redeemer Presbyterian Church East Side	New York City
Steve Shaffer	Director of Community Groups, Redeemer Presbyterian Church	New York City

Name	Title and Organization	Location
Mattox Shuler	Content Manager, Mars Hill Church	Seattle, WA
James K. A. Smith	Professor of Philosophy, Calvin College	Grand Rapids, MI
Linda Stanley	Leadership Community Director, Leadership Network	Denton, TX
Kenny Stokes	Lead Pastor, Bethlehem Baptist Church	Minneapolis, MN
Owen Strachan	Assistant Professor of Christian Theology and Church History, Boyce College; Executive Director, Council on Biblical Manhood and Womanhood	Louisville, KY
Tim Suttle	Lead Pastor, Redemption Church	Olathe, KS
Don Sweeting	President, Reformed Theological Seminary	Orlando, FL
Justin Taylor	Associate Publisher, Crossway Books	Wheaton, IL
Bruce Terrell	Executive Director, Redeemer Presbyterian Church	New York City
Phyllis Tickle	Author and lecturer	Millington, TN
Steve Tompkins	Lead Pastor, Mars Hill Church	Seattle, WA
Mike Tong	Director of Downtown Campus Ministry, Bethlehem Baptist Church	Minneapolis, MN
Mark Van Steenwyk	Cofounder and Spokesperson, The Mennonite Worker	Minneapolis, MN
Jeff White	Assistant Pastor, Redeemer Presbyterian Church	New York City
Willie Wilson	Lead Pastor, Mars Hill Church	Seattle, WA
Jesse Wisnewski	Copywriter (Content Manager), Mars Hill Church	Seattle, WA
Mike Wittmer	Professor of Systematic Theology, Director of the Center for Christian Worldview, Grand Rapids Theological Seminary	Grand Rapids, MI
Anonymous	Female Deacon, Mars Hill Church	Edmonds, WA
Anonymous	Female Deacon, Mars Hill Church	Seattle, WA
Anonymous	Video Producer, Mars Hill Church	Seattle, WA
Anonymous	Founder of Quarters (Twenties Ministry), Redeemer Presbyterian Church	New York City

b) Did both biological parents raise you? Divorce? Adoption? Etc.

c) Did your parent(s) have a positive influence on your faith?

d) Where did you grow up? Was it rural, suburban, or urban?

e) Did you attend public school, Christian school, home-school?

f) What did your parent(s) do for a living? Full-time?

g) Would you say you grew up working, middle, or upper class?

h) How far did your parent(s) go in school? Their highest degree?

i) Do you think you've done better economically than your parent(s) did?

Education and Career

(6) Have you earned a bachelor's degree? [IF YES] Which college or university did you go to? What did your studies focus on (majors and minors)? Why did you choose to study that?

(7) Do you have any graduate degrees? [IF YES] What degrees do you have? What are they in, exactly? Where did you earn them? What years?

(8) Take a minute or two to trace your professional journey from your days as a student up to now. Did you feel a strong sense of "calling" from God to what you are now doing for a career?

Marriage and Family

(9) What is your marital status right now? [SINGLE, ENGAGED, MARRIED, DIVORCED, OR SOMETHING ELSE?) [IF MARRIED] When did you get married?

(10) Do you have any children? [IF YES, AND NOT CLEAR] How many? What are their ages?

Religious Identity

(11) How would you describe your personal faith to someone who doesn't know you?

(12) [IF NOT CLEAR] Do you consider yourself an Evangelical? Why or why not? What does that term mean to you? In other words, what makes someone an Evangelical Christian?

(13) [IF NOT CLEAR] Did you have a religious conversion experience? [IF YES] At what age? [IF NO] Or have you come to your current faith gradually since a young age?

(14) [IF NOT ALREADY CLEAR] Do you identify with any particular denomination, or not? [IF YES] Which one, and why? [IF NOT] Why not? Do you "lean" close to a denomination?

(15) Do you consider yourself a Calvinist? [IF NO] Why not, exactly? What is it about Calvinism that doesn't describe your theology? [IF YES OR KIND OF] In what ways, exactly? What does being a Calvinist mean to you?

WE'RE STILL ON THE PART ABOUT YOU AS AN INDIVIDUAL, SO YOU'RE NOT NECESSARILY SPEAKING FOR YOUR ORGANIZATION. FOR THIS PART, I HAVE SOME QUESTIONS ABOUT THEOLOGY. I'M GOING TO MAKE A SERIES OF STATEMENTS. FOR EACH ONE, SAY A NUMBER FROM (1) TO (5), WITH (1) MEANING "STRONGLY DISAGREE" AND (5) MEANING "STRONGLY AGREE." (3) CAN MEAN EITHER "NEUTRAL" OR "DON'T KNOW." IF YOU'D LIKE, YOU CAN EXPLAIN YOUR ANSWERS, BUT THAT ISN'T EXPECTED FOR THIS.

1	2	3	4	5
Strongly Disagree	Disagree	Neutral/DK	Agree	Strongly Agree

SO HERE THEY ARE:

Elements of Reformed Theology

(16) Total Depravity: Every aspect of each human person—including emotions, desires, thinking, and the like—was spiritually distorted and turned against God by humanity's fall into sin.

(17) Unconditional Election (a): God predestined "before the foundation of the world" which particular people would be saved or rescued from their sins and reconciled to God.

(18) Unconditional Election (b): When it comes to salvation of individual people, God initiates salvation prior to and apart from any preconditions or human cooperation.

(19) Double Predestination: Before the foundation of the world, God predestined certain people to salvation as well as other people to condemnation in Hell.

(20) Single Predestination: Before the creation of the world, God predestined certain people to salvation but left other persons, by their own fault, to suffer the due penalty for their sins.

(21) Limited Atonement: When Jesus was crucified on the cross, He died only for those persons who would eventually become Christians, not for every person in the world.

(22) Irresistible Grace: If God wills a certain person to be saved and bestows His saving grace upon him or her, that person will definitely come to faith in Jesus and be saved.

(23) Perseverance of the Saints: If someone at one time is truly a regenerated Christian, then that person cannot become unregenerate or, in other words, lose his or her salvation.

Other Proposed Distinctives of the New Calvinism

(24) Complementarianism: God designed men and women to have complementary roles in the home and the church, with men as loving heads or leaders and women as submissive helpmeets.

(25) Spirit-Filled Lives (a): The Holy Spirit is present and active in the lives of Christians today, facilitating miracles and empowering Christians to live lives that are pleasing to God.

(26) Spirit-Filled Lives (b): Continuationism: The supernatural gifts of the Holy Spirit, as enumerated in 1 Corinthians 12, continue to be available and operative in the lives of Christians today.

(27) Missional Churches: The members (or mature Christian congregants) of local churches should be actively engaged with an evangelistic mission in their own communities.

NOW I'M GOING TO SWITCH FROM QUESTIONS ABOUT YOU SPECIFICALLY TO QUESTIONS ABOUT YOUR VIEWS ON [ORGANIZATION], THE NEW CALVINIST MOVEMENT IN EVANGELICALISM, AND CULTURE MORE GENERALLY.

Mission and Motivation

(28) I know that this is probably on your (church's/seminary's/etc.) website, but how would you summarize the mission and vision of [ORGANIZATION]? What are they trying to get done?

(29) What would you say are the deep motivations for [ORGANIZATION]'s mission? *Why* are you/they striving toward fulfilling the mission you just talked about?

Projected Trajectory

(30) Looking ahead, what is next on the horizon for [ORGANIZATION]? Are there any recent developments we'll see in the next year or so? New projects? New methods? New ideas?

(31) How about five years from now? What do you hope or expect [ORGANIZATION] will be doing then? And if you had to guess, where do you envision [ORGANIZATION] in, say, twenty-five years?

The New Calvinism

(32) Are you familiar with the term "New Calvinism" or what has also been called the "Young, Restless, Reformed" movement in American Evangelicalism? [IF NO OR KIND OF] I mean the increasing prominence of Calvinist or Reformed preachers and churches—pastors such as Mark Driscoll, Tim Keller, and John Piper, and the churches they lead. Have you heard of these pastors and the attention they've been receiving? [IF YES] What do you think, generally speaking, of this pocket or trend in Evangelicalism?

(33) Why do you think the New Calvinism has been receiving so much attention and visibility within American Evangelicalism? And how about in the national media?

(34) Can you tell, from your best understanding, why the New Calvinism as a religious trend has arisen over time? Over the last twenty years or so, what has brought it about?

Positions in and on Culture

(35) In your view, how should Christians relate to culture? In other words, how should they live in the world while navigating the various cultural mores that surround them?

(36) What role or importance do you think tradition or a "long view of history" should play in Christian life and faith? How should Christians relate what they do and believe today to earlier centuries?

(37) Likewise, what role or importance do you think "culture making" and innovation should play in Christian life and faith? Is there a particular Christian task in the development of new culture?

Positions in and on Evangelicalism

(38) What kinds of things does [ORGANIZATION] do that make it unique in the broader field of American Evangelicalism? How does it differ from most other churches?

(39) Do you think American Evangelicalism is in a state of crisis? If so, how, exactly? What do you see as some of the most pressing problems in Evangelicalism, writ large, today?

Closing Matters

(40) Is there anything else you would like to discuss before we end? Is there anything you would like to know about this project?

Thanks for taking the time to talk with me.

Reflexivity and Privilege

Part of the tradition of field theory and of qualitative research more generally is to reflect upon and be honest about the ways who one is as a person influences—for good or for ill—the work one produces as a researcher and scholar.[2] Throughout the entire research process but especially during participant observation, I could not help but notice how this played out in my case. The gist of it is this: My own personal characteristics, interests, and privileges made conducting this research far easier than it would have been otherwise, and much of it I suspect would not have been possible at all. I am a highly educated, upper-middle-class, heterosexual, nontransgender, able-bodied, younger,[3] white, male, native-born American citizen—all of which in various ways helped immensely during the long process of examining this particular conservative American Christian movement. Moreover, while I don't think being a traditional, catholic Christian affords much privilege in the United States anymore, the fact that I am one likewise was advantageous in this case.

I do not doubt that I would have experienced more challenges and roadblocks while "in the field" if I happened instead to be, say, a black woman, economically disadvantaged, vaguely nonreligious, or in a wheelchair. Fitting and blending in among the church crowds, building trust and rapport, physically maneuvering around the cities I visited, subleasing an apartment in Lower Manhattan, and securing interviews with Evangelical leaders—among other things—all were made easier because of who I am. This should not be taken to reflect negatively on the motivations, care, or hospitality of my "research subjects" nor of the other people I encountered on my travels. Without getting caught up in the logics of intersectionality and identity politics, about which I have some reservations, I nevertheless think it is only fair to recognize the operation of unearned advantage when it happens.

---

[2] Pierre Bourdieu and Loïc J. D. Wacquant, *An Invitation to Reflexive Sociology* (Chicago: The University of Chicago Press, 1992).
[3] I began fieldwork in October 2012, when I was twenty-six years old.

Nine (or So) Alternatives to Calvinism

Within Protestant Christianity broadly, there are a number of theological belief systems and approaches that serve as historic alternatives to the Calvinist system. For the sake of grasping the New Calvinism more clearly, and for better understanding its competitors in the Evangelical field, this Appendix very briefly outlines those alternatives. This section cannot even broach many of the details, debates, and nuances involved in these schools of thought—the kinds of issues that fill the pages of professional theological journals. What follows here is painted only with the broadest of strokes, although I trust it will prove beneficial.

To start, Calvinism's nearest cousin is Lutheranism, which was founded a generation before Calvinism. Analyzing Lutheranism somewhat anachronistically through the grid of the five points of Calvinism, we can say that classical, early-modern Lutheranism affirmed total depravity and unconditional election, but not Calvin's double predestination. And moving even slightly beyond the earliest generations of Lutheranism, one finds Lutheran scholastic theologians rejecting unconditional election altogether, instead arguing that God's election of persons unto salvation is conditioned upon His foreseeing their faith. Confessional Lutheranism has consistently rejected the doctrine of limited atonement or particular redemption, but in his writings Martin Luther himself was less consistent on that issue. Also, when understood with proper nuances and caveats, one can say that Lutheranism affirms irresistible grace or effectual calling, although that matter too is up for debate. Finally, Lutheranism rejects the perseverance of the saints, teaching instead that genuinely born-again persons can fall from grace and lose their salvation.[1]

A second alternative to Calvinism is Molinism. Named after a Spanish Catholic (Jesuit) priest named Luis de Molina (1535–1600), Molinism was an attempt to reconcile God's predestination with human free will. This position emphasizes that God not only knows the future, but that God also knows counterfactuals. That is, God knows what humans would (freely) choose—or would have freely chosen—when placed in various hypothetical circumstances or life conditions. For example, Molinists would claim God knows, for some specific person who did not go to college, "If you had gone to college, you would have chosen to major in sociology." This knowledge of counterfactuals is called God's "middle knowledge" (or *scientia media*). Molinists believe that prior to the creation of the universe, God "surveyed" all possible worlds and, by using His middle knowledge, actualized the universe in which humans freely choose what God wanted to occur. This stance is especially seen among more philosophically inclined Protestants, including philosophy

[1] James M. Kittelson and Hans H. Wiersma, *Luther the Reformer: The Story of the Man and His Career*, 2nd ed. (Minneapolis, MN: Fortress Press, [2003] 2016); Martin E. Marty, *Martin Luther* (New York: Penguin, 2004); Martin E. Marty, *Lutheran Questions, Lutheran Answers: Exploring Christian Faith* (Minneapolis, MN: Fortress Press, 2007); Douglas A. Sweeney, "Was Luther a Calvinist?" *The Gospel Coalition*, July 15, 2014, https://www.thegospelcoalition.org/article/was-luther-a-calvinist, accessed August 4, 2016.

professor William Lane Craig.[2] Still, unlike Calvinism and Lutheranism, Molinism did not develop into its own branch of Christianity.

A third alternative to Calvinism—the alternative against which it is most often contrasted—is Arminianism, named after Dutch theologian Jacobus Arminius (1560–1609). The key concept for Arminianism is *prevenient grace*—a special grace of God that "goes before" in order to unlock human wills from their depravity so that all persons may freely choose whether or not to place their faith in Jesus for salvation. Arminianism traditionally affirms the doctrine of total depravity, but this has been overcome by God's prevenient grace. Similarly, Arminianism affirms election, but God's election is neither predestined nor unconditional. Arminians believe in the atoning sacrifice of Jesus on the cross, but that atonement is—in Calvinistic terms—unlimited. From Arminius's times forward, the perseverance (or preservation) of the saints has been and remains a debated question for this tradition. Aside from Arminius himself, arguably the most prominent adherents to this school of thought historically are the Wesley brothers, John (1703–1791) and Charles (1707–1788), who left an Arminian imprint on the Protestant denomination they helped found: Methodism. Today, significant segments of Evangelicalism are implicitly or explicitly Arminian in orientation—including the Church of the Nazarene, The Salvation Army, much of the Anabaptist tradition, much of Pentecostalism including Assemblies of God and the Vineyard movement, many nondenominational churches, and roughly half of the Southern Baptist Convention (the other half, roughly, is Calvinist).[3]

The fourth and fifth alternatives to Calvinism reach further back into history by more than one thousand years ultimately to Pelagius (ca. 354–420), a contemporary of Augustine of Hippo whose views were condemned as heretical by the early Catholic Church.[4] The milder version of this perspective—known as semi-Pelagianism—still finds a home in much of American Evangelicalism today. Unlike classical Arminianism— which, despite caricatures by some to the contrary, places the initiative for the possibility of saving faith in the (prevenient) grace of God overcoming humanity's total depravity and rebellion—semi-Pelagianism places the first step toward salvation fully in the freely choosing human will. Original sin is rejected, or at least not acknowledged. This view, like those just mentioned, still believes in the necessity of personal salvation by faith through the atoning work of Jesus on the cross. And it typically holds that divine grace is needed to enable and sustain a Christian life of faith and good works after being converted. But saving faith, at the initial moment of conversion, on the semi-Pelagian view, ultimately comes from a unilateral act of human will, untouched by God's grace.[5]

---

[2] William Lane Craig, *The Only Wise God: The Compatibility of Divine Foreknowledge and Human Freedom* (Eugene, OR: Wipf and Stock, 1999); William Lane Craig, "The Middle-Knowledge View," in *Divine Foreknowledge: Four Views*, ed. James K. Beilby and Paul R. Eddy (Downers Grove, IL: InterVarsity Press, 2001), 119–143; Thomas P. Flint, *Divine Providence: The Molinist Account* (Ithaca, NY: Cornell University Press, 1998); Kenneth Keathley, *Salvation and Sovereignty: A Molinist Approach* (Nashville, TN: B&H, 2010).

[3] Roger E. Olson, *Arminian Theology: Myths and Realities* (Downers Grove, IL: InterVarsity Press, 2006); Roger E. Olson, *Against Calvinism* (Grand Rapids, MI: Zondervan, 2011). See also the Society of Evangelical Arminians at http://evangelicalarminians.org/, accessed September 14, 2015.

[4] Pelagius was condemned as a heretic at the Council of Carthage in 418 and at the Council of Ephesus in 431.

[5] Olson, *Arminian Theology: Myths and Realities*. The Catholic Church condemned the semi-Pelagian view of salvation (although not by that name) as heresy at the Second Council of Orange in 529.

The fifth alternative to Calvinism, then, is a more thoroughgoing Pelagianism. As with semi-Pelagianism, this perspective rejects the doctrine of original sin (and thus also its more intense variant, total depravity) and places the impetus for being in a right relationship with God fully in human free will, not in divine grace. But this position goes beyond semi-Pelagianism in that there is little or no conception of atonement or conversion. Instead, on this view, one need only freely choose to live a good, devout life for God. As Horton put it, for Pelagianism, Adam is a bad example and Christ is a good example.[6] Salvation is often still the goal, but salvation is attained not by God's grace but rather by living a moral life by one's own untainted free will.[7] Thus, this view is not synergistic, like Arminianism (and the traditional Catholic view of salvation). Instead, it is a kind of *inverted monergism*—that is, only one agent is working toward salvation, but that agent is man, not God. Very few leaders in contemporary American Evangelicalism are self-avowed Pelagians, although some are. It is more common to come across this belief as a kind of folk interpretation of what Christianity is all about.[8]

In addition to the aforementioned five alternatives, there are a host of other perspectives and ideas in American Evangelicalism against which Calvinism can be understood. Most of these views do not fit easily along the spectrum of "will and grace," from Calvinistic monergism, through Arminian synergism, ultimately to Pelagian (what I called) inverted monergism. Some of these have to do with salvation. For example, a minority of leaders in American Evangelicalism understands salvation to be fundamentally a corporate or collective phenomenon, not primarily a matter of individual election.[9] British theologian and retired Anglican bishop N. T. Wright and his "new perspective on Paul" offer a distinctive view that emphasizes being included as a member of God's covenantal people through Christ's faithfulness.[10] Other leaders are Christian universalists and argue that salvation, however the mechanics of it work, will eventually come to all people, not just to some. Some of the more progressive Evangelical leaders I interviewed joked that they have no problem with the Calvinist dogma of unconditional election as long as it is understood in the sense that God sovereignly elects *everyone* for salvation.

Other alternative beliefs have less to do with salvation proper and more to do with the extent of God's sovereignty and providence over human affairs. Some Christian leaders hold to "open theism," which says (depending on whom you ask) either that God does not know the future or—more technically—that God knows the future as it really is which is as a range of real unsettled possibilities. Some of the most progressive pastors and leaders within American Evangelicalism are uninterested in and unmoved by the old "Calvinist-Arminian debate" because they reject the very questions to which those

---

[6] Horton, *For Calvinism*, 31.

[7] Smith's "moralistic therapeutic deism" and Ammerman's "Golden Rule Christianity" might both be thought of as American therapeutic culture mixed with Pelagianism. Christian Smith with Melinda Lundquist Denton, *Soul Searching: The Religious and Spiritual Lives of American Teenagers* (New York: Oxford University Press, 2005); Nancy Ammerman, "Golden Rule Christianity," in *Lived Religion in America: Toward a History of Practice*, ed. David D. Hall (Princeton, NJ: Princeton University Press, 1997), 196–216.

[8] Brad Vermurlen, "Perceptions of and Objections to Christianity among Unchurched and Dechurched Adults," *Review of Religious Research* 57, no. 1 (2015): 161–162.

[9] William W. Klein, *The New Chosen People: A Corporate View of Election* (Grand Rapids, MI: Zondervan, 1990).

[10] See for starters N. T. Wright, *Justification: God's Plan and Paul's Vision* (Downers Grove, IL: InterVarsity Press, 2009); N. T. Wright, *The Paul Debate: Critical Questions for Understanding the Apostle* (Waco, TX: Baylor University Press, 2015).

theological systems have been historic answers, preferring instead to renarrate the traditional Christian storyline in a new way that does not involve sin, atonement, and salvation. Still other Evangelical leaders *do* hold to that traditional narrative but simply are undecided or uninterested and wish not to speculate into the mysteries of the spiritual-causal mechanisms by which God saves sinners. Who can know, they say. Others, like Shane Claiborne and Peter Rollins, take a different tack and argue that what matters most is not what Christians believe but how they live and love in the world.

With this overview, readers can see how Calvinism is one, albeit a major one, among multiple perspectives and options in contemporary Evangelicalism for thinking about how exactly salvation happens and God's role over human affairs. For the purposes of this book, it is not necessary to understand the intricacies of these perspectives beyond what is said here—the way a theologian or Christian historian might. The point is only to provide an introductory familiarity to these varying perspectives and, along with the broader argument of this book, to get a good, thorough sense of just how diverse—or divided—the American Evangelical field is today on one of its most fundamental questions: What must I do to be saved?

Twitter Followers

Tables C.1–C.5 display the number of Twitter followers for major leaders and organizations within the four main expressions of American Evangelicalism. Due to the theological distinctiveness of the corner of mainstream Evangelicalism which ministers at the intersection of Pentecostalism and the "prosperity gospel," those actors are presented in a separate table (Table C.3), although one may still consider them "mainstream." For the sake of comparison, Table C.6 likewise shows Twitter followers of select elements of popular American culture. The numbers presented here were accurate as of mid-November 2015.

Table C.1 Twitter Followers of the New Calvinist Movement

Leader or Organization	No. of Followers	Twitter Handle
Lecrae	1,051,500	https://twitter.com/lecrae
John Piper	792,400	https://twitter.com/JohnPiper
Mark Driscoll	502,400	https://twitter.com/PastorMark
Matt Chandler	350,200	https://twitter.com/MattChandler74
Desiring God	349,300	https://twitter.com/desiringGod
Trip Lee	258,900	https://twitter.com/TripLee
Tim Keller	239,600	https://twitter.com/timkellernyc
James MacDonald	191,900	https://twitter.com/jamesmacdonald
The Gospel Coalition	169,800	https://twitter.com/TGC
Passion Conferences	167,400	https://twitter.com/passion268
Tedashii	158,100	https://twitter.com/Tedashii
Albert Mohler	110,500	https://twitter.com/albertmohler
Tullian Tchividjian	107,400	https://twitter.com/PastorTullian
The Resurgence	88,800	https://twitter.com/theResurgence
Joshua Harris	84,700	https://twitter.com/HarrisJosh
Francis Chan	79,400	https://twitter.com/crazylove
Kevin DeYoung	74,800	https://twitter.com/RevKevDeYoung
Ligonier Ministries	74,000	https://twitter.com/Ligonier
Mark Dever	66,800	https://twitter.com/MarkDever
Mars Hill Church	59,800	https://twitter.com/MarsHill
Crossway Books	52,300	https://twitter.com/crossway
The Village Church	52,100	https://twitter.com/villagechurchtx
C. J. Mahaney	49,200	https://twitter.com/CJMahaney
Acts 29 Network	48,300	https://twitter.com/Acts29
Darrin Patrick	47,000	https://twitter.com/darrinpatrick
R. C. Sproul	45,900	https://twitter.com/rcsproul
Tim Challies	45,600	https://twitter.com/challies
ESV Daily Verse	44,600	https://twitter.com/esvdaily
9Marks	42,700	https://twitter.com/9Marks
Shai Linne	41,300	https://twitter.com/ShaiLinne
Justin Taylor	38,700	https://twitter.com/between2worlds
Ligon Duncan	36,900	https://twitter.com/LigonDuncan
Matt Carter	33,500	https://twitter.com/_Matt_Carter
Dustin Kensrue	32,800	https://twitter.com/dustinkensrue
Tabletalk Magazine	32,500	https://twitter.com/Tabletalk
Trevin Wax	32,500	https://twitter.com/TrevinWax
Thabiti Anyabwile	30,400	https://twitter.com/ThabitiAnyabwil
Jackie Hill Perry	30,100	https://twitter.com/JackieHillPerry
Eric Mason	29,900	https://twitter.com/pastoremase
Sovereign Grace Churches	24,800	https://twitter.com/SovereignGrace

Leader or Organization	No. of Followers	Twitter Handle
Together for the Gospel	23,900	https://twitter.com/T4GOnline
White Horse Inn	23,100	https://twitter.com/WhiteHorseInn
Redeemer Pres. Church	20,100	https://twitter.com/RedeemerNYC
The Austin Stone	15,400	https://twitter.com/TheAustinStone
Banner of Truth	14,900	https://twitter.com/BannerofTruth
Michael Horton	14,100	https://twitter.com/MichaelHorton_
Kings Kaleidoscope	12,900	https://twitter.com/kingsKmusic
Owen Strachan	12,100	https://twitter.com/ostrachan
Collin Hansen	11,400	https://twitter.com/collinhansen
Léonce Crump, Jr.	10,100	https://twitter.com/LeonceCrump
Matt Smethurst	9,900	https://twitter.com/MattSmethurst
Trillia Newbell	7,900	https://twitter.com/trillianewbell
Jason Meyer	7,700	https://twitter.com/WePreachChrist
CBMW	6,800	https://twitter.com/CBMWorg
Ref. Afr. Am. Network	5,600	https://twitter.com/RAANetwork
Sam Storms	4,900	https://twitter.com/Samuel_Storms
Bethlehem Bap. Church	4,800	https://twitter.com/hopeinGod

Table C.2 Twitter Followers of Mainstream Evangelicalism

Leader or Organization	No. of Followers	Twitter Handle
Rick Warren	1,735,600	https://twitter.com/RickWarren
Max Lucado	1,219,400	https://twitter.com/MaxLucado
Hillsong United*	1,042,900	https://twitter.com/hillsongunited
Chris Tomlin	866,700	https://twitter.com/christomlin
Dave Ramsey	694,500	https://twitter.com/DaveRamsey
Hillsong Church*	693,300	https://twitter.com/hillsong
Beth Moore	685,200	https://twitter.com/BethMooreLPM
Ed Young ("Jr.")	634,800	https://twitter.com/EdYoung
World Vision U.S.A.	531,800	https://twitter.com/WorldVisionUSA
Louie Giglio	527,000	https://twitter.com/louiegiglio
The Dave Ramsey Show	520,800	https://twitter.com/RamseyShow
Andy Stanley	500,500	https://twitter.com/AndyStanley
Brian Houston*	457,200	https://twitter.com/BrianCHouston
Daily Bible Verse	435,100	https://twitter.com/Daily_Bible
Hillsong Worship	419,700	https://twitter.com/hillsongworship
David Crowder	375,000	https://twitter.com/crowdermusic
Judah Smith	360,100	https://twitter.com/judahsmith
Steven Furtick	259,700	https://twitter.com/stevenfurtick
Christianity Today	256,900	https://twitter.com/CTmagazine

Leader or Organization	No. of Followers	Twitter Handle
Craig Groeschel	252,100	https://twitter.com/craiggroeschel
Billy Graham (BGEA)	251,400	https://twitter.com/BillyGraham
Bill Hybels	250,400	https://twitter.com/BillHybels
Donald Miller	237,100	https://twitter.com/donaldmiller
Relevant Magazine	234,000	https://twitter.com/RELEVANT
Ravi Zacharias	218,200	https://twitter.com/RaviZacharias
Ed Stetzer	172,700	https://twitter.com/edstetzer
Pete Wilson	151,600	https://twitter.com/pwilson
Perry Noble	151,500	https://twitter.com/perrynoble
Hillsong NYC	145,100	https://twitter.com/hillsongNYC
The Christian Post	138,500	https://twitter.com/ChristianPost
Carl Lentz	130,800	https://twitter.com/carllentzNYC
Lee Strobel	130,200	https://twitter.com/LeeStrobel
Paul David Tripp	121,100	https://twitter.com/PaulTripp
Mark Batterson	103,200	https://twitter.com/MarkBatterson
Catalyst	102,700	https://twitter.com/CatalystLeader
Chuck Swindoll	98,200	https://twitter.com/chuckswindoll
Elevation Church	85,800	https://twitter.com/ElevationChurch
Focus on the Family	81,200	https://twitter.com/FocusFamily
Russell Moore	76,600	https://twitter.com/drmoore
Robert Morris	75,200	https://twitter.com/PsRobertMorris
Elevation Worship	74,300	https://twitter.com/elevation_wrshp
BGEA	69,100	https://twitter.com/BGEA
Chris Hodges	68,900	https://twitter.com/Chris_Hodges
Gungor	66,900	https://twitter.com/gungormusic
Erwin McManus	64,500	https://twitter.com/erwinmcmanus
NewSpring Church	60,100	https://twitter.com/newspring
Josh McDowell	53,500	https://twitter.com/josh_mcdowell
Passion City Church	52,600	https://twitter.com/passioncity
Zondervan Publishers	46,000	https://twitter.com/Zondervan
Salvation Army USA	42,800	https://twitter.com/SalvationArmyUS
Jonathan Merritt	42,300	https://twitter.com/JonathanMerritt
Lacey Sturm	42,100	https://twitter.com/LaceySturm
Jud Wilhite	39,800	https://twitter.com/JudWilhite
Willow Creek Assoc.	37,200	https://twitter.com/wcagls
CBN News	35,400	https://twitter.com/CBNNews
Kyle Idleman	33,200	https://twitter.com/KyleIdleman
Kerry Shook	32,200	https://twitter.com/KerryShook
Greg Surratt	31,400	https://twitter.com/gregsurratt
James Dobson	31,400	https://twitter.com/DrJamesCDobson
Stovall Weems	31,200	https://twitter.com/stovallweems

Leader or Organization	No. of Followers	Twitter Handle
Verge Network	31,100	https://twitter.com/VergeNetwork
Willie George	30,900	https://twitter.com/Willie_George
Exponential	29,300	https://twitter.com/churchplanting
The 700 Club	29,200	https://twitter.com/700club
Leadership Network	28,200	https://twitter.com/leadnet
World Magazine	24,700	https://twitter.com/WORLD_mag
Eric Geiger	23,600	https://twitter.com/EricGeiger
Cross Point Church	22,900	https://twitter.com/crosspoint_tv
Willow Creek Church	22,700	https://twitter.com/WillowCreekCC
Dave Ferguson	22,400	https://twitter.com/daveferguson
Chris Seay	22,000	https://twitter.com/PastorChrisSeay
Hillsong Conference	22,000	https://twitter.com/hillsongconf
Ben Stuart	19,100	https://twitter.com/Ben_Stuart_
Andy Crouch	17,800	https://twitter.com/ahc
Dave Stone	17,700	https://twitter.com/DaveStone920
Jim Daly	16,800	https://twitter.com/DalyFocus
Geoff Surratt	16,700	https://twitter.com/GeoffSurratt
Vineyard Worship	16,600	https://twitter.com/VineyardWorship
Assoc. Related Churches	15,500	https://twitter.com/arcchurches
Breakaway Ministries	15,100	https://twitter.com/breakawaymin
Gabe Lyons	14,300	https://twitter.com/GabeLyons
Larry Osborne	13,800	https://twitter.com/LarryOsborne
Jon Tyson	11,700	https://twitter.com/JonTyson
Urbana Missions	11,300	https://twitter.com/UrbanaMissions
InterVarsity USA	10,800	https://twitter.com/INTERVARSITYusa
Cru	10,600	https://twitter.com/crutweets
Micah Fries	10,600	https://twitter.com/micahfries
Wheaton College	10,000	https://twitter.com/WheatonCollege
Southeast Christian Church	10,000	https://twitter.com/southeastchrist
InterVarsity Press	8,000	https://twitter.com/ivpress
Marvin Olasky	5,700	https://twitter.com/MarvinOlasky
TEDS	2,500	https://twitter.com/TEDS

*These are based in Sydney, Australia, not in the United States.

Table C.3 Twitter Followers of Prosperity Pentecostalism

Leader or Organization	No. of Followers	Twitter Handle
Joel Osteen	4,090,800	https://twitter.com/JoelOsteen
Joyce Meyer	3,807,100	https://twitter.com/JoyceMeyer
T. D. Jakes	2,031,000	https://twitter.com/BishopJakes
Creflo Dollar	513,200	https://twitter.com/Creflo_Dollar
Paula White	443,500	https://twitter.com/paula_white
Benny Hinn	426,200	https://twitter.com/Benny_Hinn
Kenneth Copeland	228,400	https://twitter.com/CopelandNetwork
John Hagee	221,000	https://twitter.com/PastorJohnHagee
Lakewood Church	156,100	https://twitter.com/lakewoodch
Jesse Duplantis	155,100	https://twitter.com/jesse_duplantis
Rod Parsley	70,000	https://twitter.com/RealRodParsley

Table C.4 Twitter Followers of Neo-Anabaptist Evangelicalism

Leader or Organization	No. of Followers	Twitter Handle
Shane Claiborne	61,800	https://twitter.com/ShaneClaiborne
Kurt Willems	52,100	https://twitter.com/kurtwillems
Tony Campolo	40,400	https://twitter.com/TonyCampolo
Scot McKnight	35,700	https://twitter.com/scotmcknight
Geoff Holsclaw	27,900	https://twitter.com/geoffholsclaw
Greg Boyd	22,900	https://twitter.com/greg_boyd
Englewood Rev. Books	21,700	https://twitter.com/ERBks
J. R. Woodward	16,000	https://twitter.com/dreamawakener
David Fitch	15,200	https://twitter.com/fitchest
Brian Zahnd	14,600	https://twitter.com/BrianZahnd
Zach Hoag	12,700	https://twitter.com/zhoag
Bruxy Cavey	12,400	https://twitter.com/Bruxy
The Simple Way	11,500	https://twitter.com/theSimpleWay
Neil Cole	10,900	https://twitter.com/Neil_Cole
Red Letter Christians	10,300	https://twitter.com/RedLetterXians
Missio Alliance	8,300	https://twitter.com/missioalliance
Preston Sprinkle	6,800	https://twitter.com/PrestonSprinkle
The Meeting House	5,000	https://twitter.com/TheMeetingHouse
Aaron Niequist	4,600	https://twitter.com/aaronieq
Jonathan Wilson-Hartgrove	3,800	https://twitter.com/wilsonhartgrove
Mark Van Steenwyk	3,700	https://twitter.com/markvans
Northern Seminary	2,600	https://twitter.com/nseminary
Tim Keel	1,700	https://twitter.com/timothykeel
Debra Hirsch	1,700	https://twitter.com/debrahirsch
J. R. Rozko	1,400	https://twitter.com/jrrozko

Leader or Organization	No. of Followers	Twitter Handle
Tim Suttle	1,100	https://twitter.com/Tim_Suttle
Pangea Communities	1,100	https://twitter.com/SeattlePangea
EVANA Network	100	https://twitter.com/evananetwork

Table C.5 Twitter Followers of Progressive Evangelicalism

Leader or Organization	No. of Followers	Twitter Handle
Rob Bell	154,100	https://twitter.com/realrobbell
Sojourners	91,600	https://twitter.com/Sojourners
Rachel Held Evans	81,800	https://twitter.com/rachelheldevans
Brian McLaren	44,800	https://twitter.com/brianmclaren
Nadia Bolz-Weber	38,900	https://twitter.com/Sarcasticluther
Jim Wallis	27,600	https://twitter.com/jimwallis
Sarah Bessey	27,200	https://twitter.com/sarahbessey
Peter Rollins	20,500	https://twitter.com/PeterRollins
Kristen Howerton	19,300	https://twitter.com/kristenhowerton
Jay Bakker	17,200	https://twitter.com/jaybakker
Tony Jones	15,800	https://twitter.com/jonestony
Diana Butler Bass	15,400	https://twitter.com/dianabutlerbass
Christian Piatt	14,800	https://twitter.com/christianpiatt
Mike Morrell	14,200	https://twitter.com/zoecarnate
Emergent Village	12,100	https://twitter.com/emergentvillage
Wild Goose Festival	9,300	https://twitter.com/WildGooseFest
Doug Pagitt	8,600	https://twitter.com/pagitt
Brandan Robertson	8,600	https://twitter.com/BrandanJR
Frank Schaeffer	7,500	https://twitter.com/Frank_Schaeffer
Lisa Sharon Harper	5,300	https://twitter.com/lisasharper
Patheos Prog. Channel	4,400	https://twitter.com/PatheosProgXn
John Shore	3,100	https://twitter.com/johnshore
Ctr. for Prog. Renewal	2,900	https://twitter.com/progressrenew
Revolution Church	2,900	https://twitter.com/Revolution1994
Darkwood Brew	2,600	https://twitter.com/darkwoodbrew
Michael Toy	600	https://twitter.com/mtoy
Kyle Roberts	600	https://twitter.com/kylearoberts
Eric Elnes	500	https://twitter.com/ericelnes
Christianity 21	500	https://twitter.com/Christianity21
Stephanie Spellers	300	https://twitter.com/SSpellers
The JoPa Group	300	https://twitter.com/TheJoPaGroup
Convergence U.S.	200	https://twitter.com/ConvergenceMvmt
CANA Initiative	200	https://twitter.com/CANAInitiative

Table C.6 Twitter Followers of Popular American Culture

Person or Organization	No. of Followers	Twitter Handle
Katy Perry	77,840,100	https://twitter.com/katyperry
Justin Bieber	69,588,900	https://twitter.com/justinbieber
Ellen DeGeneres	49,681,400	https://twitter.com/TheEllenShow
Jimmy Fallon	31,361,300	https://twitter.com/jimmyfallon
Oprah Winfrey	29,659,700	https://twitter.com/Oprah
Lebron James	25,007,100	https://twitter.com/KingJames
SportsCenter	22,967,100	https://twitter.com/SportsCenter
The New York Times	21,196,800	https://twitter.com/nytimes
Conan O'Brien	18,657,600	https://twitter.com/ConanOBrien
Jim Carrey	15,212,200	https://twitter.com/JimCarrey
Tyra Banks	12,928,300	https://twitter.com/tyrabanks
Tom Hanks	10,635,800	https://twitter.com/tomhanks
Stephen Colbert	9,505,100	https://twitter.com/StephenAtHome
Wall Street Journal	8,253,300	https://twitter.com/WSJ
Pope Francis	7,950,400	https://twitter.com/Pontifex
Anderson Cooper	6,520,200	https://twitter.com/andersoncooper
The New Yorker	5,754,600	https://twitter.com/NewYorker
Neil deGrasse Tyson	4,542,300	https://twitter.com/neiltyson
National Public Radio	4,480,400	https://twitter.com/NPR
Rachel Maddow	3,571,700	https://twitter.com/maddow
Jerry Seinfeld	3,257,900	https://twitter.com/JerrySeinfeld
Magic Johnson	2,881,700	https://twitter.com/MagicJohnson
Tony Robbins	2,684,400	https://twitter.com/TonyRobbins
Bill Nye	2,556,000	https://twitter.com/BillNye
Museum of Modern Art	2,378,400	https://twitter.com/MuseumModernArt
Bob Saget	2,348,100	https://twitter.com/bobsaget
Kathy Griffin	2,063,500	https://twitter.com/kathygriffin
Target	1,730,300	https://twitter.com/Target
Sadie Robertson	1,631,900	https://twitter.com/sadierob
Nate Silver	1,293,100	https://twitter.com/NateSilver538
Richard Dawkins	1,281,000	https://twitter.com/RichardDawkins
NY Review of Books	990,000	https://twitter.com/nybooks
Simon Helberg	843,600	https://twitter.com/simonhelberg
Penguin Random House	827,300	https://twitter.com/penguinrandom
Cobie Smulders	815,500	https://twitter.com/CobieSmulders
Nickelback	749,300	https://twitter.com/Nickelback
Kristen Schaal	704,600	https://twitter.com/kristenschaaled
Josh Radnor	636,100	https://twitter.com/JoshRadnor
Billy Crystal	590,000	https://twitter.com/BillyCrystal
Ta-Nehisi Coates	359,400	https://twitter.com/tanehisicoates

Person or Organization	No. of Followers	Twitter Handle
Sam Harris	346,600	https://twitter.com/SamHarrisOrg
Dan Savage	242,000	https://twitter.com/fakedansavage
Ron White	200,800	https://twitter.com/Ron_White
Sean Astin	157,500	https://twitter.com/SeanAstin
Reza Aslan	148,100	https://twitter.com/rezaaslan
Daniel Dennett	139,800	https://twitter.com/danieldennett
Jaleel White	112,700	https://twitter.com/jaleelwhite
Jeff Foxworthy	111,000	https://twitter.com/foxoutdoors
Joe Gibbs Racing	81,900	https://twitter.com/JoeGibbsRacing
Carrot Top	59,700	https://twitter.com/RealCarrotTop
David Brooks	59,600	https://twitter.com/nytdavidbrooks
Mitch Albom	58,600	https://twitter.com/MitchAlbom
Ross Douthat	53,100	https://twitter.com/DouthatNYT
Joyful Heart Found.	43,200	https://twitter.com/TheJHF
Mateen Cleaves	38,000	https://twitter.com/Mateen_Cleaves
Mary Steenburgen	20,200	https://twitter.com/MarySteenburgen
American Soc. Assoc.	18,300	https://twitter.com/ASAnews
Primer Magazine	15,100	https://twitter.com/primermag
Adam Gopnik	12,200	https://twitter.com/adamgopnik
Kellie Williams	9,700	https://twitter.com/KellieSWilliams
Emma Green	5,300	https://twitter.com/emmaogreen
Kevin Federline	3,800	https://twitter.com/kevinfederline

Is the New Calvinism Past Its Prime?

Close and persistent observers of the New Calvinist movement know it is fair to ask whether the New Calvinism's best days are behind it. Since the time research for this book began in 2012, a number of events and changes have significantly altered the contours of the New Calvinism, arguably portending the weakening and decline of the movement.

Which events and changes? First consider the three megachurches I spent time at. Mark Driscoll experienced a dramatic and very public fall from grace, and his mega-church dissolved into a number of new autonomous churches. Driscoll has since been largely sidelined from the movement. John Piper transitioned away from being the weekly preacher at Bethlehem Baptist Church, even though he is still very active at Bethlehem in other ways. Tim Keller, likewise, transitioned away from being the preacher at Redeemer Presbyterian Church, and soon thereafter Redeemer's congregations were (strategically and proactively) "spun off" as separate, particularized churches.

Moreover, Darrin Patrick was forced out of his pastoral position at The Journey due to "a historical pattern of sin," and in May 2020 died of a self-inflicted gunshot wound. Tullian Tchividjian was removed from leadership positions at two Presbyterian churches after he and his (now ex-) wife both had extramarital affairs. James MacDonald's behavior led to his being fired from his multisite megachurch in and around Chicago. Allegations of mishandling sexual abuse continue to hang over C. J. Mahaney's head. Lecrae, Jemar Tisby, Léonce Crump, Eric Mason, and other black leaders have distanced themselves from "white Evangelicalism" altogether due to racial tensions and misunderstandings. Voddie Baucham, Jr. has moved his primary ministry to Zambia, Africa. Joshua Harris announced on Instagram that he's divorcing his wife and is no longer a Christian. And R. C. Sproul, sadly, has passed away.

In these ways the New Calvinism has certainly changed since it came on the scene (largely through the observations of Collin Hansen) from 2006 to 2008. And it is accurate to say the Reformed resurgence reached peak "emotional energy" from about 2010 to 2014, and has settled down quite a bit since then, especially after the dissolution of Mars Hill Church. At the same time, the neo-Reformed movement is by no means on its way toward extinction. There are three big reasons for this: numbers, institutions, and worldview.

One of the main arguments of this book has been that the New Calvinist movement is a relationally constructed, ontologically emergent religious phenomenon. Its force in the Evangelical field has more to do with its "acceleration" than its "mass." Still, there are millions of people involved in it, forming the on-the-ground substance of this expression of Evangelical Christianity. This core of adherents and laypersons—especially among younger American Christians—means the movement will survive even after beloved pastors retire or pass away and megachurches splinter.

The second reason the New Calvinism isn't going away any time soon is its noteworthy infrastructure and institutions. As long as The Gospel Coalition, Acts 29, the Council on Biblical Manhood and Womanhood, Desiring God, Together for the Gospel, 9Marks, Crossway, and other related organizations, networks, and conferences persist, the New

Calvinist movement will continue on, even if the label "New Calvinism" becomes less important. Additionally, the Reformed expression of Evangelical Protestantism holds notable sway and power over other institutions of American religion, including seminaries and publishers.

Finally, in the United States at least, there will continue to be demand for socially and theologically conservative, gender complementarian, culturally savvy, Calvinistic faith. Given the alternative worldviews on offer both in mainstream American culture and within Evangelicalism (which are generally more liberal or therapeutic or self-help oriented), the convictions and beliefs animating the Reformed resurgence will find a receptive audience for a long time. So even if the specific movement connected to Mark Driscoll, John Piper, James MacDonald, Darrin Patrick, Wayne Grudem, and other leaders has lost some energy over the last five years, the beliefs behind it are well-positioned to continue and thrive into the foreseeable future.

Index

Tables and figures are indicated by *t* and *f* following the page number

For the benefit of digital users, indexed terms that span two pages (e.g., 52–53) may, on occasion, appear on only one of those pages.